God the Creator

ROBERT CUMMINGS NEVILLE

God the Creator

On the Transcendence and Presence of God

Drawings by Beth Neville

STATE UNIVERSITY OF NEW YORK PRESS

Published by
State University of New York Press, Albany
© 1992 State University of New York

First published by The University of Chicago Press, ©1968 The University of Chicago

For information, address State University of New York Press,
State University Plaza, Albany, N.Y., 12246

Library of Congress Cataloging-in-Publication Data

Neville, Robert C.
    God the creator : on the transcendence and presence of God / Robert
Cummings Neville.
        p. cm.
    Reprint. Originally published: Chicago : University of Chicago
Press, 1968.
    Includes bibliographical references and index.
    ISBN 0-7914-0843-4 (hard). — ISBN 0-7914-0844-2 (pbk.)
    1. Ontology.   2. Creation.   3. God—Knowableness.   4. Religion-
-Philosophy.   I. Title.
BD331.N48   1992
    210—dc20
                                                                      90-27103
                                                                          CIP

10 9 8 7 6 5 4 3 2 1

To John E. Smith

Contents

Part Two

Part Three

List of Illustrations

Plato

Preface to the SUNY Press Edition

I.

What could prompt a person to republish a book written twenty-five years ago, the very first sentence of which is now clearly mistaken? The answer, of course, has to be, confidence in the rest of the sentences. Whether the confidence is warranted is for the readers to decide. A reflection on the mistake in the first sentence, however, sets the context in which I believe the book has more pertinence now than it had a quarter century ago.

"This book is an essay in philosophy, not in theology." Whereas it remains true that the book is a philosophic essay, in metaphysics, epistemology, and philosophy of religion, it is no longer true that the book is not theology. Perhaps it was theology even in the mid-1960s. Two things prompted me then to refuse the connection with theology. One was my conviction that theology should be truly systematic, on the model of Schleiermacher or Tillich's great works, and this book is not that. The other was that theology in those days was claimed by the Neo-orthodox school which strenuously rejected any positive contribution of philosophy "in the grand tradition," of which this book is an example. The Neo-orthodox thinkers called their opponents in theology "philosophers," people such as Tillich, Weiman, Brightman, and Hartshorne. So I thought it was just *better* to be a philosopher than a theologian if you were going to be serious about God.

The adventures of theology as a professional discipline during the last twenty-five years have undermined whatever value there may have been in those considerations. The most important change has been the recognition that theology is a public discipline.[1] Twenty-five years ago, a sharp distinction was felt between confessional theology and academic theology, the latter associating itself with the emerging discipline of religious studies. Identified then most closely with Barth and his German colleagues who had asserted the critical independence of Christianity from the cultural church of

[1] See, for instance, Van A. Harvey's *The Historian and the Believer* (New York: Macmillan, 1966; or David Tracy's books *Blessed Rage for Order* (New York: Seabury/Crossroad, 1975), *The Analogical Imagination* (New York: Crossroad, 1981), and *Plurality and Ambiguity* (San Francisco: Harper & Row, 1987).

Nazi Germany, confessional theology protected its warrant for truth by referring it to claims for revelation within some community of faith.[2] By contrast, the academic theologians were supposed to have abandoned claims to revelation that necessarily are limited to communities of faith in order to make cultural arguments open to anyone.[3] To the extent they reinforced this division, both sides accepted the underlying supposition that a secular, non-religious reductionism would delegitimate claims to revelation. Therefore, either one accepted the reduction and abandoned claims to revelation or one isolated theology from criticism from outside the circle of the faithful. Almost alone, Paul Tillich opposed this division with his "method of correlation," and he was both misunderstood and rejected by confessional and liberal academic theologians alike.[4]

Now, mainly because of the importance of hermeneutics, the reductionism that underlay the confessional-academic distinction in theology has been rejected. Perhaps Wilfrid Cantwell Smith goes too far in claiming that the test of a description of a religion is whether its adherents accept themselves as so described.[5] But there is a firm methodological requirement for honesty that commits theology to acknowledging, redescribing, perhaps even reconstructing the validity of the cognitively significant experiences important for the religious and anti-religious life. Thus, although an academic theologian can dispute the interpretation placed upon a revelatory tradition, it is not possible to dismiss the tradition or reduce it to something it is not.

[2] See, for instance, the interesting study by Rolf Ahlers, *The Community of Freedom: Barth and Presuppositionless Theology* (New York: Peter Lang, 1989).

[3] See, for instance, Charles Hartshorne's *The Logic of Perfection* (LaSalle, Ill.; Open Court, 1961) or Henry Nelson Wieman's *The Source of Human Good* (Carbondale, Ill.: Southern Illinois University Press, 1946). For commentary on the empiricist side of this position, see William Dean's *American Religious Empiricism* and *History Making History: The New Historicism in American Religious Thought*, (both Albany: State University of New York Press, 1986, 1988 respectively) and Nancy Frankenberry's *Religion and Radical Empiricism* (Albany: State University of New York Press, 1987).

[4] One of the most interesting theological documents of the 1960s was John B. Cobb, Jr.'s *Living Options in Protestant Theology* (Philadelphia: Westminster, 1962). It was mistaken about the living options, of course, because it modestly neglected process theology to which Cobb has made the premier contributions since that time. Nevertheless its importance lies in its general classifications. His name for much of what I have called "academic theology" was "natural theology," under which head he considered Neo-Thomism, Boston Personalism, and Henry Nelson Wieman. Confessional theology he called "theological positivism" and considered the thought of Berkouwer, Brunner, and Barth. Finally, he employed the classification of theological existentialism, under which he discussed Bultmann, Tillich, and H. Richard and Reinhold Niebuhr. In retrospect, I believe that existentialism was not the significant alternative to confessional theology and academic or natural theology. Barth was as much influenced by the existentialist Kierkegaard as was Bultmann or Tillich, and Bultmann himself was an academic theologian according to my description, indeed even a natural theologian in the sense that he demythologized the traditional Christian language into a kind of existential naturalism. Neither of the Niebuhrs intended to limit his work to the interests of a Christian community of faith, but both wrote from an explicitly confessional stance; see especially H. Richard Niebuhr's *The Meaning of Revelation* (New York: MacMillan, 1960). Tillich is the one person of the group who stands outside the other two main camps.

[5] See his *Towards a World Theology: Faith and the Comparative History of Religion* (Maryknoll, N.Y.: Orbis, 1989; orig. London: Macmillan, 1981).

By the same token, a confessional theologian now needs to be able to explain the confessional position to an outsider, respecting the defining commitments of the outsider's tradition (or anti-tradition). Theological argument thus takes the form of dialogue with those interested in the truth of the matter; exposition and query are instrumental to dialogue. Twenty-five years ago, dialogue was a bureaucratic practice of the ecumenical movement; now it is internal to both academic and confessional theology. Confessional theology now must continue to assert its claim to truth by presenting that truth in comprehensible ways to people with different founding truths. Otherwise, confessional theology reduces to mere sociological analysis of what the confessing group believes, the very opposite of the intent of Barth and his colleagues to preserve the truth of the Christian gospel from its cultural distortions. In short, insofar as confessional theology aims to proclaim the confessional truths, it has become part of academic theology whose community defines the public. Perhaps the most outstanding early case in America of confessionally originating theology opening out to public discussion by means of the hermeneutic of revelation is in Ray L. Hart's *Unfinished Man and the Imagination.*[6]

On the other hand, the heirs to Barth are theologians such as George Lindbeck who see the connection between theological truth claims and the structured practice of religion in particular communities.[7] Theology is not merely descriptive of divine matters but articulates the performative function of ideas and beliefs. Therefore, theology does arise out of practising religious communities, and theological disputes are in large measure disputes between or within communities about how to be the people of God, or of the Torah, or of the Book, or the Dharma. Academic theology now appreciates the fact that the living context of religious thinking is religious (or anti-religious) practice, not the university classroom or bookstore alone.

There is something of an historic irony here. The development of confessional theology into Wittgensteinean socio-linguistic models of self-understanding has associated it far more closely with a purely cultural definition immune from transcendent criticism than Barth would have liked. Indeed, perhaps on the shoulders of academic theologians with minimal confessional connection falls the obligation to say, "This is what God makes, does, and is: ..."

Academic theology has emerged as less a "discipline" than a field requiring many disciplines. Twenty-five years ago, entry into theology narrowly defined was through historical and scriptural studies. Although enthusiasm for finding "the" Biblical theology has greatly waned, Biblical and historical studies remain a crucial component of theology.[8] Whereas before, philosophy

---

[6] *Unfinished Man and the Imagination: Toward an Ontology and a Rhetoric of Revelation* (New York: Herder and Herder, 1968).
[7] George A. Lindbeck, *The Nature of Doctrine: Religion and Theology in a Postliberal Age* (Philadelphia: Westminster, 1984).
[8] See, for instance, Hans Frei's seminal *The Eclipse of Biblical Narrative: A Study in Eighteenth and Nineteenth Century Hermeneutics* (New Haven: Yale University Press, 1974).

was seen as an alternative to theology, philosophy is now recognized as an equally crucial component.

Philosophy is required in theology for two principal contributions beyond the standard need for an epistemological justification of theological claims. One is the interpretation of the phenomenology of religion. Philosophy of religion in at least one of its modes is the discipline that assesses what is gained and lost in religious abstractions, in the various simplifications involved in the selections that religions make in their responses to their traditions and their world.[9] Abstractions in ritual, community life, and theology are inevitable and philosophy of religion is needed to say what they are and to assess their costs and benefits. The other contribution of philosophy to theology is simply to provide new and better concepts of God and related matters. For all the recent talk about metaphors and symbols in theology, the understanding of their applications and limitations depends on the underlying concepts of God and God's relation to the world and human life. Therefore, theology is in need of old fashioned metaphysical attention to problems such as the one and the many, the nature of being and becoming, of difference and unity, of good and evil, of causation and creation, and of ultimate beings and categories. The difference between the mid-1960s and now with regard to philosophical theology has been effected by the rise of process theology: however one assesses Whitehead's theory of God, he and his followers have shown that the way to solve conceptual problems in theology is by getting better ideas. Precisely because the basic symbols of the religious traditions require interpretation in current terms, metaphysics as a trans-traditional discipline has an ongoing task of conceptual imagination. Although at the time it seemed as if the abstract metaphysics in Part I of this book was unique and untimely, the flourishing of philosophical theology today has justified its instincts regarding the needs of the discipline.

In addition to the public character of theology, or perhaps as a ramification of it, the need for comparative theology and philosophy is now apparent. When *God the Creator* was written, it noted that the empirical testing of its ideas would require a comparative study of world religions, and announced its failure to engage that as a limitation on its conclusions. Since that time the situation in comparative studies has changed dramatically. Most of the important texts, and some unimportant ones, in Hinduism, Buddhism, Confucianism, and Taoism have been translated into English and other European languages. Scholarship in Islam lags a bit behind but is coming along. Serious comparative reflection is now possible without universal philological expertise. The development of organizations such as the International Society for Chinese Philosophy have fostered ongoing dialogue among scholars who are spokespersons for their traditions in one sense, but creators of a new common language for dialogue in another. Theological dialogues among Christians, Jews, Buddhists, Muslims and Confucianists have begun to flourish, and have largely replaced the intra-Christian

---

[9] This is defended at length in my *Behind the Masks of God* (Albany: State University of New York Press, 1991).

ecumenical interests of the 1950s and 1960s. Now it is the case that, except in very sheltered environments, the presentation of a Christian theology needs to be sensitive to how a Buddhist or Jew would respond to it, and to organize itself in respectful anticipation of that.

Yet another crucial development in theology since the 1960s has been the flourishing of process theology. It now commands the attention at national meetings and in journals that Neo-orthodoxy had before it, yet with an extraordinary generosity. I know of no other theological movement that, on the one hand, is as sharply defined by primary texts (Whitehead's and Hartshorne's) as process philosophy and, on the other hand, has reached out on its own initiative and often with its own funding (for instance, from the Center for Process Studies) to engage other theologies so as to enlarge the arena of discourse. Process theology has engaged liberation and feminist theologies, Thomist and other classical theologies, German, Indian, and Japanese Christian theologies, Buddhists, Confucians, physicists, chemists, environmentalists, biologists, and economists. The generosity of the legitimate field of theological discussion today is due largely to this embracing passion of process theology, especially as led by John B. Cobb, Jr., David Griffin, and Lewis S. Ford.

What is perhaps most remarkable about the success of process theology, however, is that it has done all this while disciplining the discussion with careful, detailed, and systematic abstract metaphysics. Unlike most dialogical theologies and swarmy spiritual catholic effusions, process theology has set high standards for clarity of the metaphysical thought in any theology. A theologian now cannot ignore the process conceptions of God. If one does not agree with any of them, then the terms of the debate are such that one must do better, and on terms largely set by process theology. My own work owes a deep debt to process theology. Although the conception of God as creator *ex nihilo* is not congenial to that movement, my discussion is legitimated in the theological context because of the philosophic rigor with which process theology determines that context. [10] In the work of Cobb, Ford, Griffin, Schubert Ogden, and their students, the philosophical elements in process theology have been extended to cover the range of doctrinal topics. Whereas in 1968, the process theologians were about the only people who could read *God the Creator,* because of their own work, its audience is far broader now.

A final change to be noted in the theological situation is the collapse of the idea of salvation history. The 1964 translation of Oscar Cullmann's *Christ and Time* perhaps marked the high point of the doctrine of salvation history, a doctrine according to which the heart of the gospel must be understood as pointing to a unique history defining both the fortunes of humankind and the redemptive character of God. That doctrine in some form or other was central to Neo-orthodoxy. Its demise has come from many sources, most particularly those associated with the collapse of European Christendom signalled first by

---

[10] For my reasons for rejecting process theology, see *Creativity and God* (New York: The Seabury Press, 1980).

Kierkegaard who emphasized the lack of difference between Jesus' contemporaries and ourselves. But it was the death of God theology of Thomas J. J. Altizer that showed what was at stake in the idea of salvation history and that analyzed its collapse. From the early *Gospel of Christian Atheism* through masterful systematic theologies such as *The Self-Embodiment of God* to the historically sweeping *History as Apocalypse,* Altizer has demonstrated the death of the God as defined by salvation history. [11]

There have been three main lines of positive response to Altizer's work. Mark C. Taylor has taken its conclusion to be a kind of deconstruction of all theology. [12] David Tracy, responding to Altizer and to a great many other influences having to do with the decline of transcendental Thomism, has moved from first-order theology back to methodological considerations, such as in *Blessed Rage for Order* and literary considerations such as the theory of "classics" in *The Analogical Imagination.* The opening chapters of Tracy's *Pluralism and Ambiguity* constitute a conclusive argument against proceeding with a theology of salvation history. The third line of response comes from the process theologians who conclude that nature is prior to history and can support a number of different historical and anti-historical configurations for human society and culture. [13] Although few would suspect a close affinity of process theology to death of God theology, Cobb edited a Festschrift for Altizer and Altizer did the same for Cobb. [14] My own work follows the third line of response, although in ways with specific differences from that of process theology.

II.

After all these years, I am pleased to be able to suggest that the argument in *God the Creator* remains relevant. In fact, because of the wider acceptance of metaphysical philosophical theology, the conception of God as creator *ex nihilo* may find a readier audience than ever before. Process theology has created that audience, as mentioned already, and the theory of creation *ex nihilo* is a clear alternative to the basic conceptions in process theology. I have responded to process theology in detail in *Creativity and God,* and three distinguished process theologians, John Cobb, Lewis Ford, and Charles Hartshorne, have answered. [15] My own position, to which only elliptical

[11] See *The Gospel of Christian Atheism* (Philadelphia: Westminster, 1966), *Descent into Hell* (New York: Lippincott, 1970), *The Self-Embodiment of God* (New York: Harper & Row, 1977), *Total Presence* (New York: Seabury, 1980), and *History as Apocalypse* (Albany: State University of New York Press, 1985).
[12] See his *Erring: A Postmodern A/Theology* (Chicago: University of Chicago Press, 1984), and his anthology *Deconstruction and Theology* (New York: Crossroad, 1982).
[13] Cobb saw this early on, for instance in *The Structure of Christian Existence* and *Christ in a Pluralistic Age* (Philadelphia: Westminster, 1967 and 1975 respectively).
[14] *The Theology of Altizer: Critique and Response,* edited by John B. Cobb, Jr. (Philadelphia: Westminster, 1970), and *John Cobb's Theology in Process,* edited by Thomas J. J. Altizer and David Ray Griffin (Philadelphia: Westminster, 1977).
[15] "Three Responses to Neville's *Creativity and God,*" in *Process Studies,* 10/3-4 (Fall-Winter).

reference is made in that debate, is best expressed in *God the Creator*.

The chief criticism that has been made over the years to the conception of God as creator *ex nihilo* has been that the very idea of creation is unintelligible. Intelligibility, in this complaint, is defined in terms of some first principles to which the phenomenon (e.g., the existence of the world) is to be reduced. Because creation *ex nihilo* implies, as argued below, that everything determinate is created, no determinate principles could possibly explain the basic theological question. Process philosophers, for instance, therefore require that the basic metaphysical principles apply to God as well as the world, and no account is offered for why there are these metaphysical principles.

In answer to this I have to say that the idea of creation *ex nihilo* is just a different kind of idea from that of explanatory *first principles*. The idea is that, instead, explanation points to the action of creating. Creation itself is a making of something new, and is to be understood in terms of what is made, the dependency of the made on the creative act, and the creative act itself. All this is argued in the present volume. In debates about positions it is sometimes difficult to assert that one's idea is different from what others think count as meaningful ideas. The advantage of *God the Creator* is that all the arguments I know are given for why one should come to understand and prefer the idea of creation *ex nihilo* to its alternatives. A critic cannot announce in advance that the idea is unintelligible; rather, the critic must cope with the arguments in order to reject the position.

Part II of *God the Creator* is about epistemological issues raised by the kind of arguments made in Part I. Although it was written long before French deconstructionist philosophy became known in North America, a matter reflected in its language, Part II is strangely positioned to answer the kinds of critiques deconstruction has made of "the grand tradition." Partly this is due to the fact my discussion draws so closely from Charles Peirce, who had anticipated the critiques of foundationalism, the rejection of "centrism", logo or otherwise, and the theory of "textuality," which Peirce expressed as an ontology of signs.

Another and more interesting reason is that the job of the epistemological argument is to justify a non-standard kind of thinking, a thinking about the *creation* of logos rather than about its structure. The distinction between cosmology and cosmogony in the fifth chapter and the distinction between methodological and constitutive dialectic developed in the sixth and seventh argue for a flexibility of language accommodated to things in contrast to a language that demands the accommodation of things. I have developed that theme in a metaphysical hermeneutics extended far beyond the idea of creation *ex nihilo* in later works.[16] Chapter eight, on the empirical testing of the metaphysics in experience, lays out the hypothetical character of speculative metaphysics, and sets the task for Part III.

The function of Part III is to weave the idea of God the creator *ex nihilo*

---

[16] See particularly *Recovery of the Measure* (Albany: State University of New York Press, 1989).

through pervasive aspects of religion, using philosophy of religion to test the hypothesis in detail. In many respects, the discussion there is both the most dated and the most curious in the book. The whole of it was written before I was twenty-six years old, and what can a person that young understand of the important things in life? It was also written before the impact of the social sciences had been felt strongly in philosophy of religion. That impact has come from two sources. One is the conceptual success of sociology of religion in the work of Peter Berger, whose *Sacred Canopy* appeared in 1967. [17] The other is the influence of liberation theologies, especially those associated with African-Americans in the civil rights movement, feminist theology, and Latin American liberation theology. [18] Not until my second book, *The Cosmology of Freedom*, in 1974 did I study and take seriously the elements of institutions determined by the kinds of considerations open to the social sciences. [19] Thus I am bemused to find in *God the Creator* both a call for deeper understanding of the social dimensions of religion and a prototypical theory of them, especially in chapter twelve, "The Public Expression of the Religious Life."

One of the most difficult problems remaining at the end of this book is whether human beings can be free if God creates everything determinate. *The Cosmology of Freedom* was written to answer that question. It contains sections on personal and social freedom, and its original version contained an extended discussion of spiritual freedom that eventually found expression in *Soldier, Sage, Saint*. [20] The long part on social freedom in *The Cosmology of Freedom* makes a persuasive case, I believe, for the neo-Calvinist theory that God is the total creator and that individuals are profoundly free and wholly responsible. It contains a theory of revolution and participatory democracy that anticipated much of the work of liberation theology. But it does not surrender individual responsibility because of its commitment to the view that God is at the heart of every individual.

Wholly lacking from *God the Creator* is sensitivity to gender-inclusive language. Having been as careful as possible since *Soldier, Sage, Saint* to refer to the deity in non-sexist ways and to use inclusive language for persons, I read the text of *God the Creator* with singular embarrassment in this respect. Those who feel offended, for positive or negative reasons, by the sexist language of this text can take interest in the use to which the idea of creation

---

[17] *The Sacred Canopy: Elements of a Sociological Theory of Religion* (Garden City, N.Y.: Doubleday, 1967). See also his *The Social Construction of Reality: A Treatise in the Sociology of Knowledge*, with Thomas Luckmann, (Garden City, N.Y.: Doubleday, 1966). Neither of these books was known to me when I finished *God the Creator* in 1966.

[18] Although the literature in these movements is vast, examples of the best expressions of each are the following: Cornell West's *Prophesy Deliverance!: An Afro-American Revolutionary Christianity* (Philadelphia: Westminster, 1982), Rosemary Radford Ruether's *Sexism and God-Talk: Towards a Feminist Theology* (Boston: Beacon, 1983), and Gustavo Gutierrez' *A Theology of Liberation* (Maryknoll, N.Y.: Orbis, 1973). Although the pushes toward appreciating the social sciences in theology have been effective, they are not necessarily consistent with one another.

[19] *The Cosmology of Freedom* (New Haven: Yale University Press, 1974).

[20] *Soldier, Sage, Saint* (New York: Fordham University Press, 1978).

ex nihilo is put in *Behind the Masks of God* and *A Theology Primer* for the demonstration of a feminine component to religion and Christian theology. [21]

A final word about the difference in my own theology between the first publication of *God the Creator* and now. The most striking connection between then and now is the continued centrality of the idea of creation *ex nihilo*; my interest in exploring that notion has not abated. But in *God the Creator*, the metaphysics behind the theological application of that idea was almost exclusively limited to the exploration of that idea itself. Since then I have developed a rather comprehensive metaphysical position that has freed itself both from the theological language of the early work and from the languages of Whitehead and Paul Weiss, the major metaphysicians of the twentieth century. [22] In addition, I have done extensive, if perhaps amateurish, work in comparative religion and comparative theology. [23] Thus the overall form of my theology today couches itself in implicit and often explicit dialogue with non-Christian theological traditions, especially those of East Asia. Finally, although because of the comparative dimensions required for publicness in theology I take the theological task to be "world theology," not "Christian theology," I am also a Christian and a church theologian. *A Theology Primer* explicitly is church theology, designed to express Christian doctrines for Christians (and anyone else who is interested), but always in the context of the issues of validity raised in dialogue with other traditions. Would it have been possible in the mid-1960s for the author of *God the Creator* to be the Dean of a denominational Christian seminary, the office I now hold? Most likely not. But now I am pleased to say that my theological "position" requires three expressions: the traditional one of *A Theology Primer*, the comparative one of *Behind the Masks of God*, and the philosophic one of *God the Creator*. Though not envisioned twenty-five years ago, these three books form a unity. The artist of the original drawings here, Beth Neville, has revised the drawings for aesthetic purposes and used them for the cover. She has added a drawing of Plato because he is in truth a primary inspiration of the book, and a drawing of the author at the age at which he wrote the original text, an age that seems more attractive as it becomes ever more remote.

Boston University
September, 1990

---

[21] *Behind the Masks of God* and *A Theology Primer*, (both Albany: State University of New York Press, 1991).

[22] In addition to *The Cosmology of Freedom* and *Recovery of the Measure*, I have developed elements of a metaphysical system in *Reconstruction of Thinking* (Albany: State University of New York Press, 1981).

[23] For instance, in *The Tao and the Daimon*, *The Puritan Smile*, and *Behind the Masks of God*, (Albany: State University of New York Press, 1982, 1987, and 1991 respectively).

Portrait of the Author as a Young Man

Preface to the First Edition

This book is an essay in philosophy, not in theology. It undertakes speculative metaphysics, critical epistemology, and philosophy of religion. This is ambitious enough. Some readers will feel an irresistible urge to interpret it as theology, however, and it cannot be denied that the essay has many theological implications. Its general topic is at the heart of the theological enterprise.

The difference between philosophy and theology is a problem of great subtlety, not to be assaulted in a preface. Let me single out two points, however, which mark the fact that this is a philosophy book. In the first place, from the standpoint of theology there are certain central problems that are not discussed here, for instance, those of immortality and other eschatological notions, that are crucial for a proper theological understanding of many problems that are discussed. For various reasons these neglected problems cannot be treated economically within the special philosophical focus of this book; the reasons have to do chiefly with a desire to avoid detailed comparative study of religions. A theological approach would have to give these problems a more central position.

In the second place, the arguments of the book are aimed to solve problems of philosophers. Philosophers, not theologians, usually are taken as foils in the discussion. In carving out an orientation for the position taken in the book, I have gone to great lengths to locate it in the philosophical tradition, not in the theological one. Of course, these intertwine, and there is much carry-over. But the integrity of the argument is one that takes philosophical criteria into account, not theological ones. In short, although I would be happy if something of theological value is found here, the essay should be read as philosophy.

My philosophical debts are the heavy ones of a young man. It is especially true that what is good in this book is what my teachers have taught me and that what is bad comes from my own incorrigibility. This would be less true of an older person. The ideas in the main were conceived while I was a student at Yale. Certain few of the pages below come from my Ph.D. dissertation, "A Theory of Divine Creation," submitted to the Graduate School of Yale University in 1963. My debt to the faculty at Yale, especially the philosophical faculty, is enormous. I and many others owe a special tribute to Professor Charles Hendel, not only a fine teacher, but a philosophical statesman who for many years as chairman of the philosophy department at Yale provided unsurpassed conditions for genuine education in the richest sense.

I should also acknowledge my debt to Professors Paul Weiss and Robert Brumbaugh. The former has been patient and unrelenting both in his criticism and in his encouragement of my attempts at speculative philosophy. The latter has not only made me love the things in philosophy I love most, but I find that as years separate me from my schooling my own speculative thought agrees most closely with his; the closeness is evident in the argument against him in Chapter Seven below.

One does not learn only from teachers. I want to thank Professor Carl G. Vaught, who as a fellow graduate student argued clearly, profoundly, and critically in our long conversations to hammer out views point by point.

Finally, the greatest debt without doubt is to Professor John E. Smith, to whom this book is dedicated. He was my mentor from sophomore year in college through the doctoral degree. After many years of trying to disagree with him, I confess that every bit of self-criticism calls me back to his views on philosophy of religion. As I have come to understand philosophy of religion through writing this book, I see that the position he articulated in several of the essays in *Reason and God* is one that cannot be escaped. Smith once wrote of Dewey, "we should attempt to do him the only honor which philosophers ought to acknowledge, namely, to consider his ideas as sufficiently important to be the subject of continued interpretation and critical judgment." [1] It has not been difficult for me to honor teachers like Weiss and Brumbaugh this way because I know where I agree and disagree with them. But the profound philosophical culture Professor Smith tried long years to give me is too much a part of my own thought, with whatever distortion I possess it, to be clearly disengaged. He must be content, then, with my great thanks and perhaps with the small honor a teacher finds when a few of his own virtues peer through his students' work, even though in clouded form.

The readers, as much as myself, owe thanks to my wife for her art that lightens these pages.

[1] *Reason and God: Encounters of Philosophy with Religion* (New Haven, Conn.: Yale University Press, 1961), p. 92.

Introduction

The pervasive question of this book is the relation between God and the world. The answer defended is that God is the creator of the world and that all his various connections with the world ultimately refer to creation. In particular, that God creates the world means that he is both transcendent of it and immanent within it. Surprisingly, making the notion of creation central allows for much stronger claims both of transcendence and of immanence than are possible for approaches that concentrate on one or the other. For instance, the immanence lauded by the view that God is a finite individual interacting with other elements in the world does not show God to be as close to the heart of everything finite as does the view that all things exist as termini of God's creative act. Nor is the transcendence alleged in the claim that God is wholly spiritual as august and mysterious as the transcendence required of one who creates everything determinate, including his own character as creator of this world. The centrality of creation is the distinguishing mark of this interpretation of the relation between God and the world.

What *kind* of question is that of the relation between God and the world? It has been a central issue of the Western speculative tradition since the earliest days. As a speculative question the relation between God and the world has been closely connected with most of the general problems, for example, the nature of being, causation, the one and the many, and so on. The centrality of the question to speculation is such that it can hardly be raised, not to say answered, without broaching a complete systematic approach.

At the present time, however, systematic speculation is considered a dubious enterprise. Even more problematic is a speculative position that holds to a transcendent God. The tenor of philosophy since Descartes has been to take *man* as the focal point of reason, and anything that transcends man's world as much as a creator of everything determinate is called unintelligible. Therefore, in a uniquely modern sense the problem of the relation between God and the world is an epistemological problem, the problem specifically of how man's reason can know something that transcends it.

Most obviously, the question of the relation of God to the world is a religious question. There is a large truth to the claim that philosophy merely reflects on realities found in experience. The experience of man in religion is a fundamental and pervasive dimension of human life and culture, and in many ways that experience encounters the relation of God to the world. Other dimensions of experience, for instance, that of aesthetics, also raise the question, but none quite so directly and centrally as religion.

The answer to the question, What kind of question is that of the relation between God and the world? is that it is several kinds, *at least* metaphysical, epistemological, and religious (this last is handled by philosophy of religion). Consequently, any thoroughgoing assault on the problem must approach in all three ways. It is interesting to note, moreover, that those philosophical approaches which presently command the live options do in fact move in this threefold way.

In America today, there are three thoroughgoing speculative theories that give expression to religion, not counting the continuing development of Catholic Thomism. One is the systematic existential theology of Paul Tillich. A second is the Whiteheadian process philosophy of Charles Hartshorne. The third is the Aristotelian philosophy of Paul Weiss. All of these are highly original developments of traditional approaches, and all articulate essential tenets of religion in terms of well-developed speculative categories. What seems to be missing from the contemporary scene, however, is a comparable theory in the Platonic-Augustinian tradition. Tillich is much closer to this, of course, than Hartshorne or Weiss, especially in his emphasis on the utter transcendence of God. But his equal emphasis on the idealistic immanence of existential categories and his view of concrete universals and their ambiguities in existence commit him also to a different kind of theory.

It is one of the aims of the present study to begin the development of a speculative theory in which religion, especially Christianity, can be expressed, and which will represent the Platonic-Augustinian tradition in the contemporary situation. This is intended as a contribution to religion as well as a claim to truth in speculative philosophy. The present study is just a beginning because it deals only with the problem of God's transcendence and presence. There are many other problems. Furthermore, it operates on a very abstract level; the few concrete problems of religion it deals with at the end are by no means comprehensive and most of them are still so general as to be applicable to all religions. Notwithstanding these qualifications, however, it must be acknowledged that this aim pretends to a great deal.

The second aim of this study, the more intrinsic aim, is to discover the philosophical truth about the speculative problem of the transcendence and presence (or immanence) of God. This is a straightforward, although complex, speculative question and the pursuit of it should be attended with all philosophic rigor and impartiality. Even if religion is to undertake speculative philosophy for its own purposes, it cannot succeed in its undertaking unless it respects the integrity of philosophy. The actual theological employment of speculative philosophy is not a concern in this study, and therefore the form of the discussion is that simply of speculative philosophy. Accordingly, although religion will be treated both as a datum to be analyzed and as an experiential domain to test speculation, its validity, even in the latter instance, will be considered only hypothetically. Taken in large enough portions, of course, religion as a domain of experience can be limited to merely hypothetical validity only as an academic exercise. But with regard to the particulars of religion, in the context of our present study they serve as tests for speculation only on the presumption that there is some truth to them.

Any domain of philosophy has a subject matter in experience to which it would like to do justice; the ultimate worth of its categories involves their interpretive power for the experiential subject matter. Speculative philosophy, however, deals with the most general, fundamental, and ultimate categories. Its experiential subject matter, therefore, is of like breadth and depth. But the very breadth of the experiential subject matter required by speculative philosophy has caused untold difficulties. It seems far too general to have any substance over against the speculations. It is too insubstantial to be a test.

There have been many ways of responding to this problem. Speculative philosophy can retreat from its experiential subject matter and allow that its claims be merely analytical. Analytical claims, however, are interesting only when they articulate meanings already presupposed in a rich context. The context must be rich to make its analysis worthwhile. But speculative philosophy is interested precisely in the higher validity of those very general presupposed contexts of meanings. Another response is to retreat from the generality of speculative problems and limit philosophy to experiential subject matters sufficiently narrow to verify or falsify the philosophical claims. The difficulty with this move is that interest in the general speculative questions can never be squelched for very long, and the arguments that such interest ought to be squelched usually seem to be based on debatable presuppositions that have the forbidden generality. Yet another response is to lead speculation up to its general experiential level through levels of lesser generality, trusting that the lesser levels will commit philosophy to only one alternative at the top that will not have to be questioned by experience. This response, however, also seems to give up the enterprise of criticizing speculative philosophy from the side of experience, for it is those last conclusions we especially want to test.

What speculative philosophy at its best actually has done is to take as its testing subject matter some specialized domain of experience that allegedly pervades the breadth of experience and at the same time articulates its depth. Then philosophy develops its speculative categories with constant reference to the problems of this specialized domain. The specialized domain of experience is thus a recurrent theme through the speculative theory. For Plato, the recurrent theme was aesthetic or normative value judgments. For Aristotle it was the problem of thought and action. Although neither philosopher believed that aesthetics or the connections of thought and action were the only domains of experience interesting for philosophy, the thorough development of those themes gave a richness and experiential concreteness to their most abstruse speculations. Because of their development of specific but pervasive and profound experiential domains, we have a near tangible grasp of what Plato meant when he called the most general speculative category the form of the Good and what Aristotle meant when he called the First Principle pure intellect and pure act.

But neither the problems of normative judgments nor the problems of thought and action seem as pervasive or profound in our experience as they did in that of the ancients. The fact is that the conditions of our culture, and hence of our funded experience, are very different from those of ancient Greece. More to the point, the impact of Christianity on Western culture has been to make *religion,* Christian or otherwise, the experiential domain in which we interpret the pervasive traits and profundities of experience. It is in terms of religion that we experience, affirmatively or negatively, the limits and depths of existence.[1] Consequently, from the time of Augustine on, philosophical speculation has had one eye on religion. This was especially true in the last great group of speculators, the nineteenth-century idealists.

As speculative philosophy needs to pay attention to religion, religion in its turn needs to pay attention to philosophy. There are, moreover, two levels of this need. On one level, religion is a concern involving the intellect. Its practical concerns raise intellectual problems that lead naturally into philosophy's domain. To be sure many domains of experience and reality raise problems that lead to philosophical reflection, and philosophy must continually refresh itself in all of them. But religion is one of the most prominent of these domains, and throughout its history it has moved into either moral or speculative philosophy to satisfy itself in certain ways.

There are many problems of reflection in religion that lead to speculative philosophy. If religion is as pervasive and profound a domain of experience as it is alleged to be, and surely no one could deny the prima facie truth of this claim, then many of its problems for philosophy will be those of the general, fundamental, and ultimate scope of *speculative* philosophy. The history of the connection between philosophy and religion in both East and West has shown this to be the fact.[2] The need of religion for philosophy on

---

[1] Now and again, of course, the ancients stage a comeback. But Plato's aristocrat of grace and beauty is too quickly imitated as a man of manners. Aristotle's contemplator becomes an academic and his man of action suffers the misfortune of becoming *nouveau riche.* Those who touch *our* experience most deeply are those who touch our religion.

[2] History also shows that the general and fundamental questions raised by religion not only require speculative philosophy but help keep it on the right track. When philosophers as a group have retreated from speculation, it usually has been religious concerns that reraised the speculative questions. Especially has this been true for Christianity. As John E. Smith, the most astute commentator on the connection of philosophy and religion, has pointed out, ". . . Christianity has contributed its distinctive concerns and convictions, keeping philosophical thought focused upon the speculative questions, those questions which ask about the foundations of existence itself" (*Reason and God: Encounters of Philosophy with Religion* [New Haven, Conn.: Yale University Press, 1961], p. 136).

John E. Smith

6 GOD THE CREATOR

this level is illustrated by the five problems that will be taken up in Part Three below.[3]

There is a deeper level, however, on which religion needs speculative philosophy. Although it may be true that religion has its sharpest cutting edge in those situations when it has the narrowest focus and its life is heavily oriented around some specific abuse or persecution, those are usually not the situations in which religion is most *complete*. Religion seems to be nearest completion when it mediates most thoroughly in the lives of men the blessings of God it claims to bestow. It does this when it copes with all the dimensions of man's life. To say this is not a commitment to the view that religion should develop a religious culture. Many religions, including Protestant Christianity, believe that religion should have a certain critical and reforming distance from culture, even from the religion's own cultural forms. The very requirement of distance, however, means that religion should develop its critical relevance to all dimensions of life. Because intellect is an important dimension of life, religion should find its expression in arts, letters, and thought.

Since the early days of Christianity in the West, and before that in the East, the intellectual expression of religion often has taken the form of speculative philosophy. Origen, Augustine, Anselm, Bonaventura, Aquinas, Scotus, Cusanus, Hegel, Schleiermacher, Tillich, and countless others in the Christian tradition alone have moved into speculative philosophy for theological expression. Furthermore, the eras of religious philosophical speculation usually have been vigorous and productive times for religion. It can fairly be put down as a lesson of history that the self-understanding of religion, and by extension its intellectual self-expression, requires a thoroughgoing employment and development of a speculative philosophical theory of the whole of things. Religion is narrow and provincial, even on its own terms, when it lacks expression in some large-scale speculative theory. Religion needs speculative philosophy for its own fullness of life.

No thinker, be he theologian or secular philosopher, weaves his speculative theory into whole cloth; every philosophical move is related to its antecedents and is enriched by its relations. In that sense we are fortunate that our works are footnotes to the ancients. But it is a mark of the peculiar individualism of philosophical reflection that each speculative theory must be developed from within to have an integrity of its own. Although a speculative theory should be informed by its antecedents and contemporaries, it cannot be a mere patchwork of opinions. This is especially true of the philosophical speculation undertaken by theology. Contemporary American theology is often so discouraging precisely because it is a patchwork of improperly baptized borrowings from secular philosophy. The common mélange of Heidegger, Buber, and Whitehead is no credit to the integrity of either Judaism or Christianity.

[3] They are listed briefly in the Preliminary Remarks to Part Three.

It is argued by some that, because of the principle that religion must maintain a critical distance from culture, it cannot engage thoroughly in such a cultural enterprise as speculative philosophy and should instead borrow its philosophy widely and lightly. The fear is that religion will become too committed to a cultural form. But this overlooks two essential facts. In the first place, religion must reach thoroughly into culture if it is to reform it; philosophy is one of the things religion should redeem and set straight. In the second place, religion must continually re-express itself as times change even if it does not engage in philosophy, and therefore it should not fear the critical development of its philosophical enterprises. Religion should not fear to develop its speculative expression from within.

Let it be completely understood, however, that this present book is a philosophical one. Its speculation and epistemology are oriented toward the philosophical community. And it treats religion not with theology but with philosophy of religion. It is important to keep this orientation in mind.

The situation within the present philosophical community with respect to a view about the problem of God's transcendence, especially a view that attempts to solve the problem with a theory of creation, is very complex. Whereas in past centuries a theory of creation would be more expected than not, the present situation is dominated by an antimetaphysical bias, on the one hand, and by the antitranscendence bias of many of the leading metaphysicians, on the other hand. A theory of creation is now an anomaly. Skepticism about it arises on two levels.

From the antimetaphysicians there is a general skepticism about any attempt to generate enough speculative machinery to handle with precision a problem so grand as that of what transcends the world of determinate reality. The only answer to this general skepticism is to stress again the need for systematic reflection within experience itself and to point out that where systematic reflection is lacking confusion is only compounded and decorated with the title of humility. Few people are ever convinced by this kind of answer, it must be admitted. The only "existential" answer that can be given is that there is simply more speculative adventure in the air now than can be contented with the programs characteristic of the antimetaphysical position.

From the metaphysicians who can do without the transcendence that religion acknowledges in so many ways, there is a more specific skepticism about the possibility of making an argument that concludes to something transcending the determinate categories of experience and thought. The foundation for the skepticism is readily understandable when it is taken into account that what is transcended, on the view defended here, is the very structure of rationality itself. The kind of dialectical argument the present view involves is surely not without historical precedent: St. Thomas attempted it with his doctrine of analogy. Still, the whole procedure merits more preliminary skepticism than allegiance. The answer to this skepticism can only be a careful presentation of the defense of the kind of thing that is going on in the argument.

These two skeptical features in the contemporary philosophical situation, coupled with the demand of systematic reflection, determine the rhetorical form of the present study.

Part One will give a speculative theory of the transcendence and presence of God. It will deal with standard speculative problems of the nature of being-itself and the one and the many and will argue that their resolution requires a theory of creation. Part One of the study will be abstract and cannot stand on its own without a defense of the kind of knowledge involved in speculation of this sort and an application of the speculative conclusions to concrete problems.

Part Two will be "critical" philosophy, showing how the knowledge involved in Part One is possible. This discussion supplements the first part; yet it could not stand without the first part unless it were to be another of those endless discussions of how we *would* do metaphysics if we ever *were* to do it. As Kant showed, and Hegel more concretely, epistemological philosophy cannot proceed without having in hand an actual specimen of the knowledge in question. The first and second parts together cannot stand without the third if systematic philosophy is not to ignore its duty to experience.

Part Three must bring the speculative theory of creation to the experience of religion, in which God's transcendence and presence is an issue. Although all the relevant problems cannot be considered, the ones chosen will be illustrative of the interpretive power of the speculative categories. Although it might seem, rhetorically, that this part should come first, since most people are familiar with the religious problems and skeptical about the kind of answer to be offered here, new light can be thrown on the concrete problems of religion only when the abstract speculation is in hand. If philosophy is to make its advertised contribution to the problems of life, it will be in virtue of its capacity to penetrate to the abstract features that lie at the heart of all things, to deal with these features precisely, and to bring the precise abstractions to the affairs of life.

Part One

Preliminary Remarks

The nature of the transcendence and presence of God is an old-fashioned speculative problem. Although there still are some thinkers who deal with it, even they are old-fashioned in the eyes of the larger philosophical community. The fact that the problem is out of style has significance for any honest contemporary treatment of it, for the appropriateness of the problem must be justified. It surely cannot be taken for granted, as perhaps it once was, that God is in fact transcendent and present and that all we must understand is how. Rather the task today is to give legitimate speculative arguments that there is a God, that he is transcendent and present, and that this is a proper part of speculative philosophy.

This task cannot be tackled directly, however. The difficulty stems from the peculiarity of proofs for God that they require interpretation both in terms of some comprehensive speculative scheme and in terms of the experience of God in religion and elsewhere. No matter how valid in abstract form the proofs are, they do not prove what is wanted until they are interpreted. Anselm's proofs are significant only within some speculative scheme that interprets degrees of reality or ontological modes of necessity and dependence. Aquinas' proofs require interpretation within a more or less Aristotelian framework. The same point holds of contemporaries like Charles Hartshorne. Rather than begin with a proof for the reality of God, the better part of wisdom is to develop the speculative system and at the end point out that God's reality has been demonstrated along the way.

The difficulty with the indirect approach, however, is that it obscures the focus of the speculative interpretation of God's transcendence and presence. It must "back in" to its treatment of God. Fortunately, the philosophical tradition is rich with correlations between terms like God, transcendence, and presence, on the one hand, and other terms properly respected as speculative problems today. The identification of God with being-itself is almost standard. Furthermore, the relation of God to the unity of the world has such a rich tradition that in many ways the problem of the one and the many is almost a theological one. If there is any truth to these correlations, it should be possible to begin with acceptable problems and issues in the contemporary view and move through them to the old-fashioned subjects. The following speculative theory will in fact be developed this way. The truth to the correlations will be defended as we proceed.

With an eye, therefore, to an ultimate correlation of being-itself with God, we shall begin by inquiring into the nature of being-itself. One of the basic things meant by being-itself is that it is the source of the unity for all of the many real things in the world. The chief challenge to the thesis that being-itself is identical with the ontological one is that of the "analogy of being" theory. That is, if being-itself is not one thing but many things connected by analogy, then it cannot be the ontological one. I shall argue against the analogy theory. The next move is to ask whether being-itself is determinate. My argument will be that being-itself cannot be determinate if it is to be the one for the ontological many. Chapter 1 will conclude that, whatever being-itself is, it must be indeterminate.

Since little can be discovered by direct examination about something that is indeterminate, the next step is to shift from the one to the many and analyze what the many determinations of being need in the way of an ontological unity. An examination of what it is to be a determination of being will show that no determination, however complex, can be the ontological one for itself and the others; therefore, the ground of the unity of the determinations must transcend them. Furthermore, since the one must transcend the determinations of being, we find again that it cannot be determinate. Being-itself is indeterminate, and it is that of which the determinations of being are determinations. These are the conclusions of chapter 2.

How does this transcendent and indeterminate being-itself unify the many determinations of being? I shall argue that it does so by creating them *ex nihilo*. The theory of creation accounts for what the determinations need from their ontological unity; and creating *ex nihilo* is precisely what something transcending the determinations and indeterminate in itself can do. If it were to create out of its own potentialities instead of *ex nihilo*, then being-itself would have to be determinate, which it cannot be. What is created is determinate being, and determinate being contrasts with absolute non-being. But what creates determinate being must in itself be independent of what it creates, since what it creates depends on it wholly. Therefore, being-itself, I shall argue, must be beyond the distinction between determinate being and absolute non-being. That being-itself is the creator of the determinations of being in a way very like that often ascribed to God is the suggestion of chapter 3.

If all determinations are created, then is the distinction between being-itself and the created world determinate or indeterminate? If it is indeterminate, it is wholly unintelligible and our previous argumentation will have been for nought. I shall argue that it is determinate and that therefore it must be among the things that are created. Furthermore, even the role in which being-itself participates in the distinction as creator must be created. The formal structure of the creator-created distinction will be examined in detail. Furthermore, it will be exhibited as a creation theory of the kind that deserves to be called divine creation. This will justify a preliminary identification of being-itself with God, and we will indicate that the creator both transcends and is present in his creation. This will conclude chapter 4 and the whole of Part One.

The advantages of the indirect strategy are great. While the first two chapters are setting the context for the elaboration of the speculative theory, they are also eliminating the chief competitors for the prize. To conclude that being-itself cannot be determinate but must be indeterminate and transcendent of the determinations of being is to leave very few alternatives. The argument to this effect will treat in some detail many of the major philosophies that deny our conclusion. What is left after chapter 2 is little more than an argument that the best way to interpret the notion of being-itself as transcendent and indeterminate is with a theory of divine creation.

1

On the Nature of Being-Itself

The nature of being-itself is a speculative problem for us as much as it was for the ancients and scholastics. No speculative philosophy of the whole of things is complete without a theory of being-itself, even if the theory is nothing more than the claim that the problem of being-itself is misconceived. Furthermore, the problem of being-itself has long been associated with the problem of God. In certain ontologies, being-itself and God are identical. Consequently, consideration of the problem of the nature of being-itself is a promising and fair way to raise philosophical speculation about the transcendence and presence of God.

To the question, What is being-itself? a determinate answer is expected. Or if it is not expected, at least it is hoped for. The acknowledgment that we are looking for a determinate answer, however, should not commit us prematurely to a certain kind of determinate answer, namely, the answer that being-itself is determinate. There is a distinction between the claim that being-itself is determinate and the claim that the answer to the question of being-itself should be determinate, for the answer that being-itself is *indeterminate* is a determinate answer.[1] Since we shall in fact argue that being-itself is indeterminate, this is an extremely important distinction to bear in mind, and it will be defended on many levels in what follows.

[1] Why is it an advantage to use the barbaric term "being-itself" instead of the simpler term "being"? The advantage is that "being-itself" indicates the possibility of a strong distinction between the things that have being and the being that they have, or being-itself. If being-itself is determinate, then it is likely that the things that have being are constitutive of the very essential nature of being-itself; the distinction between the things that have being and the being that they have would be very weak if present at all. On the other hand, if being-itself is indeterminate, then there is likely to be a more external distinction between being-itself and its determinations. It must be kept in mind that the question at issue in the present chapter is not whether there is determinateness in being but whether being-itself is determinate. Should we answer that it is determinate, the awkward use of the term "being-itself" may be gratuitous. But should we answer no, then an important distinction is preserved. We shall, in fact, answer no.

The very distinction between the alternatives that being-itself is determinate or indeterminate marks a major division of watersheds. If we were to conclude that being-itself is determinate, there would still be many constructions of this to choose between. But the conclusion that it is indeterminate, as we shall argue in subsequent chapters, leaves only one way of making sense of being-itself and that is in terms of the theory of creation *ex nihilo,* which undergirds our speculative interpretation of the transcendence and presence of God. Because of the importance of this distinction, we shall begin our discussion of being-itself by asking whether it is determinate or indeterminate.

The question can fruitfully be posed only with some inkling of a criterion that could choose between the two alternatives. How can we initially construe being-itself so as to discover whether it is determinate or indeterminate? There is considerable weight in the philosophical tradition behind an identification of being-itself with that which unifies the diversity of the world. Philosophers have recognized that, however different things in the world might be, their very differences presuppose that they are determinate relative to each other and therefore exist in some more basic unity. At least the different things exist in the unity of having being, and whatever this entails. Any multiplicity presupposes some rudimentary unity: every many needs a one. The ontological one is what gives the multiplicity the unity it needs in order to be diverse. How a multiplicity is unified is the classical problem of the one and the many. It would be a great help to our pursuit of the nature of being-itself to correlate being-itself with the ontological one, the ground of the most comprehensive unity, and to ask what being-itself must be in order to unify the greatest possible diversity.

It is relevant, of course, to ask what the diversity consists in. But the answer to this question would involve a whole metaphysics to determine all the diverse kinds of being. Since this would be a digression from our present purpose, we can remain as neutral as possible by speaking of the many diverse things merely as "determinations" of being. Since they are diverse, they must be determinate; and since they all *are,* in some sense or other, they all have being. Being-itself is the being that they have considered in abstraction from them; whether in itself it is nothing more than an abstraction or whether it has transcendent reality of its own is the root question we shall have to answer.

Is it legitimate to attack the question, Is being-itself determinate or indeterminate? by asking the question, Must being-itself be determinate or indeterminate in order to be the ontological one for the many determinations of being? Weighty tradition, the usages of language, and convenience for our purpose urge that it is legitimate. The only negative voice, aside from attacks on speculative philosophy in general, is raised by the theory that being-itself is not in fact unified as one thing and is signified through merely analogically unified concepts. The prima facie ground for identifying being-itself with the ontological one is that, regardless of what we say a thing is and regardless of what we say are the differences between things, we say of one and all of them that they *are,* even if what they are is only a fiction.

Now the concept of being presupposed here can be used univocally, equivocally, or analogically; there are no other logical possibilities. If the concept is used univocally, then it is quite safe to identify being-itself with the ontological one, for all differences between things would be traceable to differences in their natures, not to the being-itself in which they participate. If the concept is used purely equivocally, then being-itself cannot possibly be identified with the one. But neither, on this view, can there be any such thing as being-itself, only determinate beings; the ontological one for the many would have to be provided by the determinate beings in the many, a view that we shall examine and reject in chapter 2.

If the concept of being is used in that peculiar equivocation called analogy, however, then the identification of being-itself with the ontological one is much more problematic. For if the concept of being is applied to different things only analogically, then being-itself is not sufficiently unified in its relations to the many determinations of being to unify them. The legitimacy of our identification of being-itself with the ontological one depends upon the truth of the claim that the concept of being is used univocally. We shall discuss the consequences of pure equivocation in the next chapter and reject that view. At this point, however, we must determine whether we can reject the theory of the analogy of being.

SECTION A

The Analogy of Being

Almost inevitably in the present day, discussions of the analogicity versus the univocity of being are plagued by an ambivalence as to whether the problem should be treated first-intentionally or second-intentionally. The second-intentional treatment deals with whether the concept "being" is predicated analogically or univocally, and this is the context in which the scholastics usually treated the problem. Since in many ways the scholastic treatment is the most subtle and articulate, it would be unjust not to deal with the problem on this level. Yet at the same time, since differences in the ways concepts are to be predicated are grounded in differences in the things the concepts are supposed to interpret, the problem arises on the first-intentional level, too. Because the bearing of the problem of analogy versus univocity on the issues of the one and the many stems not so much from what it says about a theory of predication as from what it says directly about the nature of being-itself, it is more straightforward to state at least one's conclusions on the first-intentional level. Parallel to the alternatives that "being" is predicated either analogically or univocally are the alternatives either that there is more than one kind of being with no common element or that being-itself is one and common to all things that are. In practice, apart from a discussion of knowing being analogically or univocally, it is impossible to keep the first- and second-intentional level discussions separate, and considerations move from one to the other.

In the beginning, however, the problem can be raised second-intentionally as that of predicating the concept of being, and we shall first consider the claims of the analogy theory. Two current uses of analogy may be distinguished: a classical or strong use, and a weak use that, though as old as Heraclitus, is very popular among philosophers today.

1. The strong use is the one associated with Thomas Aquinas, and it claims that the analogate is known *only* through the analogue. This use is for deriving or inferring knowledge about one thing when we have direct access only to another thing, its analogue. According to Thomas, the form of analogy proper in theology (and speculative philosophy about God) is that of *proportionality* in contrast to that of *proportion*. But the analogy of proportion is simpler and the contrast can be made best by explaining it first.

a) An analogical term (in the analogy of proportion) is one used in two ways; the ways are different in some respects, alike in others. As Aquinas said, such a

> term is predicated according to concepts diverse in some respect and in some respect not—diverse inasmuch as they entail diverse relations, but one in that these diverse relations are all referred to some *one term*.[2]

This "one term" referred to enters into the analogy of proportion in the following way:

> There exists a certain conformity among things proportioned to each other because of a mutual determinate distance or some other determinate relation between them, as two is proportioned to one by being the double of one.[3]

So two and one each have diverse relations to many things; but they are not diverse in that they belong to a number system wherein two is the double of one. The rub, however, is that in analogy this "determinate distance" or "one term" is what is *not* known. Or if it is, the result is a completely univocal system with no real equivocation whatsoever. Aquinas realized this in rejecting the analogy of proportion. "It is impossible for anything to be said of God and creature" by the analogy of proportion, "for no creature has a relation to God such that, through it, the divine perfection could be determined."[4]

b) The analogy of proportionality, on the other hand, claims not to depend on the distance being determinate between the analogous things; rather, the two things have similar proportions within themselves. Propor-

---

[2] *Metaph.* IV, lect. 1, no. 535, trans. James F. Anderson, in *An Introduction to the Metaphysics of St. Thomas Aquinas* (Chicago: Henry Regnery Co., 1953), p. 37 (italics mine).

[3] *De Veritate,* Q. 2, a. 11, in *ibid.,* p. 41.

[4] *Ibid.*

tionality is "a mutual conformity of two things *between which* there is no determinate proportion, but rather a mutual likeness of two proportions." [5] Accordingly, although we have no knowledge of the distance between God and man, we can nonetheless know, for instance, that God's intelligence is proportioned to his being as our intelligence is proportioned to our being.

The interpretation of this is ambiguous, however, and neither side of the ambiguity is satisfactory. On the one hand, the analogy of proportionality could be taken to assert, in the above example, that God's intelligence, like all his powers, is appropriate to his kind of being as our powers are to ours. But since we do not know the distance between man and God, we do not know what his kind of being is, and the analogy, in effect, gives no information about his intelligence at all. Nor does it say anything about God even in a backhanded way to assert that his features are appropriate to his kind of being, for "appropriateness" may be taken in a quite different sense for God than for man in this strong sense of analogy.

On the other hand, an analogy of proportionality could be understood to assert that the proportions in the analogous things are indeed similar. God's intelligence is related to his being similarly to the way man's intelligence is related to man's own being. But this is clearly false; man's intelligence is discursive and God's is immediate. We appeal to analogy instead of univocity precisely because of the differences, not the similarities, between God and man. And on this interpretation of proportionality, it is just the respect in which things are said to be analogous that similarity is to be denied.

But this argument seems too facile. God's intelligence is immediate because his being is simple. Man's intelligence is discursive because his being is discursive, that is, played out in parts. As simple being is to immediate intelligence, so composite being is to discursive intelligence; this is a perfectly coherent proportionality, and given any three terms the fourth could be worked out. The difficulty with this is the old one, however: to begin with *three* of the terms, *any* three, is to know the determinate distance between man and God. In other words, this presupposes an analogy of proportion. Austin Farrer, a contemporary thinker dealing with this problem writes:

> Proportion logically underlies proportionality. . . . The natural use of the proportion is inseparable from that of the proportionality, as the apprehension of the very fact of the divine being is inseparable from some apprehension of its mode.[6]

In this statement (a proportionality in its own right) lies Farrer's ground for asserting the usefulness of the doctrine of proportionality. To speak of the divine being at all is already to have some notion of his nature and hence of the determinate distance or proportion between God and creature. For analogy to be seen as a problem, something like a determinate distance must be known, however vaguely. John Duns Scotus put this point most succinctly:

[5] *Ibid.* (italics mine).
[6] *Finite and Infinite* (2d ed.; London: Dacre Press, 1959), p. 53.

. . . Every denial is intelligible only in terms of some affirmation. . . . if we deny anything of God, it is because we wish to do away with something inconsistent with what we have already affirmed.[7]

And analogy is introduced just because of the denial of univocity.

The upshot of this is that the classical or strong use of analogy presupposes some non-analogical knowledge of the "determinate distance," some positive affirmation outside the analogy to show that the analogy is only an analogy by denying some of the implied similarities. It cannot be the case, then, that the analogate is known *only* by the analogue, and if there is any reason at all for speaking analogically at this point, it cannot be to *infer* from what is known something not known.

2. The weaker use of analogy, like the stronger or classical use, also depends upon a non-analogical ground. The weaker use is simply where the familiar is used to illuminate or illustrate something about what is unfamiliar. Having insight into something unusual, one person conveys this insight to another with the aid of an analogy; but it is presupposed that the other can have direct access to the unfamiliar also and that the analogy only suggests what to look for. When the insight is gained, the analogical term is understood to have two clearly different though related meanings: one in the context of the familiar, and one in the unusual context newly understood. That the analogy depends on extra-analogical knowledge of both the analogue and the analogate is not questioned, and this is the issue at hand.

In both the strong and weak uses, the positive non-analogical affirmation has a dual role, as has been indicated implicitly. On the one hand, as Scotus pointed out, the affirmation is the standard that establishes what is to be denied of the analogy, that determines what parts are not similar. On the other hand, it must be the ground for asserting the analogy itself, for if the analogate could be known *only* through the analogue, how could it be known that *any* analogy applied? There must be some third perspective, however rudimentary or vague, from which the analogy can be judged applicable. In many cases apart from the analogy of *being,* this non-analogical or univocal ground is trivial, especially where the weak use of analogy is concerned, for often analogy is invoked simply to suggest lines of thought to be pursued in detail non-analogically or to set in striking aesthetic relief what otherwise is boorishly literal though important. But in certain philosophical uses of analogy, especially those dealing with the concepts of being-itself and God, the univocal ground for the analogy is very important in itself.

3. These considerations about analogy, however, have yet to be made specific with respect to the knowledge of being; here the line between first and second intention begins to blur. The concern is whether the being had by the ontological many—for instance, both by God and by his creatures—is

[7] *Duns Scotus: Philosophical Writings,* ed. and trans. Allan Wolter, O.F.M. (New York: Thomas Nelson & Sons, 1962), p. 15. See also Thomas' agreement with this, *Summa Theologica,* Pt. I, Q. 13, a. 2.

analogical or univocal. If it is true that any analogical predication of a term must have a univocal or non-analogical ground, both for asserting the analogy in the first place and for showing where it is equivocal, then God and his creatures, or any other kinds of beings, *cannot be said to be in different senses.* This is the important argument. There is no univocal concept able to ground an assertion that there is an equivocation in the respective senses in which two things are, for if "being" is not predicated univocally of two things, then no concept can be predicated univocally of them. This is because the sense in which concepts can be predicated of things depends upon the sense in which those things *are what* they are; that is, it depends upon the sense in which the things have or possess the properties or qualities interpreted by the concepts we predicate of them. But if the sense in which things are what they are is not univocal; if, that is, things differ not only in *what* they are but in the sense in which they are what they are, then no concept can be applied to them univocally. Hence, no univocal knowledge can ground the claim that "being" is predicated of two things analogically. Whatever analogical features things might have, they cannot be analogical in their being; or if they are, it cannot be known that they are. There can be no ground, then, for claiming that "being" is said of God and creatures in an analogical sense, since the analogy in the senses of being would undercut any positive univocal ground for asserting the analogy of being.

This point is relevant to more than the difficulty in knowing just that God's being is analogical with respect to ours. If "being" is analogical when applied to God and creatures, and if all our knowledge of God is by analogy with creatures (by the classical or strong use of analogy), then, as Scotus first made the point, no proper knowledge of God is possible at all; [8] for, if our knowledge of God originates with creatures, then "being" must be in the middle term of a syllogism connecting creatures' being and God's; but if "being" is analogical, then any such syllogism must commit the fallacy of equivocation.[9] For instance, in the syllogism, All rational beings love the Good, God is a rational being, and therefore God loves the Good; if the sense in which God is what he is—that is, the sense in which he possesses the attribute of being a rational being—is not univocal with the sense in which the creaturely rational beings are what they are, then the syllogism commits the fallacy of equivocation.

Defenders of the strong use of analogy recognize the force of this point, however. Aquinas, for instance, tried to meet it when he claimed that an analogy cannot be purely equivocal.[10] He argued that there must be unity sufficient to avoid equivocation in any concept that named both cause and effect. The concept would not be univocal when the cause is not in the same genus as the effect; but this would not destroy the unity of the concept, he thought. As the sun is the cause of generation in men, although not itself in

[8] Duns Scotus *De Anima,* Q. 21, n. 10; and *Opus oxoniense,* I, D. 3, Q. 2, no. 10.
[9] *Opus oxoniense* I, D. 3, Q. 2, no. 5.
[10] *Summa Theologica,* Pt. I, Q. 13, a. 5.

the genus *man,* so God is the cause of the whole order of creation, although he is not in the genus *creature.* But surely the unity needed to avoid equivocation is the unity, in this case, of the definition of the genus, and Thomas did not show what other candidate for unity there might be.[11]

4. The conclusions of this second-intentional discussion of analogy and being are twofold: (1) "being" cannot be predicated analogically of two things, for example, God and creatures, without presupposing a univocal ground that both suggests the analogy in the first place and denies what is purely equivocal in it in the second place; (2) if "being" is predicated analogically, there can be no univocal predication whatsoever with respect to those things. Hence, both the strong and weak uses of analogy presuppose that "being" is predicated univocally, whatever else may be analogical. The weak use of analogy never doubted this; the strong use had to be shown.

These conclusions can be stated in first-intentional form. (1) Although two things can differ in what they are, that is, in their determinations, they cannot differ in the sense in which they are what they are; to be different relative to each other, they must be or possess their determinations in the same sense. (2) If two things do differ in the sense in which they are what they are, then *in no way* could they be said to be alike; for the sense in which they *have* or *are* the determinations would be different. Hence, however the determinations of being differ, being-itself must be one.[12]

The conclusion that being-itself must be one removes the objection raised by the analogy-of-being theory to our strategy of identifying being-itself with the ontological one that unifies the many determinations of being. It is legitimate for us to ask what being-itself is by asking what it must be in order to be the one that unifies the many determinations of being.

Our first approach will be to ask whether being-itself must be determinate or indeterminate in order to unify the many determinations. We shall begin by considering the case for determinateness. The claim that being-itself is

---

[11] Cf. an interesting and related argument by Charles Hartshorne in *The Divine Relativity* (New Haven, Conn.: Yale University Press, 1948), pp. 17 f.: "To say, we know, not God, but something to which we know that God is analogous, does not meet my argument. Analogy involves relation, thus: —'We know there is Something to which the world is related as effect to cause.' If the relation is in God, then he is relative. If it is in the world, then the world has relation-to-God, and since this is a complex which includes God, and since God has, by hypothesis, only absolute being, the world must include this absolute being. Otherwise, what the world has is not relation-to-God, but relation-to, and nowhere, in the world or in God, is there any such relation as the analogy involves. So 'the analogy of being' fails to provide an answer to the question, what do we know when we know God?"

[12] A qualification of this discussion of analogy should be pointed out. Although it is undoubtedly true that the doctrine of analogy is connected closely with the Thomistic doctrine of creation, it is not necessarily true that the difficulties with analogy are fatal to Aquinas' creation theory. It may well be that what Aquinas claims is analogical about the relation between God and creatures can be given univocal interpretations; or it may even be that St. Thomas recognized a univocal ground himself. It will turn out, in fact, in the subsequent discussion that God is not a thing possessing his determinations in the same way that created things are what they are; rather God *is* the univocal being-itself that is common to the creatures. And this is not too different from Aquinas' own view of the matter.

something determinate has several interpretations, however; and the differences between the interpretations are far reaching and systematic. We shall consider four paradigmatic positions that espouse and interpret the claim that being-itself is determinate: the theory that being-itself is determinate as *ens commune*, that it is determinate as *ens perfectissimum*, that it is determinate as a self-structuring power, and that it is determinate but non-general.

SECTION B

Ens Commune

The simplest way of claiming that being-itself is determinate is to say that it is a property common to all beings. When it is said that all beings have being or participate in being-itself, what is meant, on this interpretation, is that there is a property or attribute "being-itself" that is a feature of all beings. Of course, on *any* theory of being, it must be possible to say that beings participate in being-itself. The distinguishing mark about this interpretation is that the being-itself in question is a determinate property alongside of or on a par with other properties. Being-itself on this interpretation is a common quality or predicate.

The claim that being-itself is a property common to all beings can be vague with respect to further interpretations of what kind of property is involved. On the one hand, it has been said that the common property is a surd, simply to be apprehended and not to be "explained" in terms of other intelligible characters. There is a kind of mysteriousness or arbitrariness about being-itself that recommends this kind of elaboration. On the other hand, it has been said that the common property is a specifiable character, like "presence to consciousness." [13] We are aware of this character from earliest times, and all we need to be told, on this view, is that this character is what we are looking for when we ask what being-itself is.

Regardless of these further interpretations of the common property, whether it is a surd or whether it is to be determinately characterized, we must acknowledge that the common property is determinate in a higher sense that puts it on a par with other determinations. That is, the common property contrasts determinately with other properties. A thing may have, for instance, the properties of "brown," "large," "live," and "being." Or it may have all those properties except "brown" or all except "being." The point of saying that being-itself is a property is to claim that things may either have it or not have it. Centaurs have hoofs but no being; abominable snowmen have large feet, but whether any have being is a matter still in question. Being may be a different kind of property from that of having hoofs, but this is like the

---

[13] For a contemporary defense of this view, see two articles by Robert R. Ehman: "On the Possibility of Nothing" and "A Defense of the Private Self," both in *Review of Metaphysics*, XVII (December, 1963), 205–13, and XVII (March, 1964), 340–60, respectively. But see also this author's "Ehman's Idealism" in the same journal, XVII (June, 1964), 617–22.

difference between "large" and "good." The differences are properly to be noted in their place, but the common characteristic of all properties, that they contrast determinately with each other, is most important to notice here.

This interpretation of being-itself as a property beside others immediately runs afoul of a fundamental dilemma of ontology, for if being-itself is a property, what is the ontological status of the other properties? The other properties, by hypothesis, contrast determinately with the property of being-itself. But to contrast with being-itself, they must have an integrity or being of their own over against being-itself. If being-itself is one of many properties, then those other properties must be, on their own and in contrast to the property of being-itself. But this is smuggling in a higher sense of being than the one in question.

Perhaps it should be said, to help this view, that being-itself is one property among others and that the others "are" only in the event that they have or participate in the property of being-itself. After all, many properties contrast with each other and yet by their natures entail the others; for instance, "red" is not the same as "colored" and yet it entails it. Or, to take the example mentioned above, if being is "presence to consciousness," it is different from the property of "squareness"; yet the property of squareness may have no being at all unless it is present to some consciousness. But what is at issue is not whether one property can participate in another, even to the point of necessary entailment; the issue concerns the ontological status of those characters of properties in virtue of which they contrast. If a property is other than being-itself, even if it has being, then that in virtue of which it is other than being must have an ontological status. The contrasting elements must be over against being-itself. Red may be a color, but it is not the same as "color" since it is different from blue, which is also a color. As "redness in contrast to blueness" is over against "color," so the contrasting properties that have being are over against being-itself. Otherwise there is no point in saying that being-itself is a property. But if this is so, then they have being over against being, which is a contradiction.

Perhaps it should be said, again to help the view, that only *substances* have being and that properties "are" only when they are properties of substances. To speak of properties having being, on this view, is merely a confusion. Substances have being, and being is a property of substances. On this interpretation it is a distorting abstraction to speak of the property of being-itself; one can speak of *being* as a property had by substances, but to isolate it and call it being-*itself* is an unwarranted hypostatization. Needless to say, this way out only occasions more difficulties of the kind that beset the previous interpretation. If substances contrast with being, what is their ontological status insofar as they contrast? And even if properties are only to be found in substances, how do they contrast with the property of being? If it is said that to be is to be a substance, that this is just exactly the property that being is, again, how does a substance contrast with its other properties? Its other properties are either exactly identical with it, all substances being alike, or they contrast; if the other properties differ from substantial being, whatever in them is other than being-itself must have some ontological status, must have being of its own. So long as being is considered as a determinate property, it must contrast with other properties and be considered in that context as being-*itself*.

If being-itself is said to be the common element in all the things that are, there is always the temptation to characterize it in such a way as to put the differentia distinguishing the beings outside of being and in contrast with it. To say that the common element is a property determinately different from other properties is to do just that. But this is always fatal, since the properties things have over and above being *are other than being*, which is to be and not to be in the same respect.

The difficulties of the common-property interpretation exhibit a basic principle that can be given explicit formulation. It can be called the "principle of the ontological ground of differences," and it is that *two differing determinations of being presuppose a common ground in virtue of which they are relevantly determined with respect to each other and from which each delimits for itself a domain over against the other*. Although both differing elements must *be* in the same sense in order to be comparable, and thus must have being in common, at the same time they differ according to their individual integrities or natures and therefore each must have its "own" being; being-itself must be such that each being can delimit it and possess its own domain. The metaphor of a "domain" indicates its meaning roughly now but can be explained fully only when our reflection arrives at a positive account of being-itself later on.

The error of the interpretation of being-itself as a determinate property is that it emphasizes the commonality in the principle of the ontological ground of differences while it pays insufficient attention to the sense in which each being has its own being. Consequently, the interpretation acknowledges the latter side unreflectively by construing the relation between being-itself and the beings as that of universal to particular or of genus to species. Put in this bald way, it is readily seen that neither of these models can suffice. For, as Aristotle saw, neither the universal nor the genus properly bespeaks the features that differentiate their instances or species one from the other; yet these distinguishing features have their being, too, over against the universal or genus.

SECTION C

Ens Perfectissimum

It is natural to look from an *ens commune* theory to its opposite, an *ens perfectissimum* theory. Being-itself on this second interpretation is the determinate completion or totality of the ontological many or plurality of beings. Two sides of this interpretation must be emphasized. First, in order to be a determinate totality, not an adventitious massing or indeterminate collection, being-itself in its complete sense must be the embodiment of a highest principle or category. This highest category cannot be exhibited fully by any limited number of the beings of the ontological many but must be exhibited by them all together. It must be a supercategory that integrates the many together and gives a determinate place to each. Secondly, the many beings included within the *ens perfectissimum* are in themselves only partial or abstract expressions or embodiments of being-itself. This is not to say that they may not be real, concrete, or capable of exercising brute force; it is only to say that with respect to being-itself they are abstract. Being-itself was construed this way by many of the idealists who wrote near the turn of the century; it is the block universe view attacked by James and others.

This second interpretation of the claim that being-itself is determinate founders, like the first, on the same fundamental dilemma of ontology, the dilemma of giving being-itself a positive characterization. This can be shown by asking whether the highest category has a significant contrast category. Is the determination that unifies all other determinations determinately what it is and not some other thing? Two answers are possible.

1. Suppose the highest category does not have a significant contrast term. But then it can have no determinateness uniquely its own whereby it internally relates, as a "third term," the abstract categories and beings it encompasses; for to have a significant determination of its own over and above the determinations of being it contains, it must have a significant contrast, contrary to the hypothesis. In virtue of what, it must be asked, does the highest category unite its contents? The answer must be, In virtue of its own determinate nature. But to be determinately what it is, the highest category must contrast with what it determinately is not. Otherwise it would contain the encompassed categories as a box indifferently contains a miscellany of things; even this analogy begs the question, since a box has a determinate principle of ordering space in virtue of which it unites its contents. The highest category, if not determinate over against a contrast term, could not of itself give an interpreting order to its contents, nor could it even be said to be anything more than the uncollected sum (already a contradiction!) of its parts. And at any rate, if it has no significant contrast and hence is not determinate itself, it cannot be an interpretation of the claim that being itself is determinate.

2. Suppose then that the highest category does have a significant contrast term. What can the contrast term be? Two answers are possible: (*a*) the contrast term could be one or all of the categories or beings contained within the highest category, or (*b*) it could be absolute non-being.

a) Suppose first that the contrast term is one of the beings or categories of being contained in the highest category. Now, although the highest category would be a significant contrast for one of its abstract parts because it would have determinations over and above any of its parts, the contrary does not hold. The abstract part has no determination over and above the whole of which it is the part, that is, the highest category; for the highest category must wholly integrate its parts and hence all of its parts are completely internally related to it. The abstract part cannot be a significant contrast for the highest category unless its limitations make it sufficiently less than the highest category. But the limitations of an abstract part or determination of being are nothing more than the totality of the rest of the abstract parts or determinations. But an abstract part together with its limitations is the same thing as the highest category, for in order that the abstract part be unified with its limitations—that is, the other abstract parts—it must be unified within the highest category. The totality of parts is the same as the highest category; otherwise the parts could not be "totalled." A thing cannot be a contrast term to itself.

b) Suppose second that the contrast term to the highest category is absolute non-being. Now by definition, non-being cannot contrast with the highest category by some determination of its own, since if non-being had a determination it would *be*. Then the contrast must be that non-being has absolutely no features, whereas being-itself does have determination. But if this is so, absolute non-being cannot be the contrast term for that specific positive determination in virtue of which the highest category unites its parts; and it is the highest category's peculiar inclusive determination that needs the contrast, not determinateness as such. If the contrast is between non-being, which has no determinations, and a category that does have determinations, any abstract category of being would contrast with non-being just as well as the highest category could, since all abstract parts and categories are determinate.

It might be objected to our criticism at this point that the abstract parts of the highest category are abstract precisely because they are *not* wholly determinate and that the move beyond them to the absolute or highest category is necessary to give them complete determination. There are two historical ways in which this objection has been defended. One says that implicit within any element of being is a drive to become determinate with respect to what is other than that element and that so long as there is some such other the drive persists. At the end the absolute is reached when no other remains with respect to which being is indeterminate. The satisfied drive for determinateness, or being-itself, contrasts with non-being; the specific determinations it has depend upon the contingent facts of what it finds as its other along the way. Hence, according to this first theory, the satisfied drive toward determinateness, called Spirit, does contrast simply in itself with absolute non-being. This is the way of Hegel and the third interpretation of the claim that being-itself is determinate that will be considered. The second defense of the objection argues that the determinate knowledge of any part of being requires us to determine that part with respect to everything else; but it is characteristic of finite knowledge that it inevitably involves general terms, which are always partially indeterminate. Consequently, complete determinateness or being-itself is unknown to us; and since the need for a contrast term is characteristic only of finite thought,

Neville '66

G. W. F. Hegel

it cannot be required of the highest category, which our finite thought approaches as a limit. This is the way of Royce and will be considered as the fourth interpretation of the claim that being-itself is determinate.

The difficulties of the second interpretation of the determinate-being claim, however, like those of the first interpretation, exhibit a general dialectical principle. It can be called the "principle of the ontological equality of reciprocal contrasts": *if two determinations of being are contrast terms for each other, then they must be on the same ontological level and the categories descriptive of them must be on the same logical level.* Of course, if the contrast is not reciprocal, the determinations of being need not be on the same ontological level. The metaphor of "levels" in the statement of this principle serves to indicate its meaning roughly; but its full explication must wait for a more complete discussion of the nature of real distinctions.

The difficulty with this second interpretation of the claim that being-itself is determinate is that it accepts a meaning of "determinate" that requires that being-itself have a contrast term. Yet there is nothing on the same ontological level with being-itself with which it can contrast. Nor is there anything on the same logical level in the order of varying degrees of abstractness with which it can contrast. We must now turn to theories of being that couple the claim that being-itself is determinate with the further claim that this is because being-itself is determinateness as such.

SECTION D

Being-Itself as Self-structuring Power: Hegel

The third interpretation of the claim that being-itself is determinate is by far the most difficult to make plausible and by far the most tenacious once plausible. The difficulty in rendering it plausible stems largely from the fact that it involves a kind of apprehension of things that belongs to another, more romantic era. The notion of a powerful, vitalistic Spirit has all but disappeared from our fund of respectable categories and has in fact taken a prominant place in the museum of quaint anthropomorphisms seen through all too well. All that is left today of that fundamental category of romantic idealism is its abstract conceptual form, which, as Hegel would put it, is reality after dusk has fallen. The problem is that the notion of Spirit has not been refuted conclusively; its hold on our philosophic imagination has only been "gotten over," and it remains to be seen whether this getting over is an advance or a lapse. The tenacity of the theory stems largely from the fact that it was most notably elaborated by one of the most massive, persistent, thorough, consistent, and sensitive philosophic minds ever to write, G. W. F. Hegel.

The genius of Hegel's theory lies chiefly in the unprejudiced attention it pays to whatever subject matter is at hand. For Hegel no knowledge of a subject matter is determined a priori, or prior to the actual examination of it. Everyone knows that Hegel held the ultimate subject matter of philosophy to be the proper form of thought and that the proper form of thought is the necessary rationality that determines the real.[14] But the "proper form of thought" has more kinship, for him, with the medieval notion of intellect adequated to its subject matter than it does to any a priori formal structure from which particulars could be deduced.

One consequence of this a posteriori approach is that the ontological categories do not retain fixed meanings throughout all domains of reality. The connotations of the term "will," for instance, change many times in Hegel's treatment of the will's development of freedom. The usual interpretation of Hegel's dialectic as a movement from a thesis to its antithesis and finally to a synthesis obscures the essential fact that in the process of dialectic even the meanings of the moves change from one moment to the next. Only in the vague domain of history, where particular thoughts are obscured and only general trends are brought to attention, does the dialectical process have anything like the simple structure of thesis, antithesis, and synthesis. The result of Hegel's claim that the categories of thought appear in many guises and that the guises are essential to the truth of the categories is that any general criticism of his theory is subject to the charge that it falsifies by taking categories out of context. Whereas Plato encouraged the abstraction of forms or essences from the particular contexts in which they are found in experience, Hegel saw this as "mere" abstraction contrary to the true aim of thought, the pursuit of the love of wisdom rather than wisdom itself.[15] It is a great surprise to many philosophers who attempt to work out a thoroughgoing nominalism to find Hegel sitting on the prize. Since Hegel claimed that the rational is the real only when the rational categories are particularized in individual contexts (and only categories so particularized are properly rational and not abstract[16]), it would seem that the only unity of the system of reflection is constituted by the rational but ideosyncratic cogency of the individual moves run through serially. It would seem that there are no universal categories that apply with a fixed sense to all domains, no unifying themes, no general principles that can be considered in abstraction from the details of the system. This would indeed be a thoroughgoing nominalism. But Hegel was a nominalist only with respect to concepts. His doctrine of Spirit claims that there is a kind of generality that is not conceptual generality but that pervades all of reality.

Spirit has an essential structure that can be described. But the structure of Spirit is a dynamic structure, a structure primarily of moves. Spirit is a move from the simple identity of the beginning to the determination of that identity with respect to what is other than its simple nature, thus making the identity complex and inclusive of its other. Prior to the move of determina-

---

[14] See *The Logic of Hegel*, trans. W. Wallace (2d ed.; Oxford: Oxford University Press, 1892), secs. 9–17, pp. 15–28.
[15] See *Hegel's Phenomenology of Mind*, trans. J. B. Baillie (rev. 2d ed.; London: George Allen & Unwin, Ltd., 1931), p. 70.
[16] See *The Logic of Hegel*, sec. 6, p. 10.

tion, the simple identity is indeterminate with respect to its other, and hence
the contrast between the identity and its other cannot be made except from
the standpoint of the move already made. Consequently, the distinction
between the identity and its other, the opposition between them, is always
abstract since there are no distinctions but determinate distinctions and a
determinate distinction is always in the context of a resolution where the
relation between the identity and its other is determinate.

The conceptualizable distinctions between the moments of Spirit's progress, however, are not the whole story, for at the heart of Spirit is power or
dynamics. Power always stems from a source or initial identity, moves
through a medium, and produces a product. This directional movement
cannot be overlooked, for otherwise the theory would collapse into the second
interpretation of the determinateness of being discussed above; it is the
distinguishing characteristic of Hegel's romantic idealism. Because of the
directional dynamics of Spirit, the stages of Spirit's movement are real,
though abstract, even where determination is not complete. Their indeterminate status must have some kind of reality for the concluding determinate
synthesis to be the result of a dynamic exercise of power. What the reality is,
is a problem to be conjured with below.

The structure of Spirit is often taken as the model for a self. But Hegel
drew a definite distinction between finite selves and an infinite self. With
suitable modifications, the structure of Spirit and its development can be
applied to finite selves, as Hegel did in his *Phenomenology of Mind* and
Philosophy of Right. But when talking about Spirit as the ontological
principle of reality, Hegel meant an infinite self or infinite Spirit. Two
additional clarifications of the notion of infinite Spirit are required.

First, considered in the first moment of simple identity, the power of
infinite Spirit *creates* its other. Considered still from the standpoint of the
simple identity, this creation does not take place according to any rational
principles, nor does it have a determinate form. From the standpoint of the
synthetic determination of the simple identity and its other, the simple
identity has its later development implicit within it; but from the immediacy
of the simple identity, its development is not even implicit, only indeterminate. In creating, then, Spirit has moved beyond its simple identity; to fix on
a moment in itself is to conceive abstractly and miss the reality of the
dynamics of Spirit. To create a determinate other, Spirit must be already at
the third, determinate, and synthesizing stage. Consequently, the dynamics of
Spirit always transcend the abstract structure of its nature. The simple
identity's other has no determinate form and hence no being until it is
determined with reference to the identity. (It is a characteristic of *finite*
spirit that its other does have a form of its own prior to being made determinate with respect to the spirit; finite spirit does not create *ex nihilo*.)

Second, infinite Spirit need not move through a temporal medium. In fact,
since it creates its other, and the other is the medium, the dynamics of infinite
Spirit apart from finite spirit cannot be temporal. Only finite spirit moves

temporally. The sense we have that all exercise of power is temporal stems from the fact that our usual understanding of power is that of finite power, which produces only novel arrangements of already existing things through time. Infinite power, which produces its product in its entirety, cannot be temporal but rather simply productive; there is no contradiction in thinking of the exercise of infinite power as atemporal.

It is interesting to note that the creative work of Spirit, which gives rational form to its product only when it has moved beyond it, is an analogue to Hegel's a posteriori method. Since philosophy works, according to him, by following the development of Spirit, the conclusions of the dialectic can never be deduced from the premises or starting point. The nature of rationality is not determined until after the determinations are all in.

As an interpretation of the claim that being-itself is determinate, Hegel's theory says that to be is to be Spirit. Spirit's essential nature is the drive to become wholly determinate. It is in virtue of the fact that Spirit is complete determinateness that it, as being-itself, contrasts with absolute non-being. Yet we can hardly speak at this point of the need for a contrast term for being-itself. Being-itself has its meaning in virtue of the fulfillment of a dynamic drive that is implicit in all the parts of being. From the standpoint of a stage prior to the end of Spirit's development, the meaning of being-itself is the determination of the yet indeterminate end. In fact, only at the end can we speak of being-itself instead of being-becoming-itself. From the standpoint of the end, being has no meaning apart from its simple identity, which is the outcome of its abstract predecessors; but to ask for the meaning of being at this point is to presuppose a standpoint beyond the end, a determinate other, which is contrary to the hypothesis that the end is the end. Absolute non-being cannot be an other. The meaning of being-itself is simply complete determinateness, and determinateness acquires its meaning from its implicit development.

Brilliant as this theory is, however, the fundamental dilemma of ontology strikes it down. A question must be put as to the completion of determination, the last step in the dialectical development of Spirit. Is this last step determinate? Two answers are possible.

1. One could say that the last step is not determinate. Spirit is always moving beyond the stage it has made determinate; the dynamics of Spirit always transcend the stage that has been made determinate. There is, in effect, no last step, since any determinate stage is transcended. The last step is a move, not a stage, and the move lacks the determinateness of a stage. Being-itself is not so much complete determinateness as the *drive* toward further determination. The more one emphasizes the romantic quality of power in Hegel's notion of Spirit, the more this interpretation is plausible. But it has two difficulties.

a) The interpretation falls into what Hegel calls the "bad infinite," a conception of infinity that is a mere formula for repetition, not a concrete demonstration or showing of infinite transcendence. Given any provisional last stage, Spirit transcends it by creating an other that is determinately related to it: this is a mere formula. On this interpretation it turns out that rationality goes from abstract principles to concrete reality and then again to abstract and finite thought. Perhaps Hegel would say that the *question* as to the completion of the dialectic of Spirit is essentially abstract; but the whole force of his argument has been to show that only the completion is concrete, only the completion is being-itself. And if he says that questions as to the last step always must deal with a particular candidate, then he has given up the claim that being-itself is determinateness as such. This may be what he would do, but it would be an adherence to descriptive philosophy to the exclusion of ontology, which puts him outside the pale of our present reflection.

b) The second difficulty with this interpretation is that it claims that being-itself is only abstractly determinate; the essential nature of being is to be indeterminate, to be transcending any explicit determination toward an implicit determination that at the moment of transcendence is indeterminate. The rational discipline of power comes after the fact, and the essential nature of Spirit or being-itself is immediate and arbitrary transcendence. The mediation of determinateness is always less concrete than the sheer transcending power itself. This interpretation, of course, puts Hegel outside the camp of those who claim that being-itself is determinate; but it also has an unusual twist for our traditional understanding of Hegel. It is not quite accurate to say, as he did, that the real is the rational and the rational is the real, where rationality is taken to mean determinate and necessary, for whereas the rational is always real, the real is rational only abstractly, since rationality is abstract. However rational the dialectic might be from the standpoint of its terminus, from the standpoint of the beginning or simple identity, the moves ahead are contingent, free, and arbitrary; every terminus is itself a starting point. Furthermore, the reality of Spirit as self-transcendence makes any stage more abstract in its determinate *terminal* aspect than in that *initiating* aspect which faces transcendence indeterminately. The essential thing to say about being is that it is indeterminate, and that its product, its determination, is abstract when considering being-itself. If Hegel is to move over to the position that being-itself is most essentially indeterminate, our quarrel with him is inconsequential at this point; it would only be to argue about how the determinations get produced and how they can be related to indeterminate being.

2. One could also answer the question whether the last step in the dialectic is determinate in the affirmative. This is the answer of most of Hegel's successors. But then the question must be, How can the last step be determinate and still be the last step? This is to question whether complete determinateness is possible. If the process of complete determination is to be completed, then it must have a determinate last step, a step that is a third term giving determinate unity to the many elements that lead to it. The unifying determination of the last step is not contained in its predecessors, and to be determinate it needs a contrast term. But this is exactly the position

of the second interpretation of being as determinate considered above. The difficulties with that interpretation are fatal for this answer of Hegel.

Hegel is notorious, however, for having an answer to every move made against him, and this discussion is no exception. The form of our argument has been to consider Hegel's theory of Spirit as an answer to the question of the nature of being-itself, and then to pose for that theory the issue whether the completion of Spirit is determinate or not. The question forces a dilemma: if the answer is no, then the theory at once denies that being-itself is essentially determinate and is led to assert an un-Hegelian irrationalism; if the answer is yes, then the theory reduces to the second interpretation of the claim that being-itself is determinate, which was already in trouble. But Hegel's typical response to a dilemma is to affirm both sides and to claim that the sheer posing of the dilemma presupposes a common ground, beyond the contradictories, which resolves them. Thus, although each side of the dilemma falls by itself, when both sides are affirmed together within a third term there is no difficulty. The truly dialectical answer to the question whether the completion of Spirit is determinate or not determinate is that it is both, since that is the very dialectical nature of Spirit. We must see whether Hegel is entitled to this response and whether it helps his case as a defender of the claim that being-itself is determinate.

The horns of the dilemma are that the completion of Spirit is either determinate or indeterminate. If the indeterminateness side means sheer power to the exclusion of determinateness, then obviously Hegel could rejoin that Spirit is beyond and inclusive of both. Yet in fact the indeterminateness side means simply that which transcends but *includes* as abstract moments the determinations of reality. Hence, the horns of the dilemma do not oppose two abstract elements but rather an abstract element versus the whole of which it is a part. There is no third term beyond Spirit.

But we critics do take up a standpoint that is beyond and inclusive of the horns of the dilemma. Hegel could argue that there must be a mistake somewhere because the very ability to frame the question presupposes a third position. The question, however, as was admitted above, is an abstract one, far removed from any concrete candidate for the last move of dialectic. And the abstractness of the question allows it to be raised without presupposing a standpoint in reality beyond the alternatives within the dilemma. Abstract thought is characterized by the fact that it treats as alternatives elements of a concrete whole that are only abstractly to be distinguished. And the justification of abstract thought is that on Hegel's theory of Spirit there is no other way of raising the question of the meaning of being-itself. Hegel might, in true nominalist fashion, conclude from this that the question cannot be raised. If so, this excludes him from the camp of candidates to defend the claim that being-itself is determinate.

But suppose Hegel is justified in making this move to a third term beyond the alternatives of the dilemma. How would this help him make out the case that being-itself is determinate? The question whether being-itself is determinate is not the question whether there are determinations of being; in fact, we presuppose that there is a determinate many for which being-itself is to be the ontological one. Nor is it the question of the relation between being-itself and its determinations; although Hegel's theory of Spirit does give an answer to this question, this is not of the present interest. The question at issue is whether being-itself is to be essentially characterized as determinate. If Hegel were to say that the truth of the matter is some third term beyond determinateness and indeterminateness, this still would make determinateness an abstract and less than essential characterization of being-itself.

"Indeterminateness" is a concept by negation, and it could be interpreted either as an exclusive or as an inclusive alternative to determinateness. We have just argued that on Hegel's theory it should be interpreted as an inclusive alternative. Any move to a third term is still a move to indeterminateness; this proves our point about Hegel. It should be made clear, however, that our discussion has accepted Hegel's account of determinateness as an abstract element of Spirit only for the end of discovering the upshot of his view with regard to the claim that being-itself is essentially to be characterized as determinate. Having discovered that the results of his view are that being-itself is not so to be characterized, his entire notion of Spirit may be called into question when we come to consider the alternative. What indeterminateness really is will be found to be something much different from self-transcending Spirit, and determinateness may be something other than an abstract element of something more concrete.

One more second intentional look must be taken at our reflections about Hegel. For systematic purposes we have taken Hegel's theory of Spirit as a candidate answer to the question we have posed about the characterization of being-itself. Yet anyone familiar with Hegel's writings will surely have noticed that he uses the term "being" to mean the very opposite of "Spirit" in its absolute form. Being, for him, is the very first and most abstract moment of Spirit.[17] Is there a more fundamental issue hidden here, or is this a mere terminological difference wherein the significance we have attached to the question of being-itself properly applies to his notion of Spirit? Could it be that Hegel would maintain that there is a more fundamental ontological question than that of the nature of being-itself? Would he ask rather, What is it to be?, and answer, To be Spirit? The more one emphasizes Hegel's nominalistic tendency, the more plausible this question becomes.

The question of being-itself, as we have systematically posed it, is the question of the one for the ontological many. And Hegel said that being in its abstract sense is what is common to all determinations of the dialectic. More fundamental for ontology is the study of Spirit, which accounts for the development and connections of the various determinations. Hegel forces us to recognize that simple commonality is not the only meaning of ontological unity, for a true theory of unity must take into account the full reality of the

[17] See *ibid.*, secs. 84–86, pp. 156–61.

various determinations, not simply what is common to them in principle. Hegel's account of how being is common to the determinations *individually* is his theory of Spirit, for Spirit is being's *explicit* presence in all things. But if this is so, then Hegel's interpretation of our question about being-itself as the one for the ontological many *is* his theory of Spirit and not his doctrine of being considered abstractly, for Spirit is being as it is related individually to all the members of the many. If it is the case that the question of being is an abstract version of the question of what it is to be, then the answer to the question of what it is to be is a concrete answer to the question of being-itself, and that was what we wanted.

The conclusion to the discussion of Hegel is that he could give a meaning to being-itself only by making it essentially indeterminate. Assuming that being-itself can be given a meaning, that is, that the question, What is being-itself? can be given a determinate answer, it is still an undecided issue whether the essential indeterminateness of being-itself includes determinateness as an essential but abstract part or whether a more external relation to determinateness is involved.

SECTION E
Being-Itself as Non-generally Determinate: Royce

There is an even more extreme theory than Hegel's that tries to get around the difficulty that being-itself as determinate needs and cannot find a contrast term on the same ontological level. This is the theory held by Josiah Royce, which claims that determinateness in its truly infinite sense does not need a contrast term, and it constitutes our fourth interpretation of the claim that being-itself is determinate.

The aim of thought and will, according to Royce, is the apprehension of being in its concreteness, and it is assumed from the outset that concrete being is wholly determinate.[18] But the distinguishing characteristic of finite thought is that it is in terms of universals.[19] When finite thought aims to know a concrete thing, like a chair, it always does so in universal terms that possibly could apply to other things; so, to know the chair as brown, straight-backed, and uncomfortable is not truly to know that concrete chair because there may be other such chairs and our present knowledge does not include the differentia.[20] Finite thought might increase its specifying universals ad infinitum, and yet in virtue of the fact that finite thoughts are universals, another possible referent for our knowledge is always conceivable.[21] Consequently, completely adequate knowledge of concrete and wholly determinate being is impossible for finite thought. Another brand of understanding is

---

[18] See Royce's *The World and the Individual, First Series* (New York: Macmillan Co., 1899), pp. 39 ff. and 295.
[19] *Ibid.*, p. 269.
[20] *Ibid.*, p. 236.
[21] *Ibid.*, p. 293.

required for knowledge of concrete being, and we approach this only as a limit.[22] The determinateness of concrete being is a different thing from the determinateness of finite thought, even though finite thought can approach it ever more closely.[23]

But what is there in the universality of finite thought that keeps it at an unbridgeable distance from concrete being? Royce explained the difficulty by pointing out that finite thought is universal because the kind of determinateness it has is determination by negation.[24] If all that thought says of a subject matter is that it is not *x*, then this thought applies equally well to any other possibility that is also not *x*, and the concreteness or unique individuality of the subject matter is inaccessible. Royce's argument that the determinateness of finite thought is determination by negation rewards closer scrutiny.

All thought, Royce claims, and most of us would agree, is of a judgmental form. The consideration of a rough classification of judgments is enough to indicate plausibility in Royce's thesis that finite determination is by negation. The classification is of hypothetical, categorical, and disjunctive judgments.[25]

A hypothetical judgment is of the form, "if *a*, then *b*." [26] Although it does not assert the truth of anything positive, it does say that reality is not such that *a* is true and *b* false. It is a determinate judgment in the sense that it says what reality is *not*.

Categorical judgments are either universal or particular. A universal judgment is of the form "all *a* is *b*." [27] But it makes no claim as to the reality of *a* or *b*; it only says that if there are any *a*'s they are *b*'s, or that there are no *a*'s that are not *b*'s. A universal categorical judgment is basically a hypothetical one and hence determinate by negation. A particular categorical judgment is of the form "some *a* is *b*." [28] This is obviously a negation if it is taken to mean that it is not the case that all *a*'s are *not-b*. But suppose we have it from experience that here is an *a* that is a *b*. Yet all intelligible experience is selected experience where the selection takes place in universal terms. We experience positive characters by recognition, and recognition involves seeing a hypothetical interpretation of experience supported. But the support of a hypothetical interpretation in a particular case can only be the acknowledgment that the hypothesis or hypothetical judgment is not falsified. We know from the above that all hypothetical judgments are determined by negation.

Disjunctive judgments are of the form "*a* is *b* or *c*." [29] This is not to say anything positive about *a* except that there are no alternatives for it to be except *b* and *c*. Thus the determinate character of disjunctive judgments stems from their negation of other alternatives than the disjuncts.

[22] *Ibid.*, p. 297.
[23] *Ibid.*, pp. 299 and 359.
[24] *Ibid.*, p. 278.
[25] *Ibid.*, p. 273. Royce means this rough classification to be only thematically illustrative.
[26] *Ibid.*
[27] *Ibid.*, pp. 275 ff.
[28] *Ibid.*, pp. 282 ff.
[29] *Ibid.*, pp. 277 ff.

Josiah Royce

This rough sketch of Royce's argument gives at least initial plausibility to his claim that all finite thought is determinate in virtue of what it excludes or negates. Many issues are raised by his theory, especially whether it is possible to negate except by a positive claim even where the form of the positive claim is negative; but the considerations before us now are sufficient to consider the consequences of his theory for the problem of whether being-itself is essentially determinate.

If the universal character of finite thought stems from the fact that its determinateness consists in what it negates, then the concrete nature of that thought which could genuinely know concrete being-itself must be determinate in virtue of something positive, not negative. Royce's own theory is that the positive determination is simple identity with concrete being-itself. But as to the general issue, if the determinateness of *genuine* knowledge of concrete being-itself is not negative, then the determinateness of concrete being-itself is not negative. Therefore, being-itself is determinate without negating a contrast term and the need for a contrast term is circumvented. Granted, the concrete knowledge of being-itself is given up as a possibility for finite thought; but finite thought can know from its own nature and shortcomings that the determinateness of being-itself is of a non-negative kind. If being-itself is determinate in and of itself without negating anything, it does not contrast with anything, and the demand that the determinate-being theory provide a contrast term is shown to be misapplying a characteristic of finite thought.[30]

The question must be raised for this approach about the significance of the claim that being-itself is determinate in this infinite sense. It is easy to see that the significance of a claim that being-itself is determinate in what Royce would call the finite sense would be that it is a denial or exclusion of its contrast term. But if being-itself is to be determinate in a wholly non-negative sense, wherein can the significance of that claim lie?

The ready answer to this question is that asking for significance is demanding the infinite to conform to the canons of finite thought; and this is what was just proved impossible. One's approach to being-itself as concrete should not be cognitive in the finite sense but rather mystical.[31] The mysticism intended is not that which harks to the simple immediacy of all things [32] but that which arrives after finite thought has ascended to its limits. Consequently, as finite thought indefinitely narrows down on the concrete individuality of being without ever catching it, we should acknowledge this and admit that being-itself is determinate beyond the possibility of negation. This is the

[30] It must be admitted that Royce says, "Being, then, viewed as Truth, is to be in any case something determinate, that excludes as well as includes" (*ibid.*, p. 296). But what is excluded here is not a contrast term on the same level but rather *in*determinateness.
[31] *Ibid.*, p. 348.
[32] See "Lecture Five" in *The World and the Individual* for Royce's criticism of this brand of mysticism.

answer Royce and others would give to the question about the significance of the determinateness of being-itself.

The answer bears certain affinities with Hegel's, for the only significance that can be attached to the claim that being-itself is determinate in this sense comes from the fact that this claim is a conclusion about the indefinite progression of finite thought. The only contrast term possible or needed in this characterization of being-itself stems from the contrast between being-itself and being-as-the-result-of-a-process. But the difference of Royce's theory from Hegel's is that the American affirms a discontinuity or break in kind between the indefinite process of finite thought and infinite being. For Royce the difference between the finite and the infinite is infinite, and it is not to be bridged by a finite number of finite steps, no matter how indefinitely high that finite number is. For Hegel the distance between the finite and the infinite is infinite, but the infinite is present in the finite to begin with and thought is properly infinite all along; even to recognize the difference between the finite and infinite is to employ infinite thought and suppose more than a mere analysis of the negativity of finite thought. The discontinuity that Royce sees between the finite and the infinite occasions a great difficulty, since the directional progress of the dialectic or finite thought is not easily carried over the gulf to the infinite.

This difficulty is made apparent by the following question. Does Royce's version of the claim that being-itself is determinate exclude the claim that it is indeterminate? Of course, it cannot exclude it, but the question is asked in return, Is there any meaning to the term "indeterminate" that needs to be excluded at this level? One calls being-itself determinate because complete determinateness is what finite thought is tending toward as it gets closer to the concrete; even if the gulf between the finite and infinite prohibits a strict carry-over of meaning, at least all warrant for the claim is not destroyed. Yet the term "indeterminate" has never meant anything in our discussion so far other than a denial of determinateness by contrast. Therefore, unless some other sense of "determinate" is specified for "indeterminate" to deny, it is more accurate to say of Royce's conclusion about the infinite distance of being-itself from the finite that it argues for the claim that being-itself is *in*determinate.

Indeterminateness often has the connotation of emptiness; but it is just this connotation that is called into question by Royce's argument when pressed, for indeterminateness could just as well mean pure fullness or positivity that is unmixed with any negative determinateness. When one characterizes finite determinateness as negativity and concludes that the infinite lacks the negativity, it is more natural to say that the infinite is indeterminate since the notion of the infinite is here arrived at by negating the essence of finitude. Perhaps if we had a kind of knowledge other than that which Royce describes as finite we could say more about the infinite. But with respect to our first characterization of finitude as determination by negation, we should say of the infinite that it is indeterminate. This eliminates the

Roycean type view as a candidate for an interpretation of the claim that being-itself is determinate.

SECTION F

The Fundamental Dilemma of Ontology

Our survey of positions that claim that being-itself is determinate has turned up a fundamental dilemma of ontology, which all the positions either falter on or attempt to cope with in ways that soften the claim that being-itself is determinate. The dilemma arises when being-itself is construed problematically as the ontological one for the many determinations of being.

We can express the dilemma in the following way. On the one hand, being-itself must be ubiquitous; absolutely everything has it in one mode or other, and nothing lacks it. If anything is determinate, even if it is an error or a fiction, it still has being, as an error or a fiction. On the other hand, any positive or determinate characterization of being-itself must have a significant contrast term to be meaningful. This is so even if the determinate characterization is that being-itself is indeterminate. The dilemma is that, since being-itself is ubiquitous, it must be present in or apply to the significant contrast to the determinate characterization as well as to the character itself. Hence, any characterization of the form "being-itself is *x*" would be false, because the expression "being-itself is *non-x*" would also have to be true. For *x* to be significant, *non-x* must be a positive or affirmative term.[33] The contrast term must always have the status of an intelligible, if not actual, possibility; and that is always a status in being.

However the fundamental dilemma is to be resolved, we discovered in our discussion of the first two positions that two principles must be respected by any resolution. The first is the *principle of the ontological ground of differences:*

> Two differing determinations of being presuppose a common ground in virtue of which they are relevantly determined with respect to each other and from which each delimits for itself a domain over against the other.

The second is the *principle of the ontological equality of reciprocal contrasts:*

> If two determinations of being are contrast terms for each other, then they must be on the same ontological level and the categories descriptive of them must be on the same logical level.

The theory that being-itself is a determinate property common to all the things that are runs afoul the first principle. For, it fails to acknowledge that

---

[33] Cf. Kant's discussion of affirmative and infinite judgments, *Critique of Pure Reason* B 97; he makes the point that an infinite judgment positively locates its object in one part of the whole extension of possible things, limited only by what is finitely excluded from it. Being's contrast term cannot be in the class of possible things, however, if it is not to be in being.

the very determinateness of the property "being-itself" requires something more fundamental to allow it to differ from other properties on a par with itself. Taking being-itself to be whatever turns out to be the most basic and fundamental category, the principle states that between any two determinately different things there is some more basic presupposed common ground from which each delimits a domain of its own. This principle will be a theme developed throughout the whole of the next chapter where we examine what is presupposed by the many determinations of being.

The theory that being-itself is a comprehensive absolute totalled up according to a highest determinated category runs afoul the second principle, the principle of the ontological equality of reciprocal contrasts; for the determinate highest category that includes and structures the whole cannot have a significant contrast since there is nothing left outside it to contrast with. Without the contrast it cannot be determinate, and without determinateness it cannot structure the whole. Coupling this principle with the first, we see that the claim that being-itself is something determinate presupposes not only something determinate besides what is in being but also that there is something more fundamental than both. If, on the other hand, being-itself is something indeterminate, we are still required to give a determinate meaning to the notion of indeterminacy by way of a contrast. How to give a determinate characterization of being-itself, with a determinate contrast to the characterization, while saying that being-itself is actually indeterminate and does not need a contrast, is the theme of chapter 3.

As we conclude our discussion of being-itself as determinate, we should consider the possibility that determinateness and indeterminateness are not exclusive alternatives with regard to being-itself. Hegel might claim them both to be aspects of the powerful nature of Spirit. He would criticize us for interpreting Spirit only at the beginning and at the end but never in process. So, when we claim that being-itself is indeterminate if it is implicit power and that it is determinate if it is fully explicit power, Hegel would argue that both of these are abstractions. Now, is it possible that being-itself is both determinate and indeterminate? A fitting answer to this kind of Hegelian argument is yes and no.

In an obvious way being-itself is both determinate and indeterminate. At the very least it is determinate in the sense in which it is determinately connected to the determinations of being as their one, the ground of their unity. And at the same time, we are about to conclude that, in itself, being-itself cannot be determinate if in fact it is to be the ground of the unity of the determinations. In chapter 4 below we shall examine in detail the sense in which being-itself is essentially indeterminate and conditionally determinate.

But in a more difficult sense, being-itself cannot be both determinate and indeterminate. It cannot be both in the sense we mean when we refer to its essential character or integrity. Its essential character is what Hegel was referring to, in our fictional disputation, when we had him say that Spirit really is something that transcends and includes elements of determinateness and indeterminateness. In the end, however, the alternatives of determinateness and indeterminateness are exclusive, and the argument we put in Hegel's mouth is absurd, for the notion of power in process is surely something determinate—it contrasts quite nicely with the possibility of a finished and completely structured universe. The only reason the argument seemed plausible was that we are prone to identify determinateness with static and abstract form; yet many things like time, value, and power are determinately different from other things and from each other and still are not mere abstract and static forms. Power is quite clearly a determinate thing,[34] and just because of this, Hegel can be pushed back into the *ens perfectissimum* camp and rejected, for he can allow no contrast term to power on the same ontological level.

Our final rejection of Hegel has ramifications beyond his own theory. It amounts to a rejection of all views that hold being-itself, and, by extention, God, to be *essentially* of the nature of a self, for all such views must have some notion of what a self is; and even if the notion of self includes that of exercising power to produce freely, it is the notion of a determinate thing. To be a self is to be determinately different from all sorts of things. By the principle of the ontological equality of reciprocal contrasts, such a self, no matter how cosmic, could not be being-itself, for its contrasts also would be in being. Of course, many people, for example, Charles Hartshorne and Paul Weiss, say that God is a cosmic self; but they also argue that he has contrasting contemporaries and is not identical with being-itself. It remains to be determined whether true being-itself can be identified with the God of religion.

Our rejection of Hegel, however, does *not* involve a rejection of the view that being-itself might be a self or have a personal character in some *conditional* sense. On the supposition that the *connection* of being-itself to the determinations of being is something nonessential to being-itself, it is quite possible that being-itself might be a self or person in that conditional connection. This is, in fact, what we shall argue in chapter 12.

What was lacking in Royce's view was any reason why being-itself should be considered determinate rather than indeterminate in the sense of undifferentiated fullness. If all determination is by negation, then pure positivity with all negation removed is purely indeterminate. But if being-itself is indeterminate, even in the utterly full sense, then it is hard to see why it is an individual, even an absolute individual, for individuality seems to be essentially characteristic of finite things beset with negativity.

We may fairly conclude, now, that whatever being-itself is, it is not something essentially determinate. This conclusion, however, has been reached only by a kind of negative elimination of alternatives, and we must wait for further chapters to exhibit its complete significance.

[34] Cf. the discussion of "power" in chap. 4, sec. B 3, below.

2

Determinations of Being

⋅⋅⊹⋪═══════════════════╠⊹⋅⋅

Being-itself cannot be conceived as something determinate, at least not in any ordinary sense of "determinate." We may provisionally assume that being-itself is indeterminate. Although this *answer* to the question, What is being-itself? is a determinate one, its determinateness is of the lowest degree. The crucial question now becomes, In what sense is being-itself indeterminate? The answer to this question depends on how we characterize determinateness. If determinateness is limited to the realm of finite things, to the realm of determinations of being rather than being-itself, then it is to the determinations of being that we must turn.

Not only is it logically cogent at this point to move to the realm of determination proper in order to discover the true meaning of indeterminateness; at the same time the dialectic of our defense of God's transcendence is advanced. Issues about the nature of God's transcendence are logically preceded by the problem whether there is any such transcendence at all. And at the heart of this problem lie alternative solutions to the dilemma of the one and the many: if the one-many problem can be solved without recourse to a transcendent God or category of being-itself, then the ground is cut away from one of the major approaches to God's transcendence.

But if the problem of the one and the many is to be solved without recourse to a transcendent one, then the unity must come from the side of the many. To say that the unity comes from the side of the many is, of course, paradoxical, for the unity is supposed to be the unity of the many. If the one *for* the many is one *of* the many, it would seem that the plurality is only multiplied, not unified, in this view. Yet to say the opposite, that a one over against the many unifies them, is equally paradoxical, since, if the one so transcendent is not just another one of the many, it would seem to be too distant from the many to unify them. We must now consider the attempt of pluralism to resolve the dilemma of the one and the many from the side of the determinations.

SECTION A
Determinateness

Our first task is to articulate more fully what is meant by a determination of being. Anything whatsoever that is determinate is a determination of being. This follows from the principle of the ontological ground of differences,[1] for to be determinate is, minimally, to have some identity over against or in difference from what is other than that identity. It follows from the principle of the ontological ground of differences that anything that so differs must be, in *some* sense of "be." Therefore, our task is to discover what it is to be determinate.

Since to be determinate is at least to have an identity that contrasts with what is other than that identity, anything determinate is involved in distinctions with what is other than itself. This means that the nature of distinctions must be treated in connection with the discussion of determinateness.

The first thing to be noted is that a discussion of determinations of being and distinctions is very abstract. It is abstract in the sense that consideration of determinations of being per se abstracts from the many kinds of distinctions in which things are determinately related. The red of a book's cover is distinct from the black of the book's printing; and hence is determinate in that respect. The red of the cover is also distinct from the totality of the book as a physical substance and as a perceived object. It is distinct from the meaning of the book's contents and from the fact that the book is owned by someone, that it is a copy of a certain edition, that it is referred to by some other book, and so forth. The red of the book plays a role in attracting buyers, and this is distinct from the role it is now playing as a philosophical example. The number two is distinct from the aesthetic quality of dual balance, from the moral quality of just distribution, and from the fact that two apples are better than one if a person is hungry enough. These examples only begin to illustrate the monumental abundance of different kinds of determinate relations or distinctions. To focus attention, then, on the fact that each element in the distinctions is a determination of being is to abstract greatly from the fullness of the being of the determinations. It is to ignore many problems that have to do with what kinds of determinations can enter into what kinds of relations and distinctions. The way a *pair* of apples is in a box is distinct from the way the *apples* are in the box and from the way the number "two" is in the box. All these elements are abstracted from in considering distinguishable things simply as determinations of being.

The second thing to be noted is that determinations of being, no matter how else they may be distinct, have *real distinctions* between them and all things other than their own identity.[2] This acknowledges, first, the demand of

---

[1] See chap. 1, sec. B, above, and Appendix, pp. 307–12 below.

[2] The term "real distinction" is taken over from scholastic philosophy where it often had the extreme connotation that the items distinguished were separable and

the principle of the ontological equality of reciprocal contrasts that each
contrasting determination of being be on the same ontological level as its
contrast; [3] insofar as two determinations of being are in determinate contrast,
regardless of their other connections, just that far they are on the same
ontological level. In this manner, for instance, sweetness and whiteness are
determinate contrasts with each other, even though they may in other contexts be inseparable qualities of some third thing, like a lump of sugar.
Calling the connection between determinations of being *qua* determinations
"real distinctions" points out, second, that, according to the principle of the
ontological ground of differences, in such contrasting determinations each
possesses its own being in opposition to the being of the others; whatever
properties the determinations might share, they at least have their own shares
of being-itself. This individually possessed being is what is prima facie
connoted by the term "real distinction."

A real distinction holds between determinations of being simply in virtue
of the fact that they are determinate with respect to each other. The peculiar
character of the determinations may involve them in distinctions over and
above their real distinctions; but just insofar as they are determinate, they are
really distinct. An analysis of what it is to be determinate will reveal the
nature of real distinctions.

To be determinate is to have an identity over against or in contrast to what
is other than that identity.[4] This entails that a determination be complex, for
a determination x must be what it is, namely x, and also must be other than
its contrast, *non-x*. Its own nature x is not determinate unless it is other than
what is not itself, *non-x*. But obviously the contrast to x cannot be simply
non-x if it is in virtue of this contrast that x is determinate. Therefore, the
contrast must be some other determination, y, and the nature of x is 'x and
not-y.' Conversely, y is determinate in that it is 'y and not-x.' Suppose there is
a third determination, z. If x is determinate with respect to z as well as y, that
is, if a real distinction holds between them, then the nature of x must be 'x
and not-y and not-z.' We can say in less formal terms that the nature of a
determination of being has an essential feature and conditional or nonessential features. The essential feature of x is 'x' and the conditional features are
'not-y,' 'not-z,' and so forth. The conditional features come from the real
distinctions that pertain between the determination and what it is determinate with respect to. It is necessary for any determination of being to have an
essential feature *and* conditional ones. If a determination lacks an essential

<hr>

that each could exist without the other. This extreme connotation does not apply in the
present use, since it will be maintained that the real distinction between determinations
means that they need each other in order to be determinate. Something *like* the
scholastic connotation is preserved, however, in our understanding of really distinct
things as having their own being over against each other.

[3] See chap. 1, sec. C, above.
[4] The tenor of this point, as well as of many points in this analysis of determinateness,
comes from Paul Weiss. See his *Modes of Being* (Carbondale: Southern Illinois University Press, 1958), p. 512.

feature, it lacks a ground for being other than what is really distinct from it. If it lacks conditional features, it lacks determinateness in contrast to what is really distinct from it.

If both essential and conditional features are necessary for determinateness, may the latter be called non-essential? The conditional features are those whose character depends in half measure on what happens to be determinate over against the determination in question. Therefore, the nature of a conditional feature depends as much on what is other than the determination of which it is a feature as it does on that determination itself. This can be indicated by calling it non-essential. But both essential and conditional or non-essential features are necessary for a thing to be determinate.

It should be recognized that this is a metaphysical analysis, and this kind of analysis should not be confused with other kinds. A perceptual analysis, say, of a red color patch might yield the result that the patch is "red all over" and not at all complex. Yet, a metaphysical analysis of the patch as a determination of being shows that its redness involves, on the one hand, its own character and, on the other hand, the fact that it is different from blue or yellow. This complexity may not be a perceptual one.

We still must ask about the distinctions between the features *within* the nature of a determination. Any determination of being seems to be complex with respect to having an essential feature (and this itself may be complex) and at least one conditional feature. Is the distinction between the essential and conditional features a real distinction? Are the essential and conditional features different from each other and determinate with respect to each other?

Suppose they are not determinately different from each other. We would account metaphysically for their difference by saying that the simple nature of the determination functions in two capacities, the capacity of being its own identity and the capacity of being over against what is other than itself. The fact that each capacity requires the other lends plausibility to this interpretation of the metaphysical complexity. Upon reflection, however, this interpretation begs the question. The distinction between the natures of determinations of being and the capacities of those determinations is not a strong one, as this interpretation would require. The metaphysical analysis of determinateness applies to capacities as well as to determinations. The distinction between determinations and their capacities overlooks the abstractness of the discussion, for it interprets determination to mean something like a substance that endures through and unifies the exercise of several capacities. This, however, is just one kind of determination. For the capacities themselves to be determinately different from each other, they must be determinations in the sense characterized above.

Specifically, it can be shown that the capacities, that is, the essential and conditional features, are determinately different from each other, for the fact that seems to support the "capacities" view, namely, that the essential and conditional features require each other, is a two-edged sword. If each side requires the other, then they cannot be the same. It is not the case that each side *is* the other, for one side is simple and positive ideosyncracy and the other is excluding negativity. It is in virtue of the positive side that the negative side excludes, and it is in virtue of the negative side that the positive side has an identity over against other identities; but these are not the same thing. If it is said that the same thing is both positive and negative, this is only to say what has been maintained in our analysis, that to be determinate is to be complex with both essential and conditional features.

SECTION B

Real Distinctions of Determinations

If a determination of being is determinate in virtue of a real distinction between it and what it is determinate with respect to, and if a real distinction involves a complexity of essential and conditional features in its terms, then several important things must be acknowledged in consequence.

1. That there are determinations of being implies that there is a plurality of determinations, for a thing is determinate only insofar as it is over against something else determinate. This implication is perhaps gratuitous, since few people since Parmenides have seriously maintained that there is not a plurality of determinations.[5] To show that determinateness involves a real distinction is to defend a basic, though minimal, independence of terms that might in other contexts enter into inclusive relations. Our metaphysical analysis of determinations of being rejects any attempt to account for determinate distinctions as nothing but abstractions from the standpoint of third terms. Even to be in an abstract contrast requires that the determinations be really distinct in the sense of our analysis.

What is not so gratuitous in the fact that determinateness implies plurality is the consequence that, within the realm of determinations of being, pluralism is a likely metaphysics. Even though the determinations of being may and do enter into tighter and more inclusive relations in virtue of their specific determinate natures, the basic pluralism of their metaphysical status simply as determinations is not to be circumvented. Every inclusive determination that internally relates its determinate parts must be acknowledged to have real distinctions between its parts. The result of this is that unless pluralism can solve the ontological problem of the one and the many, we must move from the realm of being's determinations to what in contrast must be indeterminate. We shall shortly examine the attempt of pluralism to solve the dilemma of the one and the many.

---

[5] The possible exception to this was Bradley; but our discussion has been couched in terms of *distinctions* rather than *relations* precisely to get around arguments like his that all connections are swallowed up in "third terms" that do not allow the included terms to be distinguished.

2. A second result of our discussion is that the analysis of determinations has not attempted to account for what it is to be an individual. An individual is a peculiar complex of determinations who persists and acts through time, who has a changing identity, faces possibilities, and who sometimes is guilty for what he does or does not do. To account for individuals requires far more than the abstract account of determinations.

When we speak of the ontological many for which we need to find the one or unity, the many is often interpreted as a plurality of individuals. Of course, there are individuals within the many; but the ontological character of the many that needs an account is the simple distinction between determinations as such. The problem of the one and the many appears in many guises: as the one for many men in a state, as the unity of man's many needs, and in countless like guises; but these are not instances of the *ontological* problem of the one and the many. What we are after is the ontological one for the many determinations of being.

3. Having arrived at a characterization of determinateness, we are in a position to characterize indeterminateness by contrast.[6] If a thing is determinate with respect to something, its nature includes a conditional feature that sets it off from that with respect to which it is determinate. As we shall see in the next section, this means it has an affect or modification due to that other thing. If a determination is determinate with respect to some determination and is *in*determinate with respect to some third determination, this is to say that its nature has no feature distinguishing it from that third determination. So, if determination x is determinate with respect to y and indeterminate with respect to z, its nature is 'x and not-y'; it has no acknowledgment of z. Even to speak of z as that with respect to which x is indeterminate is first of all to suppose that z is determinate in its own right with respect to something; and second, it is to suppose that z is determinate with respect to something with respect to which x is also determinate, say, y, since some common ground is presupposed to note the indeterminateness. Yet, if both x and z are determinate with respect to y, then they are at least indirectly determinate with respect to each other unless y relates its own conditional features in a wholly external way. These degrees of indirect determination, however, need not be spelled out here;[7] our present concern is with indeterminateness.

Our first characterization of indeterminateness applies to determinations that are determinate in some respects but not in others. We can only say, according to this characterization, that a thing is partially indeterminate, not that it is wholly so. Yet if we are to say that being-itself is indeterminate, it would seem from what has been said that complete indeterminateness is what is meant if such indeterminate being-itself is to be the one for the many that includes all determinations of being. Consequently, the analysis of indeterminateness must be pushed further in our discussion of being-itself.

[6] See chap. 12, sec. B, below, for a further discussion of indeterminateness.
[7] See chap. 10, sec. B, below, where the relations between individuals and their environment is discussed.

4. A fourth conclusion from the analysis of determinateness is that any determination of being is infinitely complex. If any determination includes features that are themselves determinate with real distinctions between them, those features must themselves be complex and so on around. Any determination, then, is a unity of other determinations. This fact, however, does not commit us to the view of infinite complexity that takes the analysis of a complex necessarily to be a move to elements *less complex.* The move *may* be to the less complex, but not necessarily so, for the complexity involved in the features of a determination may be elements of a system of determinations that comes around again to the original determination and its contrasts. A circle is as infinite as a straight line. Thus, if *x* is determinate with respect to *y*, and its features are *a* and *b,* the features of, say, *a* could, either immediately or with the mediation of a system, be *x* and *y.* Any necessary or self-sufficient facts or principles are determinations of this sort.

It might be argued at this point that we should say that a determination of being is in*def*initely complex, not infinitely so. The reason behind this argument would not necessarily be a scruple about the limits of our knowledge. More likely it would stem from the motive of defending the possibility of contingency, for it would be urged that if a determination of being is contingent, then an infinite analysis of it should be impossible. This contingency seems to require that a determination be indeterminate, not in the first instance with respect to something with which it contrasts, but with respect to one of its features in virtue of which it is determinate over against its contrasts. Put formally, if the nature of *x* is '*x and not-y*' and the nature of, say, *not-y* is '*a and not-x,*' and if *x* is contingent, then a real distinction does not pertain between *a* and *not-x.* How this is so is inconceivable, but this is just to say that *x* is contingent. Consequently, it would be argued, we should say that determinations are indefinitely complex, allowing for the possibility of at least some determinations that are contingent.

But if this qualification is allowed, then we would have to give up our analysis of what it is to be determinate. Our analysis says that to be determinate requires really distinct components, each of which is itself determinate, which distinguish the determination from that with respect to which the determination is determinate.

On the other hand, if we persist with our analysis, then we must be able in some other way to allow for the possibility of contingency; since experience delivers so strongly that many things are contingent, their possibility should not be ruled out by such an abstract analysis as this.

A remark about the character of analysis itself is sufficient to reveal a kind of contingency. To move from a determination to its components by analysis is to leave something behind. And what is left behind is precisely the unity or harmony of the parts prior to analysis. As we shall see shortly in our consideration of the attempt of pluralism to solve the problem of the one and the many, the harmony of the parts cannot be given by one of the parts, and the harmony or unity is just what is broken in the analytical move. Therefore, from the standpoint of the analysis, the harmony of the parts of a determination is always contingent. Although it may be presupposed by the parts, it is still there contingently; it is still a *de facto* unity.

Of course, that this unity is ultimately contingent is a question to be decided in a broader context than the one of analysis of determinateness as such, for what is at issue is the ground or reason for the determinations in general. This is a problem that must be reapproached later on when we have dealt with the attempt of pluralism to solve the problem of the one and the many.

5. As we have seen, a final result of the analysis of determinateness is that the problem of the unity of a determination has not been faced. This is for good reason, however, since that problem is the same as the problem of the one and the many. If the features of a determination of being are really distinct from each other, then the problem of their unity is the problem of the unity of really distinct determinations. If the realm of the ontological many, the realm of determinate being, is characterized at base as a domain of real distinctions, then the problem of finding the one for this many is the problem of finding the unity of really distinct determinations of being. The solution to the ontological problem of the one and the many is the same as the solution to the problem of the unity of a determination's features.

No one would doubt that there are determinations of being. Hence, no one would doubt that each is unified as a matter of fact and that there is some kind of unity of them all together. But this kind of unity, as far as our reflection has progressed, is a mere *de facto* unity, a togetherness. When we seek an *account* of this *de facto* unity, we are asking for an explanation of how the unity came to be the way it is. What the question means fully, of course, can hardly be understood until we have the answer. However, we must acknowledge at least the felt distinction between a mere togetherness and a genuine unity, that is, a unity that is self-sufficient or fully explained.

The first philosophically sophisticated guess we probably would make at the nature of the unity is that it is a unifying determination. Thus, the unity of a determination's features would be a superfeature that internally relates its parts, and the unity of the determinations of being as a whole would be a supercategory that internally relates them all. This was the move we considered first in trying to characterize being-itself: we tried to see whether the one for the many could itself be determinate. The inadequacies of that move with respect to the unity of being apply equally to the attempt to account for the unity of a determination with a special unifying feature.

The first philosophically *un*sophisticated guess men make for the explanation of the *de facto* unities in the determinations of their world is simply that "they were made that way." The lack of sophistication in this view has been shown up by the advances of science, which explain *how* things came to be made the way they are. If this response is to be made sophisticated, a distinction must be drawn between the kind of explanation offered by science and the one implicitly aimed at in the response.

But before any attempt is made to defend the unsophisticated guess, we must pay attention to the attempt of pluralism to solve the problem of the one and the many in its own terms.

SECTION C
Weiss's Theory of the One and the Many

The most serious and thorough attempt to provide a pluralistic solution for the problem of the one and the many is to be found in the work of Paul Weiss. Justice, therefore, to the pluralistic position urges that his solution be considered in detail. Since many of the key points of our discussion of the nature of determinateness owe their intent, if not their form, to Weiss's analysis, a few words can connect his terms for solving the one-and-many problem with our own. Weiss believes that all determinations of being range themselves into four types or modes. His formal characterization of the modes of being for the purpose of addressing the problem of the one and the many coincides at the crucial points with the analysis we have given of really distinct determinations of being. Therefore, his search for the unity of the modes of being can be taken as parallel to our search for the unity of the determinations that are really distinct.

Few philosophers have maintained that the general kinds or modes of determinations of being are irreducibly different and yet are not derivatives from a single unifying source. Most of those who have, like Plato in the *Philebus* and the *Timaeus,* have ignored the problem of the unity of the modes per se and have concentrated on their togetherness in the world of experience, a togetherness itself the product of one of the modes (for example, of the demiurge or the "cause of mixture"). Weiss, in contrast, has acknowledged that there is a problem of the unity of the modes as such, over and above their unity in a particular occasion. If it is maintained that the modes in themselves were but abstractions from a concrete experience, abstractions whose differences were grounded in the nature of the knowing subject, then there would be no problem of the unity of the modes as such; there would be only the problem of the unity of the subject. But if it is maintained that the modes are *really* distinct, as we do with Weiss, then there is a problem of the togetherness of the really distinct modes; acknowledgment of a *de facto* unity or togetherness is not enough.

Weiss begins his argument with relatively formal considerations. "Any single mode of being would be radically indeterminate were it not over against some other," he points out, with our agreement. "To be determinate is to be opposed to and opposed by." [8] This is to say, a universe could not be made of purely simple modes; if there were two modes in the universe, x and y, then the nature of x would have to be 'x *and not* y,' and the nature of y would have to be 'y *and not* x.' This is the crucial thesis defended by Weiss's

[8] *Modes of Being,* p. 512.

position and on his interpretation of it hangs the entire enterprise. He agrees that to be determinate is to be together with something else; therefore, *that* there are really distinct modes (or determinations) necessitates that they be together.

The '*x and not y*' must be interpreted in two ways, according to Weiss. On the one hand, the *x* must be contrasted with *y* as something over against it (Weiss symbolizes this interpretation as *x,y*). This contrast can only be made from a point of view where *x* and *y* are merged together so that there is a common ground. This merged togetherness (symbolized as *x.y*) is the other interpretation of the '*x and not y*.' Of course, it cannot be pointed out that the x and *y* are merged except from a position wherein they are initially contrasted. Therefore, the *x,y* can be characterized only from the standpoint of *x.y* and vice versa.

How are the two forms of togetherness united? The two togethernesses, the *x,y* and the *x.y,* themselves constitute a many. If they were one thing, if a unity could be made out of the apparently two forms of togetherness, the *x* and the *y* would be divided each against itself; if they were not so divided, there could be no ground for even the apparent contrast. The unity of the two forms of togetherness, argues Weiss, is supplied by the very modes they unite, the *x* and the *y*. Hence, there are two ways in which the forms of togetherness are unified, an *x* way and a *y* way.[9] The forms of togetherness are not *directly* related to each other. "The relating of the ways of togetherness is via the items which are related; they mediate these ways just as these ways relate the beings to one another."[10]

But how does each of the items relate the two ways in which it is together with the other? Each item is a unity of what it is in itself, thus as contrasted with the other (*x,y*), and of what it is as present to and for the other, thus as merged with it (*x.y*). If it were not the unity of these two things, it could not mediate them. Thus it seems necessary that there is a division within the unitary items, a division between inside and outside, so to speak. Weiss, however, wants to deny this, thinking that a division into "an inside and an outside, a process and a terminal point," amounts to "the dissolution of all the modes of being."[11] He attributes this dissolution to an attempt to make a "single neutral concrete Many" out of the two manys, the manys of the two forms of togetherness. But there are two mistakes here. First, the division of each item into an inside and an outside comes from the fact that each one mediates in its own way the forms of togetherness. Each item would be divided even if there were, as Weiss claims, two ways of uniting the many of the forms of togetherness, an *x* way and a *y* way. He may be perfectly right in pointing out that the overarching unity of the many ways of uniting the forms of togetherness presupposes a standpoint neutral to the items that unify the forms of togetherness, a standpoint that can never be perfectly achieved.

[9] *Ibid.*
[10] *Ibid.*, p. 513.
[11] *Ibid.*, p. 515.

But he is wrong in thinking that by admitting this, he avoids dividing the items into an inside and outside; otherwise they could not relate the forms of togetherness at all. Second, he is mistaken in thinking that a division into an inside and outside constitutes a dissolution of the modes of being, for each mode must also unite its inside and outside or else, again, it could not relate the forms of togetherness, lacking a common ground in itself. Granted, the unity of the inside and the outside has not yet been accounted for, but it need not be accounted for to make the point at issue here. The account of it, if our discussion in the previous section is right, is the same as the account of the unity of the modes, since the unity of real distinctions is the issue in both places.

As a matter of fact, Weiss resorts to a distinction between inside and outside to account *in concreto* for the ways in which the modes do relate. He claims that there are not two but four irreducible beings or determinate modes. Each mode has some nonessential features (corresponding to our "conditional features") that come from its relations to each of the other modes. A relation between any two modes is affected by the other two modes, and Weiss calls this affection "mediating." Therefore, the nonessential features a mode has in virtue of its direct relations to the other modes are complemented by further nonessential features that reflect how each of the other modes functions twice indirectly as a relator. Now Weiss's presentation seems to indicate that the x,y and $x.y$ ways in which any two modes are together are supplied by the two remaining modes respectively.[12] But if this is what he intends, he is misstating his case. For, he insists, and rightly for consistency, that the forms of togetherness are simply the x and y together. "The togetherness of beings is the being of them together. . . . Such a togetherness is not a new, distinct entity; it is a fact constituted by the demands or thrusts of each to the others as met by their counter demands and counterthrusts."[13] So if the two modes of togetherness of x and y are simply x and y together, the "." and the ",", cannot be two more modes w and z. Hence, if two more modes are involved, even as relating x and y in some further way, they are still related to each of those first two in a twofold way, that is, as $x.w$ and x,w and $x.z$ and x,z, and so forth. Therefore, although the two ways in which two modes are together can be affected or influenced by the remaining two modes, those remaining modes do not constitute the two forms of togetherness of the original pair.

If it *were* true, however, that the fundamental ways of togetherness of two beings lay in two other beings, then the way in which each mode unites the two forms of togetherness relating it to some other mode could be laid to the nonessential features coming from the remaining two modes. Thus, if $x.y$ were constituted by w (perhaps via its nonessential features coming from x and y), and x,y by z, then the way in which x, for instance, is the unity of $x.y$

[12] *Ibid.*, p. 517.
[13] *Ibid.*, p. 514.

and *x,y* could be the way in which it unites the nonessential features it has because of *w* with those it has because of *z*. This is perhaps the solution Weiss wanted to purchase in his treatment of the four modes together; but as has been shown, it will not do, for it simply raises the problem once again.

It is not the case, however, that a better solution is not to be found in Weiss's system. The solution is that the form of togetherness in which the two determinate modes are merged is constituted by the nonessential features each receives from the other, and that the form of togetherness in which the two determinate modes are contrasted is constituted by the essential features of each over against the other; for their common ground is their mutual affection, and their contrasting ground is what each is that the other is not. The way in which each mode is the one for the many forms of togetherness is the way in which each is the unity of its essential and nonessential features. This allows the two modes to be related in two ways without the relations being two more things, which is of the essence of Weiss's position. And what is the distinction between essential and nonessential features but that between "inside" and "outside"? An essential feature is what a thing fulfills in itself, and a nonessential or conditional feature comes from a "need" it has and cannot fulfill, a need therefore that turns it outside itself for fulfillment of its determinateness. A nonessential feature cannot be what a thing is essentially, nor can it be what it does not need, for if all its needs were fulfilled then it would be perfect and nothing could be added to it.[14] "Need" can be interpreted here as what is necessary in order to be determinate.

All this has been said in interpretation of the basic point that "to be determinate is to be together with something else." What has been shown is *how* what is determinate is together; two things are determinate as over against one another and as conjoined. Weiss is right in arguing that there are really distinct things, and his theory accords with our analysis of what a real distinction is. If things were only abstractly distinct, as Hegel held, they would have *only* nonessential (or conditional) features, and to be at all they would have to be together as the essential features of some third thing. But if they have nonessential features, then those nonessential features may serve as common ground for contrasting their essential differences.

What is the solution this theory offers to the problem of the one and the many? If each mode unifies the ways by which it is together with the others, then each mode is a one for the many others. As many modes as there are, that many ones are there. There is not a single one for the many but many ones. Yet if the modes are what is real, and their togetherness is to be accounted for in terms of the modes' features, then there is no context over and above the modes for which a unity of the many ones is to be sought. To ask for a unity of the many ones is to ask a question so abstract as not to have

[14] For an explicit discussion of "inside" and "outside," see Weiss's *Nature and Man* (New York: Henry Holt & Co., 1948), chap. 3, pp. 39 ff. This is Weiss' early discussion of the problem of the one and the many, and though it focuses primarily on the togetherness of actualities, much of the theory is carried over into *Modes of Being*.

any basis. If to be is simply to be determinate, and being-itself is nothing over and above the determinations, that is, *is not transcendent of the determinations,* then each determination is the ontological one for the many in which it is involved, uniting the many ways in which that many is together. This is the essence of ontological pluralism.

SECTION D

Difficulties with Weiss's Theory

This solution seems to fall into three main difficulties.

1. The first applies not directly to Weiss's theory but to the rider our own analysis has attached to it, namely, that the features of a determination of being are themselves determinate and hence really distinct. If it is the case that a mode or determination unifies the ways in which it is together with the ontological many, then it must be the case that its own unity is likewise the unity that each of its features gives to the complex of features. Thus, the unity of a determination x whose nature includes 'x *and not-y*' is really two unities, the unity constituted by 'x' and the unity constituted by '*not-y*' (and by all the other conditional features). But then each of those unities is again a plurality of unities, and so on down.

The difficulty is that the unity in each case is again reduced to a *de facto* unity or mere togetherness. The unity of x is simply the togetherness of the features of its nature, and the unity of each of them is again the togetherness of their own component features, and so on. The togetherness is only acknowledged; it is not accounted for as a genuine unity.

2. The second difficulty does apply directly to the pluralistic position as Weiss defends it. That each mode or determination of being unifies the various ways in which it is together with the others of the ontological many is not sufficient for that mode to account for the being and the unity of those others.

In the first place it does not account for the unity of the others of the ontological many, for each of those others unifies the many in its own way. That way may be reflected in the conditional features of the first mode, and perhaps even in the way that first mode unites its essential and conditional features, but the reflection loses the immediate presence of the other mode's unity in the reproduction. Moreover, the way the other mode unifies its ways of togetherness is distorted and qualified when it is integrated with the things that must be unified in the first mode's way of unity.

In the second place, the fact that each mode unifies the various ways in which it is together with the others of the ontological many does not account for the being of those others. The one for the ontological many must not only unify the *ways* in which the presence of the many modifies it; it must also account for the *unity* of the *being* of the others. This is the inexpungeable insight in the view that being-itself must be common to the many in order to unify them. But on a pluralistic view like Weiss's, it is precisely this commonality that is denied in favor of an independence in being of each mode or determination from the others. We should examine the ways in which the pluralistic theory attempts to get around this requirement of commonality in the one and the many.

It might be argued, first, that of the two ways in which the modes are together, the way of comparison or merging does affix the being of the many in the unifying one. Yet, at best it is only the non-essential or conditional features of the many that get encompassed by the one, since by definition the conditional features are those that result from the merging of the two determinations and the essential features are those that each has in *contrast* to the other. The essential features of the many other modes are precisely those that are not encompassed by the unifying one. And at worst, perhaps even the conditional features of the many are not encompassed by the unifying mode; to say that they are is to move dangerously close to affirming that the connections between the one and many are real and partially independent third terms. If the connection is not somewhat independent of the one and many, then the conditional features of the many, when encompassed by the one, are resolutely cut off from the essential features of the many, thus destroying the unities that each of the many in turn provides.

It might be argued, second, that it is not the togetherness of merging but rather the togetherness of contrasting that brings the being of the many into the one, for really distinct modes are together as over against each other as well as in a modifying conjunction; and if a mode unifies the ways it is together with the other modes, it must include the way in which the others are over against it. This argument, however, overlooks the fact that the way in which a mode of being is over against others is simply by excluding them. The exclusion is done in virtue of the merged and modifying features so that the essential features of the other modes are not contained at all in the unifying one.

Finally, it might be argued that the two ways of togetherness, the merging and the contrasting, taken not singly but together as unified, do bring the being of the many into the compass of the one; for to acknowledge a distinction between the ways of togetherness is to acknowledge that in the way of contrast the being of the many is excluded from the one, whereas in the way of comparison it is merged with it. Yet the being of the one unifies the ways of togetherness; it does not, except perhaps abstractly, contrast them. If the one were to contrast the ways of togetherness as well as unify them, its unity and diversity would be on the same footing. That this is so is probably true, but this pushes the theory back to the position refuted in our first objection. The unity of the many ways of togetherness with their own unity is a mere *de facto* unity or togetherness, and the explanation sought is not at hand.

This general difficulty about Weiss's pluralism can be put in terms he uses in explaining the possibility of knowledge on his view. Let X and Y be modes of being, and suppose they are the only modes of being. Let x be the guise X has for Y and let y be the guise Y has for X (the lower case letters indicate whatever of the other mode is brought into the initial mode by both forms of togetherness). Of these distinctions Weiss says:

> X deals with the Y through the mediation of y; reciprocally, Y deals with X through the agency of x. X-y, X as facing and possessing the datum y, is related to Y, as a form to a content; Y-x is similarly related to X. This means that X-y and Y are reciprocals, each exhausting the import of the other, allowing nothing over but the fact that there is an X which is imposing the X-y on the Y, and that there is a Y sustaining the X-y. The form, X-y, both in reality and in knowledge, together with the content, Y, of which it is the form, constitutes the being of Y as that which is over against X. The content Y is the content for just that particular form, X-y, the form which X imposes.
> The form and content make a single entity, the Y as related to the X.[15]

This statement illustrates the dilemma pluralism falls into when attempting to account for the being of the many when the one that does the accounting is itself one of the many. We must put the question: Is the "single entity" that is made up of the form and content an ontologically real being or is it an abstract version of such a real being? Two answers are possible.

a) It can be answered that the "single entity" is not an ontologically real being; it can be said that the X-y and Y make up not the full being of an ontological entity but rather only "the Y as related to the X," as Weiss says. This implies that there must also be the Y as not related to the X, and that the real ontological entity would be the Y as both related and unrelated. But if this is so, there is something surd about the being of the modes, namely, the being they have as not related to each other. Yet Weiss clearly maintains that "there is no surd in the universe."[16] If there is such a surd, then there is some being of the many not in relation at all to the one, and therefore the one is not the one of the being of the many.

b) It can be answered, on the other hand, that the single entity made up of form and content is indeed the ontologically real being and that it is *false* that "X-y and Y are reciprocals, each exhausting the import of the other, allowing nothing over but the fact that there is an X which is imposing the X-y on the Y, and that there is a Y sustaining the X-y"; nothing, according to this answer, is left over. But then the real distinction between X and Y as modes of being is collapsed into a single entity in which each mode is reciprocally form and content for the other; form and content are one and ontologically not to be distinguished. This gives up the pluralism in favor of a monism, and pluralism's solution to the one and the many is given up at the same time.

If a mode of being is the one for the many by being completely one with that many, with nothing left over, then the force of pluralism is gone. We

[15] *Modes of Being*, p. 528.
[16] *Ibid.*, p. 531.

must return to the search for a one that is not itself one of the many. And if form and content do not exhaust the being of a mode, that is, if a unifying mode plus what it contains of the other modes does not exhaust the being of those other modes, then the unifying mode is not the ontological one for the many; it only unifies itself and the modifications it receives from the others.

3. The third difficulty with the pluralistic view is that it exhibits, upon reflection, a different locus for the ontological unity of the many than the one it advertises. However lacking in rational explanatory power a mere *de facto* unity or togetherness is, it still is *a* kind of unity that demands an explanation. To acknowledge a *de facto* unity or togetherness is at least to acknowledge a problem yet to be solved. Pluralism of Weiss's variety claims that the locus for the unity of the ontological many is in each one of the many, that is, that each determination unifies all the others in its own unity. But not only is each determination a *de facto* unity or togetherness, the whole of the determinations constitutes a *de facto* unity. If each of the many is the one for the many, then there are many ones, each unifying the whole; where there is a many, there is a one; therefore, there is at least a *de facto* unity of the many ones. This last *de facto* unity is one that goes beyond what the pluralistic theory takes itself to account for. But the unity of the plurality of unities is surely an ontological unity, in fact the most basic one. Therefore, pluralism exhibits a *de facto* unity more basic than the unity it tries to account for.

Pluralism would attempt to rebut this objection by pointing out that this *de facto* unity of the many ones presupposes a standpoint completely above and neutral to the many determinations of being; furthermore, this standpoint cannot be real. If it were real, it would be determinate, distinct from other allegedly more biased standpoints; yet, as determinate, it would itself be one of the many, not above them but among them, not neutral but biased. Therefore, if this presupposed standpoint cannot be real, then the *de facto* unity of the many ones must be only a fiction of the abstract thought that extends the principles of the many beyond their proper domain. If this rebuttal is valid, our objection does not hold.

There are two insoluble problems for this rebuttal, however. In the first place, the very statement of the pluralistic position, namely, that there are many ones, presupposes both the allegedly neutral standpoint and the *de facto* unity in question; that is, to say that the determinations are many, or that there are many ones, is to presuppose the unity of the many involved in calling them many. Manyness is perhaps the loosest kind of unity, but it is still a unity, for it encompasses all the determinations. To call the determinations many is to presuppose the standpoint relevant to them all, and the many they are called is itself a *de facto* unity.

In the second place, the principle used in our first objection to Weiss's pluralism is a two-edged sword. On the one hand, it argued that the unity of each determination is only a *de facto* one, whose real principle is to be sought in unities of the parts ad infinitum. On the other hand, it now argues that, since the unities of the really distinct components of a determination make up the *de facto* unity of the determination, the unities of the many determinations, each of which unifies the many, therefore make up a *de facto* unity of all the ones together. To say, then, that an impossible neutral standpoint is presupposed in our argument is to say that such an impossible standpoint is presupposed for each *de facto* unity, even the unities of the determinations taken individually. But if this is so, then pluralism not only cannot *account* for the unity of each of the many determinations; it cannot even allow for the possibility of such a unity—it cannot acknowledge a *de facto* unity to each of the many. This would reduce pluralism to an absurdity.

Since the rebuttal to our objection fails, what shall we say about the *de facto* unity of the many ones that we are forced to acknowledge? Our purpose here is not to push beyond the *de facto* character of the unity to some explanation but only to see what is involved in the *de facto* character itself. There is an element involved that is over and above the specific determinations unified. It can be minimally called a context of mutual relevance. It is the context wherein the determinations are contained as mutually determinate with respect to each other. The determinate relevancies are, of course, constituted by the really distinct determinations, but such mutually relevant determinations presuppose a unifying context for their relevancies. The context, in its turn, presupposes the determinations that bear the mutual relevancies, for it would not be a context unless it were a context for something. The *de facto* unity of the many determinations in their one context is the kind of unity that itself presupposes a plurality to be unified. But it is in the context of mutual relevance that the many determinations find their ontological unity. Therefore, we should expect to find the character of being-itself as the ontological one for the ontological many manifesting itself in some close connection with the context.

SECTION E

The Requirement of Transcendence and Indeterminateness

Let us recapitulate our argument up to this point. We want to justify and elaborate a theory of divine transcendence and presence. To do this philosophically, it is necessary to show that there is such a thing as transcendence that can be correlated with the transcendence of God. What is to be said for the case *against* the reality of transcendence? In the first place, it could be argued that there is no philosophical issue whose resolution requires the acknowledgment of transcendence. To answer this argument, all that is needed is to produce an issue whose resolution does require acknowledgment of transcendence. We have chosen to show this with respect to the most fundamental problem of ontology, the problem of being-itself.

In the second place, the case against the reality of transcendence could be argued by claiming that the chosen problem, that of being-itself, is already a misconstruction, because the term "being" is really an analogical one, and hence that there is no such thing as being-itself. We examined this argument and found it wanting, for "being" is not an analogical term and there indeed must be some one thing that can be called being-itself.

In the third place, the case against the reality of transcendence could be defended with the argument that the problem we have chosen does not, in fact, require acknowledgment of transcendence. We have undertaken to rebut this argument by showing that being-itself must be transcendent if the dilemma of the one and the many is to be resolved. Our argument considered first the contention that being-itself is determinate, and we showed how the four interpretations of this contention that seem to be the most powerful and popular could not solve the problem of the one and the many. Then our argument turned to develop the notion of determinateness and what it is to be a determination of being. The determinations of being comprise the ontological many for which the one is sought, and we considered the claim of pluralism that each determination is the one for the many of which it is a member. This alternative, too, we have found wanting. The failure of pluralism to solve the problem of the one and the many by saying that the one is one of the many determinations and that there are as many ones as there are determinations brings us back to the problem of being-itself.

We are now in a position to characterize more fully the indeterminateness that must be ascribed to being-itself. The indeterminateness of a *determination* is that it lacks a determinate real distinction from some other determination. But being-itself must be indeterminate with respect to *all* determinations. This is an important thesis that requires careful consideration. The failure of pluralism to solve the problem of the one and the many shows that the one for the many determinations cannot itself be a determination. Yet, it must be the common unifier of the many determinations. Suppose that being-itself as the one is determinate with respect to the determinations. If it is itself determinate with respect to the determinations even in the least bit, then there is a real distinction between it and them. But it is precisely the real distinction that prohibits one determination from being the ontological one for the others from which it is really distinct. Therefore, being-itself as the one cannot in the least be determinate with respect to the determinations of being or really distinct from them.

If being-itself must be some one thing that unifies the many determinations of being, and if it itself cannot be determinate, then it must transcend the determinations; that is, if it does the unifying, it must be something real, and if it is not one among the determinations, it must transcend them in some sense. What has been shown about transcendence, however, is still vague. In fact, all that has been shown is that being-itself cannot be of a piece with the determinations. Furthermore, since being-itself must unify the many determinations, its transcendence must be of a kind that can be present to the determinations as a unifier. What being-itself is, such that it can be so transcendent and so present, is something we have yet to treat.

3

Creation and the Transcendence of Being-Itself

It is incumbent upon us now to develop and defend in a positive way a speculative theory of being-itself. Our theory must show how being-itself is the ontological one for the many determinations of being. Furthermore, it must avoid the fundamental dilemma of ontology by exhibiting the principle of the ontological ground of differences and the principle of the ontological equality of reciprocal contrasts. We have discovered two clues for the development of the speculative theory: that being-itself must be indeterminate, and that it must be transcendent of the determinations in some sense.

This undertaking is not entirely innocent. What we are after in the long run is an articulation and justification of the claim that God is both transcendent of and present in the whole world of determinations. In chapter 4, we shall state our own speculative theory in such terms that the correlation with the traditional notions of God is made and the foundation is laid for the interpretation of religion in Part Three. But in the present chapter we must give what speculative proofs are necessary to undergird our theory.

We could acknowledge that being-itself, indeterminate as we know it to be, is transcendent of the realm of determinations if we were satisfied about two conditions: first, that there is a kind of integrity to the realm of determinations that excludes the complete indeterminateness necessary for being-itself; and second, that the indeterminateness thus excluded still has an ontological status that can be called being-itself, that is, that it is not mere and absolute non-being. Along with the connotation of "being outside of," the term "transcendence" also connotes "being superior to or better than" whatever is transcended. The justification of the latter connotation must depend upon the peculiar character ascribed to the ontological status of what transcends. If this latter sense of transcendence is justified, then much has been done to support the identification of transcendent being-itself with God. Given these two conditions, at the very least we could say that what is completely indeterminate is transcendent in the sense of "being outside of" the determinations.

The problem of the integrity of the realm of determinations is one that properly requires a complete metaphysical analysis of all domains of reality. This, of course, cannot be undertaken here in our more general study of ontology. But the integrity can be illustrated, even if its details and defense are left vague,[1] by some comparative remarks about the basic ontology of Duns Scotus. He agreed after a fashion with our own conclusion that being is a univocal concept. He then argued that being is immediately divided into intrinsic modes, the infinite mode, on the one hand, and the finite modes, on the other.[2] It might seem at first that on this view the intrinsic modes are related to being in its univocal sense as species are to genera; this is not so, however, because the modes do not add any reality or perfection to being as species add the differentia.[3] Rather, the intrinsic modes are "contractions" of being-itself.[4] The nature of contraction was a problem of considerable weight for the scholastics; it is not to the present interest, however, to pursue Scotus' theory on this line, although a modern analogue to contraction will be defended shortly in a different view of the relation between finite and infinite being.[5]

What is of interest for present purposes is Scotus' claim that the distinction between infinite and finite is a distinction between modes of a univocal being. There is a mistake, both fundamental and enlightening, in the attempt to connect in this way being-itself in its univocal sense with infinite and finite being. The distinction between infinite and finite, or indeterminate and determinate, cannot be a distinction between modes. Modes are distinct ways, kinds, or determinations of being. A mode may be infinite, but only in its own way or after its kind; for instance, the mode of love may be infinite if love is present on every occasion, or the mode of space may be infinite if it has no termini. But love is not space, and conversely; hence they are finite with respect to each other. All modes, then, are finite in the sense that they are distinct ways or kinds of being.[6]

---

[1] See chap. 4 sec. A 9, for a discussion of integrity.

[2] *Opus Oxoniense* I, D. 8, Q. 3, nos. 16–17. Cf. Allan Wolter's *Duns Scotus: Philosophical Writings* (New York: Thomas Nelson & Sons, 1962), p. 2.

[3] *Opus Oxoniense* I, D. 8, Q. 3, no. 27.

[4] *Ibid.*, I, D. 8, Q. 3, no. 26.

[5] To complete a sketch of Scotus' doctrine of being, after the division of being into the finite and infinite, the finite is divided into the ten genera or Aristotelian categories. Each genus has its intrinsic mode of finite being. See C. R. S. Harris' *Duns Scotus* (Oxford: Oxford University Press, 1927), II, 66. Transcendentals, said Scotus, are prior to the division into the ten genera because they are indifferent to any intrinsic mode and apply to all; when applied to the infinite intrinsic mode they are infinite, and when applied to the finite modes they are finite according to the manner of the mode. Some transcendentals are coextensive with being and others are not. Those that are not, for example, the category of "when," are transcendental in the sense that only being is above them and the notions contained under them are so contained only incidentally. Those transcendentals that are coextensive with being are of two kinds: convertibles and disjunctives. The convertibles are 'unity,' 'truth,' and 'goodness' and are predicable of whatever 'is.' The disjunctives, on the other hand, are pairs like 'necessary or possible,' 'act or potency,' 'finite or infinite'; these are transcendental in the sense that one or the other of the pair is predicable of every being.

[6] Cf. Spinoza's distinction between "infinite in its own kind" and "absolutely infinite,' *Ethics* I, def. VI.

Consequently, the distinction between finite and infinite being is the distinction between modes or determinations, *all* of which are finite with respect to each other, and something non-modal. The infinite, in order to avoid being modally distinct from the finite, must be indeterminate with respect to the finite distinctions between the modes or determinations. The distinction between the infinite and finite cannot be a finite or modal distinction, and the infinite term cannot be finitely determinate with respect to the finite term or terms. The principle to which this argument gives rise—the principle of the indeterminateness of the infinite—suggests that what we are looking for in saying that being-itself is indeterminate in a full rather than an empty sense is an identification of the indeterminate with the infinite. The infinity in question is not modally infinite, which might well characterize elements of the realm of determinations, but rather without finite delimitations or contrasts. Whether this identification is justified, of course, depends on the character of the ontological status we ascribe to the indeterminate.

The lesson to be learned from the example of Scotus is that the realm of determinations can contain indeterminateness only in a modal way. A determination of being may be indeterminate with respect to something; but this indeterminateness is already conditioned by the determinate nature the determination has in virtue of which it is a determination at all. Hence, if a determination is indeterminate with respect to something and has the potentiality of becoming determinate in that respect, that unrealized potentiality is in itself conditioned by the determinate character of the determination. (And it would seem that the only way by which we could point out the indeterminateness of a thing in some respect is in virtue of its potentiality to become determinate in that respect.)

Therefore, if there is something *completely* indeterminate, as we have argued that being-itself is, then it must transcend the realm of determinations. For a determination can be only partially indeterminate. This guarantees the integrity of the determinations over against the completely indeterminate.

To satisfy the second condition, namely, that the ontological status of what is indeterminate and transcendent is appropriate to being-itself, is much more difficult. The criterion for an ontological status that our reflections have acknowledged from the beginning is that the thing in question stand in some appropriate ontological contrast. The obvious contrast for being-itself would seem to be absolute non-being. But if being-itself is indeterminate, then it could not have an ontological contrast, for only determinate things have contrasts. Therefore, there is a problem whether there is any such real thing as being-itself at all; perhaps our reasoning so far has involved a fundamental mistake.

What must be done first, then, to satisfy the second condition, is to prove that there is such a thing as being-itself that is both transcendent and indeterminate. In a sense, this proof will be inverting the argument of the previous two chapters, proving positively the conclusions drawn there by negative considerations. Taken in the context of our whole reflection, including the correlation between being-itself and God, this proof can be construed as a proof for the reality of God. But the proof does not stand alone; it must be taken in the context of the whole speculative scheme that interprets it, and it must also be related to the appearance of God in religion.

We shall argue in the following way. The determinations of being need a creator in order to be. The determinations are; therefore they are created and there is a creator. This creator, furthermore, must be transcendent, indeterminate, and so forth. Finally, the reason the determinations need a creator is the same as the reason they need an ontological *one;* the creator provides the unity of the determinations of being. Therefore, the creator is what we have been looking for when we have sought being-itself.

This argument will be made in section A below. In section B we shall elaborate briefly on what is involved in such a theory of creation, putting flesh on the bones of the argument. The task of elaboration will continue through the rest of our study. In section C below we shall consolidate our argument by considering six classical objections to a theory of creation that our own speculative theory must get around.

In section D we must return to the problems of the fundamental dilemma of ontology and show that our speculative theory escapes them. Specifically, we must show that although being-itself, or the creator, is indeterminate, our theory about it is determinate, and that this determinateness arises from the connection being-itself has to the determinations, that is, from the fact that it creates them. It must be shown that being-itself, or the creator, transcends the distinction between determinate being and absolute non-being. But it must also be shown that absolute non-being is a proper ontological contrast for the determinations insofar as they are connected to the creator, for it is this connection of the determinations with the creator that must be determinate if our argument is to work. The kind of determinateness of the connection is one that can have only absolute non-being as its contrast. This will complete the initial presentation of our speculative theory. What will remain is the task of showing that it is sufficiently rich to be fruitful.

SECTION A

Proof of the Reality of Being-Itself, the Creator

Our proof will take the form of proving three propositions briefly mentioned above. First, that the determinations of being need a creator in order to be. Second, that the determinations of being are; therefore they are created and there is a creator. Third, the creator provides the unity of the determinations of being, is transcendent and indeterminate; therefore, the creator is what we have been looking for when we have sought being-itself. Therefore, there is such a thing as being-itself and it is the creator of the determinations of being.

Proposition 1

The determinations of being need a creator in order to be. This proposition is proved in two parts. First, we shall prove that the determinations of being are contingent; second, we shall prove that the contingency of the determinations of being is contingency on a creator.

a) *That the determinations of being are contingent.* This is proved in five steps.

(1) The determinateness of a determination of being requires that the determination be together with at least one other determination and that they be mutually relevant to each other. As we have seen,[7] a determination of being must be a complexity of essential and conditional features; without both kinds of features it could not be determinate. Conditional features are those a determination has in virtue of which it is determinate with respect to other things; without being determinate with respect to something else, a determination cannot be said to be determinate at all, since it would not be intrinsically different from anything. Therefore, the determinateness of a determination requires that it be together with other determinations (or at least one other determination) and that they all be mutually relevant and determinate with respect to each other.

(2) The togetherness of determinations of being requires a *de facto* unity, for a *de facto* unity is nothing more than the grouping of several things together. No matter how chaotic the grouping might be, the togetherness of several things exhibits a *de facto* unity. Therefore, the togetherness of several things requires that they are together in some sort of *de facto* unity.

(3) A *de facto* unity does not account for itself. If a *de facto* unity were to account for itself, it would have to do so in one or several of three ways. It might exhibit a determinate principle that unified it and that in turn accounted for itself. It might be unified by each of the several determinations, as the pluralistic ontology claims. Or it might exhibit a harmonious pattern that accounted for itself.

(*a*) Suppose a *de facto* unity exhibits a determinate principle that unifies it. The determinate principle would have to be complex, having parts that answer to each of the several determinations it is to unify. But then what is the unity of the determinate principle? It would either be a higher determinate principle, which in turn must be complex and need a further unity, ad infinitum, or it would contain a self-explanatory harmony or intelligibility. In the former case, the actual infinite is impossible and the series would need a highest principle that would be simple and not complex; but such a simple principle could not unify the plurality of the preceding complex principle. The latter case reduces to the third alternative, (*c*), to be considered below.

(*b*) Suppose that the *de facto* unity is constituted by each of the several determinations. But this is precisely what we found the pluralistic ontology unable to make out, for although a determination might unify the conditional

[7] Chap. 2, sec. A, above.

features of the other determinations, it could not bring into its unity the essential features of the others. With regard to what is included in its own unity, the essential features of the others are surds. Therefore, the *de facto* unity of the several determinations together escapes what is unified by each and every determination. The locus of the unity of the whole collection must be in the whole, not in the several members.

(*c*) Suppose, finally, that the *de facto* unity exhibits a harmonious pattern that accounts for itself. Such a pattern could be an intellectual one, like a principle, or it could be of many other types apprehended aesthetically. It would not seem necessary that all *de facto* unities be harmonious. But suppose for the sake of argument that the *de facto* unity of the actual ontological plurality of determinations of being is in fact a harmony. A harmony is a unified complexity whose hang-togetherness is not to be explained by some determinate external factor but rather is to be apprehended immediately in the harmony itself. If the world of determinations is in fact harmonious, how does the harmony account for itself? The harmony does not account for itself by reference to some determinate external factor, for although such a factor might cause the grouping of things that is harmonious, it could not cause the harmoniousness in the harmony. Thus, we can harmonize things by intention through making them conform to some harmonious pattern; but we cannot make a pattern itself harmonious. The harmoniousness of a pattern, as we have noted, is immediately just what it is and is not derivative from something else. But the harmony does not account for itself simply in itself. In itself, the harmony is just harmonious; no account is given. It gives no answer to the question why its own pattern is harmonious and some alternative is not. A harmony simply is what it is, that is, harmonious, and this gives no account of why it is harmonious.

We must distinguish between the question *whether* a certain pattern is harmonious and the question *why* it is harmonious. The harmony, once it is grasped, answers the first question in itself; we either see the harmony there or we do not. But just for the very reason that the answer to the first question is in terms of some kind of aesthetic intuition, an answer to the second question is impossible. Neither the harmony itself nor an external determinate thing can explain why the harmonious pattern is harmonious. To the question why one pattern is harmonious we might try to answer by pointing out certain relationships within the pattern. But this is only an aid to the grasp of the nature of the pattern and contributes only to an answer to the question *whether* the pattern is harmonious. No account can be given of why a harmony is a harmony.

It might be thought that the only account a harmony should give of itself is an exhibition of its own harmoniousness and that to question further is to require reasons of the self-evident. This is mistaken, however, because what is self-evident in a harmony is the unity or harmoniousness it confers upon what it harmonizes. Why the harmony is harmonious is not at all self-evident: what is self-evident is only the fact that it is a harmony. The only answer that can be given to the question why some patterns are harmonious and others are not is that they are just made that way.

We may now safely conclude, having eliminated the plausible alternatives, that no *de facto* unity accounts for itself.

(4) What does not account for itself is ontologically contingent. By "ontologically contingent" is meant "dependent on something else for its whole being and nature." If a thing, for instance a *de facto* unity, does not contain in itself or determine something else that accounts for why it is what it is, then it would not be at all unless some further thing makes it be and contains its account, as it were. Consider the example of chance. Suppose there is a temporal world wherein something happens that is not determinately related by causal law or otherwise to what had happened before it in time. If this is possible we would say it would be a chance happening, even if it went on to determine consequences that were determinate with respect to the consequences of other things. Now, although the nature of the chance happening might not be related to anything that went before it, we would still say that it would need a cause in order to be at all. Its cause would have to be something outside of the chain of the happening's antecedents. If the happening were contingent, that is, did not fully account for itself, it would still need a cause in order to be. Otherwise, we would not only say that it was a chance happening with respect to antecedents; we would also say that it had no way of being at all—it would be impossible. Anything not accounting for itself is either impossible or ontologically dependent.

(5) The determinateness of a determination of being requires a plurality of determinations. A plurality of determinations requires a *de facto* unity. A *de facto* unity cannot account for itself and is therefore contingent. The determinateness of a determination of being is therefore also contingent. But if a determination of being is not determinate, it is nothing, by definition. Therefore, the determinations of being are contingent. This is what was to be proved in part *a* of Proposition 1.

b) *That the contingency of the determinations of being is contingency upon a creator.* This also is proved in five steps.

(1) The very being of a determination is its determinateness. Every determination of being has a specific determinate character. Its specific determinate character is the determinateness it has in virtue of which it is determinate and different from other determinations of being. But a determination of being is nothing more than its specific determinate character or nature; this is its determinateness and its whole being. When we speak of things as determinations of being on the very general level, there is no distinction entertained between the essence of the thing and its existence. This is not the level where we can recognize a difference between the form and the matter of an Aristotelian substance. Structural or substantial forms have a specific determinate character, and matter has its specific determinate character, for example, pure potentiality for being formed, and there may be determinations of being that are substances that include both formal and

material kinds of determinations. But a distinction between essence and existence can be entertained only when dealing with complex determinations that include in their specific determinate characters both essential and existential kinds of determinations. If we speak just of determinations in the abstract, the being of the determination is only its specific determinate character. Therefore, the very being of a determination is its determinateness.

(2) The determinateness of a determination of being is contingent. This is what was proved in part *a* above.

(3) The very being of a determination is contingent. This follows from steps one and two above. The significance of this step is that, without whatever it is that the determination is contingent upon, the determination with its specific determinate character would not be at all.

(4) The being of a determination of being cannot be contingent upon other determinations of being. A determination of being is conditioned by other determinations with respect to the nature of its specific determinate character; that is, the other determinations are necessary for its conditional features and hence for the possibility of its determinateness. But because a determination is conditioned by other determinations in its very nature, its determinateness is contingent upon the togetherness of the others with itself. That is, the being of a determination is contingent upon its being together with those others. The very possibility that one determination is conditioned by another means that both are contingent upon their togetherness. And this togetherness must be contingent upon some further thing, not a determination.

Suppose again, for purposes of illustration, that there is a temporal world with physical objects connected by laws of nature. Suppose also that there are two events, *A* and *B*, which happen to the physical objects, and that *A* is the cause of *B*, according to some natural laws. *A* causes *B* by conditioning what *B*'s specific determinate character can be. The specific determinate character of *B* is conditioned by the specific determinate character of *A*. And the specific determinate character of *A* is conditioned by what it can make of *B;* that is, part of its character is that it has the potentiality of determining the specific character of *B*. Now, *A* cannot condition *B*, nor *B* condition *A*, unless both of them are together in some sort of unity. Perhaps they need not be together at the same time, but at least they must be together in the same medium of mutual conditioning. This means that, although the nature of *A* conditions what the nature of *B* is to be (at least in its conditional features), it cannot give rise to the being of *B*, for the being of *B* is presupposed for *A* to condition. Moreover, and more surprisingly, perhaps, *A* cannot have the specific determinate character it has, which includes its feature of being cause or conditioner of *B*, unless it is together with *B* and *B* is mutually relevant to it, conditioning it. This means that neither *A* nor *B* can be what they are, for example, cause and effect among other things, unless they are together. And therefore the being of one determination cannot be contingent upon another determination.

(5) The contingency of a determination of being must be contingency upon a creator that creates the determination along with the other determinations in a *de facto* unity that allows for their mutual conditioning and determinateness with respect to each other. A determination of being cannot be without being determinate with respect to other determinations; several determinations cannot be determinate with respect to each other unless they are all together. Therefore, the contingency of one is the contingency of all in their *de facto* unity of togetherness. Therefore, if any are, all must be created, that is, made to be. They cannot be contingent upon each other; therefore, what makes them be must be outside the realm of determinations and create them from nothing, that is, from no determination. Therefore, the contingency of the determinations of being is contingency upon a creator who creates them all.

This completes the proof of the proposition that the *determinations of being need a creator in order to be,* which is what was to be demonstrated.

Proposition 2

The determinations of being are; therefore they are created and there is a creator. This proposition is an enthymeme whose suppressed premise is the hypothetical proposition, "If there are determinations of being, they are created and there is a creator." If this hypothetical proposition is true, and if there indeed are determinations of being, then it follows that they are created and that there is a creator.

The hypothetical proposition follows from Proposition One, which has been proved above: "The determinations of being need a creator in order to be." Proposition One did not consider the possibility that there might be no determinations of being. If there were no determinations of being, none would be determinate and hence they would not require a creator. For the sake of logical form we must consider this possibility.

But the minor premise in our argument, "The determinations of being are," rejects this possibility. It is undeniable from our experience that this minor premise is true, for there are determinate things all about us. Furthermore, it is undeniable even in principle that there are determinations of being; for the denial of it must use at least determinate terms, which are one kind of determination of being, sufficient for the argument. All that could be denied of this minor premise is that our analysis of what it is to be a determination of being is mistaken. This denial would probably also refute Proposition One. We have defended our analysis of what it is to be determinate in Chapter Two above and shall continue to do so throughout our study. Of course, a complete defense would involve a much larger and more comprehensive metaphysical system than we can elaborate in this study. But it must be remembered that the present proof in which we are engaged should be taken as such only within the context of the whole of our reflection, and reflection in speculative philosophy is never beyond the need to issue promissory notes.

If it is true that if there are determinations of being then they are created and there is a creator, and if it is true that there are determinations of being, then it is true that the determinations of being are created and there is a creator. This argument exhibits the rule of *modus ponens,* and *modus ponens* is an intellectual principle whose validity is a harmony that all philosophers recognize.

It is interesting to note that there is a difficulty in classifying this argument with regard to whether it is "cosmological" or "ontological." Its form seems to be cosmological, since it argues from the actuality of determinations of being to the reality of their creator. But as we have noted, the actuality of determinations is undeniable in principle. Hence, even without experience, the argument would work from the deliverances of intellect alone. An ontological proof of a creator argues that from the presuppositions of intellect alone it can be proved that a creator is necessary. We can agree with this but must add the rider that our argument has shown that the very structure of intelligibility itself is contingent in the sense that we have used the term contingent, and that it is because of this very fact, that, for example, even a self-evident proposition needs an account, that we must acknowledge the reality of a creator.

Proposition 3

The creator provides the unity of the determinations of being, is transcendent and indeterminate: therefore, the creator is what we have been looking for when we have sought being-itself. From the beginning we have identified being-itself with the ontological one or unifier of the determinations of being; we have furthermore found that being-itself must be transcendent of the determinations and indeterminate. We may now identify being-itself with the creator if we can show that the creator provides the unity of the determinations and is transcendent and indeterminate in the senses our previous discussions require. We shall deal with each in turn, that the creator unifies the determinations of being, that it is transcendent, and that it is indeterminate.

a) That the creator unifies the determinations of being. This follows from the fact (see Proposition One, *b* [5]) that the creator creates all the determinations of being together, mutually determining each other. That creation is this way is what is required by the arguments of Propositions One and Two above, for we found that it is all the determinations together that are contingent in their being upon the creator. If the determinations are at all, it is because the creator creates them together.

The togetherness of the determinations that is created is the *de facto* unity that they must have. The problem of the one and the many has been the problem of finding something that would account for the *de facto* unity that the many determinations have. That the determinations have a *de facto* unity is something simply to be read off, for the *de facto* unity is just the grouping the determinations happen to have. But the *de facto* unity does not account for itself; it does not say how or why it is as it is. The fact that the creator creates the determinations with their *de facto* unity does account for the being of the unity. The creator is the ontological one that unifies the determinations.

To say that the creator is the ontological one, however, is not to be committed to the view that the creator is itself something unified. As yet, that is an open question; and since we are going to say that the creator is in itself indeterminate, it must in fact be the case that distinctions such as unity versus plurality do not apply to the creator. We are committed, nonetheless, to the view that the act or process of creation must be unified to the extent that its product is unified. In the sense that the determinations are created together, they cannot be created separately by separate acts of creation.

The principle of the ontological ground of differences says that two differing determinations of being presuppose a common ground in virtue of which they are relevantly determined with respect to each other and within which each delimits a domain over against each other. Our conclusions concerning the creator exhibit this principle in the following ways. First, the creator is the common ground of the determinations in the sense that it creates all of them together. It is the ground because it creates them, and it is common because it is the creator of them all, each and every one and all together. The truth in the *ens commune* theory is the fact that it sees the necessity that being-itself is common to all the determinations. We incorporate this truth by saying that the creator is common to all the determinations of being. Second, our theory accounts for that part of the principle that directs that each determination of being delimit a domain of the common ground for itself over against the other determinations. Although the creator cannot be conceived as a substance of which the determinations are carved-out parts, still it is the case that each determination has its own being over against the others. The being of each determination is simply its own determinateness, and this determinateness each determination has in its specific determinate character. These determinate characters are related and they condition each other; yet each determination has its *own* characters. The failure of the *ens commune* theory is that it could not account for the differences between determinations without saying that they were more than being. Our theory avoids this difficulty by pointing out that the determinateness of each determination is precisely the being that each determination has; its specific determinate character is what being is for it.

To say *that* the creator unifies the determinations of being is different from saying *why* it unifies them, and it is different from saying why it unifies them *in the way* it does. The first is proved simply from the fact that the creator creates the determinations: the very being of the determinations is to be unified, and the creator creates their being. The second two claims, however, would answer the question why there is any creation at all and the question why it is as it is. As we shall see below, neither of these two latter questions allows of an answer.

b) *That the creator transcends the determinations of being.* This follows from our argument both in negative and in positive ways. On the negative side, we said in proof of Proposition One, *b* (4), that the being of a determination of being cannot be contingent upon other determinations of being. Therefore, the creator upon which the determinations are contingent cannot be among the determinations and must be outside of them or transcend them. This negative proof of transcendence is in agreement with the arguments of earlier chapters criticizing attempts to interpret being-itself as a determinate member of the many determinations of being.

On the positive side, we can show that the notion of a creator creating the determinations requires the transcendence of the creator. If the determinations of being are created, they are dependent for their whole being on the creator. Our argument has shown, in fact, that it is just because they are wholly dependent that there must in consequence be a creator on which their being depends. Since the being of the determinations is wholly dependent on the creator, the reality of the creator cannot depend on the determinations. Hence, the creator in itself must be wholly independent of the determinations. This independence is what is needed for transcendence.

To say that the creator must be independent in itself of the created determinations is not to say that it is a creator apart from them; the creator is a creator only insofar as it creates, and insofar as it creates it is connected with the determinations. But it is the case that, in order for the creator to create, it must have a reality in itself that is independent of the created determinations. The creator makes itself creator when and as it creates; in order to do this, it must be independent, in itself, of the products it creates and even of its own role of being creator. The role of creator is the nature the creator has in virtue of its connection with the created determinations.

Now, the notion of transcendence is a vague one, and we must show what interpretation of it is entailed by the theory of creation. Transcendence usually means that something is present in or takes its rise from something else and also extends beyond it. It is obviously not the case that the creator takes its rise from the determinations, for the determinations take their rise from the creator. But it is the case that the creator is present in the determinations and that it extends beyond them. It is present in the sense that its creative act or productive power constitutes the determinations and gives them their being. The determinations are termini of the creative act. The creator transcends the determinations in the sense that its being in itself is something over and above the determinations, independent of them. Instead of the creator's transcending in the sense of starting in the determinations and extending out, the direction of the transcendence is reversed, as it were; the creator starts outside and comes in. But its coming in to the determinations and its creating of them are the same.

This peculiar reversal of the usual meaning of transcendence suggests that the creator's transcendence is both conditional and unconditional. The creator is *conditionally* transcendent in the sense that it has something to transcend only in virtue of its connection with the determinations. Unless we were to acknowledge first that the creator is present in the determinations and then to see that it must transcend them, we would have no way of noting that there is anything transcendent at all. Our knowledge of the creator's transcendence must follow the usual order or direction in transcendence, beginning with the presence of the creator in something and moving to the fact that the creator transcends what it is present in. Without something to be present in, there is no sense in saying that the creator transcends anything. The creator is *unconditionally* transcendent in the sense that, since it creates the determinations, its own being must be independent of them. The creator cannot be conditioned in its essential nature by the determinations, for it cannot be conditioned in its essential nature by something whose whole being depends on it. If the creator were conditioned in its essential nature by the created determinations, it would be necessitated by that fact to create them. The conditioning of the creator by the determinations depends in part upon the determinations. Therefore, the determinations would necessitate that the creator create them; but without being created, they would have no being in themselves to necessitate that they be created. Therefore, it is a contradiction to say that the creator is essentially conditioned by the determinations. Its essential being in itself must be unconditionally transcendent of the determinations; that is, its essential being must be independent.

c) *That the creator is indeterminate.* This is apparent from the fact that the creator creates all of the determinations and hence cannot be one of them itself. We have seen that all of the determinations together need a creator and that therefore the creator must create them all. If the creator were itself determinate essentially, then it would need a creator itself, and on ad infinitum.

That the creator is indeterminate is also apparent from the fact that the creator is transcendent of the determinations, for the creator must be indeterminate insofar as it transcends what is determinate. And, the very transcendent being of the creator is that which is independent of the determinations and creates them, the creator's essential nature. Therefore, the creator in essence is indeterminate.

As noted in *b* immediately above, transcendence is attributed to the creator according to the order of knowledge. That is, we note the presence of the creator in what is contingent upon it and then acknowledge that the creator in essence must be independent of what is wholly dependent on it.

In the order of reality, the creator's essential reality is independent of determinations and extends into them by creating them. This peculiarity of the transcendence entailed by the creation theory shows itself in the creator's indeterminateness, for indeterminateness is obviously a negative quality that is attributed to the creator in virtue of its connection with the determinations. That is, in order to be creator, the creator must be transcendent and indeterminate. To say that the creator is indeterminate is merely to deny of it the character that the determinations have, that is, determinate being. The reason determinateness should be denied of the creator is because of what is entailed by the fact that the creator is the creator.

We have now shown that the creator is what we have been looking for when we have sought being-itself; for we have shown that the creator unifies the determinations of being and is therefore the ontological one that is the criterion by which we are to recognize being-itself. Furthermore, we have shown how the creator is both transcendent and indeterminate in the senses that being-itself must be in order to be the ontological one. Therefore, we may conclude that the creator meets the requirements for identity with being-itself that we have set so far. In the concluding section of this chapter we shall show how the theory of creation accounts for being-itself in a positive sense, over and above meeting the requirements that have come out of our criticism of alternative theories.

Conclusion to Section A

This section has been a proof of the reality of being-itself, the creator. The proof has been in three main steps or propositions. Proposition One is that the determinations of being need a creator in order to be, and it was justified by showing, *a*, that the determinations of being are contingent and, *b*, that the contingency of the determinations of being is contingency upon a creator. Proposition Two is that the determinations of being are; therefore they are created and there is a creator. It was justified by showing it to be undeniable that the determinations are, and that this fact, coupled with Proposition One, proves that the determinations are created and that there is a creator. Propositions One and Two prove the reality of the creator. Proposition Three is that the creator is to be identified with what we have sought as being-itself, and it was justified by showing that the creator unifies the determinations of being, that it is transcendent, and that it is indeterminate. The three propositions together prove that there is such a thing as being-itself and that it is the creator of the determinations. This is what was to be demonstrated.

It is still necessary to articulate the theory of creation to show that it gives a speculative account of being-itself in a positive sense. This involves showing how it exhibits the principle of the ontological equality of reciprocal contrasts. Before that, however, we must elaborate the logic of the notion of creation and deal with some standard criticisms of creation theories.

SECTION B

The Logic of the Concept of Creation

The logic of the concept of creation is very complex and it will be developed throughout the rest of our study. At this point, however, we shall mark out seven important features.

1. In the argument of section A above we employed a loose distinction between what the creator is essentially and what it is in virtue of its connection with the created determinations. This distinction bears several prima facie similarities to the distinction within a determination between its essential and conditional features. What the creator is essentially would seem to be its essential features, and what it is in virtue of its connections would

seem to be its conditional features, features it has in virtue of the fact that it is determinate with respect to something else. These similarities, however, do not go very deep.

In the first place, since the creator is indeterminate essentially, it is misleading to say that it has essential features, for the term "features" connotes determinate characteristics. With respect to the creator, we cannot say whether its essential nature has many features or one, what the features are or are not. The creator is essentially indeterminate and transcendent of the domain where such determinate considerations apply.

In the second place, although it is fair to call the creator's features that arise from its connection with the determinations "conditional features," it is necessary to mark out some differences from the conditional features of determinations. A determination has conditional features in virtue of the fact that it is together with other determinations from the start, as it were. Yet the creator creates the determinations with respect to which it is determinate. With respect to the created determinations, the creator is "creator," "transcendent," "indeterminate," and so forth. Since a determination by definition is determinate, it is *necessary* that it have conditional features, as we noted in the previous chapter; without conditional features, it would not be determinate. Since the creator is essentially indeterminate, there is no *need* at all for it to have conditional features. Why the creator creates and gives itself the conditional features is a question that cannot be answered. *If* the creator is to have the features of being creator, however, it *must* create and be conditionally determinate with respect to the determinations it creates. A determination's conditional features depend on its coexistence with other determinations. The creator's conditional features depend on the reality of determinations, but the creator must create the determinations with respect to which it is determinate. Hence it can be said that the creator gives itself its conditional features as it creates the determinations of being. The connection between the creator and the determinations and the conditional features to which the connection gives rise will be analyzed formally and in detail in section A of chapter 4 below.

2. Although we have shown that the creator is essentially indeterminate, it is still necessary to note that our theory about the creator is determinate. That is, to say that the creator creates the determinations, is transcendent, indeterminate, and so forth, is to say something determinate. But what is there in the creator that corresponds to the determinate things we say about it? The answer must be that the referents of the determinate knowledge are the conditional determinate features that the creator gives itself in creating the determinations of being. If the referents were in the essential nature of the creator, we could not say that essentially the creator is indeterminate. Therefore, our knowledge of the creator must be knowledge of his determinate conditional features. We must exhibit how this is so.

That the creator is the *creator* is obviously a conditional feature, for it is a creator only in reference to what it creates. Without actually creating something, the creator could not be said to be a creator at all, just as a father could not be called a father unless he fathers children. We know that a father, apart from his fathering of children, is still a man, since we can know him in other contexts than just in relation to his children. But what the creator is apart from creating we do not know. So far we have no knowledge of the creator except what we have concluded from its presence in the created determinations; and furthermore, we have concluded that apart from the created determinations the creator must be indeterminate. What we know of the creator is strictly limited to what can be known from the connection it has with the determinations it creates.

That the creator is transcendent is likewise a conditional feature the creator has in virtue of its connection with the determinations, for as we have seen, the creator must be connected with the determinations in order to transcend them. To say that the creator is transcendent, however, is to say that it has some reality apart from any connection with the determinations, and we say that it is transcendent precisely because the creator cannot have all of its reality exhausted in its connections with what it creates. Therefore, in the sense that the creator is unconditionally transcendent, it is also independent and not dependent for its reality on the connection with the determinations of being. This, too, is knowledge about what it means to be the creator of the determinations. Independence of the determinations is not an essential feature of the creator but rather an analytic component of the conditional feature of being creator.

That the creator is indeterminate also is an analytic component of the feature of being creator. Its referent is what the creator must be in order to be creator. It does not refer to any fuzziness or chaos in the creator's essential nature. Rather, it points out that the contingent fact that the creator is indeed the creator entails a contradiction in the attribution of a determinate nature to the creator apart from all connection with the determinations. It is because the creator is the creator that we must say that essentially it is indeterminate. To say that the creator is essentially indeterminate is only to say that nothing determinate can be attributed to the creator's essential nature. In fact, it is to say that there is no such thing as a determinate essential nature and that talk about the creator's essential nature is misleading; the determinate referent for knowledge of the creator's indeterminateness is part of the determinate but conditional feature of being creator.

The upshot of our second remark is twofold. First, it is that knowledge of the creator is limited to the connection the creator has with the determinations created. What the creator is apart from all such connections is a mystery. Furthermore, it is a mystery in the philosophically acceptable sense of that word. A mystery is *un*acceptable to philosophy when it means that we do not understand something well enough. But a mystery is quite proper when it means that there is nothing to understand. If the creator is indeterminate, then any alleged understanding of it in those indeterminate respects would be in error. When we identify the creator with God, it will be important to note the religious significance of this philosophically demonstrable mystery.

Second, in the light of the fact that we shall identify the creator with the God of both religion and philosophy, it is an important point that we can claim what knowledge we have to be univocal. Knowledge of the creator may be abstruse, but it is still a laying out of the determinate features involved in being creator. We have not been forced to resort to what the scholastics called "analogical knowledge." What the creator is in itself we do not know; and we have argued that it cannot be known. Analogical knowledge was called upon to articulate what God is in himself, but we have declared this to be impossible. Yet the scholastics never made as sharp a distinction as we between what God is in himself and what he is in connection with the world, and this is what gave them the hope of knowing God analogically. They admitted that when the distinction is made sharply even analogical knowledge would not help. That the distinction should be made sharply is the brunt of our argument.

3. Since the creator gives itself conditional features as it creates the determinations of being, its conditional features must be among the determinations created. The fact that this is so raises a host of complex issues that cannot be dealt with in the present study; the issues it raises demand an exact and thorough analysis of kinds of determinations of being and of the relations that can pertain between them. This analysis belongs to metaphysics proper and not to ontology. For our present ontological purposes we must limit our metaphysical considerations to remarks about what it is to be a determination of being in general.

As a matter of program, however, we can indicate what any metaphysical theory would have to account for to do justice to the claim that the conditional features of the creator are among the created determinations. In the first place, there would have to be a kind of determination that articulates the metaphysical character of the determinations in general. Determinations of this special kind would be those that would distinguish essential from conditional features, that would comprise the nature of *de facto* unities in general, that would make up the dependent and created modal status of all determinations, and so forth. Furthermore, determinations of this kind would have to be able to be components of every determination whatsoever, including themselves. Besides this kind of determination, there would have to be another related kind that would articulate the creator's conditional feature of being creator. This second kind of determination would have to be relational in character, standing to all determinations, including its own kind, as that which relates them to their common source and standing to what is independent in the creator as that which determines it conditionally with respect to the determinations. The transcendence, indeterminateness, and so forth, of the creator would have to be elements of this second kind of determination. These two kinds of determination, and perhaps more, necessary to account for what we have marked out about ontology and the metaphysical character of

78 GOD THE CREATOR

determinateness would be over and above all the kinds of determinations needed to account for cosmology, determinations that would be physical substances and responsible persons, abstract possibilities and concrete events, numbers and past facts, and all the rest.

4. The distinction is often made today, in the theological wake of process philosophy, between a "creative ground" and a "sustaining ground." This distinction is maintained by those who want to defend the latter without the former (those who defend the former nearly always take the latter to be an analytical consequence), and their motive is the broader defense of a metaphysical system wherein finite beings may imply an encompassing being-itself or God but are not wholly contingent upon it: in fact, they maintain that God is partially and essentially contingent upon the finite beings of the world. In this vein, Charles Hartshorne writes that God

> is never confronted by a world whose coming to be antedates his own entire existence. There is no presupposed "stuff" alien to God's creative work; but rather everything that influences God has already been influenced by him, whereas we are influenced by events of the past with which we had nothing to do.[8]

It is obvious that our present reflections have brought us to a theory far different from this and that Hartshorne would have to meet the arguments we have encountered and adopted. But these arguments aside, it is difficult to see by what right the term "ground" could be used by the process position at all (admittedly, it is not Hartshorne's term). The allegedly sustainer God of this position is in no way the ground or source of the being of finite things; he is only a source of influences, altering the course of events. The term "ground" connotes more than that. As we have seen in section A above, our own reflections lead us to attribute the influences of the specific features of the determinations of being to the context of determinations itself. Our theory will have its hardest time defending the religious notion of providence, whereas the process alternative has its greatest difficulty with the freedom and integrity of the creatures of the world. In recognition of this difference, we have adopted the term "creator" instead of the more modern term "ground" to dispell ambiguities.

5. What is it to be the creator of the determinations? The term "creator" is a name applied to being-itself in virtue of a function it performs with respect to the determinations. The abstract nature of a function may supply the clue to the characterization of the function of ontological creation.

A function is an activity or a doing of something. As such it is an exercise of power. This is an actual exercise, not a potential one. A power unexercised is a power that does nothing, no power at all. The function of creating is the exercise of creative power. What is created are the determinations of being, and being-itself as creator can be called, as it often has been by thinkers like Paul Tillich, the power of being; the being of which it is the power is the being of the determinations. The feature of power, like the feature of creator,

[8] *The Divine Relativity* (New Haven, Conn.: Yale University Press, 1948), p. 30.

is one of the conditional features the creator or being-itself has in virtue of its actual creating of the determinations of being. The notion of power will play a large part in our discussion to come.

6. Not only is a function an exercise of power; it is a way or *form* of the exercise of power. Functions differ from each other according to the form or nature of their exercise. The nature of the function of creative power is very problematic, however. When the nature of an ordinary function is abstracted it is like a formula or blueprint for doing something, for getting somewhere, for working up a raw material into a finished product. Yet we are entitled to no such characterization of the nature of creating by the arguments we have considered. If it is the determinations of being that are created, then no determinate plan can precede and lead up to their production. Yet it is the determinations of being, qua determinate, for which we have been forced to acknowledge a creator. Furthermore, if the function of creating had a nature like a plan or formula whose issue is the determinations of being, then creating would be determinate, the determinate function would apply to the creator, the determinate creator would be a determinate context of mutual relevance, and all our previous conclusions would be contradicted. Therefore, the nature of the function of creating cannot be like a plan or formula or blueprint.

To construe the nature of a function as a formula, however, is to construe that action of the function as a temporal thing, for it is to say that there are determinate stages through which the formula must be run. Yet all exercises of power, all activities, are not temporal, and the function of creating the determinations of being cannot be a temporal function. Time itself is a determinate dimension of being, distinct from space, the number two, the color red, and countless other things. The "move" involved in creating is from no determinations to the determinations created.

But is there no sense in which this move has a nature? The "moving" has no nature, but the move itself obviously has the nature of its issue, its product. What activity is it? It is the activity of creating the determinations of being. Therefore the nature of the function of creating is the nature of what it creates. This is not at all a difficult conclusion when it is taken into account that part of the nature of the determinations, closer to their hearts than their essential features, is their real but contingent being, their created-ness. The nature of creating is simply to give rise to the created beings, to be the power of their being.

7. Since the only nature that can be given to the creative power is that of its termini or end products, the determinations of being, creation does not proceed according to determinate principles. Just as we cannot say why there is creation, so we cannot say why the creation is as it is. Given the nature of intelligibility and harmony, we can see why things fit together in the way that they do, at least in some instances. But as was noted above, there is no way of seeing why intelligibility is as it is or why one pattern is harmonious and another not.

The consequence of this is that we must call the creation of the determina-

Gottfried Leibniz

tions of being a "free" creation. In the Western theological and philosophical tradition, free creation has been contrasted with one or several of three kinds of constrained creation. It might be said that the creator creates because of some necessity in its own nature; the creator cannot help but create. Plotinus, for instance, maintained that the One by nature overflows and emanates the Dyad, which in turn emanates the third hypostasis, *ad indefinitum*. According to our argument above, however, there can be no reason why the creator must create. It might be said, second, that the creator has a nature that determines it to create in a certain way. Some thinkers, for instance, maintain that the creator is perfectly good and therefore must create a good product; everything that is created is good because it stems from a good creator. It might be said, third, that creation has the form it does because of some set of possibilities normative for the creator to which he must conform in creating; creation on this view would be just the actualization of what is possible. Leibniz held to both the second and third interpretations of creation. He claimed that there is a determinate set of possibilities resident in the creator's mind that would be enough for a great many possible worlds; furthermore, the creator by nature is good and must select the best of all possible worlds from the possibilities he entertained. The difficulty with the second interpretation of creation is that we have seen that the creator cannot have a nature apart from connection with its created product. Therefore it cannot be constrained to create the good before it does so. The difficulty with the third interpretation is that it holds that a determination can be possible before it is actual, that is, that it can be something before it is determinate. But a determination's reality is in its determinateness, and to create this is to create the determination. Therefore, Leibniz was wrong on both counts.

It is better to say that creation is free from all three constraints. There is no constraint for the creator to create at all, since such a constraint would have to be determinate and there would thus be a determination prior to all determination. There is no constraint for the creator to create according to its nature, since it has a determinate nature only in virtue of its actual creating. And there is no constraint for the creator to create along the lines of some primordial possibility, for again there would be determination prior to all determination. Since our argument in section A above proved that *all* determinations need a creator, it is impossible to attribute a determinate constraint to the creator apart from its actual creating. If all determination is given in the creating, then the creating itself is free and, from our standpoint, arbitrary. It is creation *ex nihilo*. If it were any other than this, then the creator, being-itself, would be conditioned in itself by what it creates, which is impossible.

SECTION C
Defense against Objections

A theory of creation has a strong commitment to the thesis that the creator is independent and the created product totally dependent. Whereas "before" creation there was only self-subsistent being-itself or God, "after" creation there is the realm of finite determinations that is wholly dependent on being created. Since a temporal construction is out of place,[9] what is important is the introduction of the modalities of independent and dependent reality. Although the notion of independent reality is essentially relational, defined in contrast to the dependent, what it signifies is something prior in reality to the determinate contrast. To speak of creation as a function, then, is to speak of the introduction of dependent reality into the nature of things.

We must ask *how* the dependent and independent are related in creation. It is an answer to the question simply to note that utter dependence is self-explanatory, taking into account, of course, what the dependent is dependent on. Complete dependence on something is a more functional notion than a process of causation through a medium.[10] We can compare the notion of creation with that of contraction in order to elaborate this point. The term "contraction" is of scholastic origin and was intended to steer a course between two disastrous pitfalls that endanger all attempts to account for finite being.

On the one hand is the temptation we have noted to interpret being-itself simply as *ens commune,* that which is common to all beings. Of course, being-itself is at least that, but the consequence of saying it is *only* that is that the determinations of finite being then must be characterized as "added realities." Apart from the contradiction in speaking of added realities over and above being-itself when being-itself is common to all that is, the *ens commune* theory makes the mistake of likening the distinction between infinite and finite being to that between a genus and its species, where the differentia are the added realities. A genus can have realities added to it because it is not completely infinite, a possibility that infinite being-itself lacks. The determinations of being must somehow come from infinite being-itself. Whereas the contraction theory says that being-itself contracts itself to make the determinations, we shall say that being-itself creates them *ex nihilo.* But we agree with the contraction theory in avoiding the temptation of *ens commune.*

On the other hand is the temptation to interpret infinite being-itself as the totality of finite determinations. This view is that being-itself is infinite in the sense that there is nothing outside of it to be a limitation, since it includes everything. Pantheism of one sort or another is the acknowledged issue of this theory. But being-itself in this sense must be determinate as an ultimate category if it is to unite all the other categories. And yet it cannot be determinate without presupposing an external contrast; this argument has already been treated in chapter 1 above. Moreover, since being-itself, according to this theory, is not infinite in the sense of being indeterminate with respect to the finite categories, it is not the univocal being that distinguishes any being from absolute non-being. In fact, absolute non-being

---

[9] See chap. 4, sec. B 3.
[10] See chap. 4, sec. B 1.

cannot be spoken of on this view, and creation is not a possible problem. Against this theory, we agree with the contraction position that the determinations of being must have some other derivations from being-itself than one wherein they are always contained in infinite being in determinate form.

In Western philosophy and theology the theory of divine contraction has had a long and close association with the theory of creation *ex nihilo*. There was hardly a time when Christian thinkers who were attempting to articulate a theory of creation *ex nihilo* were not influenced by Neo-Platonic ideas of contraction. The theories allegedly differ in that contraction is the view that God makes determinate being out of himself whereas creation is the view that God's own substance is not employed but rather that the determinations are made from nothing. This difference, however, is not as great as it might seem. Although the contraction theory says the determinations are contractions of God's own infinite being, it also says that the determinations qua determinate are never contained in the infinite being of the one; the determinations are genuinely novel and the infinite being of the One or God is in no way diminished by their generation.[11] On the other side, although the creation theory says the determinations are made of nothing, that is, of no stuff, it also says that the created determinations are closely connected with their creator, being his handiwork. In terms of our own theory, the determinations are the termini of the creative act and have no being except as such termini. However true it is to say that the determinations are created *ex nihilo*, it is also true to say on the creation theory that the fact that they have being stems from the act of their creator. Contraction and creation each acknowledge the force of the other's emphasis. As we shall see, the transcendence emphasized by creation is of a piece with the presence emphasized by contraction. Both theories are in close agreement about the connection between independent and dependent reality and about the foundation of this connection in the problem of the one and the many.

This association of contraction with creation *ex nihilo* would not merit more than a historical comparison were it not for the fact that the doctrine of contraction has been the locus for some of the most salient criticisms in recent times of any doctrine of divine creation or production. These are the criticisms given by Paul Weiss in his discussion of what he calls "self-diremption," which he identifies mainly with the contraction view of Plotinus. His criticisms are oriented around the problem of the one and the many. A discussion of them will serve as a vehicle to express the meaning of creation.

Weiss makes six critical points.[12]

1. The One [corresponding here to being-itself] by itself is unintelligible. What is without division, without complexity, allowing no dis-

---

[11] See, for example, Plotinus' *Enneads*, trans. Stephen MacKenna and rev. B. S. Page (3d ed.; London: Faber & Faber, 1962), the Fifth Ennead 1.6–7.
[12] *Modes of Being* (Carbondale: Southern Illinois University Press, 1958), pp. 505–6. This passage contains all six points.

tinction—in short, containing no Many—cannot be thought or known. The theory of [contraction] must begin with what it cannot understand, proceed by principles it cannot grasp, and end with what it affirms is not altogether true or real.

It is perfectly true that infinite being-itself is unintelligible, not in the first instance because it is one, but because, as Weiss points out, it is without division, complexity, and distinction. Being infinite, it is not determinate with respect to the determinations of being. To say it contains no many is to say that it is not *ens perfectissimum*. But in this case, as we noted in discussing transcendence, the order of being is contrary to the order of knowledge. Our knowledge begins with the finite determinations and moves dialectically to infinite, unconditionally transcendent being-itself. Therefore the theory begins with what it *can* understand and moves to what it *cannot*, showing why it cannot and why there must be that which it cannot understand. The dialectical principles by which our knowledge proceeds can be grasped, although the principle of contraction cannot be grasped, and for the same reason that infinite being cannot—that there is no such determinate thing. However, the *result* of contraction in the order of being can be grasped, since it is finite, and we can know dialectically what contraction must be to produce this effect. Finally, far from ending with what is not altogether true or real, contraction issues in the only thing that is determinately real, and determination is often taken to be the most real of things. Perhaps Neo-Platonism moves from the most real to the least real, but contraction, as it bears upon our own conclusions, does not; contraction moves from the infinite to the finite, and the determinations of the finite are products of the infinite, not "mixtures" of infinite being and absolute non-being.

> 2. A One which does not act remains undivided, but in that case it surely does not engage in a self-diremption. To produce a Many the One must act. If it and its act are identical, there is no Many produced. But if it and its act are distinct, they already constitute a Many. The production of a Many by the One already presupposes a Many in the shape of the pair of the One and its act of diversification.

Here Weiss's model is too mechanical and hence inapplicable to the logic of the relation between infinite and finite. His argument questions whether it is possible that contraction can solve the dialectical difficulties raised by that relation; to answer his argument an analogy can be offered. Just as when a person acts he is one with his act, so being-itself is one with its act. Just as from the standpoint of the product of a person's act, the act can be interpreted as a sign expressing the presence of an intender, so from the standpoint of the product of the act of contraction, the act can be interpreted as a sign expressing the "intention" of being-itself, that is, the reality of being-itself conditionally transcendent of the act of contraction. Now finite being is the terminal end of the act of contraction. We can say that the unity of the creator's act is the one for the many determinations included in its terminus. Since the nature of the product is that of determinations of being, and since the determinations must be united to be determinate, the act that creates them must be one. In answer to Weiss, the one and many problem cannot be raised in consideration of being-itself as unconditionally transcendent, unconditioned by any relation to the determinations of being, for as we noted above, unconditional transcendence transcends even the functional character of being the one for the ontological many.

3. The One allows the Many to be over against it—or it fails to produce a Many. But then it must minimize itself in order to give some being or meaning to that Many. This requires it to presuppose a One which is more real than its self-diremptive being and in the Many with which it is together. It will become a One in a Many, presupposing a One for itself and the rest of that Many.

That the one allows the many to be over against it means only that infinite being gives itself the sorts of determinations that have the integrity of being determinate and contingent. That it minimizes itself means that it contracts itself. But its self-dirempted or contracted being is not really distinct from the many; *contracted being is the same as finite being,* that is, the many. If they were distinct, there would be no point for the one to contract itself, since that would not produce the many. Moreover, if they were distinct, there would be no univocal sense of being, and there could not possibly be any relation at all between the one and the many, or between infinite and finite being. It is a systematic mistake of Weiss to suppose that otherness requires a difference in the very sense of being that different realities have, instead of a difference in determination of univocal being that amounts to real distinctions. This leads him to deny the univocity of being pertaining to creator and created and hence to reject a creation view because of the difficulties to which that denial leads.[13] There is a problem in finding a one for the many and *un*contracted being, but this is the same as Weiss's second objection.

[13] Weiss is partially aware of this problem of analogy between the modes when he writes, in a passage we have discussed, "The four modes of being, because final and exhaustive, are incapable of being encompassed in some more inclusive genus, or in some other being. Analogy would seem to be the only appropriate way of dealing with them. To be sure there are analogous features in all four. But analogical reasoning begs the question one seeks to answer with respect to them—how do we know these others with their analogous features. . . . The initial question is how we get to the others, how we are to know what they in themselves demand, and thus just what concepts are appropriate to them. It surely is right to say that all things are to be understood in appropriate terms; but this is not too helpful so long as we do not occupy the positions of the others but know them only from our own." (*Modes of Being,* p. 523).

Still, his solution does not recognize the force of his own objection. He argues (*ibid.,* pp. 526 ff.) that two things, X and Y, can be so related that X, for instance, can know or grasp Y in an X-like way, as Y. Then Xy, X with its knowledge of Y, is the form for which Y is the content. But the issue with respect to analogy is how X and Y are related in the first place if they have absolutely nothing in common! Here Weiss equivocates. He suggests, on the one hand, that the form Xy and content Y are really one thing (p. 528), the Y, and that the form is distinguished from the whole by the abstractive activity of X. That form and content are but formally distinguished in a real whole is not to be denied, but what has yet to be explained is how the X can be related to the Y so as to perform an abstraction. On the other hand, he suggests that

4. The One engages in a single act or in many. If the latter, there must paradoxically be a radical plurality before the Many has been generated. If the former, there will be only two things in the universe unless the product of that first act of generation generates a subordinate one, and so on, for a series of steps. This alternative has no beings on the same level of reality or excellence; only beings of different orders. It has a sheer Many without a One, and presupposes a distinction between that One and its act. Consequently, both at the beginning and at the end there will be only a Many.

The contraction theory, insofar as it agrees with our own conclusions, says that being-itself engages in a single act of contraction, that many modes of determinations are produced in that one act, and that the product of the first act does not produce a subordinate product, and so on down in a series of steps. A contraction theory need not agree with the whole of Plotinus' position. For this reason, Weiss's comments here are not directly applicable; however, there is a problem for the contraction view that is implicitly raised by his point, a problem with two sides. First, what is the unity of the contracted finite being as over against infinite being? As has been indicated, infinite being-itself is one both in the sense that its creative act is the unifying context for the many and in the sense that, being indeterminate, it allows no internal distinction. Second and consequent upon the first, does this unity of the determinations stand over against the unity of being-itself or not? If the unity of the many is the same as that of being-itself, how can the many be unified to stand over against being-itself? But if the unity of the many is other than the unity of being-itself, what is the further one for the two unities? The answer to this, as was said, is that the unity of the act of contraction is the one unifying the many determinations. The many has a *de facto* unity; since being-itself is not determinate it is not unified: it simply is not diverse. Being-itself is the one for the many determinations because it is their common creator; but the unity is their unity. The being of the determinations is the product of the creative act of being-itself; in this sense, being-itself can be said to be unified as contracted or as become determinate.

5. The One, before it gives rise to a Many, is distinct from the One as originating a Many. But then before the Many has been produced we have Many Ones. Yet if the generating of the Many was of the very essence of the One and instantly produced its Many, there would be no act of self-diremption. A One which was always faced with a Many could be said to require that Many, but not to have generated it, and surely not be first being a mere One and then becoming a generating source

the X and Y are primarily brought together by the knowing subject, the I. But "the I is not a third thing." It is one of the things, in this case the X, and the problem at hand is how the X can be conditioned by Y so as to indicate the latter's presence. There is an X and a Y; perhaps also an X 'Y-ized' and a Y 'X-ized,' that is, each conditioned by the other. But prior to the conditioning of one by the other, they must both be conditioned by a third thing or common ground that allows for their interaction. Weiss's solution is like two of Leibniz' isolated monads, each reflecting the other in virtue of pre-established harmony but without the pre-established harmonizer.

of whatever else there be. A self-diremptive One must not only be a source of a Many but must continue to encompass it; it must have two roles, and thus itself be a Many from the very start.

This criticism points out well the dialectical relation between the concepts of the one and many. But it supposes that the conditioned and unconditioned transcendence of being-itself constitute a many. The moral of it is that being-itself, unconditionally transcendent of its giving rise to the many, should not be said to be one. Of course it cannot be said then that it is of the very essence of being-itself as unconditionally transcendent to create a many, for, strictly speaking, the unconditionally transcendent has no essence. It is of the essence of the *one* to create a many, but being-itself cannot be called one except insofar as it *is* creator of the many. In other words, being-itself constitutes itself as a one in the very act of creating a many. What being-itself is apart from any relation to the determinations is pure mystery. Dialectical difficulties such as those Weiss brings up demonstrate that this distinction between being-itself as unconditionally transcendent and as conditionally so must be drawn.

6. A generated Many is thrust away from the One or is confined within it. If the former, the Many and the One constitute a larger Many which needs a more inclusive One to encompass it. If the latter, there is no real Many, a Many collected or connected by means of a One. There is only a One. This pair of alternatives touches the core of the doctrine of creation in classical theology. If God creates a universe, he gives it its own existence and the universe no longer needs God in order to be; if the universe does not really stand apart, over against God, there is in fact no universe that he creates.

What this dilemma shows is that a finite God cannot be a one creating a many. Weiss's mistake is to think that creation means that God gives the world a being distinct from his own, that there is a *modal* distinction between the being of God and the world. The finite realm is distinct from God or being-itself because it has determinations with respect to which being-itself is indeterminate. To deny the univocity of being and say, as Weiss does, that there is a modal difference between the being of God and that of the created realm is to purchase the difficulties of the doctrine that being is analogical with respect to God and the world. A modal difference is a finite difference, and Weiss shows that the problem of the one and the many cannot be solved where all elements taken into account are finite and where the one-many relation is that of creation. But the resolution is the view we are defending: that if we can identify God with being-itself, he is infinite being, and that his created product is finite being; that the latter comes from the former by contraction or creation; that God is one for the plural world only insofar as he is creator, in virtue of being identical with the act of creation; that God cannot be one for the plural world unless he in himself is utterly indeterminate with respect to any relation to the world, for if he were determinate with respect to it, that would constitute a modal difference.

Our reflection has arrived at the point where the identification of being-itself, creator of the determinations, with at least the God of the philosophers if not the God of religion is almost irresistible. Before we pursue this identification in the next chapter, we must consolidate our reflections about the transcendence of being-itself as creator. We must determine whether we have reached a satisfactory characterization of being-itself.

SECTION D
Being-Itself and Non-being

We conceive being-itself as the one for the many determinations of being, as the infinitely full and indeterminate creator of those determinations, transcendent conditionally of what it creates and transcendent unconditionally even of its conditioned nature as creator. But before we can accept this as an adequate account of being-itself, we must consider it in connection with absolute non-being, for it is with reference to absolute non-being that being-itself is positively conceived as *being* and not just as the one for the many determinations.

A preliminary word should be said about the notion of non-being. Philosophers have often distinguished two kinds of non-being, an absolute kind and a relative kind. The latter is what we spoke of in considering Royce's claim that all determination is by negation. Relative non-being is a feature of a thing in that it is not something else. Relative non-being is a negation of something positive. Even if Royce were right that all determination is by negation, still the being of what is so determinate is something positive; our own analysis of determinateness has affirmed the disputed positivity in the need a determination has for an essential feature, even though the determinateness of that essential feature depends in part on the negating force of some conditional feature.

Absolute non-being, like relative non-being, is *conceived* as the negation of something positive. We conceive it by negating the positive determinations of everything. We conceive it by conceiving the complete absence of everything conceivable. It is doubtful that we ever actually contemplate or imagine this conception, but at least we know the rule for conceiving it, that is, to conceive of the utter absence of all determinate being whatsoever. Yet, however much absolute non-being is conceived by negation of the positive, that of which it is the conception is not a negation of the positive but just absolutely nothing at all. The utter absence of the positive would not be a negation of anything, for there would be neither anything to negate nor any positive power of negating, no essential features with the power of sustaining negative conditional features. This much we know from the rule for conceiving absolute non-being. There is no such thing as absolute non-being; it is absolutely nothing.

Furthermore, it is inconceivable that there is such a thing as absolute non-being, for absolute non-being is the reciprocal contrast to the being of the determinations—they are something; it is nothing. If the being of the determinations were not created, they would not be and there would be absolutely nothing. But the reason that there is no such thing as absolute non-being is that there in fact is something, namely, the determinations. To conceive of the utter absence of everything would still be to presuppose the determinate structure of intelligibility, the structure of relative negativity, and hence also the structure of relative positivity, all of which are among the determinate elements created. Therefore, even the statement that there is no such thing as absolute non-being because of the reality of determinate being presupposes created being. Because of the creator, there is created being, and because there is created being, it is necessary that there is no such thing as absolute non-being. It is inconceivable that there be no creation, since conceivability presupposes the determinate intelligibles. If there were no creation, then absolute non-being would be, which is a contradiction.

Let us analyze some of the claims involved in this argument about the inconceivability of absolute non-being. In the first place we should note that absolute non-being is the reciprocal ontological contrast to the being of the determinations. We have *not* said that it is the contrast to being-itself, and we shall return to this point below. But for the present we must become precise about the meaning of the phrase "being of the determinations." The phrase is meant to be an expression for the determinations of being that emphasizes the aspect of their metaphysical character that is their createdness, that is, the fact that they are contingent but created and real. Every determination of being has a specific determinate character; but the reciprocal contrasts to each specific determinate character are the other determinations of being with respect to which each is determinate. Along with its specific determinate character, each determination of being also has the metaphysical character of being a determination. For instance, each has essential and conditional features, a *de facto* unity; and most important for our present purpose, each has a contingent reality that is created together with the reality of the others. It is nonsense to speak of the metaphysical character of a determination without acknowledging that it has a specific determinate character as well, for nothing can be determinate in general without being determinately something. Therefore, we must speak of the determination of being as a whole, even when we want to emphasize its aspect as created; hence, we use the phrase "the being of the determination."

Absolute non-being is the reciprocal contrast to the being of the determinations in this sense, for only something determinate can be in a reciprocal contrast. Absolute non-being is determinate in the sense that the concept of it is determinately the concept of absolutely nothing, and the concept of non-being is all that there is of non-being: there is no real object corresponding to the concept. Furthermore, the being of the determinations is the reciprocal contrast to absolute non-being because it is the highest determinate category. The specific determinate characters of the determinations contrast with each other, not with absolute non-being, and the creator is indeterminate. Therefore, it is the being of the determinations that is the ontological alternative to absolute non-being. If there were no determinations of being, absolute non-being would be.

The second thing to notice about the argument for the inconceivability of absolute non-being is that the being of the determinations is necessary in the sense that its denial is inconceivable. And if the being of the determinations is necessary, then creation is necessary, for their being is contingent upon their being created. But in all this, the necessity involved is necessity on the hypothesis that there is such a thing as intelligibility or conceivability. Given the structure of intelligibility, the creation is necessary and absolute non-being is impossible. But we have shown in the argument of section A above that even intelligibility bears the distinguishing mark of contingency, that is, a *de facto* unity, and that therefore even intelligibility is created. Given the structure of intelligibility, creation could not have been otherwise; this is just to say that, once intelligibility is real, it is what it is. But it is also to acknowledge that no reason can be given why intelligibility is real, since no reason could possibly be relevant. This whole point is but a reflection of the force of the argument in section A above. Given the canons of intelligibility and proof, it can be proved that the determinations are created and that there must be a creator; and by the same token it is proved that there can be no necessity in the creation—it is a free creation.

The third thing to notice about the argument for the inconceivability of absolute non-being is that it entails that being-itself or the creator transcend the distinction between absolute non-being and the being of the determinations, as it must transcend all determinate contrasts. As remarked before about the creator's transcendence, it has a peculiar reversal of direction from the usual meaning of the word. It is only for our knowledge that we begin with the presence of the creator in determinate distinctions and trace its transcendence beyond them. In the order of reality, it might be better to say that the creator or being-itself is independent in itself of the contrast between absolute non-being and the being of the determinations. This point about the transcendence of being-itself is difficult to express, since being-itself is indeterminate in the relevant respects and we attribute transcendence on the basis of the requirements of the determinate connections of being-itself with the determinations. Hence, all of our words indicate a connection with the determinations that is just the thing that we want to say is transcended or negated in the essential nature of being-itself. But the point can be made paraphrastically in the way that we have. It is the same point that Tillich makes with his view that God is the prius of all distinctions.[14]

This discussion of absolute non-being brings us to the point where we can summarize the qualifications of our speculative theory of being-itself. We hold that being-itself is the creator of all determinations of being, that it is the ontological one that unifies the determinations, and that it is both

[14] See his paper "Two Types of Philosophy of Religion," in *Theology of Culture,* ed. R. C. Kimball (New York: Oxford University Press, 1959).

transcendent and indeterminate. All of these points have been discussed in section A above. Furthermore, it has been proved that there is such a thing as being-itself and that it is transcendent even of the possibility of having a determinate contrast. Now we must indicate how our theory exhibits the principles of the ontological ground of differences and of the ontological equality of reciprocal contrasts, respectively.

The principle of the ontological ground of differences says that two differing determinations of being presuppose a common ground in virtue of which they are relevantly determined with respect to each other and from which each delimits a domain for itself over against the other. Our theory does not interpret the common ground as a determinate element or perspective from which differing determinations can be compared and contrasted. Rather it interprets the common ground as the common creator or source of the differing determinations. A common ground is necessary because determinations are mutually determined with respect to each other and hence need a context of mutual relevance. The creator creates them together as mutually determined. Being-itself must be the common ground because that which all things have in common is the fact that they are; all things have being. As was indicated in the discussion of the analogy of being, the commonality of the nature of being must underlie any other common or differing predications.[15] According to our speculative theory, this means that all determinations have in common the fact that they are created and that their similarities and differences are predicated on the univocity of the sense in which they are created.

Moreover, each determination delimits a domain of being for its own, according to our theory, in the sense that its being is determined according to its own nature. There is nothing more to the being of a determination than its being as determinate. It is its own being, different from the being of other determinations, just insofar as it is what it is. Being-itself is not a stuff to be carved up into portions, nor is it a universal property instantiated in many instances. Rather, it is the creator in which all determinations participate through being created. A determination is or participates in being-itself when it is created by it. This is the interpretation our speculative theory gives to "participation" in being.

The principle of the ontological equality of reciprocal contrasts says that if two determinations of being are contrast terms for each other then they must be on the same ontological level and the categories descriptive of them must be on the same logical level. As we have seen, this principle is devastating to any attempt to construe being-itself as something determinate; it results in the fundamental dilemma of ontology, the dilemma, namely, that any characterization of being-itself, if it is significant, must have a contrast term, a contrast term that belies the claim of the original characterization to be correct. Our speculative theory of creation exhibits this principle quite simply

[15] See chap. 1, sec. A, above.

by saying that being-itself is indeterminate. Hence, it can stand in no determinate contrasts.

However, what it means for a determinate thing to be is for it to be created, and to be created is certainly something determinate. There is a difference between being-itself and the being of a determination: the former is the indeterminate creator and the latter is the created determination. The being of the determination does indeed have a contrast term, absolute non-being. If absolute non-being is, that is, if it participates in being, then three consequences follow that would be disastrous for our theory. First, if absolute non-being is, then according to our theory it would be created. But since absolute non-being by definition is not something, its creator would be the creator of nothing, which is to be no creator at all. Second, if absolute non-being is, then it would have to be together in a *de facto* unity with the determinations. But to be in a *de facto* unity with the determinations is to be a determination, not absolute non-being, since a *de facto* unity requires its members to have essential and conditional features. But by definition, absolute non-being cannot be a determination. Therefore it cannot be in a *de facto* unity with the determinations of being, as it would have to be if it participated in being. Third, if absolute non-being is and is together with the determinations in a *de facto* unity, their unity must itself have a contrast term and there would have to be something having being that was neither something determinate nor nothing at all but that contrasted with both together, which is absurd. These three disastrous consequences do *not* befall our speculative theory of creation, however, because we have already shown that absolute non-being is not and that it is inconceivable that it be. Since some things are conceivable and there is such a thing as conceivability, the possibility of absolute non-being is excluded. The contrast term to the being of the determinations can be conceived, but it cannot be conceived to be. Therefore, absolute non-being is not, although its concept is the concept of that which is in contrast to the being of the determinations.

This returns us to the point noted at the beginning of our study, namely, that the theory about being-itself must be determinate in its characterization but that it need not characterize being-itself as determinate. We have shown that being-itself cannot be determinate, and we have characterized it as the creator of the determinations of being. The character of being creator of the determinations is, as we have argued, a determination itself created by the creator in the process of creating the other determinations. It is in virtue of this created character that we are enabled to infer the creator's independent transcendence and indeterminateness. As a determination, the character of being creator is determinately related to other determinations, and all of them together contrast with absolute non-being. Therefore, our theory is determinate, although its content asserts that the creator, apart from connection with the determinations, is indeterminate.

As a conclusion, we must raise the question whether it can be said that being-itself is. The speculative theory of creation we have defended holds that for something to be is for a determination to be created. On this account, being-itself cannot be or have being because it is not a determination for which being is something to have. Therefore, we cannot say that being-itself is. Being-itself cannot participate in itself because it is indeterminate and hence not complex enough to have itself as a component. Being-itself is simply being-itself, that which creates the determinations. Nonetheless, just because we cannot say that being-itself is does not mean that it is not real. In fact, the argument of section A above has proved that it is real, even though indeterminate and transcendent of the domain of things that have being. "Reality" means what our knowledge is forced to affirm regardless of our wills, and our argument above forces us to acknowledge the reality of being-itself. But our argument gives no clue as to what being-itself is apart from connections with the determinations, and we cannot speak of what it is or is not in its unconditioned transcendence. If we were to say that being-itself is, then indeed our theory would be wrong, for then being-itself would need a contrast term. Our theory, however, denies the appropriateness of saying that being-itself is, and we acknowledge merely the reality and mystery of the fact that it creates us.

4

The Transcendence and Presence
of God the Creator

Reflection in and about religion raises problems that suggest the need for a philosophical theory of God's transcendence and presence. But there is no direct way of getting at such a philosophical theory, for philosophy cannot take for granted, as religion perhaps can, the validity of concepts like "God," "transcendence," and "presence." To construct an honest philosophy that can interpret religion it is necessary to back our way in to these concepts, arguing every step. The untidiness of this indirect approach is that there is always difficulty in showing that where philosophy has gotten us is where religion wanted us to get.

SECTION A
The Creator-Created Distinction

If our discussion has been well aimed so far, it should be possible to formulate our conclusions in terms of a theory of divine creation akin to those expressed in religion. It should be possible to articulate the discussions of the univocity of being and of the problem of the one and the many in terms of the distinction between God and the created order. Since we have seen in the previous chapter that the solution to the problem of the one and the many requires acknowledging that the one creates the many, and that the one is what we have called being-itself, we have initial reason to believe that the present task should succeed.

Just as we elaborated the nature of a real distinction in a fairly abstract fashion, we must now give a parallel abstract rendering of the distinction between God and the created order, for in the previous chapter we drew a sharp contrast between real distinctions and the distinction between being-itself and the determinations. As real distinctions were analyzed as a complex of many elements, for example, two determinations, each with essential and conditional features, and so forth, so the distinction between God and the created order will have as its elements many features, for example, God or being-itself as the conditionally and unconditionally transcendent creator, the created determinations in their specific determinate characters and in their metaphysical natures, the power of God that creates, and so forth. For want of a better name, the distinction between God and the created order can be called the creator-created distinction.

At the outset an important difference must be noted between real distinctions and the creator-created distinction. Our discussion of real distinctions was quite general. That is, in expressions like *"A* is really distinct from *B,"* the *A* and the *B* are taken to be variables or schematic letters; there are many real distinctions. By contrast, the distinction between God and the created order is unique, as we shall see. Therefore, when we use alphabetical symbols for the sake of abstractness and simplicity, they should not be construed as variables or schematic letters but rather more like constants. In expressions like *"A* is distinct from *B* as *B*'s creator," *A* is just shorthand for God and *B* for the created order.

This point is part and parcel of a more general problem in speaking of God, namely, that the uniqueness of God and what he does cannot be rendered straightforwardly in modern symbolic logic. The reason for this is that symbolic logic has not escaped some metaphysical commitments that are false in the case of God. Consider the proposition "God creates the world" and symbolize it in the usual way: $C(g)$, with C designating the property of creating the world and g being the individual constant. Ordinarily we would say that $C(g)$ is an instantiation of the propositional function $C(x)$, where x is an individual variable. But in the case of this particular proposition to say that it is the instantiation of a propositional function is misleading, since the very nature of the property designated by C prohibits the x from being general. The meaning of God, designated by g, is indeed as much a *meaning,* internally connected with creating the world, as it is a *name;* and yet it is also a name. While it is not perhaps wrong to say that $C(g)$ is an instantiation of $C(x)$, it is misleading to imply that there is any difference in the sense of the two expressions; it is misleading to give the impression that x could ever be anything other than g, since this is impossible because of the meaning of C. The difficulty here is not necessarily intrinsic to symbolic logic, but it does mark out the fact that the usual symbolic constructions cannot be placed without second thought on the language used to speak of the nature of God.

In connection with the fact that the creator-created distinction is unique and holds only between God and the created order, we should also take note of the fact that there are finite creators, for example, artists, parents, statesmen, and teachers, as well as the divine creator. But the formal structure of the creator-created distinction does not apply universally to all creators. Rather, with respect to finite creators, there is a degenerate type of the distinction, degenerate in the sense that the first and fifth points below do not hold. A finite creator never gives rise to the whole being of his created product, only to some new feature or arrangement. This is creation but not *ex nihilo.* Therefore, what is created in this finite sense is not wholly a conditional feature of the creator.

We shall examine the creator-created distinction in detail. Each point of the discussion exhibits how our speculative theory accords with conceptions of divine creation taken from religion. This compatibility will justify the more wide-ranging attempt to articulate religion in terms of the speculative theory undertaken in Part Three.

1. The creator-created distinction is between two terms, one of which, A, is in itself independent of the other, B, whereas B in itself is dependent for its whole being on A. If B is an actuality with both essence and existence, "whole being" would express both of these. If B is a collection of things, B_a, B_b, B_c, . . . B_n, such that the things are really distinct from each other, the "whole being" of each item would be its essential and conditional features harmonized in its *de facto* unity.

a) The distinction in terms of independence and dependence is a static way of exhibiting the dialectical connection between being-itself and its determinations. It is obvious that the determinations accord with the B term, since they are dependent for their whole being on A because they are wholly created by A. The difference between the static and dialectical expressions makes itself most forcefully apparent, however, in the case of the independence of the A term as it is identified with the transcendence of being-itself. The connotations of transcendence indicate a going beyond of something already given. The connotations of independence, although still essentially relational with respect to what the independent is independent of, can indicate that the independent thing is, *first*, self-possessed, *second*, brought into relation to something else, and *third*, questioned as to whether the relation is one of dependence, a question answered in the negative. The upshot is that the relational elements in the notion of independence can be attributed to our attempt to know the independent thing through its relations, whereas its in-itselfness, which is the ground for our saying that it is independent, is there all along.

The different connotations of transcendence and independence make each notion appropriate in its place. When we question whether there is any such thing as the aseity of "in-itselfness" testified to by each, we move through the things to which being-itself is related and say it transcends them. Having discovered the transcendence, and wanting to characterize the connection once this is known, we choose the term "independence"; for it testifies to the priority in being of the aseity of being-itself while not denying that our knowledge is framed in terms of the approach through the relations to the world. We can say that being-itself is independent because we know that what creates the whole being of the determinations cannot in itself be conditioned by them. In most of our reflections, however, both religious and philosophical, we do not enjoy this static view; rather, we approach being-itself in its unconditional transcendence by seeing it surpass each condition we mount to. Therefore, we mostly deal with being-itself as it transcends, not as it is independent in itself. But we must remember that the knowledge of transcendence and independence is not knowledge of some feature of being-itself in its transcendence or independence; it is rather knowledge of what is required of being-itself by the conditional feature of being creator.

b) The most basic, if not the most important, religious characterization of the relation between God and the world is that the latter is dependent upon the former and that the former is above the world in the sense that he need not be conditioned by it. Some religions, of course, and even some interpretations of Christianity, say that the dependence of the world upon God is not complete. But from our arguments in previous chapters, we see that these religions do not take into account the full extent of the metaphysical need of the world for God; on a level less general than the metaphysical, the influence of God upon the world may not be very pervasive at all. On the other hand, some religions do not acknowledge that the independence of God is as complete as it must be if he is to be the creator of all determinations of being. Again, this may be because the religions are focusing on a level less general than the metaphysical, for it is the primary concern of many religions to note how God does attend and condition himself to our comings-in and goings-out. Although our metaphysical considerations have concluded that God is indeed conditioned by creation, once created, at a more fundamental level he is beyond this. The more fundamental level is what is testified to by the experience of the mystics. The basic proposition of a theory of divine creation is that God, the creator, is in himself independent of what he creates, whereas the created realm is dependent for its whole being on God.

2. The *A* term in the creator-created distinction must have conditional features, that is, features it has in virtue of *B*. But the term "conditional features" is not used here in the same sense in which it was used in describing real distinctions. Although it indicates in both cases the features a thing has in virtue of another thing, *B* does not give *A* these features from without as one really distinct thing gives conditional features to another distinct thing, since *B* is dependent for its whole being on *A*. Rather, as *A* gives rise to *B*, it gives itself these features. Its giving rise to *B* is a self-constituting with these features. "Having conditional features in virtue of" is a form of dependence; but it is a second level kind of dependence. That is, *A* does not have conditional features in virtue of the fact that *B* gives them to it; rather, *A* gives itself the conditional features in giving rise to *B*. So *A*'s conditional features depend upon the same act of *A* that *B* depends on.

a) This acknowledges our previous conclusion that being-itself gives itself features in creating the determinations of being. Unless this were the case, the determinations of being could in no way say anything about being-itself; there would be no such thing as transcendence because there would be nothing sufficiently close to being-itself for it to transcend.

That being-itself has conditional features would seem to imply that it has essential features, as is the case with something really distinct from a determination of being. Yet all features, because they are determinate, must be conditional to being-itself, since they are all created. We saw in our argument for creation that the creator cannot in himself be determinate. Although being-itself does not have essential features, there is still a contrast between essential and conditional, for it is the character of the conditional features, in their very determinateness and hence contingency, to bespeak their dependence upon what is essential. There would be no conditionals without the essential. To point this out is to refer to the essential by way of the conditional feature of being creator of the conditional features.

b) The conditional features constitute the nature of God in relation to the world. This, in fact, is the only sense in which God has a "nature," where "nature" has the connotation of determinate features. Except as creator, in connection with the world he creates, God is not determinate even in terms of a divine life. Those thinkers who say, for instance, that the Persons of the Trinity make up the divine life as it is in itself rightly point to the presence of God in the conditional features but wrongly ignore the creation involved in begetting the distinctions between the Persons. Those who sharply separate this divine life from the created world do not see that this establishes a real distinction between God and the world that would condition the former as much as the latter.

3. Although *A* has conditional features in virtue of *B*, since *B* is dependent for its whole being on *A*, *A* in itself must be independent of *B*. The contrast between *A*'s in-itselfness and its conditional features is not the same as that between the essential and conditional features of a really distinct thing. Within the creator-created distinction, nothing positive can be said of *A*'s in-itselfness; to say that *A* in itself is independent of *B* is to say only the negative thing that *A* in itself has no determinations with respect to *B*. All the determinations *A* has with respect to *B* are the conditional features it has in virtue of *B*'s dependence on it. If *B* determined *A* in itself, it would be necessary to *A*'s very being in itself. If this were so, then either (1) *B* would be of the essence of *A* and the distinctions between them only conceptual; or (2) *B* could not be wholly dependent on *A*, for nothing can be wholly dependent on something else and still be necessary to that on which it depends, unless the dependent thing, *B*, is only a proper part of *A*'s intrinsic nature. The importance of this is that *B* cannot command that *A* give rise to it unless *B* already exists, whereupon it bears on *A* only conditionally. *A*'s self-constitution such that it gives rise to *B* entails that *B*'s wholly dependent status not touch *A* in itself; since *A*'s giving rise to *B* is a *self*-constitution, *A*'s identity in itself with its self-constituted conditional features is not a problem. To deny the independence of *A* in itself is to claim that the distinction between *A* and *B* is only conceptual, not real.

This is in agreement with our arguments for the transcendence of being-itself. Since the *B* term includes all determinations of being, the *A* term, being-itself, must transcend all determinations. Because this is so, the problem arises that we might be making an illegitimate determination of being-itself when we interpret it in terms of the structure of the creator-created distinction. The answer to the problem, however, is that, far from violating the intrinsic mysteriousness of being-itself and thereby contradicting ourselves by applying this interpretative model to it, by recognizing that being-itself is the *A* term in the creator-created distinction, we preserve and underscore that indeterminateness; the very structure of the creator-created distinction asserts the indeterminateness of being-itself in itself. The warrant for so interpreting being-itself stems from the features it has as creator that *are* determinate with respect to the created product; the dialectic of those features shows the applicability of the creator-created distinction in all its respects. No determinateness in the model of the creator-created distinction is attributed to being-itself insofar as it is supposed by the model and our dialectic to be indeterminate.

4. The conditional self-constituted features of *A* are three in number. The first is the feature of being the creator of *B* upon which *B* is wholly dependent. If *A* did not have this feature, there would be no *B* at all.

a) This is the feature we have identified with the conditioned transcendence of being-itself. As a conditional feature of being-itself, it is determinate and does not transcend the domain of the created determinations. Yet its specific determinate character is that of an element in the metaphysical nature of all determinations of being. It is the element that identifies being-itself in its independence as the source from which the creative activity comes. That being-itself is the creator of the determinations is itself a created determination, part of the metaphysical nature of all determinations. The creator transcends the determinate feature of being the creator just as being-itself, in order to be creator, must transcend all created determinations.

b) This is the feature of God's nature in virtue of which he is creator of the world of determinations. Since this is the feature that says that God transcends even this feature, it affirms that God is prior to intelligibility, for only what is determinate can be intelligible in any ordinary sense. The only reason we know that God in himself is prior to intelligibility is simply that, by the dialectic of creation, the source of all intelligibility cannot intrinsically possess an intelligible nature as created intelligible things can. He may *give* himself a nature and really be that nature, for example, the nature of being creator; but what it is that gives the nature is not a nature.

God's feature as creator amounts in the end to two things. On the one hand, it acknowledges that God is related to the realm of determinations of being as their source; without this relation, nothing at all could be known of him by us. On the other hand, what it says about God is that he is prior to the intelligibility he creates and hence is essentially unintelligible. Our claim is that God is creator in virtue of the fact that he creates and that only what he creates is determinate; God apart from determinate creation is indeterminate. But the paradox is that to be creator is to be something determinate. The resolution is to recognize that considering God as creator is indeed considering him in determinate connection with creation; part of the meaning of being creator is that God must *also* have reality apart from that determinate connection and that this other reality is prior to his reality as creator.

A further connected problem is that of the "locus" of the feature of being creator. How can we say that only created things are determinate and still say something determinate about their creator? Does not that make the creator as well as the created beings determinate? Or do we really mean to collapse this first feature into the second, namely, into the created world itself? The answer is, Neither and both. The notion of being creator is a sign that is part of the created order. Furthermore, the warrant for asserting it is the actual fact of God's creative act, the nature of which is the nature of the created world. The content of the sign ascribes to God a character that he has in virtue of the determinate creation, and in this sense his character as creator is an actual part of the created product. But the reference of the sign is God, who is source of the determinate order. Now, we often ascribe characters to things in virtue of the nature of what they do. This, however, is not to make them determinate beyond their deeds unless it involves ascribing to them some internal potentialities to do the deeds apart from the actual deeds. And the meaning of the feature "creator" is precisely to deny such determinate potentialities. Creation cannot be mere actualization of potentialities, for those potentialities would have to stem from something determinate. God does create the feature of being creator, and this is precisely what makes the feature applicable to him.

5. The second feature A has in virtue of B is B itself. Since B is *wholly* dependent on A, it must be a feature of it; if B were dependent on A in only certain respects, B could be entirely other in the non-dependent respects. That B itself is a feature of A sounds paradoxical because it appears to deny the integrity B would need to be a term in *any* kind of distinction; but it will be argued below (point 9) that the kind of integrity proper to B and sufficient for it to be a term is not denied by its status as a feature of A. Hence the paradox is only apparent.

a) This feature of the creator-created distinction corresponds to the created realm considered in its totality as created by being-itself. It is the terminus of the act of creation as described below (points 10 and 12). Since the created realm is dependent on the creator for its whole being, it must be a feature of being-itself, for it has no being not derived from the creator in virtue of which it could ontologically be other than being-itself. This is not to say that there are *no* senses in which the created realm is other than its creator; it is, for example, other in the sense that it has determinations intrinsic to it and the creator does not. It is to say, however, that nothing of the being of the created realm is *other than that to which the creator gives rise.* The sense in which the created realm is a feature of being-itself cannot be interpreted on the part and whole model either of spatial or of class inclusion. Rather, the created realm is said to be a feature of being-itself on the ground that the terminus of the creative act is still part of the act; since there is no non-divine medium through which the act of creation works, there are no grounds for separating the product from its production or producer. The unity of the source and terminus in the creative act will be discussed below (points 10 and 12).

b) The claim that the created realm is a feature of God can be explicated by comparison with the traditional Christian doctrine that God creates the world *ex nihilo* but begets the Second Person of the Trinity out of himself. In the first place, creation of the world from nothing denies that God has an *Urstoff* present in him, such as matter or potentiality, out of which he works up the world; this is quite consistent with the claim that the created world has the status of being wholly a feature of God. In the second place, creation *ex nihilo* denies that the world is made out of a *divine* stuff such that it is a limited portion of the determinate stuff of which God is composed; for instance, it denies that the world is made of degenerate forms whereas God is identical with the forms proper. In the third place, there is a special truth to the begotten-created distinction. The specific determinate character or mundane nature of the created realm is nothing apart from its dependent relation to the source; all the being it has, it has in virtue of that dependence. As begotten, that is, as coming from God, it still is not "made out of" a divine stuff; nonetheless, its being is from God. What the created realm is apart from that dependent relation is nothing. Thus, although one may detach the specific determinate character of the created realm for consideration, and act solely in that context, one cannot in so doing deny implicitly that the being of the created realm is from God.

6. *B* must have the specific determinate character or determinate being to which *A* in its first feature as creator gives rise. Otherwise, *B* would not be any determinate thing and for that reason could not determine the character of *A*'s conditional features. This is simply to point out that the created realm must have its own mundane nature. Creation must be the creation of something, and this is what it is. What the mundane nature consists in will be discussed below (points 7 and 8). But the present point is that, without the determinate nature of the created realm, there could be no conditional features of God, since God has these features in virtue of that created realm. Without the determinate nature of the created realm, the act of creating would terminate in nothing and the creator would be the creator of nothing.

7. Because *B* must be a determinate thing, it must be composed of a plurality of really distinct determinations, B_a, B_b, B_c, . . . B_n, since to be determinate is to be really distinct from something else, by the argument of chapter 2 above. A real distinction, it was pointed out, requires that each of the really distinct things be determined over against the other. If *B* is determinate, it is so in virtue of being composed of a plurality of determinations really distinct from each other. The unity of the plurality cannot itself be another determination, since this would give rise to an infinite regress in relations between each distinct determination and its unity with the others. Nonetheless, the plurality of determinations can together give *A* its conditional features.

This recapitulates the argument of chapter 3. A determination of being must be distinct from some other determination from which it differs. Hence the determinateness of the created realm must consist in a plurality of really distinct determinations of being. The unity of the plurality cannot come from their internal relation within a third term, for the intrinsic nature of the third term must contain a plurality of determinations in virtue of which it relates the really distinct plurality, and the problem of unity then breaks out within the third term. Furthermore, the ground of the unity cannot consist in the togetherness of the really distinct things (Weiss), because their relevant distinction from each other requires that they be determinations of one thing, being. To avoid the infinite regress, the being of which all the determinations are determinations must be indeterminate with respect to those determinations; the distinction between the determinations and their creator cannot be a real one but must be the one of created-creator. Moreover, since being-itself is the ground of the distinctions of all determinations from each other, it must be univocal. This univocal being-itself must be the creator of all the determinations of being.

It might seem that the determinateness of the created realm must be really distinct from God if it is to give God conditional features, since it is in real distinctions that one thing contributes conditional features to another. This, however, is to ignore the new sense of conditional that pertains to God as elaborated above (point 2), that is, that God has conditional features in virtue, not of something alien to him, but of his own creative act. The created product *constitutes,* rather than *gives,* God's second conditional feature. Being the creator of the product constitutes God's first conditional feature. The power by which he is the creator and creates the product is the third. The features are *essential* to God's *creating;* but God's *creating* is conditional, as argued above (points 2, 3, and 4). Hence, it is proper that the distinction between God and the created determinations of being is not real but rather that of the creator and created.

8. Accordingly, the natures of B_a, B_b, B_c, . . . B_n must be composed of their respective essential and conditional features (in the real distinction sense) and of the *de facto* unity of these two, by the argument of chapter 2 above. This is an elaboration of the nature of the real distinctions within the created product cited above. The integrities of B_a, B_b, B_c, . . . B_n consist in these natures, and the integrity of B consists in these collective natures. The integrity of the created realm is its created nature. This integrity is not violated by the dependence of the created realm on its source, as the next point brings out.

9. The dependence of B (and of B_a, B_b, B_c, . . . B_n) on A is not a feature of B's specific determinate character or of the specific determinate character of any or all of the B_x's. Hence, the dependence of B on A cannot in any sense interfere with B's integrity, although the dependence is the source of the integrity. The only way A can take away the integrity of B (or of any B_x) is to take away the B (or B_x) itself. The integrity of B is its own nature or being.

It seems paradoxical to say that B's dependence on A is not a feature of B's specific determinate character, for surely B's creaturely status is that without which it would not be at all. But the phrase "specific determinate character" signifies the created determinations of a thing's nature, and that the thing is created is not another such determination. B is a feature of A in the dependence of its whole being and nature on A.

The integrity of the created realm is precisely the mundane nature that it has. Hence, God's creative act, upon which the mundane nature depends, cannot meddle with the integrity of its product; the only way God's act can destroy the integrity of any element of the created realm is for it to destroy that element itself. Whatever is has its integrity *because* of the creative act of God giving being to what is, though its integrity consists in its own nature. There is a fundamental difference between this view and those of Professors Hartshorne and Weiss. Both Hartshorne and Weiss claim that unless finite things have some being independent of God they have no integrity. Both try to preserve the integrity of the non-divine beings by limiting God's creative power to dealings with already formed beings. As quoted previously, for Hartshorne God "is never confronted by a world whose coming to be antedates his own entire existence. . . . Everything that influences God has already been influenced by him, whereas we are influenced by events of the past with which we had nothing to do." [1] The problem with this view is that, however far back God's influence may extend, there is always something present that he can only influence, something that to some degree controls its own career in opposition to God's creation of its being. For Weiss, the non-divine beings are different from God in their very mode of being. Both of these theories claim that although God's will cannot be thwarted in the long run, since what goes ill "here" can be put right "there," it can still be thwarted with respect to the career of any given actuality. God is given the task of a meddling parent who follows his children about, righting their errors and creating for them ever new chances. Since God's will is omnipotent in the long run, however finite with respect to other realities, it does interfere with our freedom and integrity to oppose him; we cannot win. The attempt to give non-divine beings an integrity over against God by giving them a being independent of him only to be influenced by him necessarily fails, so long as God's will wins out by necessity in the long run. There is, on this view, no possibility of really thwarting God; yet that possibility should follow if one is to have integrity. Nor is there the possibility of damning oneself; one can only play a less-than-capacity role in bringing about God's will in the end.

The only way in which non-divine beings can have their integrity is in depending for their whole being on God's creative power. A man is a complex of determinations of being, part of the complexity consisting in the fact that he has standards to meet. If God does not give a man the freedom to cope with these standards, as befits truly human action, then he has created an actuality who is not quite or fully a man; the man does not suffer from this, he is not cheated, just because he is not a man in those respects that would suffer or be cheated. The interesting case is that of a man who is free and by his free choice loses his freedom; he thereby loses the being of his free nature, and this is damnation. The man loses himself. If God wills to restore his free nature, this is part of God's arbitrarily free creative act; if he wills not to, this again is his freedom. Whatever being a man has, he has from God, and his

[1] *The Divine Relativity* (New Haven, Conn.: Yale University Press, 1948), p. 30.

integrity consists in possessing that being; however much being he loses, what being he has left is still from God; but his loss, negative though it is, is his own.

10. *A*'s third conditional feature is the creative activity productive of *B*, the power of *A* on and by which *B* depends. *A*'s third feature differs from the first in that it is the power or act by which *A* as creator produces *B;* without it, *A* would not be the creator of *B*. The power of creating is the feature being-itself gives to itself in virtue of which the determinations are created. The feature of power cannot be separated from the products it creates or from the character of being-itself as the creative source that creates through it.

11. The structure or form (determinate nature) the power has is the structure of *B* itself. The structure of a temporal act is the form of its process to the terminus; but since in this case there is no determination until *B* is produced, the form of the process and its terminus must be wholly one. A temporal act productive of an end can be said to be the same as the coming into final determination or being of the end; hence, the bringing to be of the determinations that constitute *B* is accomplished when *B* is, and the form of its production and the production itself are one.

The "nature" a power has is the set of principles or plan according to which it produces its end. The nature prescribes the paths the power must take to accomplish its work. But God's power is immediate and eternal, as shall be argued below (point 12); since its very end is the production of determinate being, there is nothing prior to the end to mediate its passage nor time for it to take. On the other hand, the terminus of an act is still the end *of the act*. In a temporal act, what is produced may be separated from the act because there is a medium through which the act takes place and into which it delivers its product; but even with human acts, we take a person's words and expressions to indicate the intent of his will just because they are the termini of his acts; a physiologist might distinguish the expression from the act, but he would not then see it as the expression of an intent. But with God's act, there is no such medium, and the nature of the product of the act is the only nature the act has. Nonetheless, although the only determinate nature the power has is that of its product, its reality is not to be identified only with that of the product, that is, the created realm.

12. The power or activity by which *A* gives rise to *B* is not temporal, although what it produces may be time itself and temporal entities. If this latter condition is the case, as it surely is, then the activity can be said eternally to have a temporal structure or form. Hence, although its productive activity is not temporal, from a point within time the power's activity may be viewed as coming before and after and in serial order. This follows from the fact that what is productive of the determinations of being cannot be temporal so long as time is a determination of being. It cannot be temporal, that is, except in the sense in which the nature of the power is the nature of its terminus. The upshot of this is that the power, as extending from the

source to the terminus, is not temporal, although its result or terminal end is temporal.

With regard to the problem of predestination, it is by no means entailed that the outcome of a temporal process is determined "beforehand," that is, at an earlier time. With respect to the determinations at one time, a subsequent time may be fairly indeterminate. There is no order of earlier and later or before and after in the eternal exercise of the power. Although within time some work of the divine power is done so as to be after other work, the power stems from the eternity that is indeterminate with respect to time. From our view within time God may be seen as accommodating himself to us, judging and reproving, saving and answering prayer; but as our creator he does not wait upon us, since he has no time in which to wait: neither does he determine beforehand.

13. The unity of *A*'s features constituted in its creation of *B* is the singularity of that complex act of giving rise to something wholly dependent. Any feature entails the others. The source requires the product, and vice versa; and both require the power, as the power requires an origin and terminus.

a) To speak of the singularity of the creative act is to deal, first, with the uniqueness of the kind of distinction involved in creation and, second, with the unity of that kind of distinction. The creator-created distinction is unique, for the distinction between things such that one is wholly dependent upon the other is unique. There can be only one creator-created instance when the creation is so total. Consequently, we must beware of criticizing the creator-created distinction by foisting upon it the requirements of either real or conceptual distinctions. We must beware of presuming that both terms, as in a real distinction, have their own independent being and of arguing from this that the creator-created distinction is non-sense because the created term is a "mere part" of the creator term with no integrity of its own. Likewise, we must beware of presuming that both terms are merely conceptually abstracted aspects of some one thing and arguing from this that the creator-created distinction is non-sense because the distinction entails that the creator term transcend even the character of creator it has in virtue of the distinction. Both of these criticisms beg the issue whether the creator-created distinction is a possible and intelligible construction of the relation between the determinations of being and being-itself.

The unity of the elements of the creator-created distinction is constituted in the act of giving rise to something wholly dependent. The act of creating creates both the determinations and the elements distinguishing the creator from the created with the same stroke.

As will be argued at length in Part Two, our speculative theory is a stronger claim than the position that says that the determinations of being simply are and that no ground or creator need be acknowledged for them. We shall argue that the very contingency of the determinations has no being even as a possibility for a mere chance happening unless the determinations are created. The distinction implied by the concept of contingency between determinate realized being and absolute non-being has no being at all unless the action of creation realizes some being to contrast with absolute non-being. Thus, although we say that the unity of the creator-created distinction between being-itself and the determinations is a *de facto* one, it is a necessary presupposition of all thought, since thought presupposes the reality of the created determinations.

b) For religion this is the problem of the unity of the Godhead. The only way to do justice to the differences between the features and still show their unity is to exhibit the features in the creator-created distinction as the integral elements of such a distinction. The creator requires the created realm to be the creator of. The product or created realm requires the creator to depend on. The creator requires the power to produce something with, and the created realm requires the power to be produced. The power requires the creator as its independent origin, and it requires the created realm as its terminus.

SECTION B

Creation ex Nihilo

It is apparent that our reflections about transcendence have led us not only to a view of divine creation but to a view of creation *ex nihilo*. We may now discuss some of the more general features of such a view.

1. *Creation versus actualization*. The usual interpretation of coming-to-be is Aristotelian. That is, an account of something coming to be must make reference, on the usual interpretation, to certain potentialities for the thing resident in its causes. By a kind of stable-economy rule of thought, it is said that nothing really new can come to be that is not just an actualization of some potentialities already present in what is actual. The actualization might be new, but the matter for it and its forms must be already existent in some other manifestation. The principle of sufficient reason, on this interpretation, says that the effect must be contained in the cause in some sense. As Norris Clarke, S.J., has pointed out, this means that a clear separation cannot be made of cause from effect.[2] And as Hume pointed out, if this is so, and if there *is* a clear separation of alleged causes from alleged effects, then causation as usually understood is unintelligible.

The Platonic interpretation of coming-to-be differs from the Aristotelian in that it emphasizes possibilities rather than potentialities. Although the possibilities are limited or selected by what is actual, that is, by the causes, in themselves as unactualized they are in a different order of reality from the natural order of actuality. Therefore, the process of coming to be requires recognition of at least two orders of reality, the actual and the ideal.

As theologians and philosophers have nearly always recognized, neither of

---

[2] See his "Causality and Time," in *Experience, Existence and the Good*, ed. I. C. Lieb (Carbondale: Southern Illinois University Press, 1961).

Norris Clarke, S. J.

these views can be adopted in straightforward fashion to explain the coming-to-be of the created order as such. What must be done is either one of
two things. Either we must alter one of the usual views quite radically or
deny that there is a creation of the world as total as the creation we have been
considering. The process philosophers take the latter alternative and we shall
take the former.

The Aristotelian position has the most to give up, for if we have been right
in arguing that all determinations of being depend on a creator, what sense
can it make to say that the creator in himself prior to creation has the
potentiality to create the world? By hypothesis, the potentialities cannot be
determinate; this rules out the possibility that they are ideas in God's mind
that he can plug in to his creative power. Could there be then a sort of utterly
vague and indeterminate power or force that creates determinate things in
the process of its exercise? But it makes little sense to speak of a power that
has absolutely no essential exercise, which must be the case with this power if
it is essential to God prior to creation and creation itself is conditional. Of
course, it is true to say after the event of creation that God before creation
must have been able to bring it about; but what does this "ability" mean
except that God in fact did create? To say that, *because* God did create, he
must have had the potentiality to do so beforehand is not to explain what this
potentiality is; it is only to assert the very theoretical assumption that is in
question. We cannot even speak of God's power prior to creation as a restless
force, for the to-and-from movement of its restlessness must be determinate.

The real difficulty with the potentiality interpretation is that it is committed to a temporal view of the creation. To say that potentialities and
actualities are both real and different is to distinguish them temporally. Yet if
all determinations of being are created, then time, which is surely determinate, different from space, dreams, and love, is also created and the creation of
the determinations cannot be temporal. Aristotelian theologians like Thomas
Aquinas, then, give up the view that God creates out of his potentialities for
doing so; God must rather be interpreted as pure act, which is to change the
theory of coming-to-be.

Other Aristotelian thinkers, like Hartshorne, maintain that creation is
temporal but give up the view that creation involves the coming-to-be of the
world from nothing. As we have quoted him above (p. 78), Hartshorne
holds that creation means only that God continually influences a world that at
no time in the past has not already been influenced by him. For Hartshorne,
the world takes on new features in virtue of the fact that its elements can
prehend, that is, grasp and actualize, features previously exhibited by God as
the world's potential. The features are new for the world but old potentialities in God. God, in his turn, surpasses himself to enjoy the world's new
elements and furthermore can think up new potentialities for the world to
realize in virtue of his infinite sensitivity to the world's needs. But it seems
unclear in Hartshorne where these new potentialities come from. That they
are new, he would not deny. But then they would either come from nothing,
and not out of some higher level potentiality in God, or they would come

from some deposit of forms that has its integrity over against both God's abstract and necessary nature and his contingent, relative, and concrete nature. The former is a hypothesis inimical to the whole of process philosophy, for the coming-to-be of the potentialities would be by no process whatsoever but by absolute spontaneity. The latter hypothesis is the one clearly opted for by Whitehead.

For Whitehead, the forms or eternal objects comprise a completely structured and mathematically determinate domain independent of the actual process of events. God, however, has access to this domain and selects the forms that would make good possibilities for the world. Selecting possibilities to be relevant to the world, God's nature becomes a lure that is the aim of the world. God selects the forms as possibilities and his selection makes them potentialities for the world. Entities in the world actualize these potentialities by prehending them in their actual occasions as attractive parts of God. Whitehead, thus, is a curious blend of Platonism and Aristotelianism. With Plato he holds to a clear distinction between the orders of being of formal possibilities and the actual process. Yet, with Aristotle he insists that the possibilities must become potentialities resident in some actual being, that is, God, prior to their proper actualization. His Platonism allows him to say that the natural process of events has novel elements in it, but only because those novel events are eternal elsewhere. And his Aristotelianism requires him to say that what is novel in the world of process must be the actualization of what is potential in God, who is both in and out of the flow of events. Whitehead's view is very like that of Plato's in the *Timaeas,* but Plato intended his account to be a myth, a moving image of eternity, as it were; and to make sure no one missed the point, Plato told two myths about the same thing. Whitehead means his account literally.

If our previous arguments have been right, that all determinations of being must be created, then neither Whitehead's nor Hartshorne's views can account for the creation of the world as such, regardless of the value they might have in explaining coming-to-be *within* the created order. That is, the whole of the created order cannot come to be in the way they explain if it contains all determinations of being, including the abstract forms.

The theory that creation is *ex nihilo* requires absolute novelty in the coming-to-be of the being of the determinations. Within the created order there may be laws that regulate the nature of mutual determination through time; still, their being is *ex nihilo.* Within the context of finite processes of change and coming-to-be, there is no such thing as complete novelty, or so it seems. Therefore, we should admit at once that the creation of the world ought not be construed by analogy with creations within the world. The uniqueness of the creator-created distinction is precisely what we should expect. We should take pains to guard against inferring that there are analogies present when there are not, and by the same token, we should take care not to require of a creation theory that it have all the elements of a more usual causal theory.

If we admit the uniqueness of the creator-created distinction, is it the case

that we find it made out in Plato? Obviously it is not there in any straightforward way. If it is true that there are forms whose reality transcends their
instantiation, then according to our considerations about the universality of
dependence in the case of determinations, the forms must be created as well
as the world that embodies them. The *Timaeas* story of a demiurge building a
world according to the blueprint instructions of the forms must be rejected if
all determinations are created. Beyond the *Timaeas,* Plato hardly developed
this idea. Yet he did make other suggestions about the coming to be of the
world that have been noticed by those who defend a theory of creation *ex
nihilo.* In the analogy of the Good with the Sun, for instance, in the *Republic,*
Plato said,

> This, then, which gives to the objects of knowledge their truth and to
> him who knows them his power of knowing, is the Form or essential
> nature of Goodness. It is the cause of knowledge and truth; and so,
> while you may think of it as an object of knowledge, you will do well
> to regard it as something beyond truth and knowledge and, precious as
> these both are, of still higher worth. . . . You will agree that the Sun
> not only makes the things we see visible, but also brings them into exist-
> ence and gives them growth and nourishment; yet he is not the same
> thing as existence. And so with the objects of knowledge: these derive
> from the Good not only their power of being known, but their very
> being and reality; and Goodness is not the same thing as being, but even
> beyond being, surpassing it in dignity and power.[3]

Regardless of Plato's systematic intent in this passage (remember, Glaucon
laughed at Socrates when he heard it), it is an idea picked up by the
Neo-Platonists who interpreted it as creation of the forms *ex nihilo.* We shall
have more to say in Part Two about the connection between Plato's form of
the Good and God as we construe him. But we must admit here that Plato
develops the notion of the form of the Good creating everything else even
less than he develops the *Timaeas* myth. The greatest consolation we can
derive from the passage is that Plato is not against a theory of creation *ex
nihilo* and that he acknowledges with Glaucon's laughter how different an
account it is from most usual accounts of coming to be. There is, however, a
much more positive affinity between Plato's theory and our own theory of
creation *ex nihilo,* as will be evident in the discussion of the created order.

    2. *The created order.* In the discussion of the creator-created distinction
we employed a distinction between the divine nature and mundane or specific
determinate character of the created realm to articulate the integrity of what
God creates over against him. Insofar as the created realm is a conditional
feature of God (which it is in virtue of its absolute dependence on him and
the fact that he creates it), it can be called divine. The created realm is
created to be a determinate something, however, and this something is its
own nature, determinate as God in himself is not. The determinate nature of

---

[3] *Republic* VI. 508; F. M. Cornford translation.

the created realm can be called the "mundane" nature of the world. It consists in what we have called specific determinate characters of the created realm, that is, of the essential and conditional features of things unified together. The fact that the determinations of being are created is not another determination of their nature. It is not even the *de facto* unity of the essential and conditional features. Nonetheless, the fact that determinations are created is closely connected with the ground of their *de facto* unities. We must now turn to this connection.

We have argued that a determination of being must be a complex of essential and conditional features and that the unity of these features is a mere *de facto* one. The significance of calling the unity merely *de facto* is that it can have no determinate principle of unity that unites the features. A *de facto* unity is merely a togetherness of features, as has been argued in detail. It was this fact that drove us to the conclusion that determinations of being are one and all contingent upon something that makes them be, internally united *de facto* and externally united with all the other determinations with which they are determinately related. All determinations, because of this, must have a common source or creator, which we now call God.

The interesting thing about a *de facto* unity is that it is what we usually call a harmony, for the parts are harmonized together to make up one thing. This is something Plato would like. But it would seem that a harmony is precisely the sort of thing a *de facto* unity cannot be, for the connotation of a *de facto* unity is that it is an unharmonious togetherness. This connotation arises from the fact that a harmony is usually interpreted in terms of certain kinds of determinate unifying principles. We usually articulate a harmony in terms of its harmonizing pattern or rule. When explaining the harmony of a picture we abstract its over-all pattern; the same is true of a piece of music. When explaining the harmony of an action or series of events we abstract some rule of procedure that relates the parts to a beginning and an end. Furthermore, when we abstract from a complex thing its harmonizing pattern or rule we give that pattern or rule a determinate articulation. But to say that the unity of a determination is a determinate harmonizing pattern or rule seems contrary to the hypothesis, namely, that the unity is not another determination.

This difficulty is only prima facie, however; a *de facto* unity is indeed a kind of harmony. To show that there is something wrong with the claim that the harmonizing unity is another determination, we can begin by replaying an argument we have used before. If the harmonizing pattern or rule is determinate, how is it unified with the things it patterns and rules? For it to "ingress" into the determination so as to unify it, it must itself be unified with the items that without it would be diverse and separate. Therefore, if a pattern or rule is what a harmonizing unity is, then it is not the unity we were after. There are, of course, patterns and rules to things, but these are just more determinations of being.

Furthermore, a pattern or rule is *not* exactly what *harmonizes* the parts to be unified. In fact, the pattern or rule is simply the abstract statement of the *de facto* unity in question, an exhibition of the togetherness of the parts. It is perhaps abstract in the sense that, when considered in itself, it is vague with respect to the ideosyncracies of the parts in which it is embodied. But this is only to say that certain determinations of being take on new determinations when related to certain other determinations. Where then is the unity of the pattern or rule? To say that a pattern is repeatable is not to exhibit its unity. When acccounting for the unity of patterns of parts that are together, appeal must ultimately be made to some criterion that is not another determination.

Why are some patterns unified ones whereas others are merely conglomerations? The answer is that some patterns have a kind of aesthetic hang-togetherness that others do not. The aesthetic quality of hang-togetherness in a unified pattern is not just another pattern; that would add another more complex *de facto* unity. If the pattern or rule is a matter of intelligible connection, ultimately intelligibility comes down to a matter of insight. You either see the intelligibility of a thing or you do not; more explanation after a certain point does not help. This appeal to intuitive intelligibility is on a par with the appeal to the aesthetic quality; in *neither* case is the appeal made to another determination of being. We shall return to this problem shortly in discussing the doctrine of transcendentals.

If, then, harmony is not just a harmonizing pattern or rule but something to which aesthetic and intellectual intuitive appeal is made, what has this to say to the problem of the unity of a determination of being? First, it says that the ground for asserting that a pattern or rule harmonizes a complex determination is the same as the ground of the *de facto* unity of the determination. Thus, the ground of aesthetics and intellection is the same as the ground of determinate being; of this we will speak more later. Second, it says that the harmony or the *de facto* unity of the determination of being is not another determination. Yet it is fair to say that the *de facto* unity is a harmony, for we have shown that even ordinary notions of harmony fall back upon the same appeal to an indeterminate ground of *de facto* unity. Third, it gives us a new statement of what it is to be a determination of being. To be a determination of being is to be a harmony of certain other determinations of being. Without the harmony there would be only those others. Those others in turn are harmonies of yet further determinations, and so on down or around, as the case may be. Determinations harmonize their parts in virtue of the power of being they have; this is an analytic statement. That some parts can cohere to form a determination with a *de facto* unity, that other parts or features cannot so cohere to form a determination of being, are just facts of being, part of the nature of what it is to be. That aesthetics or intellectual intuition is ultimately the arbiter of what is possible is not a surprising conclusion or one without precedents.

Our conclusion is that harmony *is* at the heart of the connection of determinations of being with God; for that which God gives a certain determination of being when he creates it is its harmony in virtue of which the determination is a composite of other determinations.

Of course, there are many kinds of determinations of being. Numbers and logical forms are quite different from physical objects and growing animals, and all of these are different from determinations like space and time. It is a mistake to think that only logical forms are determinate, for anything that is different from anything else is determinate. As there are many kinds of determinations, there are many kinds of harmonies for things, and the harmonies proper to men and states should not be interpreted as if they were harmonies for symphonies or for quadratic equations. Still, any determination of being has a *de facto* unity which is a harmony. We must now ask how the harmonies come to be.

3. *The creating power.* The notion of power is used to define the fundamental structures of whole domains of intelligibility; and because it stands at the limits and foundations, it is itself very hard to define in terms of those domains. In terms of the usual categories of thought, it is very nearly a primitive and undefinable notion, although we can characterize the meaning it has for the things it itself defines.

One thing is obvious from our above discussion, and that is that power, especially God's creative power, cannot be identified with potentialities or potencies in a divine substance. Potentialities and potencies are always *for* something, and this is too determinate to be prior to the actual creation. Furthermore, a potentiality or potency in a substance always indicates that the substance is conditioned by what the potentiality or potency is for. Even were the potentiality or potency so utterly vague as not to be determinate with reference to some object for actualization, it would still condition the substance toward the actualization of some object in general. If potentiality or potency is something essential to God, then it is essential that he must create. But as we have seen, this is self-contradictory: if God is necessitated to create, he must be conditioned by his creation essentially. But since the whole of the being of the created realm depends on God's creating, it cannot condition God essentially. Therefore, the power of creating cannot be construed as some potency or potentiality essentially part of God's nature. But then if it cannot be an essential part of his nature, neither can it be a conditional part given in creation and still be only a potency or potentiality, for the conditional features are those that God has when creation is an accomplished fact, when it is real. Yet, if creation is real, then the potentialities and potencies are no longer such but are actualized. Therefore the creative power of God can in no way be construed as a potentiality or potency.

If the creative power of God cannot be given an ordinary interpretation, can it then be done away with entirely? Can we say that there is only God the creator and his created product, with no power by which the creator makes the product? As we have seen in our discussion of the creator-created distinction, this move would leave out something important and necessary. At the end of the last chapter, we noted that the notion of absolute non-being is distinguishable and determinate only over against the actual determinate being of the world. And as so determinate, non-being is impossible, since by definition of non-being some determinate being is. The contrary is also true, that absolute non-being is the contrast term to the being of the determinations. There would be no created determinations unless absolute non-being were an alternative state of affairs. The fact that absolute non-being would be unintelligible if it were real does not militate against the fact that, if it *were* real, there would be no created realm, since the demands for intelligibility would not be real. Now, the upshot of this contrast between determinate created being and absolute non-being is that the former must have a power that makes it be and contrasts it with the state of affairs of non-being. This is the primitive sense of the notion of power. As we have seen, this power is the creative ground of all determinations of being and is common to them all. Without power creating the determinations, there would be no created realm and the creator would not be creator. The notion of power is inseparable from the notions of creator and of the created realm. The unity of the conditional features of God cannot be sundered.

One conclusion from this is that the divine creative power is something that comes to be in the actual creation. The power is what does the creating; it is not something that "can" do it. The creative power is a conditional feature God gives himself in the actual creating.

Another conclusion is that, of the many kinds of determinations of being, power is a very peculiar kind. The nature that we ascribe to power is the nature of what it does. Now, most power we see exercised through a medium of events and time, and we describe its nature in terms of the determinate path its exercise takes. Yet God's creative power has no medium apart from its product, the created realm. Hence, to describe the character of God's creative power, over and above its general contrast with absolute non-being, is to describe what it creates. As we shall see, this allows us to ask whether the created realm indicates that the character of God's creative activity is personal, whether the personality is loving, majestic, and so forth.[4]

The fact that God's creative power is without a medium reaffirms our conclusion about creation *ex nihilo*. The coming-to-be of the determinations is a novelty on the ontological scene. They come out of nothing, and there is no process with middle stages through which they are made. They are created through power and the power is immediate. This means that creation is eternal, that is, not in time.

The eternality of creation is a complex point. A minimal definition of eternity is that it have no temporal determinations. We know, on this account, that creation must be eternal in its coming to be because there are no determinations whatsoever, and hence no temporal ones, until the created realm is. A more complete description of eternity can be gained from

[4] Chap. 12, sec. B 3.

considering the activity of creative power. *Any* exercise of creative power that makes something new, or that makes something *ex nihilo* (those being the same), is eternal, that is, non-temporal. Consider even a finite thing in a finite and temporal framework, creating something absolutely new. If there is, by hypothesis, a moment when the new thing is not, then the moment when the new thing is must immediately succeed such a moment of absence; there can be no in-between moments for stages halfway between not-being and being. Even a finite and temporal creator *ex nihilo*, if there is such a thing, creates eternally, for between the moments of not-being and being, when the creating is going on, there is no time. Of course, there is very little, if any, *ex nihilo* creation in the ordinary world of events. Most creation of novelties is implicated in a vast and complex structure of old things. We create anew by reordering the old. Furthermore, the things that we intentionally create are usually quite distant in terms of increments of novelty from what at the start is actual. Hence, we plan ahead and aim at creating something that will take several steps. When we see the end we have in view slowly emerge through a process of many deliberate actions, it is not the case that the end is the first new thing that comes; each step has brought some novelty. Rather, it is only the *intended* new thing that we see coming closer and closer to full and clear being. But at each step in the process, something new and instrumental must be present. Otherwise, we would not take so many steps to reach our result. However unique God's creation might be, the notion of its eternal character should not be alien to us. Every creative exercise of power is eternal if it brings about something really new. In fact, it may be that every exercise of power is an exercise of God's power.

Although creation is eternal, a good bit of what gets created is not. Most of the striking features in the world are temporal, as are most of the problems of men's lives. Some of the determinations of being, like men and states, are such that their being is not complete at one moment of time. Many problems, like that of responsibility, stem from the fact that although men and states never have their whole being at one moment they live out their being one moment at a time. There is no difficulty, however, in conceiving of the eternal creation of temporal things, for what gets created is the temporal determinations of the things. For instance, if a person is created, he has the determinations of coming at a certain time in history, of certain parentage, and so forth; and at any single moment he has a future ahead of him that may be indeterminate from the standpoint of what is already actual. From any point within the temporal flow, things at other times may seem to be created at those other times. But this is just to recognize that they are created with other temporal determinations and hence *are* at other times. The creation of their determinations is eternal. This fact does not commit us to a view that time is unreal or that it is merely relational. Time may have all of the vitality, uncertainty, and novelty in it that Bergsonian philosophers claim. But it is the things in time that are temporal; time is not temporal—it is eternal. Time has no past, present, or future. The time of a thing or event that is temporal has a past, present, and future, and it may be filled with the uncertainties and vitality characteristic of temporal things. Yet time itself is not after anything or before anything. Things in time are temporal because of the determinate connection with the nature of time. Time simply is. It is the product of an eternal creation.[5] God's creative power creates in eternity.

SECTION C

Transcendence, Presence, and the "Transcendentals"

Because the created realm is dependent for its whole being on God the creator, the creator in himself must transcend what he creates. Yet because the determinations are in fact created, the creator is present in and to them. He is present in his power of creation, which gives them being. Now, what is there in the creating of the determinations that manifests God's presence?

Let us return to consideration of the harmonies that the determinations of being are. As determinations they have merely de facto unities. Yet, as we have seen, these de facto unities are harmonious; otherwise, the alleged determination of being is not really a determination. God is present in the determinations of being as that which makes their unities harmonious. He is present as that which contributes the quality of hanging-together to the features in a determination of being that hang together. This is the power that makes the determinations be. What is it that makes the pattern of a unity hang together or be harmonious?

The scholastic philosophers and theologians interpreted the general presence of God in the world according to a doctrine of transcendentals. The transcendentals are characteristics common to all things and are eminently close to the nature of God. The traditional list includes Being, Unity, Truth, Beauty, and Goodness. The presence of the transcendentals in something indicates the presence of God, according to the schoolmen.

Our usual response to the doctrine of transcendentals today is to consider it the expression of a monistic, closed-universe metaphysical outlook that is no longer tenable. We are much more pluralistic in our acknowledgment of many different values and kinds of value, many different senses of being and unity. Yet our own pluralistic metaphysical analysis of determinateness has led us to a view remarkably similar to that of the doctrine of transcendentals.

To account for a determination of being as the harmony of a complex of other determinations is to admit into discussion all the problems of accounting for the notion of harmony. As we said in section B above, harmony involves a power of holding parts together that must be simply seen. The harmony is not another determination of being operating as a third term. The pattern in a harmonious whole is determinate, but what makes it a harmonious pattern instead of a conglomeration of parts is not determinate.

It is easy to see how this harmony can be the transcendental Being for the

---

[5] See the discussion of indeterminateness in chap. 12, sec. B 2.

determinations, since the being of a determination is its harmonizing of component determinations. Without the harmony, there would be only those other determinations, not the determination they together are supposed to comprise. The being of a determination, over and above the being of its components separately, is its harmonizing of them. Determinate being is determinate harmony; abstract the harmony and you have the being abstracted from the determinations; and there would be no determinations left.

It is equally easy to see how this harmony can be taken for the transcendental Unity, for the harmony is what unifies the parts of a determination. Anything that is must be unified, since to be is to be the unity of other determinations of being. And the unity of a thing is the same as that in virtue of which it is, namely, its harmony.

It is more difficult to see how the harmony involved in being is to be taken as the transcendental Truth. Certainly it is not to be identified simply with truth in the sense of knowledge corresponding to the facts. Yet another sense of truth is the validity-of-meaning connections or sheer intelligibility. Although any intelligible connection between two things can be mediated by asserting a third thing as the whole of the first two things connected, to see that the whole is itself intelligible is not helped by a further mediation. The inference from one thing to another, or the assertion of the warrantability of the inference, is not another determination taken as a premise but rather a rule of inference. The rule of inference is either a brute action and no rule at all or it is an intelligible rule. But if it is intelligible, then, since its intelligibility is not another determinate premise, its warrant is something apparent to intuitive insight. And what can we say that we see intuitively but just the intelligibility? The intelligibility is not another determinate thing. Intelligibility is the harmony of determinations of being that constitutes their knowability. If to know a thing is to apprehend its connection of parts, then intelligibility boils down to the harmony of the parts (plus all the factors that go into making the determination approachable by minds, and so forth). In the sense of this intelligibility, Truth is a transcendental, identical with a determination's Being and Unity.

If the case can be made out for Truth, it can also be made out for Beauty. Intellectual intuition has often been likened to an aesthetic sense. American philosophers like Jonathan Edwards and Charles Peirce have been very explicit on this point.[6] The intelligibility of a thing differs from its beauty as the thing is apprehended in a context of knowing its connections rather than appreciating them. Appreciation is a very complex notion; but at least it involves two moments of apprehension. First the plurality of parts must be

[6] See Edwards' doctrine of spiritual sight in the *Religious Affections,* ed. John E. Smith (New Haven, Conn.: Yale University Press, 1959), pp. 266 ff., esp. pp. 272–73; see also his doctrine of the appreciation of secondary beauty in *The Nature of True Virtue,* ed. W. K. Frankena (Ann Arbor: University of Michigan Press, 1960), Chap. II. Peirce maintained that all logic is based on ethics, and that ethics is based on aesthetics. See the *Collected Papers of Charles Sanders Peirce,* ed. C. Hartshorne and P. Weiss (Cambridge, Mass.: Harvard University Press, 1931), I, 180–92.

seen and then the harmony of them. In art, as Dewey pointed out, this entails recognizing the many factors that are means to a total effect and also recognizing how the total effect is the consummation of the many means. As Dewey also pointed out, it is our personal identification with the need for the means to be consummated that gives us the sense of satisfaction with the consummation. It is one thing to recognize that a work of art or a determination of being unifies or harmonizes its components, and it is another thing to say that this unity is good. But if the problem of unifying becomes a problem for us, then the consummation of the unity is our consummation, too. This is not the place to discuss how we enter into the problem of the means or identify with their search for consummation; but we can note how such an identification fits into the notion of appreciation of beauty. Beauty is a transcendental in that the consummation of the parts of a determination in their need for a harmony is a character of all determinations, since it is a character of all harmony.

Goodness is perhaps the most difficult of the traditional transcendentals to make sense of. But it is not difficult to see that the nature of a determination of being, that is, its harmony, has a normative status for the determination as a complex of parts. In order to be, a determination must live up to its harmony. Its harmony is its being. Where the being of a determination, that is, its harmony, is the sort of thing that can fall into jeopardy, as it is with man, then the normative status of its harmony is a significant thing and can be called its good. It is essential to acknowledge that good in this sense is no absolute good or particular final end. One of the primary deliverances of experience is that there are many goods or values in the world; a monistic reduction of these to some one cosmic, determinate, and universal good is a mistake.[7] Still, the abstract and formal character of each of the plurality of values is that it must be a harmony of some sort. Any problem controlled by some value or norm, whether it is an artistic, political, ethical, personal, or other problem, takes as its sought after value some consummating harmony. To say that every determination of being, in virtue of its harmony, is or has a good is not to say what the specific character of any good is. That must be decided with reference to the particular characters of the determination in question. It is, however, to point out that goodness in the abstract and in general, as the normative harmony of each determination, is a transcendental.

The question now is the sense in which these transcendentals constitute the presence of God. The medievals said that although the transcendentals are present in created things in finite and privative ways, in their purity they are one with the nature of God. According to our own metaphysical conclusion, we cannot agree that the transcendentals are one with the nature of God as he is in himself. Perhaps even the medievals did not mean this. The transcendentals are transcendental or universal characteristics of all created determinations of being. Hence they are characteristics of created being as such, characteris-

[7] Cf. this author's "Man's Ends," in the *Review of Metaphysics*, XVI (September, 1962).

tic of God's creation. Since the product of creation is the nature of the creator's power, the transcendentals are God's general presence in the world. Not only is God generally present in his created realm, he can also be specially present. His general presence, through the transcendentals, is a metaphysical dimension of all reality. Yet, what he creates also has its specific determinate character, its mundane nature. However one finite thing is conditioned or caused by another, God is still the creator of the being of the whole. Therefore, he is present to the particularities of creation as their creator. This is significant only if there is some special quality to the creation, for example, if it seems like the creation a personal kind of being, with a particular personality, would do. As an empirical matter concerned with the mundane nature of creation, we must turn to religion and elsewhere to consider this kind of presence in detail.

The very dialectic of creation that shows the presence of God in the created realm shows by the same token his transcendence. In Part Two we shall examine the nature of this dialectic. In Part Three we shall deal with the glory for the religious man of God's transcendence and presence. These discussions will probate our claim that the speculative theory of being-itself accounts for the transcendence and presence of God.

Our speculation has led us to what might be considered two opposing and very extreme emphases. On the one hand, we have found God to be so transcendent in himself as to be indeterminate with respect to the world. This distinguishes our theory sharply from the panentheistic and personalistic positions current today. On the other hand, we have found every determinate thing to be the creative presence of God; there is nothing whose whole being is not the immanence of God. This distinguishes our theory from that of popular piety according to which God is a superindividual aiding us in the battle against evil.

Our speculation does, however, reinforce some other old positions. Just because God in himself is indeterminate and transcendent, all we know of him is his created manifestations. If God has a character, for example, is loving, or if he works miracles, for example, saves someone, this is indeed a contingent miracle, from free grace, not from necessity.

The speculative theory of creation *ex nihilo* is committed to both the extreme transcendence and extreme presence. A theory that lies in between would not be able to say that all depends on the free grace of God. That is, if God were not so transcendent, his creative grace would be necessitated by the world; and if he were not so present, not all of the world would be dependent. Although the speculative arguments given above should be the philosophic reasons for holding our theory, its religious consequences should not be lost on theologians.

Part Two

Preliminary Remarks

No philosopher today can attend to his trade without coping with the claims of Kant's "critical philosophy." This is not because many, or any, are traditional Kantians. Nor is it because there is significant support in the philosophical community for Kant's conclusions apart from his arguments; those who have recently supported his conclusions, the positivists, have never taken the metaphysics Kant declared impossible with enough seriousness to challenge it to a fair fight. Still, it is a historical fact about our present situation that everyone feels compelled to make a stand vis-à-vis Kant perspicuous in his work.

The aim of Part Two of our study is "critical" in the sense that it asks how the knowledge alleged in Part One is possible. This is not as general a question as Kant asked, for there are certain peculiarities of our speculative theory that must be taken into account. The chief of these is that we have maintained that a *de facto* unity of determinations of being needs an explanation in terms of something transcendent. In order to cope with this peculiarity, we shall have to develop a theory of investigation and explanation, that is, a theory of philosophical dialectic, that shows how, in the very structure of philosophical thought about the problem, the kind of explanation we have in fact given is required.

We shall begin by contrasting two fundamental views of speculative explanation, which we shall call "cosmology" and "cosmogony." Cosmogony, of course, is explanation by a theory of creation. Then we shall defend a view of dialectic as a method of philosophical speculation that accords with what was done in Part One. Since, however, no philosophical method is discontinuous either with the nature of its subject matter or with the doctrines it arrives at, we must go on to defend the view that our speculative dialectic is constitutive, that is, that it reflects the natural joints of the subject matter as it was articulated in Part One. This requires showing that proper speculative dialectic must go beyond cosmology to cosmogony. Finally, we shall discuss in some detail how speculative philosophy, including our own conclusions, is connected with experience so as to test itself and prove its interpretative worth.

5

Cosmology and Cosmogony

God is not an explanation, as we are often told by those who aim to preserve the integrity of the Deity from dissolution by philosophical analysis. He is a reality to be confronted and will not be bound by what our explanation would have him be. In fact, if there is truth in our earlier reflection that God is to be identified with completely indeterminate being-itself, then no determinate explanation can apply to him directly, at least in any ordinary sense. Yet, even if our *only* contact with God comes through unpredictable experience, that we recognize the experience to be one of God entails that we have some knowledge of him that is more than pure experientially given content. In our knowledge of most things, the extra-experiential elements that select, recognize, and articulate the content of experience gain their force and trustworthiness from pointing out experiential connections, potentialities for our purposes, and contradictions of our expectations. The conceptualizations employed in interpreting most experience acquire their trustworthiness in experience at large. At various periods in history, not likely to occur again, theological concepts were taken to be among those whose general worth was so attested by experience that they were not in need of further justification. Needless to say, this is not the case today; naïve acceptance of the validity of theological concepts has been under attack, in one way or another, since the time of the pre-Socratics and probably earlier.

What kind of justification can be given to concepts whose more or less immediate validity for experience has been brought into question? The most convincing justification is an unequivocal experiential instance of the concept in question: a quart bottle of phlogiston would make the physicists sit up and take notice. But in the case of God justification is more difficult; since it is the very concepts that articulate the experience that are in question, the experiential example would be challenged. The antireligious strength of both Freudian interpretations of religious experience and the analogies of such experience with drug effects comes from the fact that they challenge the prima facie interpretation of the experiential content by offering alternative interpretations.

The justification of theological concepts usually takes two directions at once. The most powerful line of justification is that of the cumulative and pervasive force of experience that lends itself to religious interpretation. Although it is doubtful that momentary experiences of isolated individuals can be given theological interpretations, the cumulative experiences of a lifetime, which become integrated throughout many, many dimensions of life and which are supported by many persons, do lend trustworthiness to theological concepts. (The consequence, on the other hand, of interpreting this same cumulative and pervasive experience in terms of Freudian or drug-affect theories is an unavoidable conclusion that a tremendous number of us, especially the powerful and creative personalities, are insane or given to flights from reality. The harder these interpretations are pressed, the more implausible they become until they finally turn full circle and undermine the rationality of the interpretations themselves.) There are three drawbacks to this first line of justification, however. Few people are willing to wait a lifetime to test the validity of religious concepts; and unless, at the beginning, critical judgment is suspended in some sense and such concepts are "taken on faith" they are seldom borne out.[1] Furthermore, the complex connections involved in the cumulative and pervasive character of allegedly religious experience require an elaborate connecting theory. It is this elaborate theological theory that leads to the second line of justification.

When the trustworthiness of religious concepts is in question, one of the most rational and discursive ways of ascertaining their warrant is to exhibit connections such that the concepts in question are seen to be explanations of something commonly accepted. This is the line taken by those theologians who have offered proofs of God's existence. It is one of the special contributions of philosophy to religion to offer this kind of justification, and the first part of our study has been directed at justifying the notion of a transcendent God, prima facie presupposed by the problems of religion; our argument showed how that notion was an explanation of the ontological problem of being-itself. In this sense, God can be said to be an explanation for philosophical problems. This does not dissolve the reality or integrity of God into a bunch of philosophical concepts, and it should not substitute the practice of philosophy for the practice of religion.

But if we acknowledge God to be an explanation in this sense, what kind of an explanation are we dealing with? This question is not directed to the general problem of God as an explanation but to the more specific one of how he functions as an explanation in the speculative theory developed in Part One.

SECTION A

The Distinction between Cosmology and Cosmogony

To understand the kind of explanation involved we must revive an old distinction that has fallen out of use, the distinction between *cosmology* and

[1] See the discussion of faith and certainty in chap. 11, secs. C and D.

cosmogony. The reason the distinction has fallen out of use is that no one indulges in cosmogonic explanations anymore, and yet this is the kind of explanation given in the above reflections. The most common objection made against that kind of theory is that it requires and offers a kind of explanation that is no explanation at all. Therefore, it is necessary to draw attention to the peculiar character of a cosmogonic (literally, "creation of the world") explanation.

In the distinction between cosmology and cosmogony, what is intended by the former is any theory that explains by reducing its subject matter to determinate first principles, principles that require no further explanation themselves because they are "first." When the subject matter is ontology, a cosmological explanation is one that finds the basic structures and principles that explain everything else. What is meant by "explain" in this sense is that the subject matter to be explained is reduced to the first principles or is shown to exhibit them. The subject matter of ontology, interpreted cosmologically, has its diversities articulated by the first principles and its unity demonstrated by the interconnections of these principles. In our day, Whitehead and Weiss well illustrate this approach, although it has not been the dominant approach of modern philosophy.

Cosmogony, on the other hand, takes the so-called first principles to be in need of explanation themselves. Since they are "first," the kind of explanation given them cannot be the same kind that they give to the subject matter they explain. Cosmogonic ontology *does* presuppose that metaphysics can arrive at first principles that explain the fundamental structures of things. But it requires that the first principles be given *further* account, on the ground that simply to acknowledge them as presupposed by the rest does not account for their being. If it is the case that to be determinate is to be contingent, as we have argued in the previous part, then the *determinate* first principles need an account of how they are at all.

It is obvious from our criticisms of the claims that being-itself is determinate that our own theory puts us into the cosmogonic camp. This is supported by our defense of the claim that to be determinate is to be contingent. Yet, now that we are taking a "critical" look at our previous reflections, we must consider the possibility that our commitment to cosmogony is a commitment to something impossible. If this is so, then our previous reflections must contain some profound mistake. But if it is not so, then our previous reflections make a stronger and more unusual claim than appeared on the surface.

SECTION B

The Argument of Cosmology

The weight of the issue can be shown by drawing up the preliminary battle lines of both positions. The cosmologist maintains that his first principles cannot themselves be explained because they are first. They are not necessary in the sense of deducibility from some higher necessary principle. But then

Paul Weiss

they are not contingent either, the cosmologist says, for to be contingent means that it is conceivable that the first principles are not real, neither constitutive of the being of things nor applicable to things in our knowledge. But the unreality of the first principles is not conceivable, since to deny them is to presuppose them. Therefore, the first principles cannot be contingent but are necessary in the sense that they are undeniable.

The cosmologist can strengthen his position with illustrations of his point taken from our own arguments in Part One. Consider the claim we made that absolute non-being is impossible because the determinations of being, especially the intelligibles, are real. What is this, the cosmologist asks, except a rather negative version of the ontological argument that concludes to the necessity of the being of the intelligibles? In that argument, the very denial of the reality of the determinations that is involved in the assertion of the reality of absolute non-being presupposes the reality of the determinations. This is what our previous argument was pointing out. If it is the case that absolute non-being is absolute non-sense, as we claimed, then it is inconceivable that the basic metaphysical determinations or first principles not be. As Weiss has pointed out,[2] the cosmologist says, this ontological argument proves the necessity of the system as articulated by its first principles; but it does not prove a transcendent creator, for the necessity applies to the real determinations, and their contingency is inconceivable.

Our preliminary defense on behalf of the cosmogonist takes three steps.

1. First, we can acknowledge that a version of the ontological argument is to be gleaned from our reflections in Part One. But the interesting thing about this version is that it makes perspicuous the fact that the ontological argument is a hypothetical one, although hypothetical in an unusual sense. The hypothesis in question is the reality of those determinations of being that make up the determinate structure of rationality. Given the structure of rationality, the necessity of something is undeniable (whether this "something" is God is not to the present point). Admittedly, the assertion that absolutely nothing is possible presupposes the structure of possibility, a determinate something. But an account must be given of the hypothesis. How do we account for the fact of the structure of rationality? That it is real cannot be questioned. But it may be real because it is contingent and actually created.

2. Second, we have, in fact, argued that any and all determinations of being are contingent, which would include those making up the structure of rationality. They are contingent because their *de facto* unities and the *de facto* unity of them all together presuppose something that is not a determination of being and that, we argued, is being-itself, their creator. This is not contingency in the sense that the denial is conceivable, for we surely cannot conceive of the utter absence of the determinations without presupposing them. Since we think according to the determinate structure of rationality,

[2] *Modes of Being* (Carbondale: Southern Illinois University Press, 1958), p. 308.

absolute non-being cannot be conceived. *Given* the determinations of being, absolute non-being is impossible.

But this is not to claim that the givenness of the determinations of being is not in need of further account. As we represented him above, the cosmologist distinguishes two kinds of necessity, the necessity of deducibility and the necessity of self-presupposition in denial. Although the latter kind of necessity can be accepted as such within the ontological argument, the cosmogonist argues that it must also be considered as a kind of contingency. Like necessity, contingency has two kinds. There is the contingency of a thing whose non-being is conceivable; this is parallel to the first kind of necessity that depends upon a deductive argument showing its non-being to be inconceivable. And there is the contingency of that which does not in itself account for its own being, although its non-being cannot be asserted without presupposing its being. Any determination of being as such falls into this category, if our arguments in Part One were right. In this way the first principles could be both necessary in one sense and contingent in another sense. The claim that the first principles are contingent in one sense depends on the possibility of a kind of explanation or accounting of them that is not recognized by the cosmologist.

3. Third, we must re-emphasize the extent to which the impossible being of absolute non-being is dialectical. The meaning of absolute non-being is the complete absence of determinations; this is meaningful only in contrast to the determinations. But given the determinations, the very meaning of absolute non-being entails that it not be. Yet if there were no determinations, it would be meaningless to say that absolute non-being is, that is, that there is absolutely nothing, for the meaningfulness of this depends on a contrast with determinations. If the determinations are themselves contingent and are real in virtue of being created, then *apart* from his function in creating, the creator is not faced with or in contrast to absolute non-being. Non-being only becomes a possibility, so to speak, in the context of creating; but that very function of creating is one of the things created, and given something created, non-being is impossible. Therefore, against the cosmologist, the dialectical relation between absolute non-being and the determinations means that the contingency of the determinations drives us beyond both them and absolute non-being for an account.

The importance of this point is that the cosmologist might insist that if a first principle cannot be given an account, and is contingent in this sense, then it *must* also be contingent in the sense that it might not be. If its non-being is inconceivable, then there might be a difference between conceivability and real possibility. The cosmologist could interpret our remarks to be an assertion that although absolute non-being cannot be conceived as real, this is because the determinations actually are. Yet if the determinations are still contingent, then, in some prior-to-conceivability sense, it was possible for them not to be. They would then not be first, and the cosmologist would repudiate the need to defend them as such. Against this, the force of the dialectical character of the relation between the determinations and absolute non-being is to point out that absolute non-being is not prior to the determinations but concomitant with them and because of them impossible. Therefore the connection of real possibility with conceivability is preserved.

SECTION C

Cosmological Explanations of Transcendence

This exchange between the cosmologist and the cosmogonist, however, is only a preliminary tactical maneuver. The real battle is to be joined over the issue of the kind of explanation necessary to penetrate to the heart of the problem of being-itself. The cosmologist has four alternative moves.

1. First, he could construe being-itself as something determinate; but as we have seen this cannot be a one for the ontological many.

2. Second, he could construe being-itself in pluralistic fashion, saying that there is no one thing that is being-itself but that every ontologically real entity is a one for the many of which it is a member; this move we have also seen fails to solve the problem of the one and the many, and besides, it presupposes something as a context for the many that is more real than the candidate it presents for being-itself.

3. Third, the cosmologist could give up the task of ontology and limit himself to metaphysics, that is, to constructing a system of the fewest possible primary categories, putting aside the question of what being-itself is; Charles Peirce, and perhaps A. N. Whitehead, have taken this move. Although we have not dealt with this alternative, three considerations make it a poor move in the present context.

a) In putting aside the question of being-itself, it suppresses a question that perennially challenges the philosophical spirit. That this move goes so counter to instinct, when properly understood, renders it initially implausible and suggests that it should be considered an alternative only in the last resort.

b) Since the metaphysical system would consist in determinate categories, it would fail to solve the problem of the one and the many. So, for example, Peirce claims that all things can be accounted for in terms of three primary categories, but he does not attempt to account for the unity of the three categories. He tries to show how they grow out of each other, but insofar as they are three, he gives no account of their ontological unity. If it is said that when metaphysics gives up the task of ontology it gives up the problem of the ontological one and many, this difficulty reduces to the first one.

c) Metaphysics without ontology would prohibit a philosophical account of a transcendent God, for God would be construed either as one of the elements of the metaphysical system or as beyond it altogether. If God is one of the elements of the metaphysical system, he does not transcend the realm of mutually relevant and interconnected determinations. If God is beyond the metaphysical system altogether, the attempt to give a philosophical account of him is given up. The former consequence is one that is espoused by thinkers like Hartshorne and Weiss, but it fails to do justice to the prima facie instincts of religion. The latter consequence combines philosophical rationalism with religious irrationalism and results usually in the denouncing of religion by philosophy or the denouncing of philosophy by religion.

4. The fourth alternative that can be taken by the cosmologist is the Heideggerian-type "show-itself" doctrine. Having arrived at a metaphysical system of first principles, the cosmologist can wait for the fundamental being-itself to show itself in a pure form. The metaphysical system can determine where not to look for being-itself and what being-itself is not. In addition, a phenomenological analysis of experience, correlated with the metaphysical system, would indicate where in our experience we should be "open" to being-itself. But there are no philosophical or rational connections that allow us to move from metaphysics to being-itself, and ontology cannot properly be called a discipline. This fourth alternative is perhaps the best one open to the cosmologist. On the one hand, it acknowledges that metaphysics must be complemented by a transcendent being-itself and that being-itself is not connected to the metaphysical categories in any deductive fashion. On the other hand, it acknowledges the claim of religion that there is something of the character of revelation in our grasp of being-itself and that being-itself is so concrete as to be grasped only in concrete experience. The difficulty with this fourth alternative is that it bifurcates philosophical reflection into what can be apprehended in terms of rational connections and what merely shows itself. Yet our reflection has as its aim to be more of a piece. Even if its parts are to be apprehended phenomenologically from experience, philosophical reflection must work upon what is so apprehended if philosophy is to make an advance. Philosophy comes from a curiosity about what is experienced, and the curiosity must be satisfied by something of the nature of an explanation. The Heideggerian alternative begins the move from cosmology to cosmogony, and the move must be completed by making out the sense of explanation philosophical reflection requires over and above the explanations of metaphysics in terms of first principles.

SECTION D

Cosmogonic Explanations

The explanation sought by cosmogony concerns the difference between a *de facto* unity and a genuine or self-accounting unity. The distinction between the two kinds of unity is not meant to signify that the latter is a real one and the former is not. Rather, a *de facto* unity is a real one but one that does not contain in itself anything that accounts for how or why the unity is what it is. A genuine unity is a self-sufficient unity. Hence, a *de facto* unity needs something besides itself to be explained, and the explanation, if it is to solve the problem of the one and the many, must include reference to a genuine unity. To say, then, that we seek to bring a *de facto* unity to a genuine unity is to say that we need to supplement the account of the former with connections to a genuine self-accounting unity.

It would seem that the easiest way to express what is lacking in the *de facto* unity is to say that it lacks a unifying principle. For, we usually account for the unity of collections by determining a unifying principle that holds the separate elements together. But a unifying principle must be both complex and unified. It must be complex because it must have different parts, each of which is homogeneous with the elements of the collection to be unified. And the unifying principle must have a unity of its own to unify its own different parts. Now, the unity of the principle might be some further principle; but then that further principle would need its own unity, and we would fall into an infinite regress. On the other hand, the unity of the principle might simply be the togetherness of its parts, a *de facto* unity. This is the status of most of the first principles of metaphysics. To call them principles is only to say that the *de facto* unities are universally pervasive and always applicable.

This is so even to the extent that the complexities of the principles are those by which we define terms. Consider, for example, the principle that the whole is the sum of its parts. The unity of this is often alleged to be that "the sum of its parts" is identical with what we mean by "whole." However, in order for this principle to apply to anything or to unify anything, there must be a difference between "whole" and "summed parts," for "whole" must be homogeneous with one of the elements to be unified and "summed parts" with the other. If "whole" and "summed parts" mean exactly the same, then they cannot unify different things; yet if they have slightly different connotations, then either there is a third term that they have in common, and the infinite regress starts, or their identification is *de facto*. If there is an infinite regress, then each stage in the regress is a *de facto* unity.

Philosophical traditions like pragmatism have recognized the *de facto* character of principles and have concentrated on ways of justifying their acceptance. But regardless of the justification for accepting and employing such first principles, philosophy, in quest of the solution to the problem of the one and the many, must press on to account for the reality of *de facto* unities. The attempt to account for what is lacking in *de facto* unities as a unifying principle is analogous to the attempt to account for the ontological unifying function of being-itself as a determinate thing, and it fails for analogous reasons.

The clue to what an explanation must provide for a *de facto* unity can be seen from a consideration of the traditional "paradox of explanation." The paradox is that the explanation of something, *A*, is either *A* itself or something else, *B*. If the explanation of *A* is simply *A*, then no advance is made, and nothing is explained that was not explained before; if something in itself is contingent, then it cannot explain in itself how it is real. If the explanation of *A* is *B*, then we have to know further how *B* is the explanation of *A*, and this further knowledge is *C*; but then, if *C* unifies *B* and *A* by identifying B as the explanation of A, then this is explained by D, and so on. The usual solution to the paradox is to say that the procession of explanations is circular and eventually leads around again to A. Thus, any part in the system is explained by the other parts. In a way it can be said, even on this interpretation, that the explanation of A is A because the circle leads all the way around; but the explanation is mediated by all the steps in the process.

It is apparent, however, that this solution does not apply to the problem of explaining the unity of a *de facto* unity, for the circular system of explanations as a whole is not explained. All its parts are explained in terms of each other, and the elements of the circle have a *de facto* unity. But it is the unity of the whole that we are after in seeking to go from the metaphysics of first principles to ontology. The theory of a circle of explanations may well solve the problem for the explanation involved in metaphysics, that is, the explanation of things according to a system of first principles. But for ontology, cosmogony sees a different solution to the paradox to be required.

From the paradox of explanation we know that a cosmogonic explanation must meet two requirements: First, what explains the first principles (or the determinations of being qua determinations) must be other than the principles themselves; otherwise no advance in explanation is made. Second, what explains the first principles must be one with them in some sense that makes it evident that the explanation applies to the determinations without presupposing yet a further explanation.

A preliminary survey of the explanation given in Part One indicates that our explanation has tools to meet the requirements. The first requirement strikes an answering chord in the claim that the *de facto* unity of the determinations comes from a creator who transcends them; the explanatory advance is from the determinations to the creator of the determinations. The second requirement, which is the more difficult of the two, is addressed by the claim that the elements of the creator that relate him functionally (and as an explanation) to the determinations are themselves created determinations. They have the function of pointing our curiosity beyond the determinations while being one with them. It is in the nature of determinations to embody these characters that testify to the transcendence of the creator.

This is just a preliminary survey of the correspondence of the cosmogonic explanation given in Part One to the requirements that arise from the paradox of explanation. The unusual particulars of the explanation of Part One must be justified as required by the kind of cosmogonic explanation given. There are three such particulars that differ from what would be expected by the view that the explanation of things is in terms of first principles.

In the first place, we said that the determinations of being are contingent and require something transcending them that explains how they are real. Yet what transcends does not explain how the determinations come to be as they are. Creation does not proceed according to principles such that the principles explain why the creation is as it is, for all determinate principles are among the things created. Therefore, our investigation of the nature of a cosmogonic explanation must determine what one thing can explain about another without explaining its nature.

The second point follows from the first. Since it is not the nature of the determinations that is explained, it is their contingent reality that is accounted for by the creator. Yet their reality is not separable from their natures, and the creator gives rise to their whole natures. We must therefore determine how a cosmogonic explanation accounts for the reality of something without accounting for the principles according to which the nature of the effect is determined.

Lastly, in order to avoid an infinite regress of explanations, we must account for how the terminus of the explanation does not itself require an explanation. That is, we must show how cosmogony is complete as an explanation of its subject matter without representing the creator as something that must in turn be explained. The problem here is that the terminus of the explanation, being-itself or the transcendent God, is heterogeneous with respect to the other elements in the explanation. It is in virtue of the heterogeneity that the procession of explanations is halted, for there is nothing in the indeterminate transcendent, such as a *de facto* unity, that allows the explanation to move out of the transcendent term. But the difficulty with the heterogeneity is how any knowledge can be had of it at all, that is, how the explanation of the determinations of being can move to what is heterogeneous with the very determinate terms of the explanation.

The heterogeneity of God with the created realm for which he is the explanation entails that the explanation must be "one way." That is, we can move from the determinations to what they need, but we cannot move from what they need back to them. This is a characteristic of dialectical arguments, in a sense of dialectic employed by Plato and, at times, by Hegel. Our examination of the cosmogonic explanation, then, must turn up an elaboration and defense of the peculiar kind of dialectic that meets the requirements of cosmogony.

As the history of philosophy has shown, however, all theories of method are much more closely connected with theories of reality than is indicated by a methodological or "critical" discussion. When philosophical discussion attempts to be only or primarily critical, the attempt to abstract from the problems of reality often results in shallow thinking, even about method. Nonetheless, the necessity of a "critical" moment in philosophical reflection justifies moving at the problems from the side of method. We must bear in mind, as a corrective to methodological abstraction, that our critical discussion will close with our theory of reality in the end. If it does not, or cannot, then we shall know that our reflection has taken a wrong turn.

6

Methodological Dialectic

"Dialectic" is a word of many meanings. One meaning refers primarily to philosophical method and indicates the approach that plays the abstract and concrete off against each other and justifies theories in the light of alternative theories. Another primary meaning of dialectic refers rather to the subject matter of philosophy; in this sense, *reality* may be said to be dialectical. The former may be called "methodological dialectic" and the latter "constitutive dialectic."

The "critical" examination of the speculation of Part One requires a look at both kinds. Constitutive dialectic, to be dealt with in the next chapter, lies at the heart of cosmogony, for it must be shown that the realities acknowledged in speculative explanation require a "dialectical" change in the sense of explanation involved. Methodological dialectic calls for prior consideration, however, for there are several important questions of method raised by the particularities of our speculation.

In the first place, we must raise the problem of the extent to which our seemingly abstract ontological discussion is based upon experiential confrontations with the subject matter. Second, we must discover the extent to which our reliance on analogy in Parts One and Three is affected by our criticisms of analogy in chapter 1. Third, we must elaborate the nature of the methodological support that dialectic and analogy give each other. Fourth, it must be shown how methodological dialectic involves experience and analogy. In the end, we will be in a position to determine how the conclusions of Part One guide our methodological dialectic into a recognition of constitutive dialectic.

SECTION A

Religious Experience

What part does experience, especially "religious" experience, play in our knowledge of the transcendence of God? It is impossible, even in the last analysis, to separate philosophical knowledge of God from its origin in religion. To be sure, much can be known of God that does not have its base in religious experience; but to be worked into systematic philosophical knowledge this must be integrated with our experience of God that does come from within a religious context. Philosophical knowledge of God that begins with experience cannot be scrubbed clean of its religious associations. The onus of having to acknowledge the foundations of one's knowledge in religious experiences is twofold.

1. On the one hand, religious experience is relatively private. But there are many private experiences, such as that of beauty or love, that are philosophically acceptable to all but those extreme thinkers who take as paradigmatic the natural scientist's experience of his subject matter—and that in its textbook description. So there would be little bite to this element of the onus of religious experience were it not for the other element, namely, its lack of universality.

2. Many thinkers deny the legitimacy of including religious experience in one's philosophical subject matter simply because they have not had such experience; and this is an excellent philosophical argument in its place. But the interpretation to be made of this lack of universality is a problem. It might be accounted for by the fact that there may be no such experience to be had by anyone, and that those who think they have it are deluded. But then those who do have it are often mightily convinced by it. It is as pervasive and fundamental an element of their over-all experience as the experience of beauty or love or personal dignity or tragedy; they would be loathe to reject the experience as delusion simply on the grounds that the only philosophical theory they can defend could not account for its possibility. Surely a kind of experience so thoroughgoing and rich, enriching and consequential, cannot be rejected as delusion simply because of the kind of experience it is; if it is to be rejected as delusion, it must be shown on independent grounds that the person is disturbed and likely to delude himself in this way. That some notorious examples are so deluded cannot be denied; but that many people, even a majority, are deluded in their religious experience is far from apparent. It would seem that religious experience should be accepted at face value unless there is independent evidence of delusion to the contrary.

Then can we account for the lack of universality in religious experience in other ways? It might be the case, and surely is for some people, that a person is so prejudiced against the possibility of religious experience that he would not and could not recognize it if it were all about him. Or it might be that a person is committed to a reduction of the significance of experiences to a domain that excludes religious significance; this is often true of people who argue that religious experience is "merely psychological." That *any* experience is psychological is a trivial truth; but this may not be the only significance a given experience has and the case should not be prejudged. This is true even of the more sophisticated psychological reductions of the meaning of an experience to the genetic origin of the signs involved, for example, the "father image." Perhaps in other cases the lack of universality of religious experience can be accounted for by a crucial ignorance of the *categories* expressing the religious significance of the experience. Perhaps some people are too rushed, harried, or callous to bother to make religious interpretations at all. Perhaps God even hides himself from some people.

At any rate, there are many ways of accounting for the lack of universality of religious experience that leave the validity of the experience more or less intact. Furthermore, since philosophical knowledge of God cannot be separated from at least some experiential foundations, it cannot be complained that some less than universal experience is at the heart of a philosophical discussion. If an artist disciplined his thought to produce a philosophy of art, his special sensitivities and kinds of experience would be considered advantages, not a prejudicial perspective necessary to be exorcised. So should it be with the knowledge of God.

But the role of experience in philosophical knowledge of God is not unambiguous. It may well lie at the beginning of a person's quest for a philosophical understanding of God, as it is for those who begin in faith and seek understanding. But it is not necessary as the origin of the philosophical quest as such. The philosopher may require experience as the confirming terminus of his inquiry; but it need not be present explicitly at the beginning, so long as the philosopher has some relevant subject matter to work on. And even Augustine, the paradigm of the man of faith seeking understanding, put it this way, "We begin in faith, we are perfected in sight." [1] This would indicate that for him the direct experience comes at the end, not at the beginning, however much it might have been present in a misunderstood form all along. But if experience is to be the confirming terminus of the inquiry, questions must be raised and faced concerning the process of inquiry itself, the understanding by analogy and dialectic that leads to the "sight."

SECTION B
Analogy

Analogy cannot have all the connotations in the theory of Part One, which denies the analogy of being, that it might have in a theory that affirms it. The difference comes from this: in an analogy-of-being theory, the ground for the equivocation in the analogy lies in the things known; in a univocity-of-being theory, it lies in the understanding. For the analogy of being, there is an analogical connection between the beings of the things known. For the univocity of being, the analogy in the understanding is the understanding's attempt to get at a univocal difference in the things known; this univocal difference can be only with respect to the natures of the things, not with respect to their being. For the analogy of being, non-analogical knowledge is false, whereas for the univocity of being, only non-analogical knowledge can finally be true; whatever value the analogy has is only as a preliminary for the truth or as a second-best substitute for some non-analogical knowledge

[1] *Enchiridion* I.

that to us may in principle be inaccessible. It is a mistake to think that the univocity of being denies *all* senses of "real" analogies; there may, for instance, be an analogical relation between two instances of a universal. But with respect to the univocity of *being-itself*, analogical knowledge cannot be the last word. We can distinguish two legitimate functions of analogy that are consistent with the view that being-itself is univocal.

1. The first is involved in articulating a new or unusual domain to which we have direct access and to which we compare some familiar domain. It must be emphasized that there *is direct access* to the new domain and that the analogy is used only for purposes of articulation. To be sure, the articulation is part of our understanding, in fact, part of our experience of that new domain; but the analogical terms acquire new meaning as the new domain becomes familiar. For instance, the great increase in the birth rate after the Second World War was articulated by the popular press as a "population explosion"; but no one was inclined to think this meant blowing up people. As the population explosion comes to be understood, the term "explosion" takes on new meaning, and the fact that the similarity in the analogy may have to be denied in just the crucial explanatory respect does not militate against the use of the term with its newly acquired meanings. The analogical term becomes a clear-cut equivocation where the two univocal senses are properly understood in their respective contexts. This function of analogy plays a large part in the piety of a religious person; such a one can come to think of God as a father in purely Godlike fatherly ways and never confuse this with the way in which his human father is a father, even though this was the sense in which his understanding of God began. A term applied analogically to articulate a new situation can acquire its own univocal new meanings as we become familiar with the features of the new situation.

Perhaps the use of this function of analogy that is most essential to philosophy comes in what Peirce called Explication of the Hypothesis.[2] His point is that before the truth of some proposed understanding or articulation of something can be investigated, its own internal logical structure must be laid out. This laying out of the logical structure cannot proceed according to an argumentation with formulated rules of procedure, for the logical structure of the premise from which the argumentation would proceed is just the thing in question. Rather, explication proceeds (and this Peirce did *not* point out) by finding in the hypothesis or proposed articulation logical analogies with other familiar functions. As explication nears completion the peculiarities of the hypothesis in question become apparent by the use of many analogies, and the analogical terms acquire new univocal meanings appropriate to the subject matter at hand. Many contemporary philosophers hold that this "logical mapwork" is the main part of philosophy.

2. The second major function of analogy that is legitimate for the univocity of being is closely allied with methodological dialectic. Not only are

---

[2] *Collected Papers of Charles Sanders Peirce*, ed. C. Hartshorne and P. Weiss (Cambridge, Mass.: Harvard University Press, 1935), VI, 471.

analogy and dialectic legitimate in some forms, even beyond the first function of analogy described above, but each *requires* the other.

It will be remembered from chapter 1 that the strong or inferential use of analogy, whether the analogy of proportion or that of proportionality, requires univocal knowledge of the determinate distance between the analogical terms. The proportion in the analogy of proportion is just that determinate distance itself. And the knowledge of any three terms in a proportionality analogy, from which the fourth term is to be inferred or determined, already includes the determinate distance between the pairs of terms. The critical result of this is that either the analogy is reduced to a complex univocity (by univocal knowledge of the determinate distance) or the inference cannot be drawn. Put in a way that does not do away with analogy altogether, an analogy that involves an inference claim such that knowledge is advanced to where it was not before must be based on a univocal foundation.

On the one hand, this univocal foundation can be simply direct experience of both sides articulated by the analogy; when this is so, the analogy is the same as the first function of analogy described above. On the other hand, the univocal foundation for an analogy can be *dialectic*, and it is this latter foundation that is our chief concern.

SECTION C
Dialectic

We distinguished above between methodological and constitutive dialectic. Yet the term "dialectic" has had many more senses than just these two. Excepting the sense it had for Aristotle and Kant, for whom it meant a specious argument, most of its important senses can be viewed as elements of methodological dialectic. A teacher often uses "dialectic" in the sense of a *therapeutic* device for stimulating a student to think in a fresh way, as did Socrates, the midwife. Often therapeutic dialectic is turned back upon the dialectician, as is the case with every reflective self-critic who learns from his own mistakes. A "dialectic" is the name given to the *procedure* of presenting a thesis in which the initial statement of a problem and its solution is vague or paradoxical and the final statement is precise and straightforward; the procedure consists in altering the terms in which the problem and solution are usually conceived. Kierkegaard was the master of this sort of dialectic. Or dialectic can also mean the kind of argumentation that justifies a thesis by comparison with alternatives, showing that to the extent that the alternatives are true one's own thesis is presupposed. This sort of dialectic is nearly always employed in defending any wholesale thesis.

Methodological dialectic works in the many ways indicated above to transform the categories of initial reflection into those that fulfill the ideal of system. It proceeds with one eye on the ideal of system that would complete understanding and with the other eye on the categories with which we begin. It is to be doubted, at least for a realist, that philosophy can be *only* dialectical; the categories with which the dialectic begins must first prove their worth in interpreting experience before pure thought can drive their ramifications to conclusions beyond experience. But given a critically developed fund of experience and interpretative categories (which we are never in reality without), a philosopher can draw conclusions that press toward making our knowledge complete and systematic.

1. Dialectic in this inclusive methological sense can provide a univocal ground for an analogy, can set the determinate distance, in the following way. A dialectical conclusion has the status of truth *if* the ideal of system can be fulfilled with respect to the initial categories the dialectic is to explain. If the dialectical conclusion can then be interpreted as an analogy to something else, the dialectical argument will supply the non-analogical basis for the analogy. For instance, our dialectical argument, beginning with the metaphysical analysis of determinations of being and showing them to depend on a creator that is indeterminate, is the univocal ground justifying an analogy between the world's dependence on God and the dependence of children on their parents. In chapter 1 we saw that an analogy needs a non-analogical ground in two ways, both of which are supplied by dialectic. In the first place, there must be a non-analogical ground for asserting the analogy at all. A dialectical argument gives this kind of knowledge of its conclusion, as, for instance, the dialectic of finite determinations and their creator gives some knowledge of the nature of the creator, knowledge specifically of the conditions the creator must fulfill to be related dialectically to the finite determinations (indeterminate, transcendent, and so forth). In the second place, there must be a non-analogical ground for denying the complete identity of the analogue and the analogate, that is, for claiming that the analogy is *only* an analogy. Again, dialectic furnishes this, as when the dialectic of finite determinations and their creator shows that the creator must be indeterminate with respect to the finite determinations, *un*like a father who is of the same determinate species as his offspring. Methodological dialectic, then, can be both the positive and negative ground for an analogy.

2. But if dialectic has an essential contribution to make to analogy, that is, by providing the required univocal ground, does analogy in its turn contribute essentially to dialectic? If it does not, why bother to move to the analogy at all, since to do so requires that we have the dialectic beforehand? That analogy does contribute essentially to dialectic can be seen from the following considerations. A dialectical conclusion is necessary if the ideal of system is to be fulfilled with respect to the categories from which the dialectic begins. But the only knowledge dialectic gives of that which is concluded to is the set of conditions the conclusion must fulfill in order for it to explain the categories from which the dialectic took its start. For instance, all we know dialectically of the creator of determinate being is what it must be in order to be that creator, that is, in order to explain the dependence of the finite realm. Now it is *not* the case that an analogy would give us extra features of that which is dialectically concluded to, for this would require yet another non-analogical

ground. But an analogy does allow us *to detach the conclusion in thought from the argument that sets the conditions it must fulfill.* For instance, the analogy of the creator to a father allows us to treat the creator without in the same breath considering the product. It allows us temporarily to neglect the argument that produces the conclusion and to deal only with the conclusion. We must admit that all names for God in his aseity, for example, the transcendent God, being-itself, the ground of determinate being, are analogical in this sense. they speak of God as if he were a subject with predicates; but their content is only what God must be to create the world, and he must not be a subject with predicates. This is not so much to conceive the conclusion *in itself,* which would be impossible for conclusions about the creator of determinate being, but rather to conceive the conclusion *by itself.*

The advantages of conceiving the conclusion by itself are two. On the one hand, it allows us to focus on the conclusion when we want to without the connected premises from which the conclusion was derived. This is especially important for the sort of concerns that quicken religion and that make a great distinction between the relative importance of the conclusion and premises. Put into the analogical terms with which we are used to dealing separately, the conclusion of a dialectical argument can be worshiped, prayed to, and so forth. On the other hand, the detachment of the conclusion of a dialectical argument allows us to move the conclusion into contexts different from the one of the original premises and argument. The analogy can be employed to suggest new connections that might cast light on the conclusion. Of course, the new connections in turn must be justified dialectically, and the analogy is only an organon of discovery. But if the conclusions of a given line of dialectical argumentation are to be worked into a comprehensive system that connects all reality, then the new connections must be pursued, and analogy has traditionally played a fruitful role in this pursuit.

The conclusion must be interpreted finally with the initially analogical terms in a univocal way that reflects the connotations peculiar to the dialectical conclusion and that does not reflect the connotation of the analogy that must be denied. In part this univocal attribution is controlled by the dialectical argument itself. But in every systematic philosophy, most things dialectically derived can be concluded to from many directions. That which is seen as the source of finite being might also be seen as the goal of human life, the quintessence of perfection in general, the savior of man's most heartfelt losses. As the conclusions of these different dialectical approaches are brought together, their analogical expressions must be integrated, common analogies found, and the deliverances of the various dialectics woven into a consistent fabric of detachable conclusions. In fact, the dialectical category that solves only one problem, for example, God as creator, is far more suspect than one that solves many problems, for example, God as creator, savior, perfection, and man's end. This requires that terms introduced analogically find univocal senses appropriate to the new subject matter; as further investigation brings greater familiarity, the analogical terms find univocal application. This point is well attested by those philosophers who claim to reason by "analogical extension" or "synechistically."

SECTION D
Dialectic in Experience

However plausible a dialectical conclusion is rendered by being concluded to from many dialectical routes and by being articulated univocally through analogy in the first sense described above, its greatest plausibility lies in its use in experience. A dialectically derived category is most securely in our confidence when it is used as an interpreting sign in a direct experience. There is no greater confirmation of the theory that God is the creator than the experience of him as such. This is the great insight of the mystical and Neo-Platonic tradition, which places the direct experience of God at the end of the process of dialectical and analogical inquiry as well as at points along the way that confirm and direct the progress and that prevision the end. It is a mistake to think of such direct experience of God as either immediate or even vague; it is the most concrete and determinate experience of all!

The direct experience employing the dialectically derived categories again points up the function of analogy in its first sense, the sense, namely, that drives toward univocity. Such a category must be *explicated* into its logical constituents. A concept, as Kant pointed out, is a unification of other representations; and the experiential employment of a dialectical concept involves experiencing its constituent representations. When our direct experience is interpreted with a dialectically derived category, we know *what* we are experiencing *by the explication* of that category. It well may be that no experience is infallibly interpreted, and hence no experiential confirmation of a theory is final; but no theory can be happier than the one whose terms are on all fours in experience with "red," "heavy," and "soft," or at least with "friendly," "beautiful," or "indicative of one's heart."

SECTION E
From Methodological to Constitutive Dialectic

We have discussed, up to this point, the way in which methodological dialectic is involved with analogy and with the ideal of system. The crucial question now is whether and how our conclusions about the involvement of methodological dialectic can be extended to constitutive dialectic; for the involvement of dialectic with the ideal of system contains the clue to the kind of explanation required by cosmogony, and the involvement with analogy is the clue to the connection of our ontological conclusions with religion (which will be pursued in Part Three). The transition from methodological to constitutive dialectic can be begun with some considerations of the way our constitutive speculative theory is treated on the contemporary scene.

Our fundamental problem concerning the relation between God and the world turns, in part at least, upon the kind of knowledge we claim to have of God; these connected issues lie at heart of the crucial difference that separates two of the leading contemporary philosophers of religion, Charles Hartshorne and Paul Tillich. Tillich maintains that God is the power of being that transcends all structural determinations of being. Even the most general determinations of being, what Tillich calls the polarities (individualization and participation, dynamics and form, freedom and destiny), are created by God as the power of being.[3] It is not the case for Tillich that God is, in a perfect way, the kind of things we are in imperfect ways; rather, God transcends all determinate ways of being. Tillich draws the consequence of this for knowledge that all knowledge of God as he is in himself must be symbolic; any knowledge that was either analogical or literal would commit God to a determinate structure. Although there are difficulties with the view that all knowledge of God is symbolic, difficulties that the theory of constitutive dialectic in the next chapter is calculated to avoid, the claim that God in himself transcends all determinate being is close to our own conclusions.

Hartshorne, on the other hand, holds the opposite view on these points. God, he claims, is the perfection of the categories common to all possibilities (the metaphysically necessary categories) and the perfection of the contingent features God has by being related to a contingent world. Thus, although God may transcend certain elements of *contingent* reality, for Hartshorne he is wholly immanent within the necessary structures of being; God is the perfection of determinate being, not its creator. Accordingly, although Hartshorne thinks that there are some things said of God only symbolically (for example, that he is a divine shepherd), he also thinks that metaphysical truths are true of God literally, as, paradoxically, are some analogical truths. These two kinds of literal knowledge of God must be examined in greater detail.

Metaphysical truths, according to Hartshorne, are those that deal "with what is common and *necessary* to all possible states of affairs and all possible truth."[4] Although metaphysical truths are analytic and positive, they do not deny any contingent fact. An example would be the principle "that any possible world will actualize some possibilities, and thereby exclude the actualization of certain other possibilities."[5] Whatever contingent facts there are must illustrate this principle, and the principle excludes no possible contingent fact. Hartshorne goes even further to claim that "God is the *one individual conceivable a priori.*" God has, for him, a "metaphysically unique status and character," that is, "one whose distinctiveness can be defined through purely universal categories."[6] God is distinguished from all other beings by the fact that the metaphysical categories fit him perfectly whereas they apply to other beings only relatively.

[3] See his *Systematic Theology* (Chicago: University of Chicago Press, 1951), I, 203.
[4] *The Divine Relativity* (New Haven, Conn.: Yale University Press, 1948), p. xiii.
[5] *The Logic of Perfection and Other Essays in Neoclassical Metaphysics* (LaSalle, Ill.: Open Court Publishing Co., 1962), p. 284.
[6] *The Divine Relativity*, p. 31.

For whereas creatures exhibit the categories only in a nondistinctive fashion, one creature being relative (for example) in the same categorical manner as another, and thus sharing the category with that other, God is relative in a categorically unique manner, which is shared with nothing else. What can this mean, if not that the referent of the category is something original with God, in some fashion God himself? Other creatures *participate* in being as expressed in the category; God *is* that being.[7]

Although this is not the place to determine whether the notion of "a perfect being" is self-consistent or whether the dialectic of perfection entails that what is perfect cannot be *a* being, certain other less specific difficulties with Hartshorne's view on this point can be singled out. The first has to do with the claim that God's distinctiveness can be defined through purely universal categories. If a metaphysical truth is one that is common to all possible worlds, then there would seem to be an equivocation in "common" when all beings other than God *participate* in the categories whereas only God *is* them. Hartshorne would argue, of course, that the metaphysical truths are God's very nature, and hence *he* is common to all possible worlds. God is not simply *a* being beside others; he is *necessarily* beside others, no matter which contingent others there happen to be. But if that which can literally be known of God in the metaphysical sense, that which is common to all possibilities, is God himself, even in his abstract nature, this is not to describe him as a being but simply as the sum of necessity in all possible worlds. It takes a further argument to show that the sum of necessity is one being, *the* being that is God, rather than simply some fundamental principles defined by the nature of necessity.

The second difficulty has to do more directly with Hartshorne's notion of metaphysical truths. What he takes to be an absolute distinction between metaphysical and contingent truths is, in fact, only a relative one.[8] Any alternative sets of contingent facts may presuppose common, and therefore "metaphysically necessary," categories; but what is necessary relative to these sets of contingent facts may in itself allow of alternatives. This situation is only complicated, not intrinsically changed, when the contingent alternative sets of facts in question are all possible worlds, for the alternative to what is common to all these, the alternative to possibility *überhaupt,* is the total absence of possibility. But this is the very issue in question when the claim is being debated whether the intelligibles themselves, metaphysical possibility itself, is created or original. Of course we cannot conceive of the alternative to conceivability in general; but this only shows that there *are* intelligibles and that part of our nature is to be intelligent. It does not show that what is necessary for there to be any possible worlds is necessary and uncreated in itself; it does show that since there is one possible world, at least, there are

---

[7] *Ibid.,* p. 34.
[8] Absolute in principle: Hartshorne recognizes that the distinction may be problematic in practice; see *The Logic of Perfection,* p. 284.

some necessary things relative to it. If God is to create any possible worlds, such creation has necessary elements; but it could be that those necessary elements would not be at all were there no creation. The issue as to whether the intelligibles are original or created is not to be decided by showing that there are common elements to all intelligibility—this is to beg the question in favor of cosmology—rather, it must be decided by some kind of dialectical argument as was given in Part One. Since this is so, the issue as to the knowledge we have of God depends on ontological considerations of the structure constitutive of reality.

The second kind of literal knowledge of God that Hartshorne supports, and which must be examined, is what he calls "analogy." The paradox is that he claims that such knowledge is literal with respect to God and analogical with respect to creatures. Analogical knowledge has to do with features that relate one thing to another; God is perfectly relative and finite creatures are imperfect, at least in part, because they are *imperfectly* relative. Therefore, such features as "knowledge" and "love," which are essentially defined by their relativity (knowledge and love are always relative to their objects), can be had in their essential form by God only, and they can be had by us analogically.[9] It must be pointed out that for Hartshorne God is not only necessary in nature; he has contingent features as well. It is necessary that he be perfectly relative to every contingent fact, but which contingent facts there are for him to be relative to is a contingent matter. Since it is only with respect to creatures that these relativities are attributed analogically, they can be said of God with literal metaphysical necessity, thus reducing this kind of knowledge of God to the first kind discussed above.

But Hartshorne still has not gotten around the problem that our knowledge of perfect relativity, for example, of what perfect knowledge or perfect love is, is derived by analogy and dialectic from what we see in broken form in us. Our knowledge does not begin with a perfect theory of what perfect relativity is and then accommodate itself to explain the lack of perfection in us; it begins with an examination of what we have ourselves and then proceeds by analogy and dialectic to determine what perfect forms our own condition presupposes. This is not to claim, of course, that God is not perfect in respects in which we are imperfect, or that perfection is not in some instance perfect relativity; Christians argue, in fact, that God *shows* us what perfect love is. But it is to claim that if God does not show us through finite manifestations the perfect form of what we are imperfectly, then we must figure it out dialectically and by analogy. This again returns us to constitutive arguments about reality.

It seems then that Hartshorne's doctrine that we have literal knowledge of God in himself is not adequate. In terms of the conclusions of Part One, we have knowledge of God's necessary nature insofar as God is interpreted in terms of his conditional features. But it has been argued throughout that the

[9] See *The Logic of Perfection*, p. 141.

creator in himself is prior to intelligibility and to the determinate structures of being. If Hartshorne's view that we have literal knowledge of God as he is in himself were true, it could not be the case that God in himself is prior to the determinate structures of being. But since the difficulties with Hartshorne's theory of metaphysics limit its applicability to the domain of the intelligibles, this theory of the nature of metaphysical knowledge cannot itself decide whether the intelligibles are created or uncreated. This latter issue must be decided on grounds like those given in Part One. Standing with our previous argument that creation implies that the creator is prior to the product and that the product in this case is the whole of determinate being, we find ourselves on Tillich's side in his dispute with Hartshorne.

But if we find ourselves with Tillich, we must make up accounts with Tillich's doctrine that all knowledge of God, except perhaps the claim that God is being-itself, is symbolic. To say that it is symbolic is to have some univocal ground for denying literal univocity. This ground for Tillich is the ontological theory that God is being-itself and that being-itself or the power of being transcends the determinate structures of finite being. Since this ontological theory grounds the claim that other knowledge of God is symbolic, it itself cannot be symbolic. Yet if God does transcend all determinate structures, the ontological theory cannot be literal and articulate God in his transcendence. The Tillichian position therefore shares with our own position from Part One the task of justifying a constitutive ontological dialectic that shows that the determinate role of being creator presupposes a transcendent God who is indeterminate without at the same time showing that the transcendent God is essentially determinate.

7
Constitutive Dialectic

Constitutive dialectic, in contrast to methodological dialectic, can be characterized generally by two points. First, it is connected with reality in a way that methodological dialectic is not. As denoting a method of philosophical inquiry, the latter is relatively neutral with respect to the alternative conclusions to which it is prejudicially committed by its very form. Of course, no method is completely externally related to its conclusions about the subject matter; every method prejudices the possible outcome by its own structure. But insofar as it is a method and not identical with the conclusions themselves, methodological dialectic is compatible in form with many possible conceptions of its subject matter. Constitutive dialectic, however, refers to a dialectical character in the subject matter of the inquiry and hence is identical with the conclusions of the inquiry when those conclusions are adequate to the subject matter. The conclusions are not immediately on a par, though, and there is an essential order in which they must be run through, as we shall see below. Therefore, starting from our methodological dialectic, our philosophical explanation of the subject matter is a linear affair. To speak of constitutive dialectic is to speak both of the dialectical structure of reality and of the dialectical structure of our philosophy that exhibits reality's structure.

Second, constitutive dialectic is characterized by the shift in the significance of its terms from one level to another. The significance of the subject matter on one level itself forces us to a new level where the significance is different. As in methodological dialectic, there is a single goal that leads our reflections on; but the appearance of the goal changes or develops from level to level.

The nature of philosophical reflection itself exhibits the structure of constitutive dialectic in the encounter of metaphysics and ontology where the justification of cosmogony must be made out. The shift in the significance of dialectic from the methodological to the constitutive levels is an instance of constitutive dialectic.

The justification of cosmogony requires showing that the view of explanation held by cosmology must undergo a shift in meaning and significance and that the cosmogonic explanation is the result. To this end several elements in the dialectical nature of explanation must be examined: (*a*) the shift in the conception of the goal of reflection or the ideal of system, (*b*) the shift in the nature of what suffices to explain the subject matter, (*c*) the shift in the continuity of the process of explanation from homogeneous elements to heterogeneous elements, and (*d*) the shift in the relation between the order of explanation and the order of being, where the latter means the order of ontological dependence of one element of being on another. Each of these elements in the dialectical character of explanation is connected with constitutive problems discussed in Part One; they will be noted in each instance. If our examination of these points can justify the shift in each case, then we will have justified our conception of cosmogonic explanation.

SECTION A

The Ideal of Explanation

The most apparent difference between cosmology and cosmogony is in the ideal each has for its explanation. Each has its own view as to the form its explanation of the subject matter should take. Since both cosmology and cosmogony aim to give systematic accounts of the nature of all reality, this difference is about the conception of the ideal of system. Cosmogony would partially be justified if it can find the seeds of its view in the claims of cosmology.

1. It would be foolish to attempt a detailed characterization of the ideal of system that governs cosmology, for there is neither a thorough-going consensus as to the nature of the ideal current in the philosophical community nor a very specific commitment implied in our own speculative theory of Part One. We can note some general distinguishing marks, however.

First, the cosmological ideal of system entails separating out and clearly distinguishing the various general principles that interpret reality. This is a job primarily of analysis and clarification.

Second, the cosmological ideal of system entails determining the ways in which these general principles fit together to make up the things in the world, for example, how actuality and potentiality are combined in a substance, how rules and goals are combined in normative behavior, and so forth. This task involves laying out the complex natures of things and describing the coherence of these natures. Nearly always, this task is done in conjunction with the first.

Third, the cosmological ideal of system entails arranging the general principles in systematic form, defining them in terms of each other and measuring their mutual consistency and coherence together. Often, this element of the ideal of system is not distinguished from the first two. On theories of a nominalistic bent, the fundamental metaphysical principles would have no being or status apart from their co-operation in making up the things of the world. Yet on other theories, the move is to distinguish this element of the ideal of system so clearly as to be identified with the whole of that ideal to the exclusion of the other elements we have noted. Whitehead gives an example, though perhaps not quite this extreme, in *Process and Reality* when he begins with a list of all the categories to be used in his cosmology.

The end result of these elements is that the cosmological ideal of system is to develop a set of interrelated categories that can be employed in giving a philosophical interpretation to all the things in the world and to the world as a whole. The cosmological ideal of system recognizes a subject matter and a set of categories to explain it. The character of the explanation is the reduction of the subject matter to the set of explanatory categories.

2. The cosmological ideal of system accounts for the *de facto* unity of its set of explanatory categories or first principles when it sets forth their interconnections and relations. But it cannot account for the genuine unity of these categories in the sense of explaining the reality of their contingent *de facto* unity. It cannot explain why the harmony of the pattern of the *de facto* unity is harmonious. Yet this is the very thing cosmology would want to explain. The reason for this inability is that the only explanation allowed by cosmology is a categorial one, and a determinate category is precisely the kind of thing that cannot account for the unity of the determinate categories, as we have seen over and again.

Still, cosmology does attempt to give an account of the unity of the things that are made up of the fundamental general principles and elements of the system. And the *de facto* complexity of the things of the world that cosmology attempts to explain is the same sort of complexity that pertains to the first principles considered together by themselves.

The account of the *de facto* unity of the first principles of the system unfortunately cannot be of the same kind that the set of first principles gives the things that it explains, for there are no categories beyond the first ones to explain them. Therefore, *either* a different kind of explanation must be found, the meaning of explanation must undergo a shift and the ideal of system be seen to include something different from what it appeared to include from the inside of cosmology, *or* the first principles are themselves to be admitted as inexplicable. Since the hypothesis that something is inexplicable is to be admitted only in cases of desperation, cosmology should look first for something that transcends its own conception of itself, a new conception of the ideal of system.

3. The cosmogonist's ideal of system includes both the cosmologist's ideal and the explanation of the reality of the contingent determinate first principles. Because cosmological first principles are determinate, their unities, both individually and together, are *de facto* and their reality is therefore contingent. Since cosmology has removed any doubts as to the fact of the reality of the first principles, because this reality is contingent the explanation of it is truly presupposed by cosmology. Our reflections about what explains the determinateness of things in Part One concluded that the explanation must be

the ground or creator of the determinations. The word "cosmogony" means the ground or origination of the basic elements.

The point here is not so much to spell out the explanation that cosmogony adds to cosmology in enlarging its ideal of system as it is to show that the explanation involves an argument about the structure constitutive of reality. We have already given the arguments in this regard in Part One. The point is that the aim that is implicit in the cosmologist's approach to the nature of reality and that he thinks is fulfilled by a system of explanatory categories is not in fact fulfilled by those categories. The aim cannot be fulfilled without an explanation of the determinate categories qua determinate. The cosmogonic ideal of system is the one that includes the explanation of the first principles per se.

It is an interesting point that the enlargement of the conception of the ideal of system coincides with the appreciation of the problem of the one and the many as the central problem of ontology. The unity that is sought by our dialectical explanation and that is required by ontology is one that includes or unifies all elements of the determinate things, including their reality or groundedness.

A further interesting point is that since a *de facto* unity is a harmony, the cosmogonic ideal of explanation is that of finding the ground for harmony. With Plato we can say that our ultimate explanatory principle is something like the form of the Good, the ground of all determinate harmony. With Plato, we acknowledge that the search for the ground of unity is the motive force in dialectic.

SECTION B
Kinds of Explanations

Closely connected with the shift in the conception of the ideal of system is the shift in the conception of the sort of thing that suffices as an explanation. The question of the ideal of system concerns the systematic nature of the explanation. The question of the kind of explanation concerns how the systems are taken to explain the subject matter. A corresponding shift from cosmology to cosmogony is evident in the latter issue.

1. For cosmology, the systematic philosophical explanation sought is an axiomatic-deductive theory. The first principles, when established by all the arguments available, have the character of axioms from which the philosophically relevant characters of reality can be deduced. This statement of the cosmological view is perhaps too specialized in itself to serve as a handy selective principle for such a large and varied collection of positions as that which we have identified as cosmological. But certain qualifications can render it a fairly useful characterization.

Instead of calling the first principles axioms, many philosophers would prefer to call them hypotheses. This is an acceptable qualification of our statement so long as the distinction intended by the qualification is recognized and the distinction not made for reasons of false modesty. Three things might be intended by claiming that the first principles are hypotheses in contrast to axioms.

a) The first principles should be called hypotheses when our philosophical reflection is at an explicitly tentative stage and when we have criteria that would indicate the end of the tentativeness. In this sense, we call our first principles hypotheses when our methodological dialectic is still midstream and we are conscious of difficulties in the principles at hand that must still be worked out; the principles are only hypothetical because we know that they must be changed somewhat before the cosmological ideal of system will be satisfied. But in this sense, the hypothetical character of the first principles will be given up when the dialectical difficulties are resolved.

b) The first principles should also be called hypotheses on a view like the pragmatists', for which the process of methodological dialectic is infinite. All results of philosophical reflection, for this view, are tentative because of the nature of the method of philosophical reflection. There can be many different ways of claiming that philosophy is always tentative in this sense, but for all the ways it is fair to say that the first principles at hand at any time are hypotheses. Nonetheless, however hypothetical the status of the first principles might be in the workings of the infinite community of investigators, the status they have as explanation of the subject matter is that of axioms from which the philosophically relevant features of the subject matter are to be deduced. They might best be called "hypothetically asserted axioms." In the infinite long run, which is not possible in any finite time, their hypothetical character will be irrelevant and they will be significant only as axioms.

c) The first principles, finally, could be called hypotheses when the whole structure of the cosmological system is taken to require some further explanation and when the structure of a given cosmological system might be rejected if the further explanation cannot be found. Here the tentativeness of the first principles rests not on considerations of method but on considerations of the constitutive character of reality that show the cosmological structure to be dependent upon something that transcends the domain of cosmology. But once the explanation is found that transcends cosmology, the cosmological system is taken to be axiomatic for its subject matter.

For all three senses in which the first principles might be called hypotheses, the first principles do have the status of axioms once the cosmological system is properly established. This is true whether the proper establishment of cosmology is simply a matter of time, or is impossible in any finite time, or requires the transcendence of cosmology.

We must also admit qualifications of the notion of deduction as used in our characterization of the cosmological kind of explanation as an axiomatic deductive system. Two general qualifications are necessary.

First, although for some extremely rationalistic views, the whole of reality is thought to be deducible from the axioms, for most views this is not so. Most philosophers maintain that what is deduced from the system is only the philosophically relevant or interesting elements of reality, and this implies that something is left over. There are two fairly traditional attitudes that have been taken toward the leftovers. Some philosophers, with Hegel, say that the criterion of philosophical relevance is whether the subject matter embodies the workings of the first principles; that which does not is called chance and is said to be insignificant for philosophical reflection.[1] This sort of view develops the first principles not so much according to adequacy to an external subject matter as according to some internal principle of development. The second attitude holds that some things do happen by chance such that their particulars are in no sense deducible from first principles, but it holds also that the first principles must account for how things happen by chance. For this view, the freedom or arbitrariness in particularity is itself a matter of first principles. For both attitudes, however, the first principles are axioms from which the philosophically relevant characters of reality are deducible.

Second, the nature of deduction itself is a matter of much dispute. For all cosmology, the *ascertainment* of the first principle is not deductive but speculative (or abductive or retroductive, as Peirce called it). The deduction comes in testing out whether the first principles do in fact explain their subject matter. For some philosophers, the deduction from the axioms is a fairly formal affair, and many philosophers today, excited by symbolic logic, hope to make the deduction perfectly formal with a translation from the formal system to experiential or scientific terms coming at the end. For other philosophers, the deduction is quite informal and may not even be an explicit move separate from the dialectic by which the first principles are ascertained. Often the only explicit deduction is the prediction of previously undiscovered elements of the subject matter suggested by the first principles. But for all senses of deduction there is the common theme that the elements of the subject matter that must be explained are to be explained through derivation by a combination of first principles.

2. If the model of cosmological explanation is that of the axiomatic-deductive system, what about the explanation of the first principles of the system itself? Must we not ask the self-reflexive question about the explanatory system? One can, of course, answer no to this and say that the first principles are meant to explain and not to be explained themselves, since by definition they are first. Yet, as we have observed before, although the principles stand first in the order of axiomatic-deductive explanation, they themselves exhibit the same need for explanation that is exhibited by what they themselves explain. Something needs an explanation when it seems to have an incongruity or when we have the feeling, if not the intellectual conviction, that it is less than *sui generis*. The first principles are real but contingent, as is evidenced by the merely *de facto* character of their individual and collective unities. Because they are contingent, their reality needs an account.

[1] *The Logic of Hegel*, trans. W. Wallace (2d ed.; Oxford: Oxford University Press, 1892), sec. 16, p. 26.

If, then, the explanation of the axiomatic-deductive system must be other than an axiomatic-deductive system, what shall it be? Cosmology itself has a suggestion, and so does cosmogony. Whatever it shall be, we know that the shift from one kind of explanation to another will reflect a shift from one constitutive element of reality to another; for the axiomatic-deductive system is exclusively concerned with the determinate and yet it is precisely the determinateness in the first principles that cannot be accounted for with a determinate axiomatic-deductive scheme. So the explanation of the axiomatic-deductive theory will have to be grounded in something real but not determinate, at least not determinate in the same sense as the determinations of being articulated by the cosmological axiomatic-deductive system.

The truth of this need to go beyond what we have called cosmology to something else that can handle self-reflexive problems has been recognized almost since the beginning of philosophy. Cosmology we have characterized with more than a passing recollection of Plato's description of *dianoia,* or theory construction. Plato's dialectic, which has *dianoia* as its subject matter, has been at least the *inspiration* of our use of the term "dialectic" in describing methodological and constitutive dialectic. Following Plato, we have characterized dialectic as a method of philosophical reflection that ultimately raises questions whose answers require the structure of the method to be constitutive of reality. Like Plato, we have said that the reality to which constitutive dialectic ascends transcends the subject matter of axiomatic deductive *dianoia* and even is more real in the sense that the object of *dianoia* is ontologically dependent on it. But what is Plato's answer to the kind of explanation dialectic gives? Some interpreters, like the Neo-Platonists, have gone so far as to give a reading of Plato that puts him unequivocally in the camp of cosmogony. Others have emphasized a side closer to cosmology, a far different side, and this latter interpretation is of primary critical interest to us.

The most astute thoroughgoing interpreter of Plato who takes the non-cosmogonic line is Robert S. Brumbaugh; he interprets Plato's program as the sort of thing A. N. Whitehead was attempting, which was a kind of cosmology, and yet he recognizes the difficulties with cosmology alone. Brumbaugh holds that what is lacking in the cosmological or dianoetic approach is the inclusion of structures of value and that this lack poses the insoluble problems of self-reference. In his commentary on the *Parmenides* he says,

> It has already been remarked, in commenting on Plato's hypotheses, that a system of the hypothetical-deductive sort, which contains no forms of value, appears to generate infinite regresses when it tries to understand itself. For, in the first place, we would need a new set of hypotheses from which to deduce our definitions or theorems; so that, for example, to define "one" as anything which participates in the abstracted property of "oneness," which is itself "one" property, triggers off an unending chain of properties ascending in type. . . . Nor can we ever make non-

Robert S. Brumbaugh

hypothetical evaluations: we can only show that *if* certain axioms are accepted, certain theorems will contradict them.

On the other hand, in constructing and using logical and mathematical systems, we do have definite criteria in mind, and we do find certain properties necessary, though indefinable.[2]

Brumbaugh goes on by analogy to extend the normative criteria from logical and mathematical systems to social planning and government, to aesthetics and formal system-building; there is something analogous to criteria of simplicity, consistency, and completeness in each sphere, and these criteria are not definable within the systems they govern.[3] Even beyond these "working" criteria that govern hypothetical-deductive structures, Brumbaugh says there remain

> . . . the further normative concepts of wholeness and unity. We can say that certain structural properties are necessary conditions for the realization of the good; but to think of them as sufficient conditions, or as equivalent to the good, overlooks the presupposition of a normative demand that they cooperate to form an ordered whole.[4]

Brumbaugh's proposals agree with the cosmogonic approach that the fatal flaw in cosmology or the axiomatic-deductive system lies in the problem of the one and the many: the structural many presupposes a normative one or unity or ordered wholeness that cannot be accounted for within the terms of the many of the system. But where the cosmogonic approach emphasizes the ontological dependence of the dianoetic many on the one, and thus calls the one "being-itself," Brumbaugh's approach emphasizes the normative quality of the function of the one in the many and calls the one "value" or the "Good." Where cosmogony supplements cosmology with an ontological treatment of being-itself, Brumbaugh supplements it with a theory of value. Since Plato called his highest term the Good more consistently than he called it Being, Brumbaugh is probably more accurate than the cosmogonic Neo-Platonic tradition as an interpreter of Plato; but when it comes to the philosophical truth of the matter, our reflections incline us more to cosmogony, and we must see how cosmogony will deal with Brumbaugh's position.

Brumbaugh is right that the notion of oneness or unity functions normatively to drive our explanations on; it is at the base of the ideal of system. He is also right that the one is normative in a constitutive sense in that it is what the structural many presupposes or needs in order to be. But it is a mistake, we must argue, to think that the one or ordered wholeness is constitutively normative in the sense that explains *why* the many is as it is. It is not normative in the sense that it is a value that explains in the way a selective principle explains. The *de facto* unities are indeed harmonies, but why they are harmonies is not to be determined by principles of selection. They are

2 *Plato on the One* (New Haven, Conn.: Yale University Press, 1961), p. 201.
3 *Ibid.*
4 *Ibid.*, p. 202.

harmonious because they are real and this is what harmony means. To see why this is so, we must ask what it is in the *dianoetic* many that needs explanation and what kind of explanation suffices.

3. Brumbaugh would agree that the difficulty with the *dianoetic* or cosmological system is that it is a many with a *de facto* unity, a certain order, the principle for which cannot be determined within the system of the many itself. Now what is the explanation of this? There are two interpretations. The cosmogonic interpretation says that what needs to be explained is how the contingent many with its *de facto* unities or harmonies can be real, and the explanation it gives is that being-itself is the creative ground of all determinations of being. Since all determinations exhibit *de facto* unities, all must be created. There are no aboriginal determinate principles according to which the creation is as it is and which explain why the *de facto* unities are the ones they are or why the harmonies are harmonious. (Of course, there are determinate laws governing how one determination determines another, and so forth, but the first principles of this state of affairs to which the laws are to be traced are contingent in the sense of having *de facto* unities.) According to cosmogony, what explains the difficulties in cosmology or *dianoia* is what explains how the many is real, its *de facto* order or unity being contingent.

The other interpretation, Brumbaugh's and perhaps Plato's, says that the explanation must explain why the *de facto* unities are as they are, and that what explains this is an ontologically primitive form of value. The *de facto* many is as it is because it is good to be that way, or because its nature is to participate in some value form. Now, we must ask whether this primitive value, the Good, is determinate or indeterminate. It obviously cannot be a determinate structure, Brumbaugh would agree, for then it would be on all fours with the ordered structures it is supposed to govern; we have already agreed that it cannot be interdefinable with or determinate over against the determinate many it structures. But if it is not determinate, can it be completely indeterminate? The answer here again is obviously no, since if it were completely indeterminate it could not select one order as opposed to any other. What Brumbaugh and Plato propose is a middle ground between these two horns of a dilemma. Absolutely in itself, the Good can be completely indeterminate. But the Good is never absolutely in itself, for it is related to the systems of *dianoia* as a selective principle. Insofar as it is related to the structures of the determinations, it must be schematized in terms of them, as it were. The schemata the Good takes on are, first, determinate forms of wholeness or unity that serve as the one for the determinate many and, second, the schemata of wholeness or unity for the specific things that need to be normatively ordered, these schemata being analogical variations on simplicity, consistency, and completeness. Like good schemata, the Platonic ones combine the heterogeneous elements of the poles related; they combine the normativeness of the Good with the determinateness of the many; they are what Brumbaugh calls "normative forms." But good schemata also need a middle ground homogeneous with the elements related, in virtue of which the heterogeneous elements are combined. The need for this middle ground exhibits itself in the fact that of the many determinate orders possible some must be selected as normative; for example, why is wholeness better than partiality? Yet what can be the middle ground, homogeneous to the completely indeterminate Good and the determinations in the cosmological system? The answer that Plato sketches in the *Republic* is that the Good is the creator of the determinations and that the creative act is the middle ground. This is the side of Plato taken up by the cosmogonic Neo-Platonists. But as our own cosmogonic reflections have discovered, the consequence of this line is that there is an arbitrariness in the selection of the orders that are to be normative. That the Good creates the determinate forms, including the schemata as normative forms, explains how some forms can have a normative status with respect to the other ones; but it does not explain why they and not the others have that status. This is a very un-Platonic consequence, as Brumbaugh well sees, and even the Neo-Platonists like Plotinus hesitated to draw it out. Brumbaugh recognizes the seeds of the cosmogonic approach in Plato and acknowledges that it is intended to cope exactly with the problem of the homogeneity in the schemata; but he puts it down to a problematic mystery.[5]

The *de facto* unities of the determinations are harmonies, and these harmonies are normative; harmony itself is normative. But the fact that harmony is the form it is and that certain patterns are harmonious whereas others are not depends contingently on the nature of creation. Once the nature of harmony is determined, it is normative for the rest. But the nature of harmony is itself contingent in the sense that the explanation of why some things are harmonious and others are not cannot be given in terms of prior selective principles. We must grant, if our discussion of transcendentals is correct,[6] that harmony of some sort is a metaphysically necessary and universal characteristic of the entire created realm. But the very argument that shows the created realm to be contingent and therefore created also shows that a harmony is not a self-explanatory thing.[7]

The point can best be put in Platonic language. Since there are many harmonies, for example, at least one for each determination of being, there must be such a thing as the form of harmony (or the Good) itself, Plato would argue. But what is the form of harmony? It is what is common to all the harmonies, that is, that which makes their patterns harmonious instead of not. But if the form of harmony is just some higher order form, like consistency, coherence, or any of those used by Whitehead to characterize what all harmonies have in common,[8] we must still ask what makes these characteristic of harmony. The form of harmony itself, no matter how well

[5] *Ibid.*, p. 203, n. 20.
[6] See chap. 4, sec. C.
[7] See chap. 3, sec. A.
[8] See Whitehead's chapter on "Beauty," in *Adventures in Ideas* (Cambridge: Cambridge University Press, 1933), pp. 324 ff.

mediated by determinate forms of a higher order than particular harmonies, cannot itself be determinate if it is going to answer the question it is supposed to, that is, why are harmonious patterns harmonious? Because if it were, it would begin an infinite regress. Yet it must be determinate if it is going to select harmonious patterns. The answer we are proposing to this difficulty is that the form of the Good or the form of harmony is what it is because it creates the particular harmonies. It creates them with a character that we know as harmony. In fact, the created character is what we apprehend as determinate being: intellectually it is the nature of truth itself; aesthetically we see it as beauty itself; practically we see it as normativeness itself; and philosophy sees it as the nature of true unity, manifested in real, true, beautiful, good, and unified things. But the form of harmony is determinate only in determinate things; apart from them (and it must also be apart, since they depend for their character on it) it must be indeterminate. Plato may have had this in mind when he wrote about the awarding of prizes in the *Philebus.* What the cosmogonic theory emphasizes, however, is that the dependent connection between the form of harmony itself and the particular harmonies is one of creator-created; only this can supply the homogeneous middle term. This is no mystery. It is at the heart of the solution.

Brumbaugh's approach seems consistent with cosmogony's solution to the problem of homogeneity in the normative forms as schemata relating the pure and indeterminate Good with the world. In terms of the ontological creation theory of cosmogony all determinations are on a par insofar as they are created and have their determinate characters over against each other (for example, a determinate norm must have some determination for which it is normative). What remains is the more metaphysical and less ontological problem of sorting out the first principles of the determinations, relating determinate values to structures, and so forth, all of which concern the content, not the ground, of the created realm. In the metaphysical analysis that would be required for this, we might well agree with the Plato-Brumbaugh interpretation of the relation of determinate values to structures through schemata, with a series of schemata relating a single value to many contexts.

Of the kinds of explanation to be offered to fulfill the needs of dianoetic cosmology, the kind proposed by Brumbaugh's interpretation of Plato by itself does not say enough. It either makes the values primitively determinate, and hence reduces them to the status of the structural system that cannot contain them, or makes the primitive value so indeterminate that it is discontinuous with what it is supposed to order. It should supply the continuity with a cosmogonic view and thereby reduce to the kind of explanation to which it was supposed to be an alternative. This last move puts all norms, insofar as they are determinate, on the side of created being and the explanation of their normativeness on the side of the creator. This does not explain why the normative forms are normative. It only explains how they are normative, and the same thing explains the "how" or contingent reality of the *de facto* unities of all determinations, normative and non-normative; this is the cosmogonic interpretation of what the explanation of the cosmological first principles is supposed to do. What needs to be explained, the contingent reality of the determinations of being, is precisely what the cosmogonic theory of creation aims to explain. The needs of explanation, then, exhibit the very constitutive structure that our ontological reflections in Part One brought us to recognize.

SECTION C
Continuity in Explanation

The third shift in the meaning of explanation involves the continuity of the nature of the explained and the explanation.

1. Cosmology holds that there must be a kind of homogeneity between the subject matter to be explained and the explanation. The terms in which both are articulated must be on a par such that they can be interconnected with each other. This does not mean that one cannot be abstract and the other concrete, or one general and the other specific. But it does mean that there must be such a continuity or homogeneity of logical structure that the explanatory system can serve as the set of premises from which the elements of what is to be explained can be deduced, in a formal or informal sense of deduction.

2. The difficulties with this homogeneity are readily apparent, however, after our previous discussion. They are twofold.

a) Whatever the terms in which both subject matter and its explanation are finally to be articulated, the basic requirement of homogeneity is that both be determinate. Otherwise they could not be related determinately one to the other. But as we have seen, it is the very determinateness of the axioms of the explanatory system that need a further account, for the determinateness involves *de facto* unities, which bespeak the contingent reality of the first principles. Therefore, the homogeneity of a cosmological explanation requires the very determinateness of the first principles that demands that cosmology be transcended.

b) But what kind of continuity is there between the cosmological system and the transcendent reality that, according to cosmogony, explains it? Here we are faced with what appears to be a dilemma. On the one hand, the transcendent explanation must be homogeneous with the cosmological system. Otherwise, the terms of the transcendent explanation could not be connected with the cosmological system enough to explain it in any sense. On the other hand, the transcendent explanation must be heterogeneous with the cosmological explanation. Otherwise, the regress of finding an explanation for the transcendent explanation commences and there is no principle to stop it.

This dilemma provides the dialectical foil for those philosophers who criticize any attempt, including cosmogony, to pursue ontology beyond cosmology. Holding to the demand for homogeneity, they criticize ontologists for not being able to cut off the infinite regress with any intelligible principle. Thus, they say to theologians that if God is the explanatory cause of the world there must be an explanatory cause of God. Or if the ontologists admit the need for heterogeneity, the critics club them for not making an intelligible connection between the cosmological system and its explanation which requires the homogeneity of interdefinable intelligible terms. If the poor theologian then says that God is the explanatory cause of the world but is himself self-caused, he is bludgeoned on the other side for introducing a notion like self-causation whose aseity is unintelligible in terms of the connections of the world.

This dilemma *must* be resolved, however, because of the first difficulty entailed by the homogeneity between the cosmological explanation and what it explains. That is, the cosmological explanation does need a further explanation itself because of the homogeneity of its terms with the determinations of being it explains. Those who employ the dilemma to discredit the enterprise of ontology beyond cosmology have no ground to stand on.

3. We are now in a position to see that cosmogony is the kind of ontology that can get around the dilemma. Cosmogony admits that the terms of transcendent explanation of the cosmological system are homogeneous with the system, even to the extent that they are determinate. Thus, terms like creator, power of creating, indeterminate, and so forth, are determinate terms that connect with our analysis of the fundamental structure of the cosmological system, its own determinateness, and its need for a ground for its contingent reality. As we remarked at the beginning of chapter 2, our answer to the question of being-itself must be determinate, even if the answer is that being-itself is not determinate.

On the other hand, cosmogony claims that the determinate terms of its transcendent explanation in themselves require a distinction between themselves and the reality that they articulate. Thus, to be determinate creator of all determinations, the creator in itself must be indeterminate since it cannot essentially be what depends upon it. The creator must transcend its determinate status as creator in order for it to have that status in any way (even conditionally); and that it have the status of creator in *some* way is required to explain the determinations of being. In order for there to be a creator, the creator must have a side of aseity in which he is so unrelated to the world as not even to be creator.

This last claim of cosmogony points to another dialectical shift from cosmology to cosmogony.

a) Within cosmology, both what is to be explained, the cosmos, and what explains, the axiomatic system, do not recognize any difference between their determinate natures and their reality. If a substance, for instance, has a distinction between its essence and its existence, then the principles of the cosmological system should account for both elements—essence and existence, or nature and reality. Likewise, if there is a difference between the determinate nature of a first principle and its actual functioning to regulate the cosmos, then some other first principles must take account of both sides. Were the determinations not real, there would be no natures for them to have; therefore to deal with the natures of the determinations of being is to deal with their *de facto* reality. To explain the contingent reality of the determinations is the job of what transcends cosmology, but cosmology itself must acknowledge the reality of the natures of the determinations.

b) Since what explains the cosmological system, however, must be heterogeneous with the system in order not to need a further explanation itself, the transcendent reality that explains cannot be identical with the determinate nature it has as explanation. Thus the reality that explains must be indeterminate and in itself incapable of requiring further explanation. There must then be a difference between the essential reality of what explains and the character it has as explanation. Paradoxically, this fact seems to reverse the usual dictum that in finite being there is a difference between essence and reality whereas in God or infinite being there is no such difference. But the paradox is explained by recognizing that in finite reality, although there is no difference between a determination and its reality, there is a difference between contingent reality and that which is not contingent, and that in God, although there is a difference between his reality in itself and the nature he has in virtue of connections with creatures, there is no ground for raising a distinction between essence and reality in God's aseity because no determinate distinctions are possible in that aseity.

c) Cosmogony, as we have seen in Part One, asserts a distinction between the creator in himself and the creator as creator, claiming that the latter is a conditional feature, a determination created along with the other determinations. The structure of the creator-created distinction elaborated in chapter 4 is aimed specifically at meeting this requirement of a distinction between God's reality in itself and the nature he has in virtue of which he is the explanation of the cosmological system. Cosmogony surmounts the dilemma of the required homogeneity and heterogeneity by affirming both sides. The nature of God as creator is the homogeneous explanation of the determinations of being, including the axioms of the cosmological system and their systematic *de facto* unity. Yet the nature of God as creator requires that the reality that creates in itself transcend any determinate character like that of creator, and hence the cosmogonic explanation demands a distinction between the explanatory character of God and his reality. This distinction affirms the other horn of the dilemma, the requirement of heterogeneity, for God in his aseity, apart from any connection with the cosmos, is heterogeneous with the cosmological system and what it explains.

As we found in our reflection about Brumbaugh's alternative to cosmogony, however, any heterogeneity requires a homogeneity if the heterogeneous poles are to be brought together in any way. *Now we must account for the identity of the explanatory character of God as creator with God's reality;* that is, we must show that the conditional feature of being creator is indeed a feature of that which essentially has no determinate features. We need a homogeneity not only between the cosmological system that needs explanation and the character of God that explains it but also between the determinate explanatory character of God and God's reality. As we pointed out in our discussion of Brumbaugh, this homogeneity consists in the fact that God in his aseity is that which creates the determinations of being, including his determinate character as creator; God moves out of his aseity by creating and, having moved out, is creator. Since, as we saw in Part One, the process of creating is an immediate thing, there is no sense to the question as to what God is while he is creator before he has created the determination of creator. Cosmogony can be said to schematize God in his aseity to the world with its theory of creation; the homogeneity required by the schematism is that both the schema and the world are created by God from his aseity.

The heterogeneity between God's reality in his aseity and his explanatory nature as creator is sufficient to stop the infinite regress of explanations, for it is the reality of what explains that would require a further explanation if such a further explanation were possible, which it is not. Now it might be said that it is not God's aseity that needs explanation but only his explanatory feature as creator. What explains that feature? The answer is that it explains itself. That God creates the determinations of being explains the determination he has as creator of the determinations of being. What is required of a self-referential explanation is that it characterize what explains it without characterizing something other than itself. When the feature of creator entails that the creator cannot *essentially* be creator, this is a characterization of the complex requirements of its own determinate nature. To say that God in himself must be indeterminate in order to create the determinations of being is to say nothing positive or determinate about God in his aseity; it is only to say something about the complex feature of being the creator. Cosmogony involves no knowledge about God as he is in himself; it knows God only as he is expressed in his conditional feature. Since the transcendence of God's aseity over any determination is a determinate part of the complex feature of being creator, what explains God's explanatory and conditional nature as creator is that nature itself. The cosmogonic explanation is perfectly self-referential.

SECTION D
The Order of Explanation

The fourth shift in the meaning of explanation concerns the relation that the order of the explanation has to the order of the subject matter, that is, whether some things must be explained first, whether the steps from the first thing explained to the last can be retraced and the move made from last to first, and so forth. One would expect the order of methodological dialectic to fit rather loosely onto the structure of the subject matter and constitutive dialectic to be intricately bound up with the order of the realities it knows.

This is true; what may not be so expected, though equally true, is that the intricate connection between constitutive dialectic and its subject matter requires a peculiar asymmetry, namely, that the order of explanation is directly contrary to the order of being, where the latter means moving from the less dependent to the more dependent. We have noted this point before in discussing the peculiarity of divine transcendence. This shift in the meaning of explanation is crucial to showing that what supplements cosmology is cosmogony and not something else.

1. Within the domain of cosmology there are two stages when the order of explanation bears a distinctive relation to the order in the structure of the subject matter: when methodological dialectic is in the process of trying to work out the first principles, and when the systematic explanation has been made adequate to its subject matter and is being presented (this is the first appearance of constitutive dialectic).

a) When the cosmological explanation is in the stage of its tentative development, its order follows all the turns, excursions, and backsteps that have been described in chapter 6. The order of explanation here reflects the degrees and areas of our own confusions and insights more than any structure in the subject matter. In fact, there is usually a fluttering back and forth between what we anticipate as the end of our dialectical reflection and the detailed arguments of the contemporaneous concerns.

b) When we settle on a systematic conclusion to our reflection, however provisional that conclusion might appear to the results of later thinking, we make the claim that the order of presentation of our explanation is coincident with the various orders in the structure of the subject matter. Depending on how far we may separate the elements in the ideal of system, there can be at least three orders of presentation: the order of analysis of the various first principles of the system, the order of showing how the first principles combine to make up the elements of the world, and the order presenting the interconnections, consistency, and coherence of the first principles. All of these orders must reflect the structure that in combination they are supposed to determine.

But over and above these various orders of presentation of the system there is the order of presenting how the system as a whole explains its subject matter. As we have seen, the system here is an axiomatic-deductive theory that explains its subject matter by deducing the philosophically relevant phenomena, as it were. The explanation is the axioms plus the deductions. The order of presentation here is reciprocal with the subject matter. We can move from the subject matter to the axioms and deductions that explain, or we can move from the explanations back down to the subject matter. There is a difference between the moves: the subject matter does not explain the axioms and deductions, though perhaps it justifies them, and the axioms and deductions do not justify the subject matter, only explain it. Nonetheless, the route from the explained to the explanation can be traveled in either direction.

Insofar as we can say that there is an order of being involved such that the explained world *depends* upon the realities characterized by the axiomatic system, the order of explanation proceeds up the order of being; and our reflection can proceed back down the order of being by reversing the steps of the explanation and following the order of deduction. The order of deducing the elements of the subject matter from the axiomatic system is the same as the order of being, going from the less dependent to the more dependent.

2. The realities characterized by the axiomatic first principles, however, are not completely independent or highest in the order of being, as we have seen. Their *de facto* unities require further explanation by something that transcends the axiomatic system itself and what that system explains. Yet what is the order of the move that explains the cosmological system? We have noted a circular movement within the parts of the system, and a reciprocal movement between the system and what it explains. To be sure, the move from the cosmological system to be explained up to its transcendent explanation is a straight-line move, not a circle, for a circle is possible only among elements all on the same explanatory level and the move from cosmology to what explains it is a move from one level to the next.

The question is, Can the move from cosmology to the transcendent explanation be reciprocal; that is, can the steps be retraced as they can within an axiomatic deductive system? The answer is that they cannot, for reason of the heterogeneity that we noted in the previous section. If the reality of what explains the cosmological first principles is heterogeneous with those principles and with its own character, which explains the cosmology and is homogeneous with the determinate principles, then it is impossible that there be connecting steps that lead from the reality of the explanation back down to what is explained. For such connecting steps would require a homogeneity of determinations between the reality of what explains and the character it has as the explanation, and there cannot be such a homogeneity without initiating an infinite regress of explanations. Therefore, although the move from cosmology to the *explanatory character* of what explains it is reciprocal, the move from there to the *reality* of what explains is not.

3. Cosmogony is compatible with this shift in the significance of explanation, and in fact it is the only theory that is compatible. The move from the determinations to their creator is reciprocal when the creator is interpreted as the determinate character of what creates them. But the move from the determinate character of the creator to what by necessity transcends it is not reciprocal.

We know from the nature of being creator that this nature is dependent upon a reality that cannot be dependent on it. If we were really to move positively to what transcends the nature "creator" and is independent of it, the independence would prohibit us from ever connecting again with the world. We, ourselves, would have to be "created" back into the world. As we noticed in Part One, to say that this reality is transcendent, independent, or even that it is complete in its aseity is not to do justice to what is required by that which creates all determinations, for all these characterizations are relational and characterize by negation. We have no word that indicates the essential reality of God, because all words signify determinately and God cannot essentially be determinate since he is not essentially conditioned by anything with respect to which he can be determinate.

In reality, we do not make an actual move from the conditional feature of creator to the reality of God. We only move around within that feature, noting the self-negating character it has in virtue of its own dependence. This self-negation is enough to make the distinction between the feature and the reality and to establish the necessary heterogeneity; but the content and object of thought always remains within the determinate feature of being creator. There is always the temptation to think that calling the reality of God indeterminate is a way of saying something positive or direct about that reality. But the temptation should always be resisted by recalling that to say that the reality of God is indeterminate is only to say that the determinate feature of being creator cannot, by its own nature, serve as a sign that determines what it depends upon.

Once the distinction between the feature of being creator and the essential reality of God is made, it is necessary that that distinction exhibit some homogeneity. This homogeneity, as we saw in the previous section, consists in the actual creation of the determinations of being by the real God. It is obvious, however, that this homogeneity is strictly in terms of the feature of being creator and does not presuppose any knowledge of God as he is apart from that feature. Again, the self-referential character of cosmogony is apparent.

SECTION E

Summary

We must now bring together the strands of our discussion of constitutive dialectic. With reference to the shift in the conception of the ideal of system, cosmogony conceives it as needing an account of the reality of the cosmological principles, which is but an epistemological way of putting the argument of chapter 3. With these references to the shift in the kind of explanation required to account for the cosmological first principles, cosmogony's answer is that the kind of explanation must be one that accounts for the reality of the principles, not for why they are as they are, which was part of the argument of chapter 3. With reference to the requirements of continuity between the explanation and what it explains, cosmogony answers that the continuity must be both homogeneous and heterogeneous, as is the case only where a homogeneous character is created by a heterogeneous reality; in no other way can the identity of the homogeneous and the heterogeneous elements be accounted for. With reference to the relation between the order of explanation and the order of being, cosmogony's argument that the explanation be not reciprocal because the terminus of the explanation is heterogeneous with what is explained is another way of putting the conclusion of chapter 4.

The most crucial conclusion of our study of constitutive dialectic, however, concerns the way it handles the problem of self-reference. Logicians have argued that a system cannot have demonstrable consistency and completeness at once. Cosmogony abides by this argument in allowing that no system of determinations is complete, for the determinations make necessary reference to what is not a determination but the ground of the reality of the determinations. Yet what is left out of the system of determinations can never be included within our philosophical system to render demonstrable consistency possible because it can never be reached directly or positively. Our only approach to it is through the character of the created determination of being *creator,* a character that negates itself, as it were, through its own dependency. And though we approach the supradeterminate reality through the determination of being *creator,* we never get beyond that determination, for our approach is bound to the terms of the function of creating. We know the indeterminateness, the absolute transcendence, the independence, the aseity, of God in himself only insofar as it gets incarnated in the created determination of being *creator.* And the relational character of those terms that are supposed to bespeak unrelatedness testify to the incarnation in determinateness of our knowledge of God.

The conditional feature of God as creator explains the cosmological system insofar as it needs explanation, that is, insofar as it is determinate with the contingent reality of determinations. The explanation of that conditional feature would also be required to explain it just insofar as it is a determination. And therefore it explains itself and is self-referential.

The paradox of explanation, as we noted far above, requires that the explanation of something both be different from the thing explained in order that an advance be made and be the same as the thing in order that it not be false in identifying something with its contrast. Cosmology resolves the paradox with the circle of explanation, but it cannot account for the contingent reality of the circle as a whole. Cosmogony accounts for that contingent reality and resolves the paradox by advancing beyond the thing explained to the creator, counting the creator both as determinate among the things explained (hence one with them) and as real beyond them. But the difference between what is beyond and what is among the determinations is determined by the determination of being *creator,* and hence the required identity is re-established. Only the identity of a creator with his product (his creating and the determinate status as creator being part of the product) can identify the difference between what is explained and the reality of the explanation. This is the theory of cosmogony.

8

The Testimonies of Experience

Philosophical reflection is not pure argumentation. If it were, rare indeed would be philosophical conviction. No matter how recondite, philosophical arguments must meet the approval of experience if they are to be more than moves in a game. Even the rules of argument gain their trustworthiness primarily from the fruits they bear in experience. Experience is an almost ubiquitous element of dialectic. Exactly where it fits in has been the occasion for great confusion in philosophy. The nature of experience itself is one of the most hotly contested of philosophical issues, and when the experience in question has to do with God and religion, the heat of the contest is often of the lightless sort.

The early pragmatists seemed to have a clue when they claimed that the function of argument is to get us into the position where some worthwhile experience is possible. Although this thesis was intended to have a very general range, including moral, asthetic, and cultural experience, we need to consider it only insofar as it applies to philosophical experience, that is, the experience that warrants philosophical conviction. Philosophical ideas and principles, theories and systems, are terms for interpreting experience; they are "interpretants," to use Peirce's word. Without the proper interpretants to articulate it, a subject matter cannot be experienced. Thus, at least one of the functions of philosophical reflection is to develop interpretants that make the experience of certain things possible. The actual experience, in turn, provides warrant for accepting the interpretants. Whatever the ultimate motive, whether to get the experience or to find the true theory, experience and argumentation do have this back-scratching relationship.

SECTION A
Religious and Philosophical Interpretations

A person must be interested in interpreting a subject matter in certain respects if he is to make any interpretation of it at all. Therefore, we must pay attention to the common interest in interpreting the created realm with respect to its created status. What kind of interest this is, is a crucial problem. Although the interest involves interpreting the created realm as a sign of God, it would be a mistake to identify this interest with the religious concern. Religious concern usually is a person's concern for salvation. It has especially to do with the relation of a person to God, and although this relation may involve that of "being the creature of," the focus and emphasis is different from the philosophical interest in interpreting the created realm as a sign of God. The philosophical interest need not be abstract in a bad sense, nor the experience it means to interpret an empty one. Admittedly, the signs that carry off the interpretation may be as complex as a whole theory and the experience may be so articulate that only a philosopher could have it. Moreover, the philosophical interest may not be so important for the person as the religious interest. But this is not to say anything against either one.

However much the philosophical interest in interpreting the created realm is not to be confused with a person's interest in his own salvation, the opposite error of thinking them to be totally unconnected or even contrary concerns is also to be avoided. In principle there is a continuum between the two extremes that covers the whole ground in the middle. This point is abundantly clear when attention is drawn to the mystical or Neo-Platonic tradition. Is the driving concern governing the thinking of Bonaventure, for instance, philosophical or religious? Surely it is religious, even though it goes far beyond "accepting Jesus Christ as Lord"; yet on the other hand, his thought is philosophical, in fact dialectical in the extreme. Communion with God is impossible without the stages of the prior discipline, according to this tradition, and at the end we have not only communion but the understanding as well. According to Richard of St. Victor: "We shall make progress gradually by the effort of work, by the effort of mediation, by the effort of prayer, and at length we shall obtain perfect knowledge." [1] Without doubt he means the end product of his work, meditation, and prayer to be communion with God, but he calls it perfect knowledge.

Certainly enough has happened in the Western tradition since the heyday of the contemplators to make this blend of religion and philosophy an unstable thing. The drive to make philosophy an antiseptic science and the opposing drive to secure the saving word from dissolution into pure theory have given rise to the belief that, if a person's philosophical and religious concerns are not clearly segregated, they should be. Yet, if knowledge is not pure reason but essentially involves experience, then the things of God and creation cannot be known properly without that experience to which religion lays partial claim. And on the other side, religion must acknowledge that although the problem for most people is first to see that the medium of salvation is at hand and to appropriate it, for some people, especially those who have accepted salvation and say, Now what? the problem is to know what they have. Piety cannot exist without understanding. So while the

[1] "Benjamin Minor," *Richard of St. Victor: Selected Writings on Contemplation*, trans. C. Kirchberger (London: Faber & Faber, Ltd., 1957), p. 117.

interest in interpreting the created realm as a sign of God is to be pursued
with all philosophic rigor, it is still bound up with the interests of religion, at
least when the latter is interpreted in a broad sense.

SECTION B

Abstract Philosophical Interpretations

As we would expect, the fundamental interpretation of the created realm as a
sign for God as creator involves an apprehension of real distinctions with an
acknowledgment, perhaps explicit but nearly always implicit, of some or all
of the features pointed out in chapter 2. The basic interpretation is that God
is present as the creator of the really distinct things. For any two things to be
really distinct, two relations must hold between them; on the one hand, there
is a relation of contrast where they are seen as different; on the other hand,
there is a relation of mutual involvement, what Weiss calls "merging," where
they are seen as connected. The standpoint from which the contrast is seen
must be the common one of mutual involvement; and conversely, the acknowledgment of the mutual involvement must accompany and cannot precede an appreciation of the differences. The contrast relation acknowledges
the different essential features of the distinct things over against each other;
the mutual involvement relation acknowledges the features each has in virtue
of the fact that it is involved with the other. The two relations are unified by
whatever it is in each of the distinct things that unifies its essential features
with the conditional ones it has in virtue of its involvement with other
things. The presupposition of the relations on which the real distinction is
founded is being-itself as the common creator. This creator God is at the
foundation of any really distinct determinations of being, and many aspects
of such a real distinction testify to his presence, as we shall catalogue. There
are at least as many logical types of interpretations of the created realm as a
sign for God as there are features of a real distinction that testify to the
contingency and dependence of the determinations. A brief description
should be given of each of the features of real distinctions that testify to God.
This schematic approach will be supplemented with a more thorough discussion in Part Three.

  1. The essential features of a thing, in contrast to the essential features of
those things from which it is distinct, can testify to the creator's grounding
the distinction. This is exemplified in experience of a work of art or a unique
personality. In experiences like these the essence of the testifying object is
focused on and the contrast of the idiosyncracies of that essence over against
all else is the principle of focus. The contrast terms are usually vague, but it is
the contrast of the uniqueness of this thing over against all else that gives
force to the experience. Although it is not usually understood *how* God is the
foundation of this essence, the essential features are taken as testimony to his
creation.

  2. The conditional features of a thing stemming from its mutual involve-

Charles S. Peirce

ment with other things can also testify to the creator. This is the kind of experience of mutual involvement and connection so impressive to scientists and inquirers; Charles Peirce has the classic discussion of this kind of experience in his "neglected argument," although his treatment of connections is highly general. His argument, in fact, is based upon the naturalness with which the apprehension of mutual involvement of distinct things leads to the suggestion of God.[2] This experience should not be confused, although the distinction is only one of degree, with an intense appreciation of the integrity of systematic connections, an experience more akin to the aesthetic one discussed just above. The experience of interconnection is forceful in the sense now being considered when the mutual involvement is *discovered* where before chaos seemed dominant.

3. A third kind of testimony to God within real distinctions is the *de facto* unity of the essential and conditional features. This is the experience of awe at the fact that a thing can maintain its integrity in the midst of an environment that threatens to reduce it to a confluence of influences. More than an appreciation of its involvement, this experience appreciates the unity of these two. The most forceful example of such a thing is the hero, conquering or tragic. Most poignant is the appreciation of integrity in those cases where it is lost after the utmost defense, in tragic heroism. However much the dissolution of the hero's integrity into the external arms of fate and circumstance is due to his own mistakes, the greatness of the struggle testifies to the power of God. Without a doubt, this kind of experience in the religious domain is mixed with many other factors—judgments of justice and justification, pleas for mercy, and acknowledgment in awe of man's helplessness in the last analysis—but fundamental to all these factors is the appreciation of the unity or integrity that men may fulfill or lose as creations of God.

4. An added dimension that can be present in any of these three experiences is the factor of contingency. This is the experience of being filled with wonder that the object focused on in the experience is at all. Certain experiences involve a sense that the feature at hand might not be, that there is no rationale why it should not be absolutely nothing. This kind of experience builds upon the three types previously mentioned in that what is focused on as a sign of God's creating activity is isolated and considered in its own nature apart from the background in which it is implicated. The experience of contingency does not deny that its object is in fact implicated in a causal nexus; but the object is experienced as not wholly reducible to the causal influences. This sort of thing is experienced in a focus on the essential features of a distinct thing when, for instance, we admit that "the grass withers, the flower fades"; it is experienced in a focus on the mutual interplay of distinct things when we see a great solar system burst and fail; and it is

[2] See his paper "A Neglected Argument for the Reality of God," in *Collected Papers of Charles Sanders Peirce*, ed. C. Hartshorne and P. Weiss (Cambridge, Mass.: Harvard University Press, 1931), VI, 452–92.

experienced in a focus on the integrity of a man's inward nature together with the impingements of his context when we see a tragic figure fall. The contingency is always highlighted when being fails or is jeopardized.

A scheme now has emerged of the logical types of experiences wherein the created realm gives testimony to a creator. Three formal features of determinations of being really distinct from each other can testify to a creator, and each of these in two ways. The essential features of a thing, the interplay of two things that gives rise to their conditional features, and the union of these two in the integrity of each thing are experienced as testimony. And for each of these three features, either the determinateness of the determinations can be the testimony or the contingency of the being of the determinations can testify (this latter was pointed out as a dimension added to the former). These two ways in which features of really distinct things can be taken as signs of God focus respectively on that aspect of creation wherein the power of being is itself productive of the determinations and on that aspect wherein the being of the determinations is contrasted with absolute non-being by their creator's power.

The experiences in which something of the created realm is taken as testimony for a creator's presence are not clear cut and distinct; often such experiences mix several of the types singled out above. The point cannot be emphasized too much that the logical grounds upon which these features of the created world are taken as signs of God's presence are usually obscure or even totally implicit. The grounds are particularly hard to find in analysis of a given experience when that experience is of only one aspect of the really distinct things, for the grounds are to be understood with respect to the whole. God is no less the source of the essence of a thing than he is of the conditional features, and the essence by itself can testify to him. But to understand *how* he is the source of the essence is to understand how he is the source of all those elements that go into making up a determination of being really distinct from other determinations. A person experiencing God in one of these testifying signs need not know the argument about the dialectic of creation given in the above chapters; but the critical justification of such an interpreted experience requires laying out that dialectic. This is the same situation as when one interprets a person's words as a sign of friendship without explicitly understanding why those words do express friendship. But on the other hand, just as one would not interpret a person's words as a sign of friendship unless one had at least some reason to suspect they meant friendship, so a person would not take parts of the created realm as signs of a creator unless at least something like the dialectic of creation were implicit in the interpretative experience.

The vividness of a flower, or its transience, the intricacy of the solar system, or the tragedy of a great man fallen can be appreciated for what they are and nothing more. But if they are understood to be caught up in the dialectic of the ontology of creation, then their very determinateness can become an interpretant for articulating the presence of God as creator. To focus on any of the elements of a determination of being that we have catalogued is to become vaguely aware of the others and of their *de facto* unity, which testifies to God. Men in all ages have taken factors like those we have singled out as elements of testimony. Of course, besides the testimony we need the arguments that take us from the testimony to the conclusions about God; many thinkers and less reflective people have not been conscious of these arguments or even of the need for them. But the arguments have been defended in Part One.

SECTION C

Religious versus Philosophical Experience

Experiences like the ones discussed in the past section are important and should not be overlooked by theologians and religious thinkers. But their importance is not great for the justification of philosophical theories about the transcendence of God, for they are too close to the "premise" end of the argument to provide much convincing warrant for the theory. The most they can do is indicate that the theory of divine creation is a natural and easy suggestion that occurs to man. The naturalness of the cosmogonic suggestion is surely sufficient to give it considerable initial plausibility and to justify its thorough investigation, but it is not enough to warrant conviction in a critical philosopher.

What is needed for critical conviction is experience on some higher and speculatively more contentious level. Some of the articulated conclusions need to be connected with experience. Of course not everything in a complicated philosophical theory is the sort of thing that we should be able to experience directly. On the other hand, many of the philosophers who have done noteworthy thinking about the problems of God's transcendence, those in the Thomistic tradition, seem to have been unnecessarily limited in what they considered as experienceable. True, much of what we experience comes through our senses, but modern philosophy and science have shown that what does come through the senses is much more complex than just sights, sounds, smells, tastes, and touches. After the work of the pragmatists, we know, for instance, that the grasp of a situation as tense or poignant, the feeling that a person is friendly or happy, and our intuitions of the "mood of the country" are closer to sensations than they are to explicitly reasoned inferences. And we also know that the sensation of colors, sounds, and the obvious sensibles involves a kind of interpretative response to a bunch of unconscious data with a conscious sensible sign. The line between brute sensation and reasoned inference is now recognized to be a blurred one, and insofar as it can be made, it is drawn not so much in terms of the kinds of entities that are thought but in terms of the degree to which the interpretative process is subject to critical control. When we are unable to exercise critical control over some interpretative response, we say that it is on the side of sensation, and our critical inabilities constitute its bruteness. And when we are able to exercise critical control, subjecting our principles of interpretation to standards, we say that our experience is shot through with conscious inference. Many interesting problems are posed by the fact that in some domains of experience, for example, art appreciation, critical control can be learned.

The upshot of this recent expansion of the notion of experience is that preliminary confidence is warranted for the possibility of experiencing directly (though with the mediation of signs or interpretants) any real thing whose nature can be articulated or recognized by some complex interpretant. As we noted before, theory construction, in philosophy as well as in art, morals, and so forth, now has the added task of working out conceptual structures that can serve to articulate some possible experience. Nothing is ever experienced unless it is experienced *as* something; and if the conception in terms of which the thing is to be experienced is impossible to us, the experience itself is impossible.

There is hope that some of the crucial elements of our theory of divine transcendence are subject to experiential encounter. This hope must be acknowledged, at least in principle, even by those who explain away alleged religious experience as a manifestation of something else. No one can deny that those who claim religious experience do experience something. Whether the reality of what is experienced is an undigested bit of beef, as Scrooge thought, or a surge of guilt about one's failings to the father image, as some Freudians argue, or the true divinity itself is a matter to be decided by a complexity of factors. These include the persistence, consistency, and pervasiveness of the experience but also and not least the over-all adequacy of the theory in terms of which the experience is articulated. Therefore, if some theory should show the experience of something to be possible, and even likely under certain conditions, it is implausible that all alleged experiences of it should be interpreted as misinterpretations of something else, however much some of them seem to be so.

The question now is, Where do we look for confirming experience for our theory of divine transcendence? In chapter 4, we made a correlation between the explicit terms of our ontological theory of being-itself and the traditional terms of a theory of divine creation that come from religion. This would suggest that there are two places to look for the confirming experience, in religion and in "philosophical experience." Theoretically both should be possible.

Philosophical experience is a strange notion, but it is not unheard of. It would be the experience of a reality by a philosopher who has developed conceptual categories that make its apprehension possible. Philosophers do not often focus on such experience, but it is evident that many have had it about various things and have been guided and convinced by it, even with respect to an abstract theory about God. Spinoza is an example of a man whose piety and devotion shines through the "geometrical" demonstrations.

This is the kind of piety that comes only from pervasive, life-transforming experience, not just "an" experience but the cumulative and varied experience of a lifetime.

It was the strategy of Schleiermacher, probably the most systematic and sensitive religious thinker of the nineteenth century, to translate the dogmas of traditional religion into connections with a philosophical theory of the absolute dependence of the created realm on God, an absolute dependence that could be "felt" or experienced. He translated the terms of the religious life into those of a philosophical theory and located the convincing experience in the philosophical terms. His motive was to remove the crucial tests from the arena of religion where they were rather defenseless against skeptical attacks and locate them in a philosophically defensible arena that was both the skeptics' alleged home ground and the ground where Schleiermacher thought the skeptics could be refuted. In many respects this was a successful strategy in Schleiermacher's day, and it even has much force today. But in the long run, for the sake of conviction with respect to theories about God, the best strategy seems to be to emphasize the translation in the other direction.

There are several difficulties with philosophical experience. To begin with, although it enjoys the advantage of being very articulate, its very articulateness renders it abstract almost to the point of barrenness. Yet the experience that convinces must be so much a part of life that to deny it borders on self-contradiction. Furthermore, philosophers are more likely than not to prejudice their experience by their theories, overlooking the obvious in focusing on the abstruse. Finally, and most importantly, concentration on philosophical experience, paradoxically, gives up a kind of objectivity and publicity to experience of God that can ill afford to be given up, for the experience of religious traditions is immense, pervasive, and colossally well documented. The better strategy for philosophy is to render an account of things that allows the testimony of the religious tradition to be taken more or less at face value rather than to limit itself to the experiential tests of private philosophers.

Therefore, in Part Three we shall develop the correlations of the ontological theory with the terms of religion and elaborate the role this plays in the experience of religions. This is no depreciation of the possibility, legitimacy, and conviction of strictly philosophical experience for some people. It is only an attempt to make clear the broadest possible base for experiential conviction. One of the difficulties with Schleiermacher's strategy is that it is often a mistake to think that the home base for religious skepticism is philosophy, although the skeptics would have us think that it is. Rather, skepticism has no home of its own but is parasitic on what it attacks, and this is the case with much religious skepticism. Therefore, the proper place to counter it is to straighten it out about religion and open to it the religious avenues of experiential conviction.

SECTION D

Experience, Proof, and Criticism

There have been some thinkers, notably Tillich, who have maintained that conviction about the transcendent God, whether from the philosophical or the religious side, is not primarily a matter of experience at all, and still less of proof. Conviction about the reality of God is not a matter of proof because the very context in which a proof is possible, the context that allows the question of God's reality to be raised, presupposes God as its ground.[3] The distinction between the knowing subject and the object of experience likewise presupposes God as the prius or ground of real distinction, argues Tillich.[4] Hence the reality of God is too close to us for our convictions in its regard ever to be weighed in any argumentative or experiential balance.

Happy as this position would be if it were true, the experience of generations unfortunately forces us to admit that the situation is not as easy as all that. A brief thought brings us several reasons why.

1. Concerning specific proofs for God's reality, as with any proofs, the conclusions are presupposed in the premises plus the contexts of the arguments (the contexts of the meanings of the terms, the acceptance of the rules of inference, and so forth). If the conclusion were not presupposed, the reasoning would be logically invalid. Our interest in proofs is not to produce a conclusion out of nothing but rather to discover in fact whether it is presupposed by what is already accepted. The difficulty with proofs for the reality of God is not that they are circular in this sense but rather that the acceptance of the premises and the context of argument must be justified; it has been the experience of the philosophical tradition that the full justification of this cannot stop short of the defense of a complete philosophical view. That is, the justification must include a theory of logic to give the argument its form, a full speculative interpretation of the realities involved to give the terms of the argument meaning, and a comprehensive theory of knowledge that can justify both the logic and the speculation. Those periods in history when specific proofs for the reality of God have had their heyday have been those when comprehensive views like those of Aristotle, Plato, or eighteenth century mechanism have been taken almost for granted. Today, when no such comprehensive view carries the victory, proofs for God's reality must be much more expansive and thoroughgoing in their philosophical analyses.

2. This brings us to another difficulty with Tillich's view. Although God may actually be presupposed by any rational consideration of him, the theory that he is so presupposed is one theory among others and must be justified as

[3] See Tillich's *Systematic Theology* (Chicago: University of Chicago Press, 1951), I, 204–8; and his *Theology of Culture*, ed. R. C. Kimball (New York: Oxford University Press, 1959), p. 25.
[4] See *Theology of Culture*, pp. 24 ff.

the true one. When conviction is the point at issue, the issue depends upon justifying the comprehensive philosophical view in terms of which God is the presupposition for the question of God. Outside of the context of a justified full-scale view, the claim that the question of God presupposes the reality of God can only sound dogmatic in the bad sense.

3. With respect to the claim that God grounds the distinction between subject and object in experience and hence cannot become merely an object for experience, if this claim is true, then God is present in the experiential situation and, as the mystics have recorded, can be recognized experientially in that situation. But that God is the presupposition of all experience cannot be a staunch conviction unless again the theory articulating him as such is justified. And the theory is necessary for recognizing him in the encounter with all experience. The warrant for holding the theory that God is present in all experience might come in part from the actual encounter of him there; but the encounter requires that we be equiped with the right interpretants in terms of which we can recognize him. Here again argument and experience must co-operate to produce conviction.

The very quickness of these objections to Tillich's view, however, suggests that his view should be interpreted on a deeper level. This suggestion is reinforced by the fact that Tillich himself did not rest with the truth of the claim that God is presupposed by the question of God but gave one of the most elaborate and powerful apologetics for this view that the twentieth century has seen. He has been strikingly successful in rendering the philosophical view required by his theory about the prius comprehensible in modern terms, and persuasive.

Furthermore, our own conclusions support the contention that God is presupposed in any argument or experience that concerns him, for God is the ground of real distinctions. And there must be a real distinction between the subject who knows and experiences and the object known or encountered, since without a real distinction there would not be enough integrity in each side for the knowledge or experience to make a difference in the state of affairs. Therefore, if experience of one thing by another is possible, or if an argument is to be not only valid but also true by virtue of a reference to a real object, then the real distinction is presupposed and God is the ground of that. If our ontological theory about the contingency of determinateness and the creatorly nature of God is true, then Tillich's point about the ubiquitous presupposition of God is also true. But to be convinced of the latter requires prior conviction of something like the former, which means that the argumentation and experience that reflection brings to the problems of religion are not without their importance.

If Tillich's theory about the ubiquity of God is true, then there must be something more profound going on than appears superficially in his claims about the function of argument and experience in conviction about God. Let us return to the conclusion of the previous section, which was that conviction concerning the ontological theory about God requires corroborating experience and that this experience is best found in the religious traditions. The difficulty with the *experiences* of the religious life is that they require philosophical reflection to render an account of them and to justify their prima facie interpretation. It was this observation that began our whole study. The philosophical reflection must make a difference to the religious experience. The experience that gives conviction to our philosophical conclusions may be the same as that which required the reflection in the first place, but it is considerably refined and chastened when we return to it the second time. The experience of the religious traditions is preferable to "philosophical experience" in part because it is closer to life; but philosophical reflection must render the experience of life so clear and articulate that its deliverances are critical. This is the job of philosophy in all domains, not only that of religion. The move from philosophical reflection to experience in living religion and back again is not a swing of a pendulum from one extreme to another but rather more like a series of sorties in many directions at once. After a while, conviction does not depend so much on the success of a reference to an external test as it does upon cumulative reinforcement of continuing articulation in every move.

This wedded union of reflection and experience, however, is only an ideal today, not a real possibility. Not since the days of the medieval contemplators has communal life had sufficient unity to take reflective argument and experience together. For us, they must be kept external as tests for each other. Yet the medieval ideal is the one by which our present efforts are guided and is what would fulfill those efforts. The kind of conviction that we would like with respect to both our reflective arguments and the more immediate interpretations of our experience is the conviction that can come only when reflection and experience are perfectly wedded as the medieval Augustinians thought they were.

Tillich is well known for his identification with the medieval contemplators.[5] And the critical conviction he has in mind is on the level where the medievals operated. In our present situation, where experience and reflection must be kept external to each other as checks, his claims about the needlessness (and even perversity) of proofs and experiential tests are plainly inappropriate. But having reached the level of the contemplators, they have their point. If the terms of our ontological speculations of Part One, for instance, should be so reinforced by continual experience and reflection that any alternatives to them would quickly be seen to be impossible, then to ask whether the proof for the transcendence of God is valid would be to assert a doubt where no reason for a doubt could be found; the effect of this would be perversity. Likewise, having wrought in our speculations the convictions of the contemplators, if we asked for a specific experience of God, this would be to tear the whole fabric of our experience through which God is pervasive and to render both that specific part and the whole from which it was torn subject to distortion and doubt.

[5] See *ibid.*, chap. 2.

If we were to reach the happy union of experience and reflection characteristic of the contemplators, both philosophy and religion would be transformed. Philosophy would lose its abstractness and become concrete and
philosophical experience would be as concrete as, and in fact identical with,
religious experience. Religious experience would not only take on the articulateness philosophy would require of it, but it would also reach a profounder
level. Religious experience would be so much at the heart of the essentials of
life that what we can understand of people's religious experience by reading
their accounts of it would appear a superficial travesty. We have a sense that
there is something slightly inappropriate in citing the recorded experience of
the religious traditions as confirming experiential evidence for a theory. This
feeling comes from the fact that genuinely profound religious experience
cannot be described except in abstract terms, which are precisely the terms
that do not convey the real thing. Although we may cite the relatively public
experience of the religious traditions as confirming evidence for our relatively
abstract ontological speculations, what those speculations ultimately need,
both with respect to their own form and the kind of conviction they should
have, is a level of experience that transcends anything so publicly communi-
cable.

Given the present situation, the most that can be done is to show how both
speculation and the experience of the religious traditions tend to converge at
a higher point. Considering abstractly what this convergence would be like,
we can say from the side of the ontological speculations that conviction
would have progressed up the ladder of explanation to the point where it
possessed God as creator. At this point, the ground for the conviction would
not be the prior explanations but the ground for the feature of being creator,
which is the unconditionally transcendent God himself. Here Tillich would
be right that the ground for the conviction would be neither argument nor
experience but the reality that makes the question of the conviction possible.
On the side of the religious experience, we would expect the problematic
character of religious experience, that is, the quest for salvation in some form
or other, to be overcome or resolved when the object of the quest is attained.
The content of the religious experience would no longer be apprehended in
terms of the quest for salvation but strictly in terms of the reality that we had
looked on before as the source of religious fulfillment. In religious terms, we
would expect to apprehend God in his own glory and not in our glory as
those he saves. Whether this expectation as to the outcome of religious
experience is warranted is the main problem to which we must turn in Part
Three.

Critical philosophy requires a conviction that in turn requires a level of
experience that transcends or amalgamates the usual distinctions we make
between philosophical reflection and the experience of the religious traditions. It may be a tragedy that the whole cloth of experience and thought is in
shreds today. But the adventure of our time is to reweave it.

Part Three

Preliminary Remarks

————————————

Speculative philosophy is both an end in itself, satisfying its own curiosity, and a means employed by other concerns of life to understand themselves. In terms of its own curiosity, speculative philosophy needs a specialized domain of experience to try its conclusions in. Religion proves itself a fitting testing ground for speculative problems, especially those of the transcendence and presence of God. Furthermore, religion is one of the concerns of life for which speculative philosophy is a means of self-understanding. On both accounts, therefore, we have cause for discussing certain problems of religion in terms of our speculative theory of the transcendence and presence of God.

To bring philosophy and religion together, however, requires that we find a prima facie integrity in religion as a subject matter that can stand over against speculation as a testing ground. There are two more or less distinct loci of religion's integrity over against philosophical reflection.

The first is the complex of the orthodox theological traditions. The significance of the term "orthodox" here is that the theologians in question take as their task the elaboration and defense of religion as it is focused in the canonical texts and historical *kairoi* of their peculiar religious traditions. The theologians would thus identify themselves as Muslim theologians or Jewish or Christian. The significance of the term "theology" is that it is a disciplined reflection that seeks to articulate the religion in more or less intellectual claims that connect up with the best in the whole of the intellectual culture. This may take a rather poetic form, as is the case with religious thinkers like Aeschylus; but more often it reaches its highest quality in those thinkers who connect religion with philosophy. The significance of speaking of the "complex" of the orthodox theological traditions is that the traditions, at least in the West, have influenced each other so much that the intellectual terms in which they formulate their claims are often common to them all. Thus, for instance, the Muslim theologians first claimed Aristotle and the thirteenth century Christian and Jewish theologians, in employing Aristotelianism, were hard pressed to defend their purity over against Islam.

The second locus of a prima facie integrity of religion over against philosophy is in what is often called the phenomenology of religion. By this is meant the various manifestations of religion as recorded by thinkers like William James,[1] G. van der Leeuw,[2] Mircea Eliade,[3] and others.[4] The integrity of the phenomenology of religion consists neither in the purity of a phenomenologically bracketed description (a notion not defended by any of the thinkers mentioned) nor in the wholeness or completeness of any selective principle. Rather, the integrity consists in the very lack of such a powerful principle that might prejudice the case in favor of some philosophical scheme; the phenomenology of religion serves as a good test for philosophical theories because its massing of data, when the work of several phenomenologists is considered, is too inclusive and naïve to be based on a question-begging selective principle. Of course, this independent integrity of the phenomenology of religion is only a relative matter; no one can escape entirely the selective principles built into the very structure of experience. But since the price for complete independence would be lack of communicability between philosophy and religion, we can make the best of our relativity.

We should be careful to bear in mind that the integrity of both theology and phenomenology is only prima facie or provisional. Both theology and phenomenology lead to philosophy for fulfillment. In particular, theology aspires to be the knowledge of God, and not just the testimony about him given by one tradition, in which the distinction between these two is apparent; therefore, theology, even if it remains primarily kerygmatic, must include philosophy for its integrity to persevere to the end. Phenomenology, although its strength lies in its original naïveté cannot maintain its integrity in the face of opposition unless it moves into philosophical reflection to formulate and to defend the selective principles it thinks should guide its investigation. When pressed, phenomenology must unite itself with systematic reflection.

Furthermore, the result of the discussion in Part Two was that philosophical reflection and its experiential subject matter, in this case religion, should be in integral external opposition to each other only in the short run; in the long run they must be woven together as one cloth. Consequently, the integrity of religion over against philosophical reflection should be maintained only as long as it takes us to unite them in such a way that the critical

---

[1] See his *Varieties of Religious Experience* (New York: Longmans, 1902).
[2] See his *Religion in Essence and Manifestation,* trans. J. E. Turner (2 vols; London: Allen & Unwin, Ltd., 1938).
[3] See his *Patterns in Comparative Religion,* trans. R. Sheed (Cleveland: World Publishing Co., 1963); *The Sacred and the Profane,* trans. W. Trask (New York: Harcourt, Brace & Co., 1959); *The Myth of the Eternal Return* (New York: Pantheon Books, Inc., 1954).
[4] Classic works, like those of Otto and E. O. James, are too numerous to detail. Other sources of phenomenology of religion, as this term is used here, are to be found in anthropological and historical writings.

control is solely in the hands of the total subject matter and is not a matter of method versus result.

The work of Part Three of our study is at the heart of what is called the philosophy of religion. As John E. Smith has best pointed out, philosophy of religion is the encounter of philosophy and religion wherein each is criticized and supplemented by what it needs besides itself.[5] We are in a position where both our philosophical reflection and religion have a provisional integrity over against each other. The temptations should not be strong either to derive our philosophy of religion from religion alone or to derive it from philosophy alone by a combination of a priori deduction and prejudicial selection of supporting facts. These temptations nearly always are the corruption of philosophy of religion. The only way they can be avoided is by proper restraint. If philosophy of religion is attempted straight from the side of religion, before philosophical reflection has developed itself to the limits of its internal systematic ideal, the attempt usually results in a philosophical generalization of some particular religion; not only is this parochial in itself, but it denies philosophy its own creative integrity and often makes impossible the connection of philosophy of religion with other domains of philosophy. On the other hand, if philosophy of religion is postponed until after the philosophical system in hand has deduced what it thinks religion ought to be, the result is usually a sterile conception that no genuinely religious man would acknowledge. Philosophy of religion must postpone its work until philosophical reflection has discovered the integrity of its internal ideal; but it must begin its work before philosophy can jump to make its external tests internal ones only.

We must still ask what the product of philosophy of religion should be. Scientifically minded philosophers might be inclined to argue that the product should be a comparison of religion's data with speculation's conclusions. This conception has the advantage of unprejudicial objectivity, but it also has several disadvantages. On the one hand, religion's "data" is hardly well formed according to scientific principles. Even the simplest testimonies of religion, either in theology, phenomenology, or religious experience, are shot through with philosophical influences and with the attempts of aesthetic imagination to articulate things vividly. Religion's data must be taken up internally, not compared externally. On the other hand, speculation's conclusions are not ready for comparison unless they have been set out with implicit appropriateness for religious subject matter. But in this case, it is not pure speculation. We must admit that the speculation of Part One is not pure and has been readied with an eye to religion from the beginning. Furthermore, a mere comparison of speculative conclusions with religious data would not get us as far as we want, for we want both to determine something of the truth of religion and something of the worth of speculation. Therefore, religion and speculation must be woven together from the inside of each.

[5] See *Reason and God* (New Haven, Conn.: Yale University Press, 1961), chaps. 7 and 13.

The new cloth must of necessity be a kind of reconstruction of religion and a specialization of the speculation at once. But both the reconstruction and the specialization must indicate clearly what is left behind in religion and speculation when the two are woven together. The generality of the speculative theory always stands over against its specialization in philosophy of religion, and the particularities of religion are left unattended to a degree when religion is reconstructed with reference to philosophical categories. The practical upshot of this is that the product of philosophy of religion cannot be taken either for speculative philosophy itself or for religion. It may be a confirmation of speculation, and it should be an aid to the self-understanding of religion; but this is a qualified contribution in each case.

Since the aim of this concluding part of our study is to suggest a close connection between the speculative considerations of Part One and religion, what follows should not be construed as an attempt at a *systematic* philosophy of religion. The selection of points has been made on the basis of what best shows the connection of our theory with religion.

We shall begin with a general discussion of the conception of God in religion, focusing on the characteristic of holiness and raising questions about what this entails for notions like divine individuality, supremacy, and so forth. Next we shall take up the problem of articulating the general notion of religion by asking about the nature of the problem religion is meant to solve. The following two chapters will concentrate on the nature of the religious life, its inner development and its public side respectively. Topics from the inner life to be considered are religious concern, conversion, faith, certainty, solitude, and bliss; those from the public religious life are religious service, liturgy, evangelism, religious dedication, reconciliation, and brotherhood. These discussions, although abstracting considerably from the general range of the previous chapters, will attempt to enrich the conceptions of God and of religion with added details and ramifications. The final chapter will take up the problem of the unity of the religious life and its connection with life's fullness.

No attempt is made in what follows to maintain a strict distinction between what religion is without the interpretations of philosophy and what philosophy has to offer to religion. Rather, at times these will be closely mixed, with philosophy showing what to expect from religion and religion showing what problems philosophy must solve. But a careful attempt will be made to keep this mixture from viciously prejudging the case. It is the interplay of religion and philosophy that we want to exhibit, and we want to do so without making philosophy of religion a third term that occupies a place of its own separating the integrity of philosophy from that of religion. The aim is to show that our speculative categories are fruitful for interpreting religion.

An important preliminary qualification should be noted. The distinction between religion in general and specific religions in particular is very complex and deserves a study of its own. Many religions claim to be true to the exclusion of other religions. If these exclusive claims were about peripheral matters, there would be little difficulty; but in fact they are often about the most essential matters. This fact alone is sufficient to cast doubt upon enterprises like Weiss's of determining *through religion in general* the pure and neutral essence of religion and God.[6] Such enterprises do not acknowledge the prima facie integrity of religion. Speculation can be pure and neutral but only at the price of abstracting from what many religions take to be the most essential matter, for example, what God has done in history.

Since our task here will involve showing that our abstract speculation and the historical peculiarities of religion are compatible, and in fact that the former is the best interpretation of what is presupposed abstractly by the latter, the religion-religions distinction is a great problem. Many of our topics will be of sufficient generality that we can deal with religion in general and give counterpart examples from several traditions. But many other topics will be so specific that religions have contrary things to say, and more subtly, different emphases to give. In these cases we must select certain religions to follow out, usually Judaism and Christianity or Christianity alone. We must leave it as just a suggestion that our speculative categories can interpret other religious traditions as well. If it should prove that they cannot, then it still is an open issue whether it is our categories or the other religions that are in the wrong. We must admit that the experience of the author is often the guiding thread.

[6] See "Introduction," *The God We Seek* (Carbondale: Southern Illinois University Press, 1964).

9
The Conception of God in Religion

The problem of the best conception of God should be distinguished from the problem of the best religious faith. The distinction, however, is difficult to make, for each problem appears in the other as occupying a necessary but subordinate place. One of the chief criteria for the adequacy of a conception of God is whether it does justice to religious faith. And religious faith involves a conception of God. The distinction between the problems should be made nonetheless, since the former problem is the intellectual domain of philosophy of religion, and the latter is in the domain of living religion itself.

The problem of the present chapter is that of the best conception of God. The general rubric within which philosophy of religion deals with the conception of God in the present day is that of the distinction between God as an individual and God as being-itself. ("Being-itself" in this context is the general problematic notion of which our version in Part One is a specific theory.)

SECTION A
God as Individual and God as Being-Itself

In the contrast between God as a personal individual and God as being-itself, there seem to be two chief traits intended by each side.

1. The intent of saying that God is a personal individual, however exalted above ordinary persons, is that God in some sense is a substance with properties and in some sense is an active agent.

a) What is meant by calling God a substance is that his individuality is given in his substantial being rather than in his properties or accidents, essential and non-essential. God is first of all a substantial individual and, second, though of necessity, has a nature. God's individuality is not a matter of his possessing a unique and unduplicable set of properties. Nor is it a matter of his delimiting a particular part of a medium that is itself a particular, as an actuality is individuated in part by the individual space it occupies. Rather it is a matter of his being first of all a substance.

No one would maintain that God is a substance in exactly the same sense that rocks or trees or persons are substances. In speaking of God's substantiality, what is to be denied of the usual sense of substance is that the predicates of the substance are different in ontological mode from the being of the substance. As some representatives of this tradition have argued, in God the substantial existence and the predicative essence are not to be distinguished. Still, one of the main thrusts of calling God a personal individual is to attribute to him the primary and self-contained individuality of a substance. A substance is what can exist as an individual by itself without the co-operation of other ontological elements, according to those who believe in substances.

b) The second main thrust of calling God a personal individual is that he is an active agent whose activity manifests a definite personal character or personality. This is a complex claim and, if taken in its totality, is a very strong one. Those thinkers who defend the conception of God as a personal individual usually defend the whole of the claim, identifying the personality of God as that of Jehovah or Allah. Later we shall take up the conditions under which God can exhibit a definite personality; for now let us focus just on that element of the claim that declares God to be an active individual whose agency affects, in some way or other, the course of the world. As van der Leeuw testifies, even the most primitive of religious responses takes the conception of the religious object to be the manifestation of power, even if it is only an extraordinary exhibition of ordinary faculties.[1] Despite the recognition of the dangers of anthropomorphism in the conception of individual agency, those who defend the conception of God as a personal individual do mean to assert that God is an acting substance.

2. To say, on the other hand, that the conception of God is primarily that of an ontological category like being-itself is to say that our conception of him is first of all structural or categoreal and second supreme in virtue of that structure.

a) The force of the claim that the conception of God is structural is not a denial that structure is involved in the alternative conception of him as a personal individual. Indeed, structural categories like individuality, activity, and substantiality are essential to the other conception. Rather the force of the claim is that the structural categories involved in the individualistic conception are not sufficiently basic or metaphysically fundamental to apply to God. The only way by which we can determine which categories are sufficiently exalted to apply to God is by a structural analysis that can determine what the most fundamental category, being-itself, consists in. To interpret God as a personal individual is to make the mistake (the claim goes) of interpreting God according to categories taken from a domain that is obviously not God; hence we must always be denying the applicability of the categories in precisely the sense in which divinity is to be distinguished

[1] *Religion in Essence and Manifestation*, trans. J. E. Turner (London: Allen & Unwin, Ltd., 1938), I, 23 ff.

from the mundane. Only after a structural analysis has done the work of establishing the character of the most exalted categories can we be in a position to determine how analogies are to apply.

b) The second portion of the claim, that being-itself is the highest of all conceptions and alone is worthy of being the conception of God, follows from the first portion. No matter what is actually maintained as the character of being-itself, the claim is that this conception alone is supreme and worthy of being the conception of God. It should be emphasized that the term "being-itself" is taken here in a general sense and should not be construed solely in terms of the discussion above in Part One.

SECTION B

Holiness

The most basic criterion for adjudicating conceptions of God is that of worthiness of worship. This criterion is recognized with appropriate shifts in emphasis by philosophy and religion alike and, within religion, by both theology and the phenomenology of religion.

To the degree that philosophy's conclusions are to gain conviction through their virtues as interpretations of the subject matter, and the subject matter is religion's object of worship, philosophy aims to articulate a conception of God as a worshipful reality. What worship means in religion depends upon what religion means, and this varies to a degree between religions. While the West emphasizes an element in worship that means the service of God and the East emphasizes an element that means the forgetting of all except God, there is a basic core common to them both. Subjectively, this core meaning of worship is what Otto called the *mysterium tremendum* that articulates our worshipful response,[2] and objectively, the core meaning is God's holiness or glory. Theology acknowledges this in the countless ways it elaborates the theme of God's majesty over against our ideal of humility.[3] Phenomenology of religion acknowledges it in its development of the conception of the religious object in terms of the awe it is able to inspire in us, each stage in the development being superseded when something more awe-inspiring becomes apparent.[4]

It was the greatest genius of Anselm of Canterbury to recognize the centrality of worshipfulness as the basic criterion for conceptions of God and to give an intellectual articulation of it: the God to be worshiped is "that than which nothing greater can be conceived."[5] To recognize Anselm's definition of God as a criterion of worshipfulness requires, of course, that we remain vague about the meanings of "greater" and "conceived" if generality

[2] *The Idea of the Holy*, trans. J. W. Harvey (Oxford: Oxford University Press, 1926), chap. 4.
[3] See F. Schleiermacher's *Christian Faith*, trans. H. R. Mackintosh and J. S. Stewart (Edinburgh: T & T Clark, 1928), for example, props. 4, 32, and 63.
[4] See *Religion in Essence and Manifestation*, I, 28–38, 172–76, 182–87.
[5] *Proslogium* II.

is to be maintained. Different people take greatness to be different things; yet their inclination to worship is guided by their conceptions of greatness. The only strict sense Anselm intended to defend for greatness in the first ontological argument is the sense in which an object is conceived to be greater when it is conceived as real than when conceived as fictitious. In the second ontological argument an object is to be conceived as greater when conceived as necessary than when conceived as contingent. But these two minimal requirements of meaning intended by Anselm allow for considerable variation in the details. Likewise, the term "conceived" in the definition can be understood broadly enough to encompass all modes in which the worshipfulness of the religious object is apprehended, for example, in imagination, in speculation, and in mystical perception. Understanding "conception" and "greatness" in this broad fashion, we can use the notion of "that than which nothing greater can be conceived" as an articulation of worshipfulness that can adjudicate between conceptions of God.

With this criterion in mind, it is apparent that neither the conception of God as a personal individual nor the conception of him as a supreme philosophical category like being-itself is wholly satisfactory, since one of the main features of each alternative renders the conception unacceptable as the conception of the object of worship.

1. The difficulty with the conception of God as a personal individual lies in the implication that his individuation comes from a kind of substantiality. An inexpungable element in the notion of a substance is that of finitude or of a contained identity over against the context in which the substance exists. If God is one individual among others this finitude is present, even when he is the best individual. That is, he is finite over against the others and with respect to their being. Less obvious is the kind of finitude that pertains to the conception of God as a substantial individual when that conception has God as the all-inclusive individual; pantheistic and absolute idealistic conceptions fall into this class, as does perhaps panentheism. It would seem on the all-inclusive conception that God is not finite since there is nothing outside of him to limit him. Nonetheless, bound up with the notion of substantial individuality is the idea that the individual must be within a context. The unity of an individual, especially one individuated through substantiality, unifies elements in a field that without the unity would be dispersed throughout the field. This, of course, is almost a spatial metaphor, and the figurative imagination that plays such a large part in the psychology of worship usually spatializes it entirely: God as a finite individual is located in space, perhaps not astronomical space but at least heavenly space. Beyond this general sense of a context we have the more specific sense that if the activity of God is the activity of a substantial individual, then he needs a surrounding context as a medium for his action. To be sure, if God is an all-encompassing individual, then the context is empty and his action cannot be external through a medium other than himself; it can only be internal digestion, so to speak. An all-inclusive conception of God as a substantial individual is the conception

of a God for whom action on externals is impossible. Yet it is still true that the conception of God as an all-inclusive substantial individual is the conception of a finite God, because we cannot imagine such a God not being in a context, albeit a context that is empty save for God.

There is a stricter philosophical reason for God's finitude on the substantial individual conception, and it lies behind the suggestions of the worshipful imagination. As we noted in Part One, if something is determinate, then it is determinate over against some other determinate thing and both determinations are in a common context. Now a substantial individual must be determinate. Insofar as it is not determinate it is not individualized over against the environment. That element of a thing that is not determinate cannot be said to belong to that thing's identity except in the case where the determinate elements of that thing bring the indeterminate element into an identifiable orientation (which can hardly be done without making the indeterminate partially determinate). Since a substantial individual is determinate, it must also be in a context over against the other things with respect to which it is determinate.

The first conclusion to draw from this, which was drawn in Part One in another form, is that the notion of an all-encompassing substantial individual is self-contradictory. Such a philosophical consideration of itself does not often function in the religious quest for an adequate object of worship; in fact, some thinkers go so far as to suggest that a felt contradiction in the conception of the object of worship renders the conception all the more adequate. The second conclusion, however, is more telling for the dynamics of worship than the first. It is that the conception of God as a substantial individual is ineradicably bound up with the fact that God must be in a context in which and with respect to which he is determinate. This is to say, as a substantial individual God is a finite articulation of a context. That God is finite, on this conception, renders the conception inadequate for worship; something greater than the finite individual is conceived when God is conceived as a substantial individual, namely, the reality that is God plus that with respect to which he is finite. This is so no matter whether that with respect to which God is finite is other individuals or a naked context (if that is possible). The greater reality is more nearly adequate as the object of worship.

It might be maintained, with the ancient Greeks cited as authority, that only finite perfection is worthy of worship, and that what transcends finite closure and self-sufficiency is too vague and chaotic to be worshipped. Aesthetic criteria of ordered complexity or integrity might be urged as the criteria of worship. But it must be remembered as a matter of history that, although the alternatives the Greeks chose were always (or at least in Plato) guided by such aesthetic criteria, the course of Greek religion moved through the finite to what transcended it. Thus, for example, in the classic tragedians the pantheon of the finite gods was taken to be less inspiring of worship than the decrees of fate and necessity that bound even the gods, and the culmination of Greek religion in Plotinus transcended even the determinations of fate and necessity. Shortly we shall trace this phenomenology of religion in greater detail. A more philosophical answer to this alternative is that aesthetic standards presuppose a distinction between themselves and what they measure. Where the distinction is accepted, the focus of worship is ambiguous; for we can either worship what lives up to the standards or worship the standards for their normative power. Yet we can worship neither adequately, for what lives up to the standards is not as great, in an important sense, as the standards that are normative for it, and the standards that are the measure of goodness are not themselves necessarily good. The Western tradition says that the standards and what they measure are identical in God and that the distinction between them is only one of "reason" as it pertains to God. But it would seem that in this case the only ground for saying that the standards and what they measure must be one in God is itself higher and closer to the heart of the object of worship than either the standards or their fulfillment. Thus, if they are identified from the motive of defending God's simplicity, for instance, then the simplicity is closer, because greater, to what it is in God that we worship. If simplicity were not greater, then it would not annul the natural distinction between the standards and what they measure. For this reason aesthetic criteria of finite perfection do not serve to make the finite an adequate object of worship. Any virtues of finitude testify to what lies beyond them, and to combine the finite with its other is to have in hand a greater reality than the finite alone and hence something more worthy of worship.

2. Just as there is a difficulty in the notion that God is a personal individual, there is a like difficulty in the alternative that he is the ontological correlate of some version of the supreme philosophical category, being-itself. The difficulty in the latter case is that the conception of God, although perhaps demonstrably the supreme conception, is the conception of a structure. That is, the content of the conception of God as the ontological correlate or embodiment of a philosophical category is just the philosophical category. To distinguish and to identify the structure with the reality it structures requires more than the conception of the structure. Although we would like to say that our conception of the supreme philosophical category is the articulation of a reality and not a mere speculative construction, knowledge of the category alone would not warrant the claim. And it would seem that what *would* warrant the claim is a higher or more supreme kind of knowledge than knowledge of the category; that is, knowledge of the reality of the category. To use the language of the old correspondence theory, knowledge of the category may correspond with reality, but knowledge that it does in fact so correspond must be higher and internally relate both the category and its real correspondent; the traditional difficulty with this is that a seemingly endless progression of higher moves checking the lower ones is started. Furthermore, more than structural considerations are involved.

The strategy of the theological tradition at this point has been to stop the progression with the ontological argument. Our speculation arrives at a structurally determined category that by its very structure entails the acknowledgment of the reality of its ontological object or correlate. The intended content of the philosophical category is one with the material content of the object, as it were, so that no distinction between the structure and the reality that has the structure is possible. No distinction is possible, with respect to the supreme category, between the structural form and the matter that is formed.

According to the strategy of the ontological argument, the difficulty in identifying God as a mere structure is overcome because the peculiar structure involved is no mere structure; it is one so rich as to contain its material reality within it. Indeed this is no ordinary structure. Were the content of our thought merely the structure whose ontological correlate we identify with God the argument would never work, since the distinction between structure and its ontological embodiment arises in the very claim that our thought-structure determines its ontological correlate. This is the difficulty that all objectors to the ontological argument have felt.

To say, however, that the ontological argument identifies God with a structure is to misstate the case. The structure involved in the ontological argument (that is, that God is that than which nothing greater can be conceived) is not a structure that we attribute to God but one that serves as a rule or criterion for sorting alternative conceptions of God. No one has ever wittingly intended to say that the essential character of God is one relative to our thinking other conceptions of him. If the ontological argument is to work, it must admit that its so-called conception of God is a conception of a rule of thinking (although to be sure, the rule is derived from conceptions of God—that he is best, insurpassable, and so forth).

The outcome of the strategy of the ontological argument is to lift the conception of God from the alternative in which it is essentially a philosophical structure. The philosophical structure is used to show that God must transcend it; the greatest of things is being-itself, which we saw in Part One to transcend the determinate structures of being. The tradition of the ontological argument thus finds itself on the side of the view that we have no determinate conception of God in himself and that we conceive him only insofar as we conceive his determinate relations. Were we to remain with the view that to call God being-itself is to identify him as the ontological embodiment of a structure, then we inevitably fail to bridge the gap between structure and ontological reality that the ontological argument would help us over.

SECTION C

The Truth in the Alternatives

Before leaving the original alternatives of conceiving God as a personal individual and conceiving him as the real correlate of a category of being-itself, we must determine whether there is not something right about these conceptions, the difficulties notwithstanding.

1. Considering our criterion of worshipfulness as that than which nothing

greater can be conceived, it is apparent that the element in the being-itself alternative that requires the supremacy of the conception of God is on the right track. Not only is it right in building into the conception of God some guarantee of supremacy, but it is also right in thinking that the best guarantee is categoreal supremacy. Even in relatively unreflective apprehensions of God, the religious object is apprehended as God and as therefore supreme only insofar as the apprehension is articulated in some general, though perhaps vague, categories. The categories can indicate God's supremacy only insofar as they structurally articulate the supreme. At the heart, then, even of unreflective religious experience is the outline of a philosophical system.

What must be remembered as a qualification of the categoreal approach to the conception of God is that the supreme category or being-itself must transcend the determinate structures; or rather, it must indicate the transcendence of God over the determinate structures, although it itself is a determinate structure. Even the category of being-itself is not a conception of what God essentially is but is only a conception arising from his relation to us that guides our approach to him.

2. On the side of the alternative conception of God as a personal individual there is something true in the idea that God acts or exercises power or expresses himself in power. The chief warrant for claiming this comes from the phenomenology of religion that notes that power is the most pervasive characterization of God and is the one best able to withstand the historical viscissitudes of special conceptions. A more specifically philosophical reason can be given for it, however, that shows power to be a necessary element of supremacy. One way of putting the difficulty discussed above in identifying God with the ontological correlate of a determinate category is that a structural category seems passive and merely formal. Yet the character of that which is supreme to ordinary things that express themselves in power must itself be more than passive. There is something in the common notion of a real thing as opposed to the notion of the idea of a thing that entails that the real thing have the power at least of maintaining its own integrity if not that of stamping its character on something else. Therefore, in our common philosophical sense, power is in some way necessary to the supreme, though perhaps only in its relation qua supreme to us. We shall have more to say of the notion of power below.

3. The adequate conception of God for religion must combine the virtues of the basic alternatives we have considered and it must avoid their faults. It must guarantee an element of power as well as show how the conception of God is the conception of that which is supreme. The conception of God must not be committed to the identification of God with a structural form alone nor must it allow the finitude of a substantial individual. Philosophy's contribution to religion at this point should be the elaboration of a conception of God that meets these requirements of theology and phenomenology of religion. We have now to see whether the conception of the transcendent God arrived at in Part One is an adequate conception for religion.

a) That our ontological conception of God accounts for the religiously required element of power is obvious on the abstract level and problematic on the more specific levels. What conception of God conveys the sense of power better than that of God the creator? Creation *ex nihilo* is the most thorough and absolute expression of power, requiring neither objects to exert power on nor a medium through which to express it. We have even seen how God can have his nature as creator expressed as the "power of being" and how this both contains within itself and transcends determinate beings.[6]

More difficult is the task of showing how the conception of God as creator is supported by and helps to interpret the phenomenological evidence coming from comparative religions. We shall devote section D of the present chapter to making out this point in detail, although the general principle can be stated here. As was noted in chapter 8, the common religious imagination often runs unconsciously through the abbreviated forms of the dialectical argument of Part One starting from various aspects of impressive determinations of being as premises. We must show how the manifold appreciations of power in religion are either examples of this many-sided recognition of the creator in the created realm or else are mistaken apprehensions that contain the seeds of their correction within them (for example, as an inferior power is mistaken for the supreme one).

b) As it is with power, so is it with supremacy in testing the conception of God as creator. On the most general level, supremacy means something like transcendence and independence, and the dialectic of Part One has already established that God's transcendence is to be accounted for in terms of the conception of him as the creator of the determinations of being and that only as the total creator of a thing can God be totally independent of it.

In particulars the test of the conception of God is more difficult; we must determine whether the religious conception of supremacy accords with the notion of supremacy current in the arguments of Part One. We have already distinguished the evidence of religion into two basic groups. On the one hand, there are the theological traditions, and on the other hand, there is the work of phenomenology of religion. Fortunately, the theological traditions, both Eastern and Western, agree fairly well with the philosophical conception of supremacy as transcendence and independence with the additions, for the Western tradition at least, of moral and providential supremacy. The philosophical justification we can take as standing on the merits, whatever they may be, of the dialectic of Part One. Moral and providential supremacy must wait upon our further analysis in chapter 12 below. The results of phenomenology, which we shall note in more detail in the next section, support the contention that the manifestation of religious power that is supreme, and therefore ultimately worthy of worship, is the manifestation of God as creator.

c) With regard to the negative elements in the religious conception of God, we turn first to the necessity of not identifying God with a structure. Here the ontological conception of God in Part One finds happy confirma-

---

[6] See chap. 4, sec. B above.

tion. The conclusion there was not only that the conception of being-itself as something determinate is impossible (chapter 1) but that the conception of God as creator entails that in his essential reality he must transcend all characters, even the character of creator. Although this is a very paradoxical point from the standpoint of philosophy and the argument to show that it is possible was a complex one, the ontological theory gains needed conviction at this its hardest point from finding that religion requires transcendence all along. One of the results of the phenomenology of religion, as we shall see shortly, is that any manifestation of God that does not also reveal that God is still essentially hidden cannot be sustained as central to religion. The dialectic of Part One shows why this is to be expected in the nature of the case.

d) The second negative point to be acknowledged in the adequate conception of God is that he not be identified as a substantial individual. There is no danger of that in the conception that arises out of Part One. God as conceived there must transcend all determinations such as individuality, substantial and otherwise. The difficulty arises on the other side; we must make some account with the claims that God, as he manifests himself in religion, does indeed *manifest* himself as an individual. Although these claims have been most central to Western religions, they find counterparts in at least the admittedly anthropomorphic conceptions of the East. What we must determine in the succeeding chapters on the presence and activity of God in various dimensions of the religious life is whether the philosophical categories necessary for understanding God as an individual at whatever level he is to be so conceived entail notions like that of irreducible substantiality, which would conflict with the conceptions of Part One.

The results of this section are that the conception of God as creator, articulated philosophically in Part One, seems to have prima facie plausibility as the adequate conception of God for religion; but whether it is finally adequate depends upon the further investigation of the presence and activity of God in the many aspects of the religious life. The general religious conception of God is too vague to give more than hope to the task of contributing conviction to the ontological theory; we must move from the general considerations to the more specific. Before investigating the specific, however, it is fit that we examine the general findings of the phenomenology of religion. The chief reason for making the examination at this point is that, because of its desire to be impartial and scientific, phenomenology of religion has done much of its most important work on a very general level.

SECTION D

Power

Many phenomenologists have noted the pervasive importance of the element of power in the religious object.[7] Especially impressive for our present

[7] For example, Otto, *The Idea of the Holy*, pp. 23 ff.; Eliade, *The Sacred and the Profane*, trans. W. Trask (New York: Harcourt, Brace & Co., 1959), p. 12.

198 GOD THE CREATOR

interests, however, is the classic analysis of religion by van der Leeuw. In the first part of his *Religion in Essence and Manifestation,* before the analysis of the various aspects of the personal and social religious life, van der Leeuw develops the thesis that the critical point in the conception of God from the most primitive to most civilized and sophisticated manifestations is the notion of power. Even in such primitive phases when the religious response is not focused on anything sufficiently articulated as an object to be designated properly by the term God, the religious response is awe or amazement at something obtrusively unusual.

> As yet, it must further be observed, we are in no way concerned with the supernatural or the transcendent: we can speak of "God" in a mere figurative sense; but there arises and persists an experience which connects or unites itself to the "Other" that thus obtrudes. Theory, and even the slightest degree of generalization, are still far remote; man remains quite content with the purely practical recognition that this Object is a departure from all that is usual and familiar; and this again is the consequence of the *Power* it generates.[8]

Quoting the missionary Codrington, van der Leeuw makes the point that the religious object at this primitive stage

> is a power or influence, not physical, and in a way supernatural; but it shows itself in physical force, or in any kind of power or excellence which a man possesses. This Mana is not fixed in anything, and can be conveyed in almost anything; but spirits . . . have it and can impart it.[9]

Van der Leeuw argues that as the conception of God emerges and grows both in religious theory and in the development of more sophisticated religious forms the conception of power develops as well. Moreover, it is the conception of power that remains as that which must be conveyed by any articulation of the religious object. As the conception at a given stage loses its capacity to embody a religious power, a new conception is sought. At the end, even the embodiment of power in form and will must be transcended.[10] What van der Leeuw calls the "absolutely powerful" is beyond personality, even name. This is the power of fate and destiny that is even above the gods of the pantheon.[11] Nor is the absolutely powerful conceivable as something external to man as opposed to internal.

> Now Power is made absolute from within as the world-soul, in conscious contrast to the powers which intrude from without:
>
> What were a God, who, outward force applying,
> But kept the All around his finger flying!
> He from within lives through all Nature rather,

---

[8] *Religion in Essence and Manifestation,* I, 23.
[9] *Ibid.,* p. 24.
[10] *Ibid.,* p. 182.
[11] *Ibid.,* pp. 183 f.

Nature and Spirit fostering each other;
So that what in Him lives, and moves, and is,
Still feels His power, and owns itself still His.[12]

[Goethe]

The crucial question for our own concerns is whether the conception of powerful agency that phenomenology of religion shows to be supreme supports the negative conclusions we have reached about the elements of structural passiveness and substantial individuality in the Godhead. That the notion of power is so dominant in the phenomenological analysis indicates that it is not inclined to suffer from an overnegative structural account. Yet it is important to recognize that the dialectics of approaches to supremacy are different between phenomenology and our own ontological analysis in Part One. Whereas ontology must approach supremacy by examining the structures of categories, reaching a structure whose nature coincides with its reality only at the end, phenomenology's dialectic proceeds by examining the efficacy of conceptions of the religious object in commanding man's worship. According to van der Leeuw, the development of religious forms exhibits an inner dialectic wherein the vehicle of divine power must continually be tested for unconditionedness; as a given conception, for example, the Olympian gods, becomes articulated in a larger conditioning context, for example, the context of the gods' fate, the direction of worship passes from the conditioned to the conditioner.

The second part of the question, whether phenomenology supports our denial of the conception of God as primarily a substantial individual, is more complex. We distinguished above two motives operative in the claim that God is a substantial individual. The first is to give the conception of the religious object a form connectible to man and to be able to interpret the expressions of power as expressions of divine will. The second is to employ the notion of irreducible substantiality to account for the divine character of "wholly otherness," which distinguishes the sacred from the mundane (or profane, as Eliade calls it). These motives must be examined in turn to determine the verdict of phenomenology upon them.

To begin with, van der Leeuw argues, the articulation of the conception of God in terms that allow the conception to have characters that are related to man's character is implicitly self-defeating. There is a kind of sacred distance between man and God that is violated whenever a form of character connectible to human life is attributed essentially to God. van der Leeuw makes the point in connection with the fall of the divine powers conceived as personalities and divine functions,[13] but it holds for any such formal characterization. In the terms of our discussion in Part One, to conceive God essentially in determinate ways that are determinately connectible with man's determinate ways is to conceive the relation between God and man to be a

[12] *Ibid.*, p. 185.
[13] *Ibid.*, p. 175.

real distinction. But a real distinction between God and man would violate the sacred distance. It would make the distance depend on man's determinate character, since the determinateness of the distance would arise by equal co-operation of God's determinate character and man's. Moreover, it would remove the foundation-shaking awesomeness of the sacred distance that comes with the discovery of the presence of the divine in the heart of the mundane soul.

The finite distance between really distinct things forms the crux of the phenomenological objection to the element of substantial individuality in the conception of God. God's own integrity as an "other" might be maintained by the conception of his essential nature as a substantial individual, but the holiness of that "other," which consists in the fact that it can be more present to us than we are to ourselves, would be impossible. A God who is a finite individual lacks holiness to the degree that we can set ourselves over against him. But the God who finds us even when we take the wings of the morning or make our bed in Sheol is thoroughly holy. God cannot be so limited by his own individuality as to be alien to us or alienable by us.

It might be argued that the phenomenological evidence that tells against the conception of God as a substantial individual does so only when that individual is conceived as something over against us, as one individual among many. We noted before that an alternative interpretation of the substantial individual view is the claim that God is an inclusive individual of whom we and the elements of our world are finite parts. Such would be the view of the pantheists and the panentheists. On theories of this sort God would be wholly other in that he would transcend any part of himself but would at the same time be found at the core of any of his parts. In fact, the more a finite element of the world is interpreted as an abstraction from a larger whole, the more the identity of the whole is seen as essential to the part and the more the part's own limited identity is seen as a relative abstraction.

Whether the phenomenological evidence tells as much against this alternative conception as against the first depends on the degree to which the alternative would attribute and account for integrity in the parts of the substantive whole. To the degree that the essential identity of the part consists in the very fact that it is a part, to that degree the distance between the holiness of God and the profanity of the mundane would be lessened toward the point of dissolution. Paradoxically, this would be because the mundane would be subsumed into God, rather than the reverse; the essence of the part would be its contribution to the divine whole. We would all be incarnations of God, as it were. On the other hand, to the degree that the essential identity of the part is something preserved over against the larger identity of the whole, to that degree the relation between the part and whole would approximate the relation between really distinct things, with the noted difficulties of such a relation.

Of course, these remarks leave it open that someone might come up with a pantheistic or panentheistic view that would establish a third position that would lie between the abolition of the integrity of the part in favor of its function within the whole and the severance of part and whole to the point of real distinction. But we have already argued that the only way between these two pitfalls is a theory like that of Part One, which denies the determinate finitude of substantive individuality in God. As was argued in Part One, the only way between an absolute monism that swallows the parts in the whole and an ultimate pluralism that has only parts is a creation theory of being-itself. Supposing, however, that another alternative were to be found, we must ask of it whether the substantive individuality of God would still be called upon to account for the integrity of the "wholly otherness" of the divine. If it is, then a completely new account would have to be given of the distance between the holy and the mundane. The theory of Part One makes up this account by claiming, on the one hand, that the essential identity of the parts or finite elements consists simply in their determinate characters whereas, on the other hand, the essential identity of God transcends, because it gives rise to, all determinate relations to the characters of finite things. The holy distance, on the account of Part One, is the distance between what is absolutely dependent and what is absolutely independent, with no determination in the distance save the feature, wholly on the side of the dependents, of dependence itself.

We must bear in mind the status of what our evidences of phenomenology "prove." Their force is in no way deductive. We must admit the possibility that the organizing principles of phenomenologists are distortive. We must admit that even an accurate description of what religion has been and is becoming is no "proof" that *true* religion is in sight, either in the past or in the future. Especially we must beware of the deceptive supposition that a genetic account of religion ever by necessity gets at religion in a pure form. It is also unwarranted to suppose as a certainty (though perhaps it is a crucial and necessary hope whose fulfillment depends on the adherence to the hope) that the ultimate development of forms in hand now will arrive in the end at pure religion. In no way will description alone warrant us in taking a given religious expression as normative. The warrant for such a normative judgment must come only from a complex critical apparatus that includes, among other things, a philosophical theory such as that we have been developing.

10

The Conception of the Religious Life

⋅⋅⊰▪══════════════▪⊱⋅⋅

When philosophers speak of God it is usually in the context of intellectual reflection. When religious people speak of God it is often in the context of God's presence, alleged or real, in the religious life of the individuals or their community. A man who is both religious and a philosopher may abstract from his religious context to speak of God philosophically. But there are two senses in which a philosopher may abstract from the context of the presence of God in the religious life. On the one hand, he may disregard the context of religion and deal with God in more general ways. This is what we did in Part One and even in the last chapter when we considered the conception of God as the object of worship but disregarded entirely the mode, motive, and nature of the worship and worshipper. On the other hand, the philosopher may abstract from the living of religion but turn his abstract attention to the context of the religious life itself and to the conception there of God and his presence.

Although it may be true, as van der Leeuw argues, that God is most adequately and ultimately only conceived as power, infinite, transcendent, and absolute, no religious man's conception of him is limited to such a general response. Isaiah's great vision of God enthroned in power and glory was accompanied by a quick recognition of his own humble and unclean state in comparison, followed by an acceptance of God's personal act of cleansing and a dedication to work God's will.[1] Although this example might not be paradigmatic for all experiences of the worship of God, it does indicate that the God of power is made personally significant by interpretation in terms of the religious life. Therefore we must examine our conception of God as creator not only in connection with the general conception of the object of worship but also in connection with the presence of God conceived in the rich texture of the religious life.

[1] Isaiah 6.

SECTION A
Religion as a Way of Life

It might seem at first that the religious life is a "way of life" on a par with the political life and the artistic life. Certainly there are people whose lives are biased in political or artistic directions. But the religious life is not quite on a par with the other two. The political life is a profession or business that only a few of us have; we may all vote and pay taxes, but this does not constitute leading a political life. Likewise, only a few of us are artists; we may all enjoy the aesthetic things of life and many of us may have the hobby of painting, but this does not constitute leading the artistic life. Yet, although there are a few of us whose profession or business deals directly with the things of religion, the religious life is possible for all and is not another profession or business. The priest, the preacher, and the religious teacher are in the business of religion, but they do not necessarily lead the religious life better than the layman. In fact, we are all familiar with examples of people who excel in the business of religion but whose lives are far from religious. Therefore, the religious life is not on a par with kinds of lives defined by professional or business activity. The religious life seems to be compatible with these other lives and indeed seems to add a religious dimension to them.[2]

If the religious life is not a kind of life in the usual sense, at least we can say that its character comes from some problematic situation considered in the light of certain ends. As the political life consists in coping with political problems in the light of political ends, and the artistic life consists in working out artistic problems in the light of aesthetic ideals, so the religious life consists in solving religious problems in the light of religious ends. But even here there is a difference between the religious life and the two other examples. The unity of the political life stems from the continuity of personal identity through the many political problems that chance, circumstance, and history throw one's way. Likewise it is the artist who makes the artistic life a unified one, not the artistic problems that swarm in from current style, chance media, and fashion. The religious life, on the other hand, is unified not so much by the continuity of the person whose life it is as by the fact that the religious life is one big problem. The problem of the religious life is a single thing and coping with it takes a whole lifetime, not to be repeated.

What is the problem of the religious life? It would seem at first that we could say it is the problem of salvation. The term "salvation" has connotations that make it seem especially appropriate for the Christian conception of the religious problem, slightly less appropriate for Judaism and Islam, and hardly appropriate at all for the Eastern religions. Yet if we keep the word

[2] See this author's article "Man's Ends," *Review of Metaphysics*, XVI (September, 1962).

deliberately vague for the time being, it can have its analogue even in the problem of attaining Nirvana.

To conceive of the religious life in terms of salvation, however, still seems too narrow. That is, suppose the religious life to consist in the problem of attaining salvation and the salvation to be attained—what then? The saved life still has to be lived, and the experience of people who have "the saving grace deep in their hearts" and who are adopted into religious communities is that there are still problems aplenty in leading the religious life. In fact, the term "religious life" is often used in a narrow sense to apply only to those who are saved already and who are living out their salvation. Regardless of the application of the term, it is clear that the problem of attaining salvation is not equivalent to the problem that forms the character of the religious life.

A general beginning to the characterization of the religious life is to note that the problem that it faces stems from the connection of men with God. The problem of living the religious life is a religious one because the decisions and judgments to be made in its pursuit are to be made in the light of standards that come from the connection of men with God. There are problems whose proper standards bear no special relation to the connection between God and man, but these are not religious problems. They are political, artistic, or some other. If men should be and do certain things for the living of the religious life, this is because of the connection between God and men.

It is the fashion today to characterize religion in non-religious ways. So, Tillich defines the religious problem as that of ultimate concern, and the existentialists conceive it as the problem of attaining authenticity. Both of these characterizations may be right in the proper context, and we shall argue below that they are. But taken at face value they do not indicate why there is anything religious about the problems they delineate. There may be perfectly good reasons why one should want to characterize religion in non-religious ways. To convince people of religion, it may be a rhetorical necessity to slip it in by the back door. And Tillich, at least, is profoundly able to show in the proper context that his characterization of religion accords with the ancient claims of the traditions. Nonetheless, a straightforward philosophical characterization of the problem of the religious life must show how that life is religious, that is, what it has to do with God.

The problem of saying what it is that the religious life leads men to do because of their connection with God is baffling from the side of religion. There seems to be very little universal agreement, either in the phenomenology of what happens or in the pronouncements of theologians, concerning the nature of the religious life. As is often the case with practical problems, the ideal put forward at any one time is conceived more in contrast with existing conditions than in balanced perspective that duly notes current values as well as those urged for the future. For instance, in a period of great religious activity and organization the ideal of the religious life is often characterized by the most exciting thinkers as a personal and internal thing.

And in a period of contemplation and monasticism the prophetic word characterizes religion in terms of its consequences for action.

The best strategy in this pass is to recur to our dialectical theory about God the creator and determine whether there might not be some clues about the religious life that come from the considerations we made there about the connection between God and the world. The plausibility for this strategy comes from the one positive thing which we have already noted about the religious life, namely, that the standards that apply to the religiously problematic elements come in some way from the connection men have with God. In this way we will bring to the test of experience not only the validity of the dialectic of Part One but also its usefulness as an interpretative tool.

SECTION B
Man as a Determination of Being

To make connection with the discussion in Part One, we must relate the conception of man to that of a determination of being, for the notion of a determination of being in general is the most concrete thing our speculative discussion has related to the conception of God. Indeed, the characterization of determinateness in chapter 2 was so abstract it did not distinguish between kinds of determination of being. It applied as well to universals and values as to particulars and complex human individuals. What is necessary now is to move from the abstract discussion of determinateness in general to a more specific characterization of how a human individual as a determination of being is related to God. It is impossible to indulge in the proper philosophical anthropology that would be needed for a comprehensively adequate account of the connection between man and God; our purposes are too limited and the discussion so far has not provided sufficient background. Furthermore, we are not even in a position to give a comprehensive metaphysical account of all the elements that go into human life, its actualities and possibilities, freedoms and destinations, ideals and responsibilities—that is, a full-blown metaphysical treatment of all the determinations of being. Still, it is necessary for our present purposes to make use of some conceptions whose full justification would require an anthropology and a metaphysics, and we must acknowledge at the outset that the best that can be hoped is that our statement of these conceptions will convey a prima facie plausibility.

1. To recapitulate our conclusions about determinateness, it is first to be noted that any determination of being is complex. For a thing to be determinate, it must be determinate in two ways. It must be externally determinate, as it were, with respect to what is other than itself, and it must be internally determinate in having a character of its own. That part in virtue of which the thing is externally determinate we called a conditional feature, and the part that is the thing's own character we called the essential feature.

Our previous discussion was vague with respect to the nature of conditional features because their nature depends on the specific kind of determination containing the conditional feature in question. For instance, if the containing determination is, say, the color blue, its conditional feature that makes it, say, "not-red" seems to be a merely negative thing; and the conditional feature that makes it "not-communist" seems even more a mere negation. We are inclined to say of the latter instance, if not of the former, that the conditional feature is contributed by the understanding of some intelligent interpreter, and that apart from such an interpreter the color blue is simply indeterminate with respect to communism. There must, of course, be a ground in the color to make the distinction from communism true rather than false, but this ground seems little more than a capacity of its essential features and of the features that determine it with respect to other colors to sustain a negative discrimination of the color from political ideologies. There seems to be a loose external relation between blue and communism, and the conditional feature of blue that makes it determinate with respect to the quality of communism seems to be supplied mainly by some third thing that relates them. Yet being not-red seems quite essential to blue and thus essential as a conditional feature. It is probably the case that for universals, considered in themselves and not as the properties of physical objects and the like, there is a sharp distinction between the external determinations with respect to which they are determinate and those with respect to which they are not essentially determinate; this is to say, they are internally related to meanings essential to their definition but are externally related to meanings with which they might contingently be embodied in actual things. Other kinds of determinations of being, that is, those that are not universals in the ordinary sense, may have different modes of connection with and distinction from what they are determinate with respect to.

2. In point of fact the case with human individuals is different from that of universals. That is, the distinction between a person's internal relations and his external relations is not at all clear cut. Science indicates that persons are rather essentially related to things that define their place, time, spatial direction and velocity, and so forth. It also seems that persons are essentially determinate with respect to their antecedents, although the character of the response people make to their pasts seems to be a little more externally related to the character of the pasts. And with respect to determinations of party affiliation, many people simply ignore this determination of their nature entirely; it is not true to say of them that they are affiliated with this party or that, or even to say that they determinately have no party affiliation: they are simply indeterminate in that respect. When Kant said that the idea of an individual was the idea of something about which every possible property could be affirmed or denied determinately, he was overlooking the peculiarities of the kind of determination of being man is.[3] Man is more or less internally related to some things, in varying degrees externally related to others, and sometimes hardly at all related to still others.

[3] *Critique of Pure Reason* B 600.

As a being in time, man must be related to a past and to a future that are somewhat external to him. As a being in space, man must be related to a natural environment that is also more or less external. Part of the natural environment is social, and man must be related both to the public or social structures in which he operates and to other persons with as much interiority as he has himself. Since man is a part of nature, the externality of the environment is a matter of degree; and likewise the social structure and the persons he takes to heart help constitute his essential as well as his conditional features.

It is a further peculiarity of the kind of determination man is that, with regard to many of the external things with respect to which he is determinate, man has a hand in his own determination. He can move around, pick his food, and select his friends; to a degree he can even develop his own education and culture. Some of this self-determination is by chance and whim, but much of it is by conscious choice with reference to standards. That element of self-determination that is of interest to reflection about the "problems of men" is of this self-conscious type. The problem of the religious life is one of these problems of men.

SECTION C
The Nature of the Religious Problem

What is the connection of God with man as a determination of being? In Part One we said that God is the creator of determinations of being. This means that for determinations of being to be they must be created from nothing by something that is not itself determinate. God, then, is connected with men as their creator. And what it means to create is to create determinations with *de facto* unities. A determination is a *de facto* unity of other determinations. We must now pay closer attention to the nature of a *de facto* unity.

The *de facto* togetherness of parts that make up a determination of being is a kind of harmony, for the parts are harmonized together to make up one thing. But the notion of harmony is very rich in connotation indeed, far richer than the abstract notion of a *de facto* unity. We have already argued in chapter 3 that any *de facto* unity is really a harmony and have sketched the presence of God to be found in harmonies. As opposed to the concerns of Part One, our present interest is with the nature of a problem within the created realm instead of with what transcends it. Hence, the richer notion of harmony will be more fruitful. If religion is a problem that man has with respect to his creator, then we can begin with the thesis that what God gives a certain determination of being when he creates it is its harmony in virtue of which it is a composite of other determinations.

The suggestion that our metaphysical discussion brings to the problem of the religious life is that the religious problem is a problem of harmony. Because a person is created by God as a determination, he is a harmony of certain other determinations that it is the nature of the determination "person" or "man" to harmonize. Therefore, if a person has a religious problem, that is, a problem concerning his basic connection with God, he has a problem of harmonizing what it is the nature of the created determination "person" to harmonize. If a person does not harmonize as he is created to, then, as the theologians say, he falls from his true or created being; and if the harmony is a problem to maintain in the face of change, development, and temptation, then the danger of falling is ubiquitous.

As we shall discover, the nature of what it is to be a truly human being is fraught with a peculiar difficulty. Man is a kind of determination of being who is bound by standards and obligations. These standards are relevant to him, in large part, because of the connections he has with other men, society, and elements in nature and culture. Yet all of these connections specify his conditional features, and there seems to be no essential limit in human nature to the number and kinds of standards that oblige a man. It is the common experience of us all that we have more obligations than we can meet and more goods possible than we can realize. The consequence of this is that there is a crucial distinction between truly human nature—what man is essentially—and ideal nature—what man ought to be in virtue of his conditional but binding responsibility to standards. As we shall see, it is part of truly human nature to fail. Coping with this frailty of human nature lies at the heart of the religious problem.

The word "man" is used loosely enough to apply to less than the complete harmony of man's true nature as a determination. Consequently, a fall from the true nature of man does not necessitate complete disintegration of a person. For instance, few people would claim that a man with an unsolved religious problem would cease to be a living animal or even that he would cease to have consciousness, memory, and ability to function in society. They might claim, however, that he would cease to have the ability to love in an ideal way or that he would cease to have the ability to understand and appreciate certain things, such as the beauty or worthiness of true virtue or God's revelations.[4]

Our problem at this point is to spell out more precisely the kinds of disharmonies that lie at the heart of being a proper man. Again we can take a suggestion from our metaphysical analysis of what it is to be a determination and look for disharmonies between the essential and conditional features of man. Although a complex determination like man has many essential features as well as many conditional ones, the first basic distinction is between essential and conditional.

As we have noted, man is determinately connected with many things external to him. His environment offers food and shelter, deprivation and destruction, pleasure and enjoyment, pain and sorrow, friends and society,

---

[4] See Edwards' *Religious Affections*, ed. John E. Smith (New Haven, Conn.: Yale University Press, 1959), pp. 269–77, esp. p. 275.

enemies and punishments. But the religious problem concerns man as he is especially man. Its concern with him as he is an animal, or as he is merely economic man or friendly man or artistic man, is indirect. The direct religious concern is with the harmony by which man as a determination of being unites all the determinations that make up his nature. Therefore, the disharmonies vis à vis conditional features with which the religious problem is concerned have to do with external things like other men and human society with respect to which man is determinately connected as especially man. This is the public side of man.

Similarly, the private side of man that is of interest for the religious problem is not all the features that man has essentially but more primarily those that bear directly on the whole harmony that is man. The relatively private problem of choosing friends is a matter that involves harmonizing certain factors, but it is not directly a religious problem. On the other hand, determining the faith or guiding principles of one's life as a whole, a faith that must take account of all the factors that go into being a person, is a religious problem indeed. But it is a problem more on the private than on the public side.

As we would expect from our metaphysical analysis, the determinations of man that are relatively conditional have connections with the essential and vice versa. Man's especially human determinations with respect to the world outside him are expressions of his essential or private side, even though they, more explicitly than his private side, take into account the external realities. And the central faith of his private side also acknowledges his external determinations, although it pays more attention to the factors peculiar to the man as a specific individual.

If the religious problem deals with the private side of man and also with the public, it must deal with the harmony of the two as well. We noted before that the religious traditions do not present for our investigations any plausible *consensus* about the nature of the religious problem or the religious life. The reason for this is that there has been a kind of pendulum swing between a rather private conception of religion and a rather public conception. Sometimes the problems of faith and the inner life are emphasized, and at other times the problems of community and public expression are under-scored. It is the problem of harmonizing both these sides, each of which deals with the harmony of man's whole nature as man, that is the religious problem at its most crucial point. The whole harmony of man as especially human can be approached from the private side, where, as we shall argue in detail in the next chapter, it is the problem of faith and faith's fulfillment. Likewise, the whole harmony of man can be approached from the side of the public expression of the essentially human, where, as we shall argue in chapter 12, the religious problem is one of hope for the proper expression of one's whole humanity in a medium or environment somewhat external and alien. But there must be a harmony of these two sides of man's humanity, a harmony of the private and public. As we shall argue in the last chapter this is a matter of love for the integrity or harmony of the determinations of being, which is at the same time love of their creator. To say that the religious problem is a matter of faith, hope, and love is not to say anything new.

It is very important to maintain the integrity of each of the elements in terms of which the religious problem is expressed. But it is also very important to acknowledge the problem of unifying the many approaches to the religious problem. This task is doubly important for its timeliness today. One of the most striking features of the contemporary religious situation is that both the public and the private sides of religion have strong advocates. Furthermore, the advocates of both sides are engaged in work that generates considerable excitement. In America the present concern with civil rights has presented a problem both simple enough in its apparent demands and difficult enough in its solutions to call forth an exhibition of public witness from all religious faiths that is as powerful and poignant as any in history. At the same time the so-called theological revolution is focusing the problems of faith and the inner life as they have not been focused for centuries. Yet the tragedy is that these seem almost to be separate movements. So often the religious advocates of civil rights are theologically naïve and offer public action as a dodge for escaping the problems of faith and the inner life. On the other side the theologians are often so caught up in the internal difficulties of their problems that they fail to give careful consideration to the guidance they offer for public expression.

Harmonizing the private and public sides of religion is so difficult because each side makes full-time demands. In the religious man's effort to throw himself wholeheartedly into "willing one thing," it is difficult to remember that both the private and public problems must be faced. Although the great public religious leaders often took themselves off to the mountains to pray and having prayed returned to the problems of the world, this is a difficult lesson for us. There is a time to act and there is a time to retreat into the inner chambers of the soul. The question is, When is the right time for each? This is the question we shall take up in chapter 13.

11

The Interiority of the Religious Life

Some distinction is almost universally recognized between religion as an affair of the inner life and religion as a public affair. Even those who claim that only one side of the distinction is valid religion implicitly acknowledge a contrast with the other side. To emphasize the matters of public worship and ethical work while calling problems of the inner life merely subjective is still to acknowledge the distinction between alleged religious phenomena on both sides. The same is true of the emphasis on the inner life that calls the public side merely practical and preparatory. Oriental religions acknowledge the holy teachers of the soul as well as the soul's holy bliss. And in the Western tradition reflective thinkers make explicit a recognition that there are private as well as public religious matters. Phenomenologists of religion like van der Leeuw are quite at home with titles like "The Sacred Community" in contrast to "The Sacred within Man" and "Outward Action" versus "Inward Action." Such a cloud of witnesses must cast some shadow.

To acknowledge that there is a distinction here is still a far cry from making out the distinction in sharply defined and precise terms. The connections between the sides distinguished are many and complex. Probably the same phenomena could be classified on one side in one context and on the other side in another. Furthermore, what lies at the heart of one side usually is expressed in some way on the other. Even the most extreme defenders of the doctrine of immediate mysticism make their private experience public by writing long books about it.[1]

We noted in the last chapter that the speculations with which this book began suggest that the religious problem of the inner life has to do with the kinds of harmonies involved in making man distinctively human particularly insofar as these harmonies are related to the essential features of man. It is the thesis to be defended here that the chief of these harmonies and the problems

---

[1] Van der Leeuw, *Religion in Essence and Manifestation,* trans. J. E. Turner (London: Allen & Unwin, Ltd., 1938), II, 459.

of maintaining them have to do with the following six topics: *Concern, conversion, faith, certainty, solitude,* and *bliss.*

The essential features of man that are closely involved with the comprehensive harmonies that make him especially man are those that have to do with his will and its principles, with what used to be called his "heart." This contrasts with religious conditional features that have to do with the specific things relative to which man is determined in his environment. Of course it is these conditional features that the will must take into account. But there is at least a prima facie difference between attending to the problems of the will and attending to those of the external determinations. Concern, conversion, faith, certainty, solitariness, and bliss will be discussed as related to the will or heart. This accounts for why they are problems of the *inner* religious life. We must also indicate why they are problems of the inner *religious* life. That they are religious means that they have to do with the comprehensive harmonies that unite all the things man must unite to be distinctively human. As noted in the previous chapter, distinctive humanity is the determination of being that man is in virtue of his creaturely connection with God, and the connection with God is the context of the religious problem. It is apparent that certain problems on the list, like conversion and faith, have to do with the total orientation of the heart. This is also apparent with concern when it is interpreted as ultimate concern and with bliss when it is viewed as perfect or eternal happiness. The case for certainty and solitude is harder. Still, certainty in religious matters is a peculiar sort of thing. Solitude, of course, must be given considerable interpretation before its religious significance becomes apparent; but suffice it for now to note that it is what Whitehead thought was the defining trait of religion.

SECTION A

Concern

Paul Tillich has characterized religion's concern as "ultimate concern." Disregarding for the moment the object of ultimate concern, Tillich points out that the ultimacy of the concern means what Mark (12:29 [R.S.V.]) conveys by the words: ". . . you shall love the Lord your God with all your heart, and with all your soul, and with all your mind, and with all your strength." [2] The "all's" in the quote indicate the unlimited quality of the concern and the "heart," "soul," "mind," and "strength" indicate that what is involved in the concern is the whole of the person. Since Tillich has drawn such pointed attention to the function of ultimate concern in religion, and since he has drawn on himself such thorough criticism for doing so, it would be well to orient our considerations of religious concern around his remarks and difficulties.

[2] *Systematic Theology* (Chicago: University of Chicago Press, 1951), I, 11; see also *Dynamics of Faith* (New York: Harper & Bros., 1957), p. 3.

1. It would seem a natural empirical beginning to note that religious concern of any kind is not necessarily the most elementary prerequisite of commerce between man and God. It is possible that God be noticed by man and responded to without any particularly religious concern at all. The evidence of phenomenology of religion that we cited in chapter 9 is that man's most primitive response to God is to him as power, extraordinariness, or mana. This power is the sort of thing that man might encounter and be struck with, and it might arouse some concerns in him; but it need not be correlated with any special concern at the outset. Man might find God without the benefit of any religious concern.

But this primitive response to the mysteriousness of the unusual is not necessarily a religious response. Whatever else it is, in terms of special concerns, problems, and the like, religion at the very minimum is a more or less well-regulated pattern of behavior. The important word here is pattern. There must be enough pattern, at least in linguistic if not in ceremonial and ethical response (and the ceremonial and ethical seem as primitive as the linguistic), for the experiences of the mysterious holy power to be compared and responded to in co-ordinated fashion. For a finding of God to be religious, and not just a chance encounter, there must be an element of universality involved, at least in man's interpretive responses. Religion is involved in the structure of this universality.

It is surely unnecessary to take the most historically primitive as the most basic and pure form of a thing. It is more likely that a thing will be found in its purity when it has been long reflected upon and interpreted through many experiences of trial and error. So, religion is most likely found in purer forms today than in the manifestations of savage cultures. But one of the chief characteristics of religion as a historical phenomenon is that it first comes to people in learning language and cultural forms. In fact, people adapt themselves either positively or negatively to religious forms and concepts probably quite long before they would have any articulate encounters with God. Like Jacob awaking from his dream and noting that God has been with him, people might recognize an encounter with God to be such only after the event; and it is possible that they might never recognize it as such at all.

The question must still be asked, however, whether men have a religious *concern* just at the point where they have religion, perhaps prior to an encounter with God. Two of the best marks by which to detect the presence of concern are intensity of passion and propensity to hark back to the object of concern when the formal pattern of behavior might lead to irrelevancies. With regard to intensity, it is undeniable in all religions that one of the cultural norms for being religious is that religious concern should be passionate to a high degree. Manifestation of passionate concern, of course, does not always take the same form. Emotional excitement is an obvious form of passionate concern, but so is the extreme quietism of some kinds of mysticism and Quakerism. To say, however, that it is a universal norm of religions that religious concern should be passionate is not to say that all those whose natures are partially made up of an adaptation to one of the religious patterns must exemplify the passion. Many persons do exemplify an intense concern; many others are lukewarm. Still others seem to have such a minimal degree of adaptation to a religion that any specifically religious concern seems indistinguishable in them. Finally, there are people whose adaptation to a religion takes the form of rejection; and although there may be considerable passion in their concern to reject, the concern is not what the religion recognizes as religious concern.

Hand in hand with intensity or passion as a mark of religious concern is the propensity to hark back to the object of concern when irrelevant alternatives are present. It is characteristic of religions that they offer many forms, patterns, and routines of religious response and behavior. But when the question arises about what responses are appropriate at a given time, even the most sophisticated and elaborate of religions sometimes fail to give sufficient rules of judgment. "Genuine" religious concern is a matter of the spirit and not of the letter. Without concern, religious behavior follows the conventional modes of response, but in so doing loses appropriateness or relevance. With religious concern, the conventional modes of response are molded to a more vital sense of reality. It is a convention of all religions that merely conventional behavior fails to be true religion.

If we take religious concern to be what religions characterize as religious concern, whereas such concern is always a norm in religion, there are many degrees of success in meeting the norm and the degrees can get so low as to be indiscernible. When religious concern is interpreted in this way, many people plainly do not have it, even though they may structure some of their actions and beliefs according to the tenets of religion.

2. Tillich has taken an approach to religious concern quite different from the rather "empirical" one of the last section. Starting from the empirical fact that the *norm* in religions with respect to religious concern is that the concern should be unconditional and surpassing all other concerns, Tillich gives a formal characterization of the ultimacy in the concern. An ultimate concern is one that will be maintained in the face of opposition when all other concerns have been given up. When the pressures of life demand choice between concerns, the one that is ultimate either rejects the others or subordinates and adapts them to itself.[3] This testifies to the intensity of passion in the concern. Another formal characteristic that Tillich notes is that the object of the ultimate concern, whatever it is, promises ultimate fulfillment. Fulfillment is the end for which concern is the need, and ultimate concern involves conceiving its fulfillment as ultimate also.

Because ultimacy in concern is such a formal characteristic, Tillich points out that many things can be the content of it, and he cites nationalism, political ideology, social success and religion as common things with which

[3] *Systematic Theology,* I, 11 f.

Paul Tillich

modern men are concerned ultimately. The formal characteristic of ultimacy is sufficient, Tillich claims, to serve as a criterion for selecting between objects as capable of providing ultimate fulfillment.[4]

One of the strongest claims Tillich makes for ultimate concern is that everyone has it. Because ultimate concern conceives its object as promising ultimate fulfillment, and because ultimate fulfillment is what religion is all about, everyone is religious whether he knows it or not. If the object of a person's ultimate concern is a political ideology, for instance, then, Tillich argues, the person is taking the ideology for God and politics is a mistaken form of religion.

We can roughly accept the thesis that ultimate concern is what religion is all about by citing our previous discussion. "What religion is all about" is the problem of achieving or maintaining the harmony of determinations that makes a man genuinely human. Since this harmony is comprehensive of all other harmonies with which man is concerned it can roughly be called ultimate for him. This is only a vague acceptance of the thesis, and there are many other problems that must be solved in making it more precise. But it is sufficient to allow us to focus attention on the first part of Tillich's argument. The question is, Does everyone have an ultimate concern?

Tillich argues that ultimate concern is an aspect of the act of faith, which is a "centered act" of the personality.[5] To say that ultimate concern involves a centered act means that the act is a movement of all the things that go into what is essential about man: consciousness, sub-consciousness, freedom, mind, will, and whatever else science and philosophy might see to be constitutive of man. An act of ultimate concern lies at the "center" or heart of all these and affects or employs them all. Yet at the same time Tillich points out that the act of faith that is ultimate concern is not to be identified with any of these or even a set of them lumped together. It is not a matter of sheer belief or sheer will or even sheer belief plus sheer will. Tillich calls the centered act of faith involving ultimate concern a matter of "ecstasy." The word ecstasy he interprets as meaning "standing outside of oneself," and this without ceasing to be oneself. The act of faith involves all the things that lie at the heart of man and also something more. What the something more is, is whatever allows the act of ultimate concern to be centered.

Our previous considerations about the nature of the religious problem allow us to recognize that Tillich has a profound point in his analysis of ecstasy. Since the religious problem is to realize the harmony of all the elements that must be harmonized for a person to be a truly human determination of being, and thus a proper creature of God, an act of religious fulfillment or ecstasy must be an act that embodies the total or "centered" harmony in question. In a sense, an act of religious concern must be an act that aims at such ecstasy.[6]

[4] *Dynamics of Faith*, pp. 8–12.
[5] *Ibid.*, pp. 4–8.
[6] We shall return to the problem of ecstasy in our discussion of "bliss" below.

The point to press now is whether everyone makes this centered act that involves ultimate concern. Unless the act is centered, the concern involved cannot be ultimate. That is, if the act is not centered, then some element of the total ideal person is left out, and the concerns of doing justice to that part are also left out. This makes the concern of the less than centered act parochial and not ultimate. It cannot subordinate or reject those concerns it does not recognize and touch.

But it would seem that an act cannot be centered unless the religious *problem* is *solved* to a degree. A centered act of ultimate concern is possible only to the person who is able to harmonize all the determinations of which, as a proper man, he should be made up. There may be better and worse harmonies, those that allow the harmonized elements their proper status and those that improperly subordinate them. But at least some degree of religious fulfillment is necessary for such a centered act of ultimate concern to be possible. It would seem also that there are many people who are incapable of such a centered act for the reason that they are far from realizing any harmony, even a poor one, of the many elements that lie at the heart of being a human person. These are people incapable of having an ultimate concern. In Western society at least, the lack of ultimate concern is a prevalent condition. As our novelists point out, utterly divided lives and loyalties, even enervating ennui and lack of *any* consistent concern, let alone an ultimate concern, are characteristic of much of the modern temper. From the heights of our religious wisdom, we can see that these people have a problem; and their problem is a religious one: they have given up something that is essential to true humanity. But they do not know that they have a problem. And what is more, they do not care. They have no ultimate concern.

Now it might be argued against this conclusion, in Tillich's defense, that, if the elements that should be harmonized in a truly human person are so disintegrated that he has no possibility of an ultimate concern, then he cannot be said to be a man at all any more. We admitted in the previous chapter that the disintegration cannot proceed so far that the person would cease to be conscious or cease to be able to function in society. If the disintegration does proceed this far, the person has so far ceased to be a true man that religion is not even a problem to him. The loss of the harmony that makes a person truly human can make him incapable of love and of appreciation of certain things, but not completely incapable of functioning humanly. The question is whether there is a point of disintegration or disharmony where a person becomes incapable of a centered act and yet is still sufficiently a human individual to have a religious problem.

A person without an ultimate concern is one who has several concerns that are different but that are not necessarily ranked so as to give one supremacy. Within the domain of action dominated by each concern, the person might be able to function well. But in those situations where a choice is demanded between concerns, the person is unable to choose. Or at least he is unable to choose consistently on the basis of anything that lies deep in his heart; chance determines his choice, and he chooses now this way and now that. This is certainly disharmonious; what harmony there is, is not a human harmony that stems from the person's heart. The man's choices are not centered. But he is still a man, and his type is easily recognizable among many of us. Even when there is a concern to make a centered act, there is often the inability to do so, and the concern fails to reach the comprehension of ultimacy. We must conclude that Tillich errs in thinking that everyone has an ultimate concern. Everyone sufficiently integrated to be called at all human does indeed have a religious problem. But not everyone with such a problem need know it or be concerned with it. The classical Western conception of damnation illustrates this point. To be damned is said to be without hope utterly. As Tillich points out, the correlate of concern is fulfillment, and viewed subjectively, this means hope. To have an ultimate concern is to have a hope of ultimate fulfillment. Yet there are those who have no hope of the fulfillment of the harmony that we have described as the aim of the religious life. That they have no hope means that their concern, if they ever had it, is dead.

3. The conclusion that not everyone has an ultimate concern although everyone has a religious problem leads us to another point that Tillich has underscored. To be capable of the ultimate concern that is necessary for religious concern, a person must have made an advance upon the state simply of having a religious problem. To have an ultimate concern is already to have a partial grasp of the harmony sought. To have even this partial grasp is to have partial religious fulfillment, and as Tillich has pointed out, this means that God must already be present. It is important that this point be understood, for it lies at the base of a distinction between two ways in which God is present in the inner religious life.

We must be clear that there is a difference between having no concern at all (of the ultimate variety), having a truly ultimate concern, and having a concern to have an ultimate concern. But although these are manifestly not the same, the kinds of differences that distinguish them are very complex. Having no ultimate concern at all and having a truly ultimate one are exclusive alternatives. But there is a sense, which Tillich duly notes, in which it is impossible to have a concern to have an ultimate concern without having the ultimate concern as well. That is, to have a concern to have an ultimate concern is to have the harmony requisite for the centered act of ultimate concern present in hope though not in much concrete fulfillment. The hope may have a very inarticulate and vague form; indeed it must, if the ultimate concern is lacking. But still, for the harmony to be present in hope is indeed for it to be present.

Because he recognizes that to have an ultimate concern is already to possess in some degree the object of the concern, Tillich is criticized for drawing the conclusion that the problem of religion is solved as soon as it is seen. This is, of course, unfair to Tillich. But it would help his analysis to emphasize the distinction, ambiguous as it may be, between the mere concern to have an ultimate concern and the actual enjoyment of it, both of which have degrees.

To have an ultimate concern as a mere hope is still a far cry from having the presence of God, which is necessary for a genuine expression of ultimate concern.

What is profoundly true in Tillich's analysis is the recognition of the presence of God wherever ultimate concern is present, even if that concern is only in hope. The classical Christian tradition has often worried over the problem that man cannot reach God if God is not already present in him; and yet if God is already present, either there is no advance made or it is God and not man who makes the advance. Since the harmony of the determinations of being that make up the determination "man" is what man is as a creature of God, God is present to his creatures as creator wherever the harmony is. If the harmony is present only as a mere unrealized lure in the depths of a man's heart, there is God present. And if the harmony is in fact realized, then it is the same source of harmony who is present at the religious fulfillment.

4. This brings us to the question whether the ultimate concern that is the motivating substance of the religious life determines its own object and fulfillment. The answer is both yes and no. Since religious concern, when it properly understands itself, is a concern for the ecstatic harmony that unites all the elements that are parts of being man in such a way that the person is truly human, the concern itself determines that its fulfillment be such a harmony. This is the "yes" part of the answer.

But the concern for the harmony is an abstract thing in that of itself it does not specify what acts, pursuits, or ways of being will result in the harmony. A person may quite well recognize that his concern is for something that will give wholeness, unity, or harmony to his life, and believe that business, marriage, politics, or art might be the way to achieve it. To choose what to do to fulfill ultimate concern requires more than an understanding of the concern itself. It requires metaphysics, anthropology, and all the arts and sciences by which we understand what life is and in what ways it might be unified. It might even require revelation or an "act of God." Furthermore, there is often a difficulty in conforming our actions to the choices that we know are right in our moments of cool reason. This is the "no" part of the answer.

Yet even though much is required beyond the mere ultimate concern itself, the character of the concern does give something of a criterion for sorting out the alternative suggestions. Although we may imagine that politics or art or marriage or some other thing will serve as the harmonizing element in life, close reflection will show that these concerns always have alternatives on a par with them. And so long as there are normative alternatives on a par, none can be the comprehensive harmonizer. The formal demands of the harmony do provide criteria for criticizing fulfillment candidates. This is the truth in Tillich's position.

There is a great error, however, beyond any we have discussed so far, in trying to make concern the key notion for understanding the inner religious life. Acknowledgment of religious concern is crucial, necessary, and primary.

But it cannot be made to do the whole work. The difficulty is that considerations of concern alone do not adequately take into account the things that structure concern, both actually and ideally. Without a discussion of those structuring elements, we are left with merely a vital force headed toward some abstract harmony. The virtue of Tillich's discussion is that he does indeed have a theory that provides the content. The difficulty with his discussion is that he sometimes speaks as if the considerations of concern alone bear the weight of all the other considerations as well. We must supplement our abstract discussion of religious concern with an analysis of the developments within it that come under the problem of salvation.

SECTION B

Conversion

Conversion is a generic phenomenon of which religious conversion is a specific, though perhaps most important, instance. Paradoxically, the classical statement of the generic nature of conversion comes not from a religious person but from Plato.

> . . . Education is not what it is said to be by some, who profess to put knowledge into a soul which does not possess it, as if they could put sight into blind eyes. On the contrary, our own account signifies that the soul of every man does possess the power of learning the truth and the organ to see it with; and that, just as one might have to turn the whole body round in order that the eye should see light instead of darkness, so the entire soul must be turned away from this changing world, until its eye can bear to contemplate reality and that supreme splendour which we have called the Good. Hence there may well be an art whose aim would be to effect this very thing, the conversion of the soul, in the readiest way; not to put the power of sight into the soul's eye, which already has it, but to ensure that, instead of looking in the wrong direction, it is turned the way it ought to be.[7]

Implied here is that conversion is an element of education, and Plato is concerned with that most general education possible to man; furthermore, he is most interested in how this education relates to political theory. Yet the conversion he mentions is rather like religious conversion. The educational view Plato attacks (the view that education is a matter of feeding in knowledge) is precisely the view that contrasts as an alternative to religious conversion. Education, for Plato, is a matter of converting the soul so that it can see something that is always present to it and or which it has the organ of seeing. What it is in the soul that needs converting, however, is not a bit of knowing but rather what we moderns call "will." How does this general notion of conversion apply to religion?

[7] *Republic* VII. 518; F. M. Cornford translation.

We would expect from our previous discussion that we should be able to mark off that area of knowledge religious conversion allows us to see. It should be the knowledge of what must be known for the soul to harmonize all the elements that, when harmonized, would make us truly human. What the heart wills depends in part on what it knows to will. For the will of the heart to be such that the whole person is harmonized, it must know what to will. The conception of "knowing what to will" is a very complex one. On the one hand, it signifies cognition in the sense of recognizing the characters of what is to be willed. On the other hand it signifies the appreciation of those characters as worthy of being willed, an appreciation so strong as to command the loyalty of the heart. "Knowing what to will," in this twofold sense, is the subject matter of the problem of faith. The problem of conversion is how a person gets this knowledge when he does not have it.

The notion of religious conversion logically implies both "sin" and "faith," for it marks the turning of the heart from one to the other. Our discussion of conversion must anticipate, therefore, what shall be said in a more systematic form about faith in the next section. "Sin," however, is a more parasitical notion, depending as it does on some conception of faith of which it can be denial, and it can be discussed here.

1. Sin is a peculiarly Western conception of the state *from which* true religion is the release and salvation. It has moral connotations that seem more or less lacking in its oriental counterparts. What roughly corresponds to the conception of sin in Eastern religions is an analysis of religion's problem as the release of man from the bondage of desire for finite pleasures and fulfillments. What is wrong with desire on the Eastern view is not that it is immoral but that its object is unreal.

Even the Western conception of sin, however, is not to be identified wholly with immorality, close though the connection may be. The popular use of the word "sins" to mean acts of moral wrongdoing has been roundly criticized by contemporary theologians. Sin is basically a religious category, not a moral one, and it connotes some sort of distortion or perversion of the proper connection between God and man. Sins are particular acts, habits, or traits that may stem from the fundamental perversion of the divine-human connection. These sins may also be immoral, but they need not be; we would say, in the Judeo-Christian tradition, that it is a sin merely to respect but not to love someone, but we would not say that it is immoral. Nor is everything that is immoral sinful, at least according to the Christian tradition. A person who is "right with God" still has problems of moral judgment, of moral tolerance, of moral concentration, and the like, and he still can err morally by faulting any of these.

Faulting the religious goal, like faulting the religious life, is not on a par with faulting other goals like those of morality. Put in terms of our metaphysics, the harmony with which religion is concerned is a total harmony. The harmonies that are the goals of moral ideals, being distinct from harmonies that are, for instance, aesthetic goals, are not comprehensive of all that goes into a truly human determination of being. Being partial, they can be achieved without the religious harmony. Conversely, the religious harmony can be achieved without the partial ones being fulfilled. We shall argue below that part of what must be recognized in faith is that men are finite and that part of being finite is the inability to realize all the norms that apply to what is fully human. We shall further argue, in opposition to several religious traditions, that religious fulfillment is compatible with the inevitable imperfection of many dimensions of man's being precisely in virtue of a faith that says perfection is proper to God and not man; our religious fulfillment consists in enjoying God's perfection.

This is, however, a general conclusion to be drawn from the arguments of this and the following two chapters. At present the point to be noted is that the Western conception of sin is not completely distinct from the Eastern counterparts because of an alleged insistence on morality.

2. Allied with the problem of sin and immorality, however, is another point on which Western and Eastern conceptions diverge rather sharply. This is the question whether the will is responsible for the sinful condition. East and West agree that it is the will or heart, the intentional center of man's self, that must be converted, disciplined, and so forth. They disagree on the question whether the condition from which the heart must be converted is a result of its own responsible action. Oriental religions tend to consider bondage to desires as the natural state of man; religious fulfillment is the transcendence of man's natural state to something not human at all, not even finite. Western religions accept the fact that sin seems *normal* for man, but they deny it is his *natural* state. Man's natural state is to be finite and perhaps immoral but not out of proper connection with God. Religious fulfillment on the Western view is not the transcendence of the human but rather the establishment of a proper connection between the human and divine. Sin does not consist in the fact that the human is not divine but rather in the fact that the human does not appreciate the presence and transcendence of the divine.

Since Eastern religions tend to interpret bondage to desires as natural, they make little point of calling the heart responsible for its condition. In no way could the oriental version of sin be called a perversion of the soul's natural state. This view, however, of the nature of man's religious wickedness does not take into account all that it should, and the Western view is more realistic. Let us argue the point.

In the first place, if we are to admit that religious fulfillment is complete transcendence of the human in man and is in no way his natural fulfillment, then the only reason that can be given for man's seeking religious fulfillment is that the natural state of man is unpleasant or undesirable in itself. This is the reason implicit in the Eastern religions. But it cannot be said that religious fulfillment is more *desirable* or *pleasant* than man's natural state, because the religious fulfillment itself is the *denial* of desire and pleasure. The view is that because desire and pleasure are never sufficiently satiated it is better to have neither. This is like saying that from the perspective of pain, lack of all sensation appears to be a good. What is unrealistic in this view is the belief that desires and pleasures are frustrating and bad. Sometimes, of course, they are; and perhaps in oriental lands life has usually seemed a burden. But desires sometimes can be satisfied and pleasures can often be fulfilled. True, satisfaction of desire and enjoyment of pleasures can lead to bondage of the heart to their pursuit; Plato's description of the fall of the despotic character in the *Republic* makes this point graphically. But as Plato also points out, proper education in temperance can keep man's appetites in a proper proportion to the other demands of his soul. Control of appetites in itself is hardly the chief problem of religion, since there is much more to man's nature than appetite alone.

In the second place, what Western religions take note of and what Eastern religions fail to appreciate is the perversity in man's heart. Man has an impulse that wittingly or unwittingly is self-destructive. This impulse proceeds on principles that not only fail to attain the harmony that is proper for man but that also prohibit its attainment. Although man's perversity may be directed in some special direction, for example, gluttony, it is an antireligious perversity in that it pursues its special direction for the sake of ruining the harmony of the whole. This need not be a conscious "for the sake of which," as modern psychology has pointed out, but may be an unconscious general principle of behavior.

The classic expression of the perversity that lies at the root of sin is the pride that goes before the fall. Out of pride man seeks to make himself something greater than he really is. And in the attempt to be greater, man loses the capacity to be even as much as fully human. The ancient Greeks developed this notion with their dramatic theme of *hubris*. The Hebrews considered it as rebellion against the worthy authority. In our day, novelists like William Faulkner depict the power of racial and regional pride to destroy even the best intentioned men and societies. Man would like to be better than merely human; yet the attempt to be better results in what is less than human, because it destroys the possibility of the properly human harmony. What the Eastern religions miss is the sense that the difficulty in human life lies not so much in man's impotence but rather in his belief that he is more potent than he is. Thus they fail to capture the poignancy in the religious problem. And likewise, they fail to articulate the difficulties in the problem of conversion.

3. Conversion is a change. This is a point everyone acknowledges. What is not so well agreed upon is the scope of the move. Some say conversion is a "rebirth," to use Jesus' term, which can take place in a day. Others argue that a person need not be "twice born" but only "once born" and that conversion might be nothing more than slow nurture from childhood in the community of faith. Yet others say that conversion is not just slow nurture, or a great crisis, but rather a series of smaller crises that are not even recognized as critical at the time, a series that is run through unevenly with successes and

failures. Great religious figures who typify these three positions and many variations are familiar to everyone.

The chief cause of this disagreement probably is that each position takes too narrow a view of the starting point of conversion. In certain societies and cultures the medium in which a religion must implant itself is alien to the religion. For example, the rough and tumble secular culture of the early American Middle West and Far West was a context from which a religious initiate could be wrenched only by a violent turning. The sharp-break paradigm of conversion "at a moment" has become standard for many of the evangelical Protestant denominations that grew to strength in the days of the river boat gambler and cattle rustler; this means that the "moment" of conversion for twentieth century Sunday school-bred people often degenerates to a matter of "mere" emotion. On the other hand, in societies and cultures where religious forms are deeply imbedded in the social fabric, the paradigm for conversion is more likely to be a slow maturation concerning the true and socially transcendent significance of the religious forms and beliefs. This is probably the characteristic kind of conversion in Anglican piety, for instance. In contemporary American society, especially among the well-educated and "culturally mature" groups, the religious forms that have become part of culture are often considered to be "merely" cultural and thus religiously hypocritical. Sometimes, of course, this is a true assessment. But more usually the problem is that the religious forms are socially parochial and for that reason unacceptable to a cosmopolitan person. A cosmopolitan person would indeed be hypocritical to commit himself to a cultural manifestation of religion too narrow to enliven the wide culture in which the person truly lives. For the cosmopolitan person, religious conversion is a matter of many small crises that bit by bit interpret the sinful condition from which he slowly must move and bit by bit put together a new form of the state of faith.

It is interesting that disagreement about the nature of conversion comes more from disagreement about the beginning of the process than from disagreement about the end. The reason for this is probably that, no matter what view of conversion is held, the view of the end of the process is vague. Most religious people are willing to admit that the development of the religious life is a process with many valid stopping places. Many people never get beyond a simple faith, simple almost to the point of simple-minded. Others live a life of great creative religious activity; these are the missionaries, the churchmen, the promulgators of religion. Still others might go so far as to attain the inner richness of the religious life that characterizes the bliss of the mystical saints. But no one will ultimately say that the end, at least in "this life," should be the same for all people.

What is necessary is that we give a characterization of the components of conversion that is vague enough to encompass the differences of construction and at the same time is structural enough to be significant. For this we can recur to our metaphysical account.

a) What a person must be converted from is the state where the principles according to which his heart operates, those principles that have to do with his whole being, do not produce that harmony of subsidiary determinations of being that would constitute true humanity. As we have noted, the disharmony a person must be converted from may be of many kinds and degrees. With young people, the disharmony may be simply that of immaturity; that is, in the process of growing up they may not have acted according to principles that harmonize all that a human being must harmonize. For all the integrity and harmony characteristic of childhood, we must admit that children are not responsible in many areas, which is to say that they yet lack the faculties of acting as a fully human being should. Sometimes, attaining the harmony of a truly human creature is simply a matter of maturing to the appropriation and use of the harmonizing principles.

With other people, the disharmony may be a more systematic problem. Often, the principles of the heart are incompatible and systematically prohibit a human harmony. In fact, there often are "superprinciples" whose content is to combine incompatible principles, thus producing disharmony. Pride, in the sense of aspiration to God's powers, is such a principle; it entails setting the principles governing our aspirations and sense of worth and accomplishment into conflict with those principles according to which our given powers are bound. The result is a perversion of our capacities from their fitting end to ends that are impossible for them; as a consequence, we do even less than is possible.

The disharmony from which a person is to be converted in most cases is a combination of many factors. Whatever the condition, conversion is a move away from it so long as it is a disharmony of the elements that must be harmonized in order for a person to be truly human.

b) What conversion moves a person *to* is the adoption of principles of the heart that produce the truly human harmony. The principles adopted constitute the content of the faith, which we shall discuss at length in the next section. Our concern here is with the nature of their "adoption."

The first thing to acknowledge about "adoption" is that adoption of certain principles is not the same thing as consistent, or even occasional, action according to them. To adopt a principle is to set the task of conforming action to it. Nothing is a plainer phenomenon in religion than the repeated experience of the converted that the discipline to which their conversion commits them is a difficult thing indeed. Sometimes the difficulty lies in not knowing what alternative conforms with the principles of faith. Sometimes the difficulty lies in self-control and personal self-mastery. Whatever the difficulties, it is clear that it is one thing to adopt the principles of faith in conversion and another thing to act consistently according to them. Conversion leads to the adoption of the principles of faith; living out the faith is another matter.

The second thing to acknowledge about "adoption" is that the person adopts principles he did not have before. If he had them before, his conversion would already have been accomplished. This is a complex point, although it seems simple at first. The complexity comes in the fact that neither before nor after conversion need it be the case that the activity of the person exhibit religious harmony. Before conversion, the person lacks the harmonizing principles. Afterward, he has adopted them but has not necessarily conformed his actions to them. It is the case, however, that we take conversion to be a significant portion of the religious life and that we do not make its significance depend wholly on the eventual success of conforming actions to principles.

One of the peculiarities of human nature is the importance that intentions have for it. For creatures with enough imagination to entertain alternative actions, intentions are the decisive factor. However much weight we must give to the effort that comes between the mere intention and the act, the intention alone is itself important. To adopt the principles of faith is to have the intention of conforming ourselves to them. Such an intention is a *sine qua non* for attaining the religious harmony. In a colloquial way we can say that conversion puts a person on the right track; it turns him in the right direction, however far he has yet to go.

A third and necessary characteristic of the adoption is that it be wholehearted. That the adoption be wholehearted is required by the very nature of the principles in question. That is, the principles are those that deal with the heart, principles that direct the actions that echo throughout man's whole being and that harmonize the whole. If the adoption were not wholehearted, then some determinations of the person's being would not be liable to integration according to the principles.

c) This point raises the question of religious concern. The result of religious conversion must be a religious concern, that is, a concern to appropriate in action the principles of faith adopted. But does conversion mark the first appearance of religious concern? This is another complex question, for religious concern has several degrees, as we have noted. Religious concern may be only a vague sense that something is missing in the way of harmony. But the result of conversion is more than this, for it means that the principles that will do the harmonizing are adopted. At the first stage of religious concern, a person may feel the problem but lack any inkling of the concrete solution. A full-blooded development of religious concern involves the concern's conformity to the content of faith. This is the wholeheartedness of the adoption of the principles. We can note that as the full-blooded development of religious concern requires first a recognition of the religious problem, so the first stage of religious concern is necessary for the process of conversion. How this is so brings us to our next point.

d) What is the inner development of the process of conversion? First must come a recognition of the lack of harmony and of the need for it. Since a person must be responsible in the process of conversion, the recognition must be conscious. Of course, the recognition may be in very symbolic terms, far removed from the rather theoretical and prosaic terms we use here; but their cash value must be the same. In fact, richly symbolic terms, quickened with the heritage of tradition, are usually far more potent for expressing the depth of understanding. A man may be unable to articulate in any clear way what it is that his life is missing and needs, but he begins with the uneasiness of doubt that may lead to despair. A man may find himself with the consciousness of a need and not recognize that it is religious; many people, in fact, are aware of the need we have characterized and argue that it is not a religious need. While this recognition is a first step in conversion, it is by no means inevitable that the rest of conversion will follow. The recognition of need may last unaided for a lifetime; or as many revival preachers will testify, it may be awakened for the first time on the crucial "night of decision."

Second must come an appreciation of the religious character of the lack of harmony. This involves two steps, though not necessarily temporally distinct. One is a recognition of the character of the trouble as something having to do with the heart. A man must see that the need he feels is no ordinary one but rather something that lies in the depths of his soul and that has to do with his very constitution as a person. Rarely if ever are the *terms* of this recognition those relating to the harmony of determinations of being; but in philosophical terms, that is what the religious understanding is getting at. The second step in recognizing the religious character of the trouble is to see that this inclusive problem of the heart is constitutive of man's connection with God. There are many symbols man can use in conceiving his relation with God, symbols that must, for this step to be taken, acknowledge God in his character as holy. Holiness, as we discussed in chapter 9, is the fundamental character in the conception of God, and man at this stage of the process of conversion must see his lack of harmony in relation to the holiness of God.

Now, how does a man come to see the connection between his lack of religious harmony and the holiness of God? He is struck at once with *awe* in the face of God and with an overwhelming feeling of *personal unworthiness* by comparison. We have mentioned earlier the classic passage from Isaiah that describes this, and counterparts are to be found almost universally. How is this response to be accounted for?

It is tempting to say at first that the connection is just a comparison of man and God on an equal footing for the purpose of shaming man at falling short of the holiness of God. But this is a superficial view. On the negative side, such a comparison would presuppose the anthropomorphizing of God to such an extent that he would have lost his holiness. On the positive side, for holiness to be on one side of the contrast, it must be acknowledged as something other and alien to man, contrary to the hypothesis. The power of God is holy just because it is so extramundane. The contrast Isaiah felt was not that God seems to be like a man who makes no mistakes whereas ordinary men do; the contrast is between the holiness of God and the unholiness of man, which is perhaps characterized by his mistakes.

To understand the connection between man's lack of religious harmony and God's holiness requires the acknowledgment of another factor, namely, the function of God as creator. To appreciate one's lack of human harmony as a religious problem is to see it as a task imposed by the fact that one is a creature of God. The task of one's authentic created being is to realize and enjoy that harmony, and to lack it is to fault one's creation. Whether or not a person possesses religious harmony, God is still holy by comparison with the man's mundane status. But God's holiness is a cause for alarm when man has done something to fault it. In the Western tradition this fault is called disobedience, and it is the Western tradition that, as we have argued, has the more realistic understanding of sin and the religious problem. Appreciation of the religious significance of the lack of religious harmony is an essential step in the logic of the process of conversion.

The third step in the process must be an apprehension of grounds for hope in remedying the situation. This means an understanding of part of the content of faith. Apprehension of the grounds for hope must precede commitment to the hope; otherwise the commitment is irresponsible. Usually in religion the grounds for hope are twofold. On the one hand, there is something the individual must do: repent, undertake discipline, and so forth. On the other hand, the individual must wait for God to do something: send his healing spirit, take the devotee up into the annihilation of nothingness, or whatever. This will be discussed in greater detail in the section below on the content of faith. The important point for present purposes is that, at this stage in the process, conversion means learning something new, the grounds for hope. Perhaps in a conversion situation this may be merely a matter of remembering something the significance of which was not appreciated before.

The fourth step in the process is the commitment to the hope. This commitment means both the will to undertake whatever the individual must do and the acceptance of whatever it is the individual must wait for God to do. At this point the process of conversion shades into the more general and prolonged task of living out the religious life in the faith. As we have remarked, sometimes the conversion is a quick and climactic event. Sometimes it is a much longer process with each phase broken down into many fits and starts. The end of conversion does not necessarily mean the complete possession of the harmony aimed at. But there are many degrees of possession, and conversion sets the person on the track of living out the harmony.

e) We have indicated only briefly the role of God in a man's conversion, and it is necessary to discuss this further. Man is a creature with certain features who faces an environment more or less distinct from him. This distinction is the basis of our division of the subject of religion into the inner life and the public life. From the standpoint of the inner religious life, conversion is the process of getting an external presence of God into the inside. It is the process of changing the lack of the presence of God in faith to some inner possession of the presence of God in faith. In parallel fashion, one of the chief tasks of the public religious life is the transference of the inwardly possessed presence of God into the external environment.

There is a standard problem with the view that conversion involves a move from a state wherein God is not real to the person nor possessed by him to the state where he is both real and possessed. This problem has two prongs. The first is that a man, lacking the presence of God, cannot on his own cook up God's presence out of some stuff that does not include it. In metaphysical terms, if a person lacks the creative presence of God in a harmony of his human determination of being, then no amount of mere switching around of pieces that are part of his nature is going to bring the harmony about. The second prong of the problem is that if the person really lacks the presence of God in religious harmony, then he will not even be interested in acquiring it. Or if he is interested in acquiring it, then this proves that God is already present.

The answer to the first prong of the problem is to admit that conversion entails an entrance of God from the outside. Whether mediated through some externally articulated word, prophet, or gospel, or whether God enters more directly through some divine afflatus, there is a point in conversion where the individual must just sit and wait. This relatively passive and receptive moment is acknowledged in nearly all religious traditions.

The answer to the second prong is more difficult, for it seems to have the logical form of a dilemma. If God is not present, then no conversion is possible; yet if he is present, then no conversion is needed. Such rigid alternatives, however, overlook the developmental character of the religious harmony. As we have noted both in this section and the last, there are degrees of actualization of the religious harmony. Minimally, the harmony makes its presence felt, because of its absence, in the form of an uneasiness and doubt about the general condition of life. Maximally, it is concretely present in a life lived in accord with the harmony in all details. Between these two there are many stages and degrees. However, the dilemma does point to a distinction that has yet to be acknowledged. So long as it is true that there is a possible presence of God that is not realized, we must distinguish between two senses of the presence of God. One is the sense in which the religious harmony is concretely possessed. The other is the sense in which there is a trace of the harmony present in the person that effects the move toward concrete possession. As it is put in the Christian tradition, it is by faith that man possesses the grace of God and it is by God's grace that we come to have faith. Conversion is a move to a state of faith.

SECTION C
Faith

The word "faith" signifies many things in the religious life. Sometimes it signifies an attitude of trust or belief in certain religious principles. This is the topic that was opened in the discussion of adoption in the previous section, and we shall return to it in the section on certainty. The word "faith" also refers to the principles themselves. To speak of a "state of faith" is to speak of both these senses together. In this section we shall discuss the content of faith, or its principles.

The content of faith is where the most explicit disagreement comes between religions. Even when it is recognized that much of the disagreement is only apparent because of the use of different symbols to indicate more or less the same thing, there is still considerable disagreement left. The disagreement may well be irreducible when it comes down to a matter of affirmations about the historical claims of the various traditions. For instance, a Jew's beliefs about Moses, a Christian's about Jesus, and a Muslim's about Mohammed are in inevitable conflict, no matter how persuasive a Hindu might be about the equality of Moses, Jesus, and Mohammed as revealers of God.

Despite the disagreements, however, some general features of the content of faith can be determined by considerations about the function of that content in the religious life. This is one of the profound truths in Tillich's approach. Whatever the content of faith is, we know that it functions so as to provide grounds for the hope that the saving religious harmony can be obtained. The next step is to turn to some more particular considerations about the nature of the religious harmony and see how the content of faith can lead to it.

Religious harmony is supposed to harmonize all the determinations that go into being a true human being. All harmonies have patterns, and every pattern that articulates the togetherness of several determinations of being is a kind of harmony. Even if a person lacks religious harmony, he still is a togetherness of determinations and hence does have a harmony of a sort.

There are many ways of having several determinations of being together. Some patterns unite determinations by giving dominance to some while subordinating or even excluding others. A unity of several determinations may be the sort that takes certain of the determinations into account only by excluding them, or perverting them, or subordinating them, or by frustrating their full realization in the harmony of the whole. A person's pattern of unity might, for instance, include certain moral demands on his activity by explicitly ignoring them. Or the only aesthetic dimension in a person's life might be gross aesthetic insensitivity. There are many dimensions and areas of man's life that are subject to norms or that call for fulfillment. Even when an area of human life is not fulfilled or is perverted or frustrated, it is included in partial form in the totality of things that together make up the character of the man; and there is a pattern of unity for each of the actually possible combinations. Where each pattern is actually operative, there is the presence of God. But not every presence of God in a unifying pattern is the one appropriate to a truly human determination of being. The creator is present in everything that is determinate, but not every determination is a truly human one, even when it is in some sense a person.

What is the general criterion for a truly human harmony? The obvious first guess is that the religious harmony sought is one that allows for the complete fulfillment or perfection or conformity to relevant norms of all areas of life, of all the determinations that go into a human being. By contrast, a person who lacks religious harmony is one whose harmony is such that some parts of life are frustrated, especially the moral parts.

But a little reflection will show that this first guess is naïve and over enthusiastic. It is an empirical fact that the conditions of human existence do not allow for this perfection of each and every part of a man's nature. There is no more common important experience of mankind than that more is demanded by human nature than it can perform, given the conditions of human existence. No matter how a man lives his life, there are parts of his nature that he must subordinate and frustrate. No matter how morally sensitive he is and careful in moral scruples, there will be situations where he must choose to deny some good in order to affirm some other good. The conditions of human life are a matter of empirical fact. There may be no necessity in principle that man must always fail; but it is certainly true that impoverished conditions provide far less possibility for fulfillment than do enriched conditions. The art of political science is that of providing the maximum external conditions of fulfillment, and perhaps in many generations the external necessities of frustration will be removed. But this is unlikely. As a matter of empirical fact, men have never lived under conditions that allow them to be perfect, and they do not now. Each man's being is created in determinate relation to the conditions of his own place and time; that is his created nature. Therefore, he cannot be created to be what is not allowed by the conditions of his created being. And therefore, religious harmony cannot be the perfection of all parts of a person's nature.

This has an important ramification for the conception of sin. For, if religious harmony is not perfection of nature, then sin is not mere imperfection of nature. It cannot be mere moral failure qua moral failure, or aesthetic insensitivity as such, or any other failing in the many dimensions of man's life. Sin must be a failing with regard to the peculiar religious harmony that we have yet to articulate.

What we have learned from the first guess about the nature of religious harmony is that any articulation of the harmony must include or be compatible with the infirmities of finite human existence. Any principles of faith that serve as the ground of hope for attaining religious harmony must allow for the inevitability, at least under present conditions, of the partiality, frustration, and plain moral failure of life. The perfection of human life is inhuman. The recognition of the infirmities and ambiguities of finite existence is the first ingredient to be noticed in the religious harmony. To err is human.

A further point is apparent here. If it is the case that many areas of human life are unfulfilled by necessity, and that the proportion of justice done to each one depends on many contingent circumstances, then the pattern descriptive of the religious harmony is not a single distinct pattern alongside other patterns of life like the artistic, the moral, the political, the philosophical. Any of those many patterns of life may be what conditions bind us to.

The religious harmony has to adapt itself to many different patterns descriptive of different ways of life. This is the same point that we noted in the previous chapter in discussing the connection of the religious life with other ways of life.

But if the religious harmony can indeed be present in many different patterns, the crucial question becomes, What is distinctive about the religious harmony? Of course, what is distinctive is a distinctive presence of God. To have a religious harmony is what man is created to be, and the creator is present in a fulfilled way when the religious harmony is present. There are several points to be made in elaboration and defense of this.

1. As a life lived in accord with religious harmony must admit, on the one hand, that it must be imperfect in the sense that many parts of it cannot be fulfilled, it must admit, on the other hand, that all the parts should be fulfilled; that is, that perfection by definition is still its norm even though impossible. Kant's dictum that "ought" implies "can" finds no acceptance in the religious man whose sense of failure is much more profound than that of simple moral errors. What ultimately must be harmonized for the religious man is his obligation to perfection and his inevitable failure. Since failure is inevitable, the actual patterns of life that can be religious are many; if any partial way of life can be religiously harmonious, a great many can. The religious harmony must include more than the actual pattern of life. It must include a reconciliation of perfection with imperfection.

2. Where is the reconciliation or harmony of imperfection with obliged perfection reached? Since man himself cannot do it, the alternatives are the rest of the world, or God, or both. The rest of the world cannot possibly do it, since by definition it is the man's nature that needs to be perfected and the conditions in which he lives do not allow it. This leaves the possibility that God in himself achieves the reconciliation or does it in conjunction with the world, and these alternatives, in one way or another, are those to which religion has turned.

Some Eastern religions tend to account for religious harmony by saying that from the standpoint of God, a standpoint attainable by man in some states, the imperfection component is unimportant and unreal. But there are several difficulties with this solution when the problem is seen in its depths. On a practical level, it is self-defeating, for to the degree to which the religious harmony must declare the actual human side to be unimportant and unreal, to that degree the harmony itself becomes unimportant for the resolution of the actual human side's practical problems. The practical problem always begins with the actual state of affairs as that which has to be harmonized.

Religions like Judaism tend to account for the harmony in terms of a conjunction of God with the rest of the world. On this view of harmony the good excluded from a man's life is realized elsewhere, as a man's evil is elsewhere atoned; this is a religious harmony because God must credit man with the good done external to him and cleanse his iniquities with someone else's bruises. Much of this thinking is carried over into Christianity in some doctrines of sacrificial atonement. Paul Weiss defends the general point. It is also the function of God on this view, especially as explained by Weiss, not only to keep the balance sheet of vicarious merit and atonement but also to arrange the course of events so that all goods do get realized in the long run.[8]

The merit of this solution is that it does appreciate the full weight of the imperfection-perfection conflict. The finite conditions of existence are seen to preclude the possibility of individual perfection; moreover, this position sees that if perfection is part of the definition of one's nature, then that perfection must be reconciled or harmonized with the actual imperfection. Perfection is nothing but the realization of the norms a thing falls under because of its nature, and if a thing has a nature that falls under norms, there is a perfection relevant to it. There is considerable dispute about exactly what norms are binding on man, but there is little denying that some do and that our failure to fulfill them is virtually inevitable. All of this is taken into account by this interpretation of religious harmony.

The difficulty with it, however, is twofold. First, it allows no possibility of final damnation. That is, if the religious harmony is a necessary adjustment of conditions to make up the good a man fails, then God is metaphysically obliged by nature to see to the adjustment. God is thus the eternal meddler, committed to the task of making sure that everything turns out well in the end. Damnation or ultimate religious failure is not a real possibility. Yet this consequence goes utterly against the religious consciousness. It amounts finally to the previous theory, the claim that the imperfection of finite life is not important and in the long run unreal. The second difficulty with this view is that the transference of credit from something external to the person is unintelligible. Its only plausibility comes from analogy with a monetary system where there is coin, indifferent in nature to ownership, that is transferred from one party to another. But a person's religious failures are precisely the things that are not indifferent to ownership. This metaphor fails for the same reason that the theory fails that says that the external world by itself makes up the value a person loses. It can never sustain itself in the religious consciousness.

3. Both the interpretation of religious harmony prominent in Eastern religions and that prominent in Judaism have many counterparts and variations in nearly all religions. But as we have seen they cannot sustain themselves when pressed, and they move by degrees to some version of a third interpretation of religious harmony.

The religious harmony in a crucial respect is not realized in man or in the world but in God. A significant part of the harmony is not realized in the created product at all. It is realized, if at all, in God as creator; God makes himself *forgiver* as he makes himself creator. Like all questions about God in his transcendence, the question about *how* God does the reconciliation cannot

---

[8] See *Modes of Being* (Carbondale: Southern Illinois University Press, 1958), prop. 2.14, and p. 14.

be put intelligibly at all. The difference the harmony makes for man, however, is that he is forgiven his imperfections and failure to realize in himself the diverse obligations of his nature. Forgiveness, if it is there, is indeed a part of creation. A person who is both imperfect and forgiven is not in contradiction and lives harmoniously with both perfection and imperfection. But the harmony is not contained exclusively in the person, and most importantly the basis or ground of the harmony is not in him but in God.

Given both the imperfection and the forgiveness, the religious problem for man is resolved; it is the man's status as a creature that makes the problem religious in the first place, and the forgiveness, coming from the creator, comes from the right source. How the imperfection and perfection are reconciled in God so that forgiveness is the issue is of course a mystery. But it is a mystery located in the right place, in God's aseity. And it is the same mystery as the one noted before in Part One, Why is there creation such as it is at all?

4. Forgiveness acknowledges the ultimate importance of the failure and imperfection by its very meaning. If the failure were unreal or unimportant, or if it would be taken up in some greater good, there would be no need for or meaning to forgiveness. Furthermore, the very lack of intelligible principles relating forgiveness to imperfection, the very arbitrariness of it, underscores the possibility of damnation. From the standpoint of any intelligible principles, whether God in fact forgives is a quite contingent matter.

5. The prime question for religion, then, is *whether* God forgives. If he does not, then despair about the religious harmony is the only accurate response. Whether God forgives some or many, others but not me, is the question to which religion must address itself. It is quite possible according to the metaphysical nature of things that God creates some persons in whom there is no reconciliation of imperfection with perfection. There may be no possibility of their realizing their natures. They may be created damned. The recognition of this possibility is a profound truth in the predestination theory, and it is because of the recognition of this truth that the predestination view goes to the depths of the religious problem. But it is the affirmation of every religion, in some form or other, that God does not exclusively damn. He sometimes, perhaps universally, forgives. Where he forgives, he does so by no necessity. It is always a surprise. Although it is human to err, to forgive is divine. If man can be truly human, it is because he both errs and is forgiven.

6. This being the nature of religious harmony, what is the content of faith that it can give grounds for hope in the attainment of the harmony? The content of faith in one guise or another must be such that it indicates forgiveness. Yet the indication of forgiveness is never so abstract as merely to be a pronouncement.

To indicate forgiveness it is first of all necessary to indicate the nature of what is forgiven. A man must first of all appreciate the nature of his imperfections and sin. We have spoken before of external conditions as the source of man's failure to perfect the many dimensions of his life. The real poignancy of man's condition is that internal conditions as well contribute to the failure. Who has not felt the utter shame of realizing that even if the external conditions were perfect he still would have erred? As St. Paul noted when he said, "the good I would I do not," our internal makeup sometimes becomes a recalcitrant stumbling block to our good will, as frustrating as any external factor. Yet even our bad nature and ignorance can be forgiven. This is the first thing we must realize. All developed religions have myths and symbols that indicate this.

Furthermore, our connection to God must be indicated in such a way that he is seen as the proper source of forgiveness. What man is, if he is so fortunate as to be forgiven, or so unfortunate as not to be, he is because of the creative work of God. This is indicated by religions in the many accounts of elements of the created world that testify to this connection by disclaiming their own power and proclaiming God's. Whether these things are elements of nature, self-denying prophets, or even a Christ who utterly relinquishes what power he has apart from God, the majesty of God as source of forgiveness or damnation is proclaimed.

Finally, some testimony to the actuality of God's forgiveness must be given. There is no need to testify to the actuality of damnation, because for the damned by definition there is no hope and hence no faith. Testimony to the actuality of forgiveness is a very difficult matter. In one sense, the only testimony is external; that is, "other people" give evidence that they are actually forgiven and that there is evidence to believe that forgiveness is promised for the hearer. Even in religions that primarily conceive of man as a member of a community who must participate in collective forgiveness, there are testimonies of the "golden age" when forgiveness was enjoyed and appeals to covenants and special revelations that promise further forgiveness. In Christianity, the saints and martyrs testify and the life of Jesus constitutes the promise. The testimony and the promise are necessary elements of faith as the ground of hope.

In another sense, the testimony and promise of faith must be internal. That is, faith must indicate the actuality of forgiveness in the person already. This is the topic of the next section on certainty.

7. To attain religious harmony, a man must adopt the faith in forgiveness with all his religious passion. The question at issue here is whether, if God's forgiveness is what makes religious harmony, the forgiveness must be appreciated consciously by man. Is not God's forgiveness enough? For the answer we must refer back to the nature of the religious problem, that is, to sin. The inevitable imperfection of man is sometimes, and nearly always in mature people, compounded with a belief in the possibility of overcoming it. This is the belief that it is man's nature to be able to be perfect. But this is false pride, as we have seen. If the imperfection is to be overcome, it is only by God's forgiveness, and man arrogates to himself God's work when he ascribes the possibility to himself. Pride, as the saying has it, goes before a fall. When pride's confidence is broken, as it almost inevitably will be, the natural move is to despair without hope or light. Religion must get the word through to

man, both in his pride and in his despair, that there is another alternative, that imperfection is overcome by God's forgiveness. Religion says that man must be humble and accept God's work. Despair is not humility but only matured pride.

If a man does not become aware of God's forgiveness, his pride will keep him from ever living in accord with it. The forgiven man, ignorant of his fortune, has the religious harmony in a moment, as it were. But if he continues to seek what he mistakenly thinks is something better, he will never enjoy the religious harmony in his life. He will not consciously enjoy the presence of God in the harmony. Since it seems part of the nature of man to enjoy his humanity, which must include the presence of God, the prideful man will needlessly be imperfect if he does not understand God's forgiveness.

It still must be admitted, however, that not to understand the forgiveness of God is merely another of the many imperfections to which man is liable. As such, it too can be forgiven, for we have no way of limiting the forgiving power of God. This is not to say that forgiveness can fail to have a palpable effect on the man's life. To forgive is to create forgivingly and this must make a harmonizing difference to the created product.

8. Properly to have faith means not only to have the grounds of hope present and to recognize them. It means also that the person must adopt them and commit himself to working out his life in the light of the content of faith. A forgiven man who does not know he is forgiven may enjoy certain benefits of the grace of God, but he is not a man of faith. Faith requires conscious judgment and action on the part of man; it is man who has the faith. Nor is a man who merely recognizes and acknowledges the content of faith a proper man of faith, for part of the content of faith is always a call to live life in all its dimensions and areas in light of the forgiveness of God, appropriating the harmony this allows. Merely to acknowledge the *truth* of faith is not properly to acknowledge it, for a proper acknowledgment leads straight to practical action.

It has long been an accepted rule of thumb in religion that the way to tell a true man of faith is by his public behavior. If the religion is one chiefly formed by considerations of community ties to God, then the man of faith is the good citizen of the covenant community. If the chief formative element is a person—teacher, prophet, or savior—the man of faith is the good disciple. In all cases the test of faithfulness is martyrdom, that is, public testimony or witness. This is the part of faith that leads from the private to the public, and our discussion of faith must interrupt itself here and resume in the next chapter when we take up the public side.

SECTION D

Certainty

No element of religion seems more offensive to the unreligious than the claims of the faithful to certainty. All of the oppression and wars, inquisitions and censorships, that unjustly have been perpetrated in the name of certainty, for all their evil, still seem not so insidious as the claim to certainty itself. The claim to certainty is seen by the unreligious to be based on evidence that is not available to them, and this seems unfair, in fact inhuman, and therefore probably false pretention. Yet there is something in religion for which the claim to certainty seems the best expression. The funded wisdom of religion indicates that there is considerable truth in each of the following theses:

Faith involves belief in things unseen, that is, belief in things for which adequate evidence is not at hand.

Faith involves belief on the basis of authority that testifies to itself.

Faith involves a will to believe, based on the view that making oneself believe contributes to the truth of the content of the belief.

Faith involves absolutely honest criticism both of personal character and of the content of belief. (As John E. Smith has expressed it, a faith that is dead certain is certainly dead.)

Despite the fact that these seem incompatible, most religions have maintained them all in some form or other. To untangle the problem of certainty in religion we shall examine them in turn.

1. *Belief in things unseen.* It must be acknowledged that at least part of what is meant by faith is that it is different from plain knowledge. Faith involves the belief or trust in something the authority for which is not wholly present. Otherwise, the connotation of faith that means trust would fall away, for there is no need to trust what is fully present and made plain. Those who have attempted to eliminate from faith the sense that in some way the faithful believe where they do not see either have reduced religion to external forms for which intelligible belief makes no difference or have turned the intellectual part of religion into sterile dogmatism. There are three questions that must be put. About what do the faithful believe when they do not see? On what grounds do they do so? Are these worthy grounds?

The first question can be given an abstract and precise answer. What one believes without seeing is that God is actually forgiving and that this forgiveness applies to oneself. It will be remembered that we determined faith to be the adoption of the grounds for hope for the attainment of religious harmony. Although adoption means more than mere belief, it does involve belief. Many of the things faith is to believe are there to be seen and do not require belief without evidence. Thus the man of faith believes certain things about the worth of his own actions and character, and although judgments of this sort are difficult, there is nothing to prevent the accumulation of sufficient evidence to make beliefs of this sort well founded. Furthermore, faith must grasp the intellectual purport of certain ideas, perhaps in very symbolic form, that connect the meaning of man's imperfect nature with his ideal of perfection, that articulate the meaning of God's forgiveness for the problem of religious harmony, and so forth. All of this should be understood, not merely trusted, in as straightforward a way as possible. Otherwise faith becomes the belief in something the meaning of which is not understood in precisely the respects it is believed; this would be non-sense, the assertion of what has no meaning. But *that* God actually forgives one is not a matter of meaning to be grasped or of empirical self-criticism; it must be believed without being seen.

Why does a person believe in the forgiveness of God? There are thought to be many reasons. The first usually cited is that a person believes because he wants to believe, and there is a truth in this that we shall discuss below. But it is easy to accuse a person of believing because he wants to when there is a deeper problem that in reality prevents him from believing. When the problem of belief is being fought out in the depths of the soul, the reason that persons do *not* believe in the forgiveness of God is not always lack of evidence. Rather it often is that men pridefully think that attaining religious harmony is their own job and that God's forgiveness is not needed. The man who is deeply concerned and who does not believe in God's forgiveness is precisely the one who does not want to believe; those who do want to believe often are those not taking a serious enough view of the matter.

Turning to the evidence, we can see that the reason why persons believe in the forgiveness of God often seems to be very closely connected with their coming to terms with some historical person who claims to have accepted the forgiveness and who exhibits great humility in doing so. Witness the story of Hosea in the Old Testament, and the story of Jesus' passion. The classic analysis of conversion to faith in Augustine's *Confessions* turns on the critical points at which Augustine heard about the public conversions of the emperor's secret service men and Victorinus the orator.[9] The humility of these men demonstrated to Augustine his own lack of humility by contrast and led him sincerely to desire God's forgiveness.

The desire to have God's forgiveness is not the same as the desire to *believe* that one actually enjoys it when this may be false; the honest man will not confuse the two. An honest man may desire the forgiveness and believe that he does not have it. In all religions, over and above the existence of holy men, there exists some kind of proclamation or promise of forgiveness for the religious man to buy into. This promise may take the form of the teachings of holy men or gurus, of community covenants between God and a people, of doctrines articulating the meaning of a life, and so on. But the promise is there, and it is what the man believes when he desires forgiveness and believes it is available to him.

The final question here is whether the promise is worthy of belief. This is the inescapable question of authority. The alleged authority is that the promise comes from a necessarily truthful God. Although the promise has an authority that is mediated by the religious tradition, it is God's authority that

[9] See the *Confessions* VIII, chaps. 2 and 6.

the tradition alleges itself to have. Necessarily the articulation of the promise is mediated by the tradition. But it has often been argued that the authority of God is precisely the thing that is at issue in the promise. How can something whose authority is in question testify to its own authority? This brings us to our second thesis.

2. *The self-testimony of authority.* In all religions, one way or another, there is an acknowledgment that something in the glory or worshipfulness of God must be seen to be believed. Regardless of how one stands with regard to rational proofs that there must be a God, a creator, or even that God must be glorious, to believe that God is glorious is less than beholding the glory itself. Sometimes the attempt is made to resolve the question of authority by saying that if one believes in God one must believe his promises to be trustworthy and, therefore, that one must believe his promises of forgiveness. What this argument overlooks is that, although one's belief in the reality of God might be independent of an appreciation of his glory, one's acceptance of his authority depends very much on a concrete response, on beholding his glory or worthiness. As it is put in the Christian tradition, the acceptance of authority must come from the testimony of the Holy Spirit.

Where is the glory of God to be seen in this connection? Schematically this question can be answered in metaphysical terms. As we argued in chapter 9, the interpretation of God's holiness and glory centers around the notion of creation. As we shall further spell out in section F below, his glory is seen in the fact that he creates the determinations of being, each of which is a harmony of other determinations. The presence of the creator, indicative of his glory, is to be found in each unifying harmony. Religion finds the glory manifested in the inner harmonies of the religious life, in its public expressions, and in the interplay of them both. Our present point is that it is possible that the glory of God be indicated in many ways. Wherever seen, God's glory is expressed as the unity, truth, beauty, and goodness that are definitive of his creation as such.

Suppose now that a person is led to catch a glimpse of God's glory somewhere or other. What is proved by this? Simply to see God's glory is not *ipso facto* to see in a plain presentation his forgiveness of oneself. Sight of the glory might be the very thing that convinces a person of his own inadequacy and sends him into despair. Apprehending God's glory, a person must still take another step to believe in his forgiveness. What the sight of the glory contributes, however, is a respect for the authority of the vehicle of the promise of forgiveness. If the vehicle of the promise manifests the glory of God in a way relevant to the promise itself, authority is given to the promise so conveyed. For example, Jews may trust the authority of the promise conveyed by Abraham because they see the glory and presence of God manifested in Abraham's life. Christians trust the authority of God's promises conveyed by Jesus because they see the glory of God manifested in him as the Christ.

We still must ask whether the vision of God's glory is an adequate logical

ground for belief in his promise of forgiveness. That it has been the actual
ground of many persons' belief is an empirical fact of which there are
countless familiar witnesses. As a logical argument, however, there are still
lacunae. However much the traditions and persons—as vehicles of the promise—might be holy men and institutions, the intellectual content of their
assertions of the promise might be mistaken, as all finite intellects are prone
at times to be. Massive general agreement of the witnesses might lend
plausibility; it might even put the probability factor on the side of belief in
the promises, such that a person would for practical purposes be a fool for
not believing them. Should a person find the presence of God deep within
himself, and feel very strongly that this presence is forgiving, still, to be
honest about the frailties of intellect and the ambition of desires, he must
admit that the argument in favor of the promise is not certain. God's glory
may be seen with certain self-evidence, indubitable without utter violence to
fundamental experience; but God's forgiveness must just be believed on faith.

Suppose, however, that one does believe. Is there any confirmation?

3. *The will to believe.* If believing in God's forgiveness is essential to
living a life that exhibits religious harmony, then the belief must make some
kind of difference to the life. And if the difference is an important one and
life is sufficiently complex, evidence should appear in the course of living to
show that the belief is well or ill founded. Therefore, the way to test the
belief, other rational ways being inconclusive, is to will to believe and see
what happens in the long run.

Making this point in his famous essay, "The Will to Believe," William
James ostensibly contrasted his view with that expressed in Pascal's wager.
The difficulty James pointed out with the wager was not that it enjoined
belief where rational evidence is inconclusive. Rather the difficulty was that
Pascal had not made his options to be adjudicated "living" ones. What James
objected to was that for himself and for his audience Pascal's view of hell and
damnation was too alien to the imagination to be much of a worry and his
view of positive religious belief as leading to masses and holy water was too
closely bound to an alien culture. If Pascal had talked of spiritual sickness and
spiritual health, James would have thought the point of his wager a valid one.

James's criticism of Pascal is important. It indicates the significance of the
fact that the conception of the promise must be put in terms relevant to the
person whose belief in it is in question. The will to believe a promise whose
terms are not significant in one's experience is not warranted by intellectual
honesty. To give up the grounds for probating the promise is to give up the
significance of the promise as something that can direct life in accord with
religious harmony. It is also to give up the honesty that is a norm for being
truly human.

4. *The life of criticism.* To believe a promise that God is forgiving with
respect to one's inadequacies is at the same time to commit oneself to live a
life of self-criticism. The religious man who believes he is forgiven and who
orders his life in accordance with this belief accepts the fact that the evidence

for his belief is not all in. But at the same time he critically examines his life to discover where the evidence should be.

In general terms, the test for the truth of the belief is whether, accepting God's forgiveness, one's life actually embodies the religious harmony. In slightly less general terms, this embodiment must express itself in the inner religious life, the public side, and in their interplay. The inner wholeness of the person has many forms. The intellectual life of the person should see the beliefs of religion grow more consistent with each other, more coherent with the rest of belief, more applicable to the many dimensions of life, and more adequate to precise and appropriate interpretation. The emotional life of a person should become more objective and accurate in response to things, more consistent with beliefs and aims, better able to integrate its sorrows and troubles into a happiness of the whole. But what these general criteria mean for a specific individual must be worked out in other terms appropriate to his own life. Only in this way will accurate criticism of a career of belief in God's forgiveness be possible.

The critical question, however, is at what point the evidence will be taken to prove the belief in God's forgiveness unwarranted. There is no specific doctrine or belief that is not to be subjected to scrutiny, if man is honest. There is no emotion that, if it is an accurate response to what happens, should be covered over or explained away. What discovery of error in a religious tradition justifies the rejection of that tradition, including the promise of forgiveness it conveys? What emotional grief is finally incompatible with the actuality of God's forgiveness? Although God's truth may be beyond human saying and his mercy beyond comprehension, where is the point at which we should take no more?

Religion gives no criteria to decide this, and since it is a matter of proximate judgment, neither does philosophy. Religion claims only that, if man believes, then as a matter of fact the confirming evidence of God's forgiving glory will come in and not the disconfirming evidence. It is impossible to say in advance when the experiment is to be over. What it is possible to say, however, is that, once it is declared over and belief in forgiveness is rejected, then the hope for the sake of which man believed in the first place becomes impossible. Living the life of religious harmony is admitted to be a lost cause. No matter how much contrary evidence is in, to accept it as final is to give up the possibility of winning. The reason man wills to believe in the first place is not so much to find out the truth of the promises, although perhaps it is that, too; rather it is to live the life of religious harmony. If this latter reason justifies the believing at the beginning, then it does so all along the way. In poetic terms, to decide that the evidence of life has shown a belief in the forgiveness of God to be unwarranted is to trade heaven for a probability. This is the point of Pascal's wager and the will to believe.

If we must consider the certainty of the man of faith regarding belief in God's forgiveness, and must do so without taking into account the actual evidence that fills his life, the certainty amounts to this: it is certain that if I do not believe all that is most important about my being is lost; and it is certain that if I do believe the most that can be suffered if my belief is mistaken is not a loss of intellectual integrity (for the will to believe is a rational procedure) but rather a blow to intellectual pride. Without God's forgiveness, life is chiefly the suffering of pride anyway.

SECTION E
Solitude

We must turn to those aspects of experience wherein belief in God's promise can show its warrant. There are two dimensions of man's inner life where God's presence as creator constitutes fulfillment of the promise and warrant for belief in it: man's solitude and his bliss.

A person is in solitude when he is alone. To be alone means to be cut off, physically, socially, emotionally, intellectually, or some other way from what is "other." In abstract terms, a determination of being is in solitude when it is cut off from active commerce with those determinations external to itself and with respect to which it is determinate. For human beings, solitude is to be cut off from those things outside the person that are significant for the person's identity, especially other people, family and friends; but also a person can be in solitude by moving to a new place, different from his home, by changing the society and social structure with which he is familiar for another. A person can be in solitude by growing beyond the human and physical environment that previously constituted the relevant portions of his world.

Certain metaphysical considerations, however, show that to be in solitude cannot mean being cut off completely from God. Although a solitary determination of being, cut off from other determinations, is cut off from the presence of God in those others, it cannot be cut off from the creative presence of God that creates its own being. If the determination is real, in any sense at all, then it enjoys the presence of God that gives it being, unifying the determinations that comprise it. If the solitary determination happens to be a human being, then it may be possible for it to enjoy in conscious fashion God's presence. Solitude means being alone and cut off from everything except the creator. This abstract metaphysical truth has immense practical religious importance.

Although there are doubtless many kinds of solitude, there are two principle classes that are of significance for religion. The first is what contemporary commentators like to call *estrangement*. In terms of our categories, this means being cut off from elements of our world in ways that frustrate our religious harmony; that is, it means being cut off in ways that keep us from being truly human or that keep us from appropriating God's forgiveness, which would allow us to live a religiously harmonious life. As we shall see in the next chapter, estrangement is part of the religious problem that arises in connection with the public side of religion.

The second class of ways in which we are cut off includes those ways that are essential to and partially constitutive of man's being as an individual. To be cut off in these ways does not constitute a failure on man's part, as do the various kinds of estrangement; rather, these ways are essential and necessary to humanity. The very fact that man is a determination of being with an inner as well as a public life means that this inner life is cut off from the world. The world may affect a man's inner life, and the inner life may be expressed in the world; but for the world to affect a man's inner life, it must be transformed into something inner, something that is no longer only public but that is intrinsically possessed by the man. The inner life may express itself in the world, but only by transforming itself into something public and objective. Either kind of transformation acknowledges an integrity in the distinction between public and interior.

There comes a time for every man to die, and this dying is a matter of the inner life that cannot be transformed into a public token; although man's public side dies with his inner life, it cannot die instead of it. Although a man's inner decisions regarding responsible action and belief should be well informed by the structure of the public world, the responsibility for determining public expressions of the inner will is an inner matter; we listen to others' reasons, but we cannot responsibly use them for our decisions unless we make those reasons our own—the blame for our mistakes cannot be shifted: Eve's reference to the serpent's seductive words was futile. Furthermore, the specific concerns of the heart about the religious problem give the inner side of a man's life a non-transferable responsibility; no one can have faith for another. Wherever individual responsibility or nature is such that a public object cannot be taken in as a token surrogate of the inner life, the inner man is solitary. He is not without God, but he is indeed without the ultimate aid and comfort of his world. This may be as frustrating to his friends in the world who would like to help him as it is to him who wants help.

To the extent that these essential ways of being cut off present problems, the problems are religious, for to be in solitude in these ways involves the workings of the heart that have to do with the harmony of a person's whole nature. There are, of course, many other places where the religious problem manifests itself, especially as a person acts in the public world. But there is something striking about the religious problem of solitude, striking enough for some thinkers like Whitehead to deem it definitive of religion. Man's solitude is one of the most poignant places where God's presence makes itself felt, and it is also a place, we shall argue, where his forgiveness is felt.

First, we must ask why solitude, in its essential forms over and above its forms of estrangement, becomes a problem. Like most large-scale problems, there are many different factors that figure in each individual case. But we can speculate about some general causes. During the process of maturing, for example, a problem arises for the young because public elements in their world have responsibility for most affairs. But the young do not recognize the public elements as public except as they mature and learn about their essential solitude. Part of maturing is learning to take into one's own responsibility matters that were previously handled by the world. Taking on responsibility is often an unwanted thing. The principal reason why it is unwanted is even more general than the problem of maturing, but it helps explain why essential solitude can be a burden.

The responsibilities of the heart all have to do with determining the unity or harmony of the person, both in his inner life and his public life. Public things and affairs also determine part of the unity, but in many respects they are beyond effective control of the heart. When the heart determines an element of the person's harmony, it inevitably must exclude alternatives, making the individual finite. Each harmony is different from every other, and when one is determinately realized the others are excluded. There is a sense in which it is comforting always to have second chances, to have many possibilities open and relevant. Yet a finite life requires that alternatives be resolved, that a single one be realized and the rest excluded. Even the best of compromises is but one way of things. To cast one's lot with one possibility and cut oneself off from all others is the depth of solitude, and it can be terrifying. The terror of limiting oneself to one thing makes the responsibility of choice a burden, to some an intolerable burden. The ultimate limitation is that we must die, choice or not; this is the ultimate terror. To die is to act in such a finite way that not only contemporary but also subsequent alternatives are excluded. The ultimate burden of responsibility is that the choices we make, good or bad, lead to death now or later. The ultimate burden is that we must be responsible for choosing some finite life that is but one life among many and that has a stop. Each man can live but a solitary life; this is the terror and burden of man whose inner life must determine but one course through the alternative avenues of the public domain.

That free determination of life is a burden and that the result of determination, free or not, is a terror, is testified to by poets, philosophers, preachers, and criminals in all ages. Every sensitive and sympathetic man has felt the burden and seen the terror in others and perhaps in himself. The fact that the burden and terror are real and common elements of experience does not, however, explain *why* they are real. Man must be alone and solitary in his necessarily finite life; but why is this terrifying?

Finitude is terrifying only on the condition that a person senses some inappropriateness about the limitation and exclusion involved. If limitation were entirely natural, if death were appropriate and welcome as the last fulfillment, finitude would hold a curiosity concerning results but no terror. There is nothing in the prospect of limitation, even of death, that in itself holds terror except under the presupposition that something is gone wrong for it to be necessary. The terror of solitude presupposes the desire to escape it and, more, the oppressing and haunting sense that nature and oneself are out of joint. It presupposes the sense that something terrible has happened to make necessary the exclusion of alternatives, the limitation, and in the extremity, the death. It presupposes utter self-alienation.

But everyone can plainly see, with or without metaphysics, that life is a course along a single path, carved out from excluded possibilities, which necessarily ends with death. In rational moments we admit that this is our nature and that we cannot get beyond it. To feel, then, that finite limitation and death are somehow appropriate implies a kind of false pride by which we would set ourselves above our nature. If we only *desire* to be non-finite and to escape death, recognizing all the while that it is not in our nature to do so, limitation and death may be a disappointment but not a terror. They are terrifying only when we both desire to escape them and believe it is appropriate for us to do so; recognition that we cannot escape them under these conditions is the terror. But pride is essential to the terror. If we do not pride ourselves on being the sort not bound in nature to limitation and death, then death may hurt but will have no sting. The conditions for the terror are not present.

We have spoken above of the pride that makes man feel he is above the limitations of his finite nature. This must be humbled if man is to recognize the relevance and power of God's forgiveness. Suppose now that a person's pride is humbled, he believes that he is forgiven the imperfections of his finite life and that he has the faith. Will he find evidence for the actuality of God's forgiveness in his life?

Religions claim that the person will find evidence in his solitude, and our metaphysics can interpret how this could be so. God's presence as forgiver must be found wherever religious harmony is actual. A person lives his life in actual religious harmony whenever he lives in acceptance of his finite, limited nature, with its own idiosyncratic limitations and inevitable finish. As we noted above, this acceptance requires as a condition that the person recognize both his actual imperfections and the perfection called for by the norms relative to the many aspects of his nature. In any life, religiously harmonious or not, God is the creative ground of whatever harmony there is. A religiously harmonious life is one that contains as one of its elements a recognition that God forgives and accepts the finite nature whose being he grounds. If a man can find in himself that recognition, he will also know that his life could not contain that recognition if God were not actually present, forgiving while creating. If God is not actually forgiving, the recognition of or belief that he forgives cannot honestly be found in the harmony of a man's life.

This is to say that a man cannot believe himself forgiven and live his life in accordance with this belief unless the belief is actually true. For the truth of the belief consists in the fact that the religious harmony is actualized. There is no way for the religious harmony to be actual if God does not forgive, and this forgiveness is the content of belief. This seems paradoxical because it seems to say that believing makes the belief true. But since the belief is one of the things created and integrated into the harmony of a person's life, and since we have already seen that the harmony of the person's life, whatever it is, is the created product of God, the life lived in accordance with the belief is created in its harmony with God and this is the religious harmony. As we have seen, the actuality of the religiously harmonious life is possible only on the condition of the actuality of God's forgiveness. Although it is true to say that to believe in God's forgiveness is to make the belief true and the forgiveness actual, it is equally true to say that the actual forgiveness and only the actual forgiveness make the believing possible.

On the one hand, we say that God's creating and contingent forgiving determine that a person believes in God's saving forgiveness. This is the truth in the ancient religious doctrine that God is the necessary and sole source of religious fulfillment or salvation. On the other hand, we say that a man must accept God's forgiveness with belief and that he must be thoroughly responsible and intellectually honest in that belief. As we have seen, actual belief in the forgiveness of God is itself the actuality of the object of belief and is evidence for the belief's truth. Not only is a man's intellectual integrity not compromised by believing in the forgiveness of God; but the belief requires that integrity. This is the truth in Arminianism.

It might be thought that, maintaining what we do, we are committed to saying that God universally forgives, thus contradicting our claim that his forgiveness is contingent and is not necessarily congruent with his creating. This would be a mistake, however, since some people do not actually believe in forgiveness. Although God might forgive them and they not know it, still the fact that they do not believe removes the necessity from the forgiveness. Only if all men believed would forgiveness be universal, and even in this event, the universality might be coincidence. If we were to accept the anthropomorphism implicit in acceptance of the problem of universal salvation, our response to the question whether God wants to save all men would be this: He wants to, to the extent that he appeals to man's intellect and will through historical promises, holy men, and the like. But he does not force the intellect or coerce the will to believe. Yet if men do in fact believe, it is the creating and forgiving presence of God that provides the harmony of their being.

In his solitude man must come to terms with the limitations of his finite existence. If he does so, accepting God's forgiveness and living the life of religious harmony, he finds the actuality of God's forgiving creative presence. Man's life includes more than his inner life in which he is alone; God's forgiving creative presence can be found in many parts of it. But as a man's most personal terror and greatest pride are found in his solitude, so God's most personal presence and humbling forgiveness are found there most poignantly. Just as in his solitude man can be most alienated from himself by pride, in his solitude he can be most at home with himself in the presence of God. Solitude has religious importance because it is the limit where man can think himself cut off utterly and yet find himself closest to God. Where he is most alone, there most clearly is God's forgiving creative presence.

SECTION F
Bliss

Bliss is happiness in the creator's glory. Mystics in all religious traditions have described bliss as the highest stage of the development of the inner religious life. Bliss, they say, transcends the specifics of religious traditions and the previous stages of the religious life. Some even say bliss transcends the internal side of religious life and is the highest stage reached altogether. We shall argue in light of the above discussions that what the mystics mean by bliss can best be interpreted as happiness in the creator's glory.

1. The phrase "happiness in . . ." conveys a sense different from both "happiness about . . ." and "happiness resulting from . . ."; yet it includes both other meanings. The old saw, "be happy in your work," means both that you should be happy about having your particular work to do and that working on it will make you happy. It also means that, while engaged in your work, you should be happy in a way that spreads the happiness around to other aspects of life; more than your work should be satisfied by your work, and all of your faculties, as Plato would say, should be virtuous as you work.

To be happy in God's glory, on the subjective side, has this rich sense of "happiness in. . . ." Bliss is happiness about the fact that God is glorious, happiness that results from the character of God's glory, and happiness that pervades all of life and transcends any direct concentration on God's glory. How is this possible?

2. Let us consider first how bliss is happiness about God's glory. We argued above that God is apprehended primarily through some grasp of the notion of creator and that the harmony at the heart of each created determination of being has an aesthetic quality. This aesthetic quality is not to be identified with the creator's glory; it is a transcendental, common to all created things, and because partly constitutive of what it is to be created, it testifies to the creator as its ground. But many other things that are part of the metaphysical nature of determinate being also point to the creator. God's glory is even more than that which evokes the mystery and awe that lies at the root of holiness. God's glory stems from the fact that as creator he does indeed create all the determinations of being and, because he is creator, must transcend even the relational nature of being creator.

To express the fact that God is creator, however, is not to express *why* the fact is glorious. It is apparent from the fact alone why it would seem awesome and full of *"mysterium tremendum."* For us to see the fact as glorious, we must not only see God in his aseity as holy but also appreciate the fact that his creation is beautiful and good. A person who is not happy in God's world and does not enjoy God's creative forgiving presence in it can see God as holy but never as glorious. To see God's glory is to see God as holy creator of the harmonies in the determinations of being. This means that to see God's glory a person must combine an aesthetic appreciation of the harmonies or beauties in his creation with an appreciation of the fact that God is their creative ground.

Harmony, we argued before, is the essential unifying factor in a determination of being. Therefore, to create the determination is to create the harmonies. God's glory consists just in the fact that he is creator. But to apprehend God's glory is to apprehend not only the fact of his creation but also that peculiar property that is the transcendental aesthetic harmony. This requires an aesthetic as well as an intellectual apprehension (although we argued above that aesthetic and intellectual intuition converge to the same point [10]).

The appreciation of God's glory, or the happiness about it, which is the same thing, can have several levels. The beauties of nature can testify to the glory of God to those whose sense of beauty about nature is keen. So can the various harmonies of life and society. But usually the most interesting, crucial, and easily jeopardized harmonies that testify to God's glory are those constitutive of each man personally. Consequently, often the most poignant moments in which a person appreciates the glory of God are those when he is aware of God's presence as the creative ground of the religious harmony of his own life, the presence that makes the harmony both possible and actual through his forgiveness. Nothing seems so glorious as one's own savior.

Even more fundamental than occasions like these, however, are occasions when we recognize what might be called the eschatological character of creation. We have discussed the limitations inherent in the finite harmonies that define all determinations of being. These limitations can also be called ends, in the sense of last things, not in the sense of goals. Each determination is what it is and the way it is, and it must stand or fall with these limitations whenever standing or falling is called for. Men are not judged by their neighbor's character but by their own. The ultimate limitation or end is death. This is when the harmony that is man's nature breaks down and resolves into the lesser harmonies that make up his non-living physical constituents. Is God's glory to be seen in the end of a man's harmony? Should we say, "The Lord giveth and the Lord taketh away: blessed be the name of the Lord"?

Part of the religious harmony is recognizing the limitations inherent in finite existence. These limitations include both the metaphysical ones man has as a determination of being and the empirical ones he has as a man, death being among the latter. It is an empirical fact of man's nature that the elements of his makeup deteriorate in their harmony and ultimately dissolve as a whole. There is no metaphysical necessity that there be changing and dying things; everything might be as eternal as the sum of two and two. But it is even the limitation of the sum of two and two that it can never be greater than four—or want to, for that matter; and it is a fact that men are not eternal but mortal. The more persistent harmonies of nature that control the changing of conditions and the inevitability of man's death are harmonies, too, beautiful intrinsically and testifying to the glory of God. For a man

[10] Chap. 4, sec. C.

to see the glory of God in the death of a loved one, however, or in the anticipation of his own death, he must not only be resigned to his own limitations and be happy with God's presence in them; he must also appreciate and enjoy God's presence in the more persistent harmonies that *call* for death. The beauties of creation, wherever they are to be seen, testify to the blessedness or glory of the name of the Lord.

Beyond this appreciation of God's glory in the "natural" grounds for death, something more must be admitted before man can bless the name of the Lord with full force. For, a man could always suggest that God might have made a *more* beautiful world had he made the harmonies of human reality as persistent as those that call for the change of natural conditions that occasions man's death. This might be suggested as an empirical improvement, and probably no one who has faced death has failed to think of it.

The answer to this suggestion requires us to recall the most striking and surprising fact about God's creation, which is that he creates anything at all. That God is creator and creates stems from no determinate principle of his nature, since all determination is itself created. That the metaphysical character of determinateness is what it is, is only because God creates it that way; its necessities, like the necessities of intellectual principles, are created necessities. That the empirical character of the world is as it is, counting both the empirical laws and the unlawful indeterminacies, is because God creates it that way. All seem arbitrary and mysterious, stemming from no principle beyond the created whole. The mystery is only one mystery, that of creation itself. That the products of God's creation have the character of harmonies is itself a mystery. Since there is no reason why God should create the conditions of human life the way he does, there is no reason why he should create them differently. To apprehend the mystery of creation is to apprehend God's holiness. The Lord giveth and the Lord taketh away; *holy* be the name of the Lord.

But it is another empirical fact that God forgives, according to religions, and therefore makes possible and actual the religious harmony that is man's happiness. Although we die, according to the promises of religion we also enjoy God's forgiving creative presence. To enjoy this beauty and to apprehend the mystery of it all is to see God's glory. The Lord giveth and the Lord taketh away; but he forgiveth and giveth happiness before he taketh away: blessed and glorious is the name of the Lord.

The part of bliss that is happiness about God's glory can be so rich as to enable us to see God's glory even in our death. The glory we see is that God creates a world with harmonies in it, graced as such by his beautiful presence. In deference to our previous metaphysical arguments, we must admit that even God's glory is a thing dependent upon creation. God makes himself glorious by creating.

3. Let us consider now how bliss is happiness that results from God's glory. God's glory consists in the fact that he creates and that what he creates is a world whose determinations, all by necessity, exhibit a harmony of their component determinations. Men are created determinations and as such

exhibit and testify to the glory of God. Happiness is harmonious resolution of diversities, and whatever happinesses man has are expressions of God's glory. If a person's intellectual work is harmonious and happy, that is God's glory. So it is with the happiness of emotional life, the happiness of a personal relation, the happiness of artistic endeavor, and all the other dimensions of human life wherein a person can be happy. The most pervasive happiness of man, that which defines human happiness per se, is the happiness of religious harmony, and if a man has that, this too expresses God's glory.

The peculiarity of a life lived in religious harmony is that it requires conscious (though perhaps highly symbolic) recognition of the creative presence of God forgiving the imperfections and sins of finite folly and thereby harmonizing the whole. Thus man's being not only is expressive of God's glory but also is such as to appreciate that glory. Furthermore, man's appreciation of the glory of God is the direct result of God's forgiving creative act that expresses the glory in the first place. That man sees God's glory expressed in him is part of the very expression of that glory.

To say then that part of bliss is happiness resulting from God's glory is to point out that the happiness we have about God's glory and the happinesses of many kinds we have in which we are oblivious of God are themselves part of creation itself and hence are expressions of the glory.

4. Happiness in God's glory includes both happiness about it and happiness as a result of it. It includes them both by mixing them into the richer fabric of a life that does many things besides contemplate the glory of God and thrill at being its expression. A life that is happy in this richer sense we say is blissful. The force of the term "blissful" consists in the fact that it acknowledges a happiness that pervades all of life, including many elements that in themselves would not be happy. A blissful life can be happy and full of grief at the same time. Not to grieve at something worth grieving about is dishonest, and this kind of evasion cannot be tolerated in a true religiously harmonious life. But in a religiously harmonious life, a true grief, honestly acknowledged and fully mourned, can be taken into a more basic happiness in God's glory. That this is so may be hard to believe, but it has been the experience of the saints.

5. What is presupposed in this basic happiness, however, is a fundamental shift in the aim of the religious life. This shift has been incipient all along and becomes explicit at this point. The original religious concern of man has to do with attaining religious harmony. But in the development of religious harmony through life, a person comes to recognize the glory of God; recognition of God's forgiveness necessitates this. Although the person never gives up the concern with his own religious harmony, he comes to see it as far less significant and important than the sheer fact that the religious harmony is an expression of God's glory. Importance is an aesthetic character, and man comes to recognize that the thing of greatest or absolute importance is the beauty of God's creation as such, greater than the importance of any limited domain of it, such as a man's own religious harmony. Apprehension of God's

absolute glory in the creation as such casts into relative insignificance the concerns for the finite religious harmony. The acknowledgment of this is a necessary part of that religious harmony itself. As the New Testament puts it, "He who would save his life shall lose it," and this can be interpreted to mean that the exclusive concern with religious harmony is in the end a selfish thing that precludes the accomplishment of its own aim.

Most Eastern religions acknowledge the absolute importance of Nirvana, but often they neglect the relative importance of man. Humanism and ethically oriented religions like Judaism see that religious concern should work some sort of improvement in man; but sometimes they fail to recognize the distinction between man's relative importance and the absolute importance of God's glory. Consequently, the mystic whose life is bliss in God's glory is sharply cut off in Eastern religions from the laymen, even though he is taken as the ideal. In Judaism the mystic is often taken as an anomaly who is close to betraying the essentially social covenant that lies at the heart of the religion. The mystic fares much better in Christianity where the blissful life is taken as the natural end result of self-forgetful and sacrificial salvation.

6. Because there is an ambiguity in the notion of bliss, it can mean either a blissful life or a moment of ecstasy. We have been discussing so far the former meaning and have paid little attention to the latter. Yet it is ecstasy that is taken to be the most striking characteristic of mysticism. Ecstasy literally means being beside oneself, standing outside oneself. There is a crucial sense in which happiness in the glory of God involves this and in which a moment of ecstasy is the epitome of bliss. Happiness in God's glory, considered from the standpoint of the attitude toward God, is the love of God. An analogy with human love can make clear the meaning of ecstasy.

Weiss has pointed out that there is a kind of purging involved in the dynamics of falling in love.[11] Falling in love calls for a distinction between what is essential to a person's identity and what is peripheral and nonessential, for a person in love wants to bring to his beloved only what is most genuinely himself. And since men live most of their lives in routines and associations that give exaggerated importance to their nonessential natures, the lover seeks to make the relationship with the beloved the essential and most genuine part of his nature. He does this by making the beloved the center of his life in the sense that his activities become the expression and medium of the beloved's interests and concerns. Or rather, the lover makes the beloved's interests and concerns his own so that the beloved becomes the center and orientation point of the lover's life. This does not mean that the lover does whatever the beloved wants, for this may not be in the beloved's true interest. Nor does it mean that the lover must forsake the routinized ways in which he lives, though this is often the misplaced ideal of romantic love. Rather, he indulges in those nonessential activities, not in his own interest anymore, but in the interest of the beloved. The lover does not lose

[11] *Man's Freedom* (New Haven, Conn.: Yale University Press, 1950), p. 297.

his own characteristic identity except to the extent that his behavior expresses what he takes to be the interests and concerns of the beloved's center or heart. The lover is ecstatic when he feels the beloved's heart to be his own. This is especially epitomized in the relationship of sex when the lover makes love for the sake of the beloved's happiness and takes the beloved's happiness to be his own. The ecstasy of the lover consists in the fact that he stands outside his own interests and happiness and makes the beloved's interests and happiness his own.

The analogy of divine ecstasy with genuine human love is an old one and well taken. God's glory has often been called his happiness, and for a man to be happy in God's glory is for him to be happy in God's happiness. Of course, this is only an analogy, and the quality of divine glory is not the same as any human happiness. Still, the analogy of the transference from one's own heart as center of activity to the beloved holds true, for God's nature, which is expressed in creation, is the center of God's glory and man can make the service of expressing God's glory the purpose of his life. As a lover sees the beauty of the beloved and makes the beloved the center of his life, so a man can see God's glory and make God the center of his life. As a lover acts in the beloved's interests, so a man can act in God's interest, that is, to express his glory in creation. This is the pure motivation for the move to the public life.

Divine ecstasy is when a man's experience is caught up with the apprehension of God's glory and the happiness that comes from taking God's glory to be the center of his life. The happiness comes in the act of appropriating God to one's own heart. Such experiences are usually few and fleeting, but they have the capacity to pervade all of life with blissful joy. Divine ecstasy goes beyond the mere enjoyment of the fact that God is glorious or the mere result of the divine creative activity that makes God glorious. It comes to the point of making God the center of life and the glory of his creation the aim of life. Of course, the finite nature of man makes the limits of the expression he can give God's glory also finite. He can do no more than to live his own life. But the creator can be the center of his being, and the moments when a man realizes this are ecstatic.

7. Many mystics, however, have given interpretations of ecstasy that lead them into grave difficulties. For example, they often describe ecstasy as immediate union with God, devoid of finite characteristics. The difficulty with this interpretation is that if it were true there would be no way of knowing what ecstasy is, no way of distinguishing ecstasy from sheer unconsciousness. Eastern mystics are fond of the analogy of ecstasy with unconsciousness but shrink from complete identification; perfect unconsciousness is death. The ecstasy that we have described accounts for the feeling of unity and identification; the nonessential aspects of a person are purged from relevance, and God becomes the center of the person's heart and will. Nothing is important but God. On the other hand, the distinction between the absolute glory of God and the finite character of the lover is never lost from sight. To admit that finite concerns and contributions to the divine

glory are relatively insignificant is not to deny them utterly. In fact, it is only by contrast with a person's finite center that love of God's glory is significant. In all mystical traditions there is a way of preparation, an ordering and disciplining of finite life that leads up to the mystical vision or ecstasy, and this preparation, which accommodates finite nature to its finitude, is essential in the ecstatic experience.

8. Mysticism is traditionally believed to be the chief element in religion that denies finite personality in God and asserts that he transcends all such determination. It is perhaps surprising then that in the ecstasy of bliss we find a move for the first time to an acknowledgment of something like personality in God. In ecstasy man acknowledges God to be in his aseity a center beyond all expression of glory. It is through the glory of creation that we move to an acknowledgment of God's transcendence, but we still take the transcendent aseity as a center of which the glory is an expression. God's expression of glory is not like human expression, which proceeds from the center according to characteristic principles, for, as we have often noted, determinate principles come only in the produced expression. But the expression itself has a character that we see as beautiful and that is part of the ground for acknowledging the glory of the creator. It is only after the fact of creation, as it were, that the creation has a characteristic glory or, rather, that God makes himself the glorious creator. But as a man can take God in his aseity as a center from which the creation mysteriously comes and can identify himself with the expression in the world of that which God in fact creates, so he takes God as a kind of personal center. The character or personality of God is determinate only in the divine expression, but this does not invalidate the interpretation of God's aseity when related to the world as a center of expression like that which a person has.

9. Bliss is an aspect of the inner religious life that requires a high degree of consciousness and awareness. Certainly it has not been a common thing in religion, and no religion except perhaps some high forms of Hinduism and Buddhism claim that it is *essential* to the religious life. We have argued above that God may create a man such that he never is conscious of the fact that he is fulfilling God's glory, which is to say that he never knows he is forgiven. Likewise, a man may never develop his awareness of the religious situation to the extent that he is happy just in the glory of God. But if he never attains bliss, this still does not diminish the glory of God that he unwittingly expresses. And if he does attain bliss, his own happiness cannot be surpassed, for his happiness is the absolute glory of God.

We have traced points in the development of the inner religious life in relative isolation from the public expression of religion. As an empirical fact they have often been relatively distinct. But at each point we have discussed, there is either a public correlate or a public extension of the inner condition of the heart. We must now turn to discuss the public expression of the religious life.

12

The Public Expression of the Religious Life

Although Whitehead was a very perceptive philosopher, he spoke too narrowly when he characterized religion as what an individual does with his solitariness.[1] Even were Whitehead to allow that religion includes the public expression of what the individual does with his solitariness, his definition would still be too narrow, for there are public elements in religion that are not mere expressions of what is private but that are primarily public and must in turn undergo a transformation to get themselves expressed in the interiority of the religious life. All religions admit this point to the extent that they claim God is related in an efficacious way to some public order, to a natural world, a religious community, or holy institution, to some political or racial community.

As was the case with our discussion of the interiority of the religious life, in dealing here with the exteriority of the religious life we must choose only a few of the many crucial questions. We shall discuss *religious service, liturgy, evangelism, dedication, reconciliation,* and *brotherhood.*

SECTION A
Service

Inner religious convictions seek to express themselves in public action. The most convincing public test of inner conviction, in religion as elsewhere, is whether a person acts in accordance with his beliefs. The first move from the inner religious life to the public world is usually the undertaking of religious service. The Buddha, directly after his Enlightenment, considered the problem of whom he should find first to teach his liberating lesson. Isaiah, having been cleansed of his iniquities, looked for a job he could do for the Lord, saying, "Here I am; send me."

We must recognize two qualifications to our general point here. Religious

---

[1] *Religion in the Making* (New York: Macmillan Co., 1926), p. 16.

service is not the only way to give public expression to inner conviction. And, on the other hand, public expression of inner conviction is not the only motive for religious service. Nonetheless religious service is most usually undertaken, in our day at least, as an expression of the inner religious life.

Religious service is a paradoxical term. Most of the charitable, educational, and personal services undertaken by explicitly religious bodies and persons are also performed by governmental and private humanitarian institutions and representatives. Perhaps it is better to say that, in our day, religious service is plain public service undertaken for religious reasons, sometimes with institutional religious sanctions. Certainly, the motivations that lead many people into the Peace Corps are religious ones, motivations that in other times would have led them into pastoral or missionary work.

How do religious motivations make public service religious? Religious harmony, developing and enduring through time, is both aided and jeopardized by change. Change allows both for improvement and for disintegration and decay. Therefore, a religious person must continually cope with his world, creatively applying to it the principles of his harmony. Any determination of being, to maintain its harmony through change, must continually apply its own essential principles to the interactions with other determinations that give it conditional features. For a religious person to apply the principles of his harmony to his life in the world means at least two things with regard to service.

First, the fact that a man has an interior religious harmony means that he has attained a peculiar freedom to pursue the standards and goals in him and in his world.[2] This freedom can be indicated best through contrast with its absence. A person lacks religious harmony if he does not accept God's forgiveness of his imperfections and whatever else is needed for the grounds for hope. He is bound by his conceit that he should be able to win perfection for himself. Hence, even his best acts are likely to be tainted with a kind of selfishness. He does what is good, not for the intrinsic good in it, but rather to make himself worthy. He loses the ability to enjoy the good he does and is left with only the ability to take satisfaction in what his good deeds do for him. He even loses the objectivity of the world in which he lives, and the world becomes primarily *his* world, a world devoted to the fight over *his* salvation. Since this is self-defeating and will cause him to lose the fight, the person has nothing to enjoy. He becomes bound even more to turn his activity to the pursuit of his own good and loses the capacity to do whatever is objectively good just because it is good. The religious man, on the other hand, working out his religious harmony, which includes God's forgiveness of his failure, is not bound to win his own salvation and is free to pursue the goods that are open to him.

Second, the religious harmony of a person naturally develops and extends

[2] See chap. 13, sec. D.

itself from those aspects of the person's being that are close to him to those that are farther away. Religious harmony seeks to harmonize the person's whole world, including those things in his world that have careers of their own apart from that world. Since harmony must allow for and fulfill the integrity of the individual things it brings into harmony, a person's religious harmony will lead him to work for the religious harmony of those around him and for all the other harmonies that go into making up the people, societies, institutions, and natural things upon which his action can bear. So, religious service takes the form, not only of evangelism, of which we shall speak below, but also of direct public service for the promotion of education, housing, cultural improvements, and so forth.

The force behind the point that inner religious conviction issues in public service is that it marks the recognition that the public side of one's existence should also be included in religious harmony. What begins as a public expression of inner conviction ends with the recognition that there is an integrity to public life that should be harmonized religiously to just as great an extent as the inner life. What begins as internal religious concern issues in public concern, given the resolution of inner conviction. And because there is an integrity to the public life of service, religious service can take on a degree of independence from the career of the inner life. Although there may be times when the inner life falls prey to doubts and uncertainties and the inner religious harmony is in danger of corruption, the religious harmony structuring public service may maintain a healthy development. This has been the experience of many religious people, who turn to concerns of public religious service when the inner concerns of the religious life are faring badly. The very ability to concentrate attention on first one side of life and then on the other has the happy effect of lessening pressure on a jeopardized domain. Of course, this independence of the public religious life from the private side is only relative. Too much crumbling of inner conviction corrupts even the most muscular religious service. Too much frustration in the public sphere can force the private side of religion into such solitude that the human harmony requisite for religion is broken down. But this does not vitiate the important point that religious service is a move of the concerns of religious harmony into a relatively public domain that has an integrity and degree of independence of its own.

To the extent that religious service is just public service undertaken for the motive of expressing inner religious conviction, the integrity of such service consists in its worth on its own account. Regardless of whether a person's personal motivations are religious, if public service is worthwhile it is because of its own worth, and the study of its integrity is properly the subject matter of ethics, social theory, and so forth. There is also integrity to a kind of public religious work that is religious not because of inner motivations but because it has itself the character expressive and constitutive of the religious harmony. It is to this "liturgy" that we must now turn our attention.

SECTION B

Liturgy and Providence

The ancient roots of the word "liturgy" originally meant holy or divine public work, the public service of the gods, and this can be interpreted to mean work that is expressive of a person or community's religious harmony. But the development of the Western religious traditions has seen the word liturgy take on a narrower meaning. It has come to mean the work done by or for a religious community, more or less ritualistic in form, that acts out, commemorates, symbolizes, or appropriates some saving event attributed directly or indirectly to God. The ancient pagan religions had liturgies to celebrate the rebirth of nature in spring, the divine potency in fertility, and great battles in which the gods gave their people victory. The Jews celebrate the Passover; the Christians celebrate Mass or the Lord's Supper. In all these cases, it is the action of God that is celebrated, and this might be the reference of the conception of "divine" in "divine work."

The power in liturgy is that it allows the participants to appropriate for themselves the saving work of God even when the liturgy celebrates God's work in a historical action long past. It may be that a covenant made long ago is kept in force by the liturgical celebration. Or it may be that the actions involved in the liturgy actually embody the same divine power that was present in the celebrated event, as in the case of the Christian sacrament of the bread and wine. Or again, the liturgy may involve the act of submitting to salvation directly, as in baptism and various forms of initiation. It is this appropriation of the saving work of God that we must endeavor to grasp.

It will be remembered from the previous chapter that an essential ingredient in the religious life is an acceptance of the actual fact that God forgives man's imperfections and takes from man the task of saving himself. This interpretation of God's saving work is a more sophisticated view than is found in some religions; but we found it to be an essential ingredient, in one form or another, in the full development of the religious life. It is necessary to face up to the major problem posed by this discrepancy between our theory of God's saving action as primarily that of forgiving and of demonstrating the forgiveness, on the one hand, and the more usual view of providence, on the other. The more usual view sees God's saving action in terms of mighty works in history, in miraculous appearances and deeds, in feats of strength and supernatural providence of natural benefits. Furthermore, it is often the quite natural benefits, received as supernatural, that are taken to be the results of saving action; salvation is not always taken to be so "merely psychological" as to mean forgiveness. It is perhaps the modern age, so antisupernatural in attitude, that has given such popularity to the view that salvation consists in forgiveness or, as Tillich has it, in acceptance. Although a view like Tillich's (and ours) might be true on its own grounds, it cannot be denied that a good portion of its appeal is that it seems to give an interpretation to the old religious categories without requiring belief in empirical events that come to pass by non-empirical means.[3] The connection between providence and forgiveness must be pursued in greater detail.

1. The doctrine of providence is the doctrine that God acts within the world to do something beneficial to some part of creation. We shall discuss the metaphysical problems of such action within the world shortly. First, certain points should be made about the connection of providence with forgiveness.

a) It should be noted in the first place that even very private forgiveness requires a kind of public providence. In the previous chapter we found that the private requirement for religious harmony or salvation is an acceptance of the fact that God forgives imperfections. But since man must be honest about his beliefs, especially in religion, there must be some objective ground for the hope for forgiveness. The objective ground, what we called the promise, is public and providential.

To pursue this matter we must raise the question about why the required forgiveness must be God's forgiveness instead of the forgiveness of some person within the created realm. No one can deny the power of forgiveness between friends and lovers to heal human hurts and cement harmonious relations. The difficulty for religious purposes with creaturely forgiveness is that it is too limited. Although one person might have an attitude of wholesale forgiveness toward another, forgiving everything in general, he is in a proper position to forgive only failures regarding his expectations and the norms constituted by the relation between the two people. If it is a third person who has been wronged, then it is the third person who must forgive if forgiveness is to be had on the creaturely level. But even if *all* the people a person has wronged were to forgive him, this would still not be enough. Man's failures are not limited to persons; he fails his culture, himself, his nation, and the world he lives in, and these are sometimes not the kinds of things that can forgive. Furthermore, man's failings are not only too large in range; they are too profound in quality. They not only add up to a sum of imperfections; they also indicate a failure to be a proper determination of being in a world of obligations. Man's failure is a wronging of the whole created order. Therefore, the profundity of man's failure requires that the forgiveness ultimately relevant to him must be God's forgiveness, the forgiveness of him whose creativity expressed by the world is wronged by man's failure. In paragraph 3 below, we shall have to consider the sense in which God is a person, the subject of man's wrongs; for if there were not some sense in which the whole world, being liable to man's failings, can be seen as an extension of the being of God, then there would be no point to God's

---

[3] Another reason for the appeal of this kind of view, which comes from the age quite apart from the force of the argument itself, is the contemporary appreciation of the fact that the depths of the soul are just as real and their phenomena just as important as empirical things in the physical sense.

forgiveness—in that case, God would not be the relevant one to forgive. If we are to understand how God can be a kind of person or self who forgives, we must understand how God can be the kind of creator who can be wronged and thereby be in the position to forgive.

We distinguished above between the experiential tests for the truth of belief in God's forgiveness and the promise we must trust in the initial will to believe. Although the experiential tests may in large part be private, the promises must be public. It is clear, in fact, that not only are the promises, covenants, and prophecies public but their very public character in teachers, leaders, and prophets mediated by long tradition constitutes the most crucial grounds for doubting them. Would that the revelations of the promises were more privately persuasive than so publicly historical! But regardless of the difficulties of verifying the promises, which we discussed in the last chapter, it is surely the case that the promises must be public and capable of being mediated to persons in some form by a public tradition.

Furthermore, religion claims that the promises are providential, that is, that it is God who is doing the promising and that the promise is intended to do something, for example, heal, teach, or enlist people. This holds as much for the enlightenment sayings of Buddha as it does for the Mosaic or Christian covenants. Whether the promises are providential in truth is, of course, another matter.

b) Private forgiveness itself is a kind of private providence. For God to forgive is for him to create or make a forgiven person (or group). A forgiven person is one whose life embodies religious harmony, God being present as forgiving creator in the harmony. Even if a person does not consciously employ his forgiveness as an organizing principle of life, with the result that his religious harmony runs great risk of dissolution through change, still he is made whole by the presence of the forgiving creator for the time being. If the person does accept the forgiveness of God and then in a sense has personal charge over the living out of his religious harmony, this means that the creator is present in him constituting the man as him who accepts. Therefore, not only does God, according to the claims of religion, provide a public and external promise, he also provides the adoption of the promise and the embodiment of it in the private religious life. Many elements of liturgy celebrate this kind of personal providence.

c) Just as religious harmony is possible for persons, so also is it possible for groups, for churches, communities, cultures, nations. Consequently, man's public life, lived in relations to people, groups, institutions, and the natural environment, can be involved in problems of a public religious harmony. Here a man may have the task of acting publicly to embody the religious harmony in the public whole; especially, he may have the task of mediating the forgiving presence of God to the others so that the public loaf is thoroughly leavened. Viewed abstractly, man's public life in behalf of the religious harmony of the public domain is service; viewed more concretely, it is brotherhood, for brotherhood is what we call truly human public harmony.

It is the main task of this chapter to trace out some of the major structures of the providential pursuit of public religious harmony. Many if not most of the liturgies of religion celebrate God's providence in the public religious life.

2. We must now ask more directly what providence is. This involves two major questions. First, how does providence differ from creation in general, and second, what is the metaphysical character of providence, relative to our answer to the first question?

a) Providence is usually thought of as the special exercise of divine creative power to bring about some beneficial result. The beneficial result on the usual view may be anything from the saving of the crops to the inspiration of souls, from the sending of true teachings to the wisdom to accept the truth. The result may be complete in itself, not requiring human judgment to fulfill it. The result may be something that must be acted upon by men to be complete, and if men do not act, there is a possibility that providence will be thwarted. Or the result may include as *part* of the divine action whatever human response is appropriate.

Distinguished from the more general exercise of creative power, providence is the special creation of something that would not have been otherwise. The qualification "that would not have been otherwise" raises many important problems, for this is the issue of miracle. In one sense, the whole created order "would not have been" were there not a specific exercise of divine power. In this sense, that there is any creation at all is a miracle and can be viewed as providential. But in another and more usual sense, providence is considered as the bringing about of what would not have happened otherwise within a context that is already on the ground. In general we should admit that the distinction between creation and providence can be made only on a sliding scale, for what is considered the created context in which something providential happens in one instance may itself be considered the providential happening in a larger context. So we might say that it was providential that Moses got water from the rock in the context of the Israelites' flight from Egypt; but it was also providential that they were fleeing Egypt in any case. At the most comprehensive limit, providence and creation would converge.

Specifically, however, we are interested in providence on a smaller scale where it has to do with the bringing about of religious harmony in private persons and public groups. Here it is convenient for the purpose of analyzing religion to distinguish miraculous events as a subclass of providential events. Whereas all providential events are those that would not have happened without a special exercise of divine creative power, only some of them are events that are quite contrary to what would naturally be expected, that is, are miraculous.

b) To articulate the metaphysical character of providence it is essential to maintain the integrity of the relative independence from each other of the specific providential event and the general created context in which it occurs.

If the special quality of the providential event is not acknowledged, then providence turns out to be just a myopic view of creation in general. And if the relatively non-special quality of the created context is not recognized, then everything that happens, with regard to its connection with divinity, is *ad hoc* divine meddling. Hartshorne's view, for instance, has no way of distinguishing providence from creation, since for him God exercises his creative powers to the limit in every event, striving to the utmost to bring about the greatest good but limited by the recalcitrance of his enemies: a sufficiently recalcitrant enemy could render God's activity so futile that it could hardly even be called providential, at least in the short run. A doctrine of providence must acknowledge the integrity both of the special providential event and the general created context in which it occurs.

The metaphysical theory that undergirds our discussion in this part claims that all determinations of being are created by God. For them to be at all means that they are created. But the created nature of a determination is determinate, and because of this it is defined in part in terms of other determinations. Suppose for purposes of illustration that Kant's cosmological theory of schematized determinate relations were correct and exhaustive. According to the category of inherence and subsistence, each determination would be a subsisting harmony with many inherent features. According to the category of ground and consequent (causality), each determination has the nature it has because of determinate rules connecting it with previous determinations. According to the category of community and reciprocity, each determination has the conditional features it does because of its determinate relations with contemporaries.

The point of this illustrative use of Kant is that God could not create a determination of being without creating the other determinations of being with respect to which it is determinate. Therefore, miracle is impossible in the sense that it would mean the creation *in toto* of a determination of being the nature of which would be to be influenced by other determinations that are not created in that specific creative act. In other words a specific providential creation taking place in the context of a more general created order cannot take credit for providing that part of the event that by determinate nature is determined by elements in the more general context. Regarding the category of inherence and subsistence, an essential inherent determination, for example, Socrates' paleness, cannot be created without the subsistent man Socrates. Regarding the category of community and reciprocity, God could not create a member of a community without the community, nor could he create any reciprocal determined thing without the reciprocal determinations. In many ways the category of causality is most interesting for the problem of miracle. Regarding causality, God could not create any determination of being, whose nature it is to be determined by some prior cause, without the prior cause; or more precisely, God could not create from whole cloth and alone a feature of a thing that requires a prior determination. So, as Weiss has pointed out, God could not have created the Garden of Eden in a moment, with no prior determinations, and still have some old trees in the garden.[4] Of course, God could have created a garden full of trees that had characters we associate with different degrees of old age; but regarding the feature of actual age, all the trees in the garden would be the same age. God cannot create an old tree without first having created a young one.

All of these limitations on providence and miracle stem from the very nature of what it is to create a determination of being. They are, however, not really very limiting. Even in many of the most extravagant claims for miracle, one of the most essential elements is that the miraculous determination is not determined by other factors in the more general created context. Part of the miracle claimed in the creation-in-time theory is that botanically mature trees were created that had *no* youth.

Although each determination of being is by nature determinate with respect to many things, perhaps even an infinite number of things, it may also be indeterminate in many respects. For instance, in the year A.D. 1000 the tallest redwood in California was indeterminate with respect to whether it was the possession of Spain or Portugal; by the year A.D. 1700 its career was affected by the fact that it was Spain's. Of course, to find an example of indeterminateness we must have recourse to either imagined or *ex post facto* determination; had the New World never been discovered or divided by the pope between Spain and Portugal we could never use it as an example of indeterminateness. But this only emphasizes the indeterminateness we are pointing out. *God's providential activity involves making determinate something indeterminate that would not have been made determinate given only the factors in the more general created context.* We can illustrate two important kinds of this providential creation by recurring to two of Kant's categories: causality, and community and reciprocity.

According to the category of causality, the nature of one event is determined by the nature of a preceding event and a rule that connects the two. But suppose there were some elements in the later event that were not determined by the preceding event and the rule, some elements that were novel but that could go on to play a role in determining future events. Of course Kant would never have allowed this degree of indeterminateness, but many subsequent philosophers, for example, Peirce, Bergson, and Whitehead, have thought that there was good reason for holding to it. Suppose for the sake of the hypothesis that some such doctrine of indeterminateness is true. Then the novel determinations in the event are created by God, as are all determinations; and because novel, they are created without the specific causal determination of prior events and hence may be providential. Of course, the novel determinations are reciprocally connected with other determinations in the event that are the direct result of rules of nature and past events, but this does not detract from their novelty, it only limits to a degree

---

[4] *Modes of Being* (Carbondale: Southern Illinois University Press, 1958), p. 244.

the kind of nature they can have. Regarding the order of efficient causes relating events in time according to determining rules, whatever determinations in an event are not determined by prior events and the natural rules are viewed as happening by chance. Chance is lack of connection to previous events by rules. But that which happens by chance still is, still exists, and hence is created. Chance and divine creation are not at all incompatible. Providence may involve chance.

According to the category of community and reciprocity, things that are together are mutually determined. But sometimes in the reciprocal interchange of relations and connections things can take on a new quality that is not determined merely by the rules governing the interchange. So, for instance, the interchange of relations and connections in a community of mutually determined things can chance upon a combination that produces a harmony of the whole. As Tillich has admirably pointed out, when nature makes the conditions right, a whole new dimension can be added to things.[5] Although such a harmony of the whole is not determined by the rules governing the interchange of parts alone, it is indeed determined by those rules plus the actual antecedent arrangements. But the qualitative harmony itself has no significance to the previous natural determinations; it is just another arrangement. Yet the harmony may be such as to affect in a new way all the parts that make it up, and it may, once the conditions for its arising are met, have the power to sustain itself and control for the sake of its own maintenance the future interchanges of relations and connections in the community. Such a harmony can introduce new rules of interchange that were not effective before. So, for instance, the rise of a national consciousness may be directly traced to the interaction of prior geographic and economic factors for which national consciousness has no significance. But when conditions are ripe for the development of national consciousness, the national consciousness takes on a career of its own, subordinates geography and economy to its own development and introduces brand-new geographic interests and economic regularities. Some new dimension or harmony can be attained that cannot be understood merely in terms of the factors that make it up; it is novel and it has a nature of its own that must be grasped on its own merits.

We have used Kant's categories of relation as illustrative of cosmological or metaphysical principles that might articulate the mutual determination, temporal and otherwise, of the many created things. A careful and precise treatment of the problem of providence would, of course, require a fully developed metaphysical theory.

However, by combining the two senses in which a new determination can come to be in our Kantian illustration, we can interpret the kind of providence that is of interest to us most, the providence regarding religious

[5] *Systematic Theology* (Vol. III; Chicago: University of Chicago Press, 1963), III, 15–17.

harmony. Were God specially to create determinations, with respect to which the more general created context otherwise would be indeterminate, and do so in such a way that conditions would constitute a religious harmony, this would be a case of providence. Without the former condition, the arising of a new determination via a new harmony would be part of divine creation but not providential, since it would have been determined by the more general created context. Without the integrity of the newly created harmony, the event again would not be providential but would merge with the more general created context as a variation on it. The combination of the two could indeed be providential.

There is yet another element of our characterization of providence that must be accounted for. An event must be beneficial in some way in order to be providential. That is, not every chance event that results in a new harmony is providential—only those that are intended to fulfill some divine intention. The notion of intention is one that is usually associated with the notion of a self or person who intends. So, in fact, is forgiveness. It is necessary now to make up accounts with the claim that God is personal.

3. We argued in Part One that because God creates all determinations of being and because the creator must be ontologically prior to his creation, God must transcend all determinations of being. As he is in his aseity, apart from all relations to creation, God must transcend even the nature he has as creator, since he has that nature in virtue of the fundamental ontological relation he has to what he creates. Therefore, God in himself must transcend the character of being something like a person, a perfect self or conscious individual; he must also transcend the character of one who has intentions or forgives.

The notion of person, at least when applied to finite persons, is a relational notion in the sense that to be a person means to be a subject relative to objects or other subjects in an environing medium. This point has been recognized even by those who want to say that God in himself is a person, for they then go on to explain God's personal aseity by arguing that God the father must beget the Son in order to have something to deal with personally, and from them both proceeds the Spirit or medium of divine personal interaction. This is one of the Christian views of the Trinity. But it seems easier to argue that God in his aseity is beyond personality and that if he has personality it is in his relation to the world. It is in his relations to the world that we would be interested in God's personality anyway. So we should not be surprised or disheartened at the conclusion that God in his aseity transcends determinate categories like personality.

If God constitutes himself creator in creating the world, there seems to be no reason in principle why the kind of creator he constitutes himself cannot be personal, intending or even forgiving. We must investigate, first, whether there is any reason to believe that God is a personal kind of creator; second, what sort of ontological status his personality would have, if there is such; and third, the connection of personality with creation and providence.

a) *Whether God is personal.* The first thing to note regarding this question is that the only ground we have for judging lies in the character of the created world. This is so whether we judge on the basis of a general trait of the created order or some particular thing in it that is supposed to be specially revelatory of God's nature. To have to judge from the character of the created world is not much of a limitation, however. The ground upon which we judge whether a finite thing is a person or what specific personality it has is its expressions in a medium public to us, for example, its ability to use language or to act responsibly. Since, as we said in Part One, the medium of God's creative activity is determinate only in the created product, the world is both the medium through which we interpret God's activity and the objects and subjects on which he acts. This seems to pose no special difficulty, since man at least is sufficiently self-reflective to consider the character of what God does to him; and things in the natural order that are not self-conscious or -reflective presumably do not worry about whether God has a personality.

Our probation can begin by considering the arguments against the view that God is a person with a personality and with the capacity to intend and forgive. There are two chief arguments. One is the argument we ourselves used in chapter 9 when we claimed that the adequate conception of God as the object of worship must transcend that of substantial personality. The other is the empirical one that some religions, for example, Buddhism, do not conceive of God as personal.

Concerning the first, our argument was that the conception of the object of worship has to be the conception of what is absolutely supreme. Since the conception of the creator who transcends even his nature as creator deals with ontologically more fundamental categories than those involved in determinate relational characteristics, this conception of God is adequate to the object of worship. We cited the mystery and awe connected with worship as appropriate to the notion of the transcendent creator but as inappropriate to conceptions like substantial personalities. To say, however, that we worship the transcendent creator is not to say that, immanently connected with the world, God is not also personal. In fact, supposing that God is both the transcendent creator and immanently personal, we would say that worship is directed to the former more than the latter.

The responses we make to the personalities of people may be those of hate or love, respect or disregard, admiration or disapproval, gratitude or disavowal. But we do not *worship* persons, even in a derivative sense. Worship is based on taking God's determinate characteristics as signs of his supremacy, transcendence, and abysmal independence of us and our claims, and this is what makes it awesome. Our response to God as a personality, if we make such a response, is loving or hateful, respectful or disregarding, admiring or disapproving, grateful or disavowing. In a rich and full religious life, of course, worship and a personal relation with God are often so intertwined that it seems impossible and even unimportant to distinguish them. But there are many people who worship who find nothing personal in God, and there are many who respond to God as a personal divinity who never are filled with worship. Most of us concentrate sometimes on one side, sometimes on the other.

It has been argued by people like Hartshorne that worship of God must be directed at that which we conceive of as a person, and that it has the character of admiration.[6] But this misses the sense of *mysterium tremendum,* which has been so well attested in worship. It might be argued further that there is this sense of mystery in our response to persons. When someone knows us better in some respects than we know ourselves, there is something uncanny about him. Suppose God were an omniscient person who knew us perfectly, far better indeed than we know ourselves; how uncanny this would be! But this kind of uncanny quality is too much bound up with ourselves; it brings too much self-consciousness. It might be astonishing and admirable, but it is not the quality found in worship. In worship the mystery and awesomeness of God so strikes us that we are brought out of ourselves and are consumed by the divine presence. This is not at all like being in the presence of an insightful friend. But it is not to say that God is not *also* like a perfect insightful friend.

Concerning the second argument that God does not seem to be a personal creator, we can interpret the claims of religions like Buddhism in two ways. On the one hand, they can be articulations of the insight that God is indeed transcendent in his aseity of any finite characterizations like personality. This interpretation perfectly accords with the mystical bent of oriental religions that concentrate more on worship than on personal relations. But Buddhism seems to exclude in a more thorough manner the possibility that God might also be personal. How are we to interpret the negative side of this doctrine? The second interpretation of the claim that God is not personal is either that the Buddhists are right and there is no positive evidence that God is personal or that there is something systematic in their view that would lead them to misconstrue what positive evidence there is. (The positive evidence we shall deal with presently.) There is indeed in Buddhism a tendency to depreciate both the reality and the worth of personality. This would tend to lead Buddhism on two counts to fail to acknowledge a personal character to God. On the one hand, it would seem to be an unworthy thing to attribute to God. On the other hand, since finite personality is considered to be both the root of all evil and unreal to boot,[7] personal relations with God as a person would seem also unimportant and unreal. Since love, the chief ideal of personal existence, is the source of all trouble, developing a love for God or having a personal God to love would be contrary to religious expectations. We have already discussed the difficulties in this conception of human nature.[8] In-

[6] *The Divine Relativity* (New Haven, Conn.: Yale University Press, 1948), p. 52.
[7] See A. K. Coomaraswamy, *Buddha and the Gospel of Buddhism* (New York: Harper & Row, 1964), pp. 39–42, 90–101, and *passim.*
[8] See chap. 11, sec. B.

Charles Hartshorne

sufficient regard for the importance of human personality leads to insensitivity toward possible manifestations of God as personal.

We now must consider whether there is any positive evidence that God is personal. There seems in fact to be considerable evidence in favor of the view that God is personal, evidence of two kinds, general and specific.

The general evidence is that the world in general seems to be the kind of ordered affair that one would expect a personal kind of creator to make. Although there are catastrophies aplenty, there still is a kind of fitness in things that testifies to an orderly-minded creator. What is more remarkable than the fact that there are goods to be achieved and beings to achieve them? Of course, as Hume pointed out, we cannot infer from order in the world to the existence of an orderer. However, in a sense we can infer from the fact that the order is contingent to the need for a ground for actual order; as Peirce pointed out, chaos is understandable, but it is regularity and order that above all need an account.[9] But we are not here trying to infer the existence of a creator; we take that as shown. Our present task is to determine whether he has a personal character as creator. To the extent that we judge whether a thing is a person by whether his deeds exhibit an order that seems to be personally intended, God seems to be a person in the character of his creation by the order of the world.

But his order is a very general thing and the argument it presents for a personal creator is abstract and tenuous, to say the least. The best it can do is indicate that, given a creator at work, the character of his work is what we would expect from a personal rather than impersonal kind of creator. In judging whether ordinary things are persons, however, we do not limit attention to such general considerations. We go on to see whether there is a specific and definite personality, an individual character. In between the general criterion of whether the creator seems to be a person because his creations seem to exhibit an intentionally designed order and the specific criteria concerning whether specific parts of creation exhibit the intentions of a definite personality, there is a general criterion concerning specificity. That is, a person is a being that does things that are characteristic of a *definite* personality. Although human persons often do uncharacteristic things because of lack of self-control, we would expect God not to have a problem of self-control and thus always to act characteristically. Indeed, so far as we can tell, which is not really very far, this is a highly selective and particular world in which the apparent empirical regularities could have been otherwise than they are. Even natural catastrophies like earthquakes are the products of regular natural laws whose regularity gives the events of the world the stamp of a definite character. As creator of *this* world, God's nature as creator has definite

---

[9] See *Collected Papers of Charles Sanders Peirce*, ed. C. Hartshorne and P. Weiss (Cambridge, Mass.: Harvard University Press, 1931), VI, 12. "Law is par excellence the thing that wants a reason."

characteristics. This point does not prove much on its own, but it adds to the general plausibility of the thesis that the creator is one we would call personal.

Furthermore, although the regularities of natural laws indicate a fairly constant character, many religions, especially those of the Middle East and West, claim that there is a particular linear history in God's dealing with men. God treats Isaac as Abraham's son, not as a man in general. According to Judaism, Christianity, and Islam, there is a linear and responsive development of God's personal relation with men leading up to and away from special messianic or prophetic moments. Of course, all the interpretations of God's historical dealings with men cannot be equally true, since they disagree. But the disagreement in many cases is more often about the relative significance of critical religious events than about whether they occurred or have any religious significance.

These considerations do not, of course, *prove* that the creator is personal. They only aim to make the view plausible. Whether we can take it as proved that God is personal depends upon our ultimate interpretation of the historical canons of promises, and we have discussed in the previous chapter the private difficulties involved in such interpretation. Our purpose in arguing for the mere plausibility of the view that God is personal is to make plausible the other doctrines to which our consideration of religion had led us, namely, that God intends and forgives. It cannot be deduced from the claim that God is the transcendent creator that he is also personal and that he intends and forgives; but neither can religion be deduced from that claim. Religion must be examined on its own ground and interpreted in the light of the metaphysical theory. That is, we aim to show the compatibility and mutual reinforcement of the religious and theoretical views.

To say that God forgives or that his character in general is loving or good is to raise further questions that cast doubt on the possibility that he is personal at all. These, of course, are the questions of theodicy: if God has a loving and forgiving character, how is this compatible with his general function as creator and with the *de facto* evil in the world? This issue is too complex to enter deeply here. But it can be pointed out that, although God might not have the personal character of making everything pleasant for man, this fact is consistent with the view that he forgives and thereby gives man religious harmony. As we shall see shortly, the reason why God has the definite character he seems to have is an utter mystery, of a piece with the mystery as to why he creates at all and why he creates as he does. Why he forgives is a mystery, too. But forgiveness is the only trait we have found religion committed to; it is not committed to the view that God's personal character is good in the sense that he must characteristically act for the good of the world, though of course he might do so.

b) *The ontological status of God's personality.* Although it is not the case that God's personality can be deduced from metaphysical considerations concerning creation, it is the case that, given the claims of religion that God is indeed personal, we must show how this is ontologically to be interpreted in terms of the theory of creation.

God's personality, being determinate, must be part of what is created, as is his very nature as creator. Personality is the characteristic expressions of a person, and just as a finite person has no personality without characteristic expression (at least private if not public expressions), so it is inappropriate to speak of God's personality apart from his expressions, that is, the created realm. But with human persons we distinguish between the characteristic expressions that give substance to personality and the person who is expressed. We say that personality is the characteristic expression of a person in a medium, allowing that the person's inner life can be a medium of expression as well as his public life. In the case of the creator, however, there is no real distinction between the medium and the actual expression: the created realm is both. With human beings, we say that the person is the whole human determination of being that expresses itself in personality through its discursive inner and public life. But with the creator, what stands for the person whose personality is expressed in creation? This is comparable to the question about the ontological status of the nature of being "creator."

Let us examine the distinction we make for human beings between the *person* and the *personality*. The person is the determination of being qua determination of being and that personality is the determinate nature of the determination, man's nature being essentially temporal or "expressive" anyway. This amounts to saying that a person is a being whose nature, that is, whose expression, is that of personality. In human beings, the "being" of the person is the total created harmony of all the comprehended determinations, including those expressive of personality. In the case of God, the "being" or person is the one whose creation exhibits personality. This is God who in himself is independent of creating and who makes himself creator by creating. Of course, when the person of God is separated from his expressed personality, the term "person" attributes nothing determinate of God. But this would make "person" a useless term; so we should not separate it from personality in application to God. Our conclusion is that to say God is a person is the same as saying that he creates with personality.

To say that a human person is a being that expresses itself or exhibits its nature as a personality leaves open the question whether something can be known of the being apart from its personal expression. To speak of God as a being who creates with personality does not leave that question open very long, for we know that the being referred to transcends the possibility of any determinate considerations. Consequently, when we say that God intends or forgives we must not be misled into believing that God has a private mind that first entertains the object of intention as mere idea and than acts to realize it. Between the idea of the object of intention and the completed fact, there is no shadow; God's thoughts are the same as his creations: his ideas are real things. Human beings sometimes express their characters first in ideas and then in more overt action; God's character is one with his expression, and that expression is the created realm.

This means that when God forgives, it is least misleading to describe it as creating forgiveness. His forgiveness is a created determination of being. We often think of forgiveness as having its reality in the forgiver instead of in the forgiven. In a sense this is true, but if it is the only truth about forgiveness, then the forgiven man is in bad shape. Forgiveness must be possessed by the forgiven as something that makes a real difference to his nature. When God forgives a man, forgiveness is in the forgiver insofar as the forgiving creator is present in his created product; forgiveness is present in the forgiven insofar as the man's reality exhibits the actuality of religious harmony.

c) Providence and personality. The question of personality was raised because we found that one of the characteristics of a providential act is that it be aimed at some good, most interestingly, at the good of the human religious harmony. Now we are in a position to ask whether providential acts, as opposed to the creation of the more general context, are specially revelatory of God's personality. This is not to ask whether providential events embody God's personality more than other events, since all creation is an equal expression of God. Rather, it is to ask whether providential acts lend themselves to instructive human interpretation about the personality of God.

It seems clear according to the claims of religion that they do. First of all, it is in dealing with human persons that God's own personality is likely to become clearest, and providence usually relates to persons. There is something more fundamental to personality in the personal traits of loving or disapproving than there is in traits like creating in an orderly manner; the former traits are the ones most likely to come out in providential events as opposed to the creation of the more general context. Second, in the general order of creation we are not as likely to notice peculiar personality traits as in providential events.

The problem raised by these considerations is that of the temporality of providential acts. We discussed in Part One the sense in which creation in general is from eternity although within time one thing occurs before another. This is because some of the determinations created are temporal determinations and from eternity have their natures temporally ordered. But what about providential acts in which God creates something to supplement the more general created order and which would not have been otherwise? Is it not necessary for God the creator to make himself into a temporal being who waits to see what man will do in order to decide what providential acts are necessary to help him out? The providential God is the one who enters into man's life, who responds to his prayers, who suffers and rejoices with him. Must this not, as many modern theologians claim, be a finite and temporal God?

If the providential God were such a finite temporal being, however much like a friendly stranger he might be, he could not be that divine power in us that is closer to us than we are to ourselves. And religion indicates that the latter is as real as the former. There must be another interpretation of the providential temporality of God if justice is to be done to religion.

It is true that the God who faces man at providential times does so in contingent and temporal ways. But as temporal, what faces us in providential events must be created; it must be part of our world. If providential events involve an encounter with God, then it must be God made finite. In fact, this is God as he is present in his creation.

The only temporal God who takes part in providential events is a revealed God, and a revealed God is God the creator present in his temporal created product. But the independent God who creates is eternal, and his act of creating is from eternity. What he creates is temporal, and among his temporal creations are providential acts that respond to the contingent temporalities of man's existence.

When we say that providential events are beneficial ones that would not have happened otherwise, we mean by the latter qualification that they are not determined by antecedent or given conditions. This does not mean that the creator would have to be in time, waiting to see what happened to determine what to do. Creation from eternity is not creation within time; it does not mean that God knows things before they happen; to say that is to interpret eternity merely as "earliest." Providential events are those created from eternity that are not determined wholly by other things created from eternity. The divine personality revealed in providential events is the personality created from eternity, although its concrete revelation is a temporal thing.

4. Our whole discussion of providence and personality in God was prompted by considerations about liturgy, for liturgy is the celebration of providential events. But part of what liturgical celebration means is that the benefit in the providential event is appropriated through the liturgy. It was the pursuit of this point that led us to the problem of providence.

The appropriation accomplished in liturgy is not private appropriation, although private appropriation can be providential. Rather, it is usually public appropriation; that is, there is a religious harmony appropriate to a public group, and liturgy is the means whereby this begins to be accomplished.

Just as a private person attains religious harmony by conversion that involves adopting the ground for hope, so a group, to have religious harmony, must adopt in some way the grounds for hope. A group, however, is made up of persons. In a group those persons express the public side of their natures, and public conversion is not so much a matter of belief as it is of profession and public embodiment of the principles of public life that the individuals believe in. Liturgical celebration is the public adoption of the principles of public religious harmony privately adopted by the individuals. Although the principles publicly adopted are related to those privately adopted, the religious harmony in question is the harmony of the group, not just of the individuals. By participating in the liturgy the individuals participate in the corporate adoption or appropriation of the saving activity of God. The group has no corporate private soul as an individual has; it has only the individuals. But in a group the individuals function publicly, and the life of the group is the public life of its members. The religious harmony of that public life should in the end be brotherhood, as we shall argue subsequently. Therefore, the providential acts celebrated in liturgy are those contributing to the founding of the brotherhood, including those that promise its perpetuation, validity, and fulfillment. Brotherhood, or the religiously harmonious public life, is possible only if the public life of the individuals as a group appropriates the principles that make the public religious harmony possible. This appropriation takes place first in liturgy.

No person is merely private; he is also public. His true religious harmony therefore must include the religious harmony of the groups in which he participates. But until the other members of the groups are prepared to contribute to the religious harmony of the whole, his own religious harmony is in jeopardy. The others will not be prepared to contribute publicly to the religious harmony of the group until they appropriate a private harmony. Therefore, an individual seeking to express his public religious harmony must evangelize his fellows.

SECTION C

Evangelism

Evangelism is a public activity aimed at bringing about both a private religious harmony in others and a public religious harmony in the group or community. Its principal means seem to fall into two classes. On the one hand, evangelism takes the form of verbal persuasion that the promises or covenants at the foundation of both private and public religious harmony are true. On the other hand, it often takes the form of demonstration of the fruits of harmony in practice.

One of the aims of evangelism is to bring about inner religious harmony in other people. Since a group is made up of individuals who have private lives, the group's concern is for individuals. Consequently, most evangelism is oriented toward bringing conviction about the promises that make possible inner religious harmony. The limitations of private evangelism, of course, are that although the evangelist can present the case, acceptance of the case must be the responsibility of the hearer. Whether the message is believed is a problem ultimately for evangelized, not for the evangelist. The evangelist might be a "means of grace" and his persuasion might excite the will to believe; but the harmony that comes with belief is indeed a matter of grace. Evangelism is perverted when it fails to respect the integrity of the evangelized and reduces them to merely emotional responders, for religious harmony is the harmony of the whole person, intellectual as well as passionate.

Because each individual has a public life, the religious harmony of the public group to which he belongs is also an evangelical concern. Evangelism for the public life aims primarily at persuading the individuals or groups of individuals to participate in the ideal structures that embody the religious harmony of the group. These structures include not only liturgical ones but all of those that contribute to brotherhood. The limitation of public evangelism, like that of private evangelism, is that its appeal must be adopted by those whose integrity as harmonious beings in some respects stands over against the evangelist.

It is clear that neither the public nor the private aim of evangelism is independent of the other. Since all evangelism is public, it uses the public tokens of the group. Even when aiming at the inner religious harmony, it proclaims the promises that are interpreted and mediated by the group and that are often addressed to the group first and to the individual only by extrapolation. Yet even evangelism aimed at the public life of man must address itself to an individual who also has an inner life; it is in the inner life that problems of belief must be coped with, notwithstanding the fact that the belief may be about how to live the public life.

In a world where organized religions compete and where religion naturally leads to evangelism, the question of who evangelizes whom is crucial. We have spoken vaguely so far in indicating that evangelism extends to the members of one's group. The difficult question concerns the identity of group membership. It is a peculiarity of Judaism, setting it apart from nearly all other major religions, that it historically has taken the divine promises of religious fulfillment to be directed rather exclusively toward the hereditary group.

Christians, as well as adherents of most other major religions, take the group to which they essentially belong and to which the divine promises are relevant to be the whole of mankind. Historical, political, geographic, and cultural problems, rather than matters of principle, have caused the actual parochialisms in the range of evangelism. It is tempting to think that such a universalistic view must be best because it is most generous and humanitarian. Certainly there are many senses, especially today, in which all men participate in the same groups. But it must be remembered that the grounds for religious harmony, in public life as well as in private, are the activities of God that forgive infirmity and make finite life blessed. If God's grace is selective, as Judaism claims that it is, then the group to which religious harmony should be extended is selective. Although other religions might be right in the claim that saving grace is universally extended, this is a contingent fact of which we are usefully reminded by Judaism's claim that grace is contingently selective. Each religion must look to the content of its evangelistic message to determine the range of evangelical operation. The range cannot be determined by a priori principles.

The form we most commonly associate with evangelism is verbal proclamation. Preachers, revivalists, door-to-door witnesses, and the like are what we know in the West as evangelists. In oriental religions the adoption of knowledge necessary for religious fulfillment is encouraged by such verbal means that the evangelists are called teachers, rather than preachers. As we have seen in our discussion of the problem of faith, belief in the principles of religious harmony, public as well as private, must be accompanied by understanding. It makes no sense to assert or believe something that has no meaning, and meaning is easiest conveyed by verbal means. Whether the content of faith is to be privately adopted in the inner life or publicly adopted as well, the content of faith must be understood to be believed.

Evangelism requires that understanding be coupled with appreciation, however, and the evangelist not only explains but persuades. There are many forms of persuasion having to do with making the advertised beliefs seem attractive and with convincing persons that their lives need the hope that faith grounds. Devices all the way from rational apologetics to emotion-bending rhetoric can be employed to proclaim the promises so long as the integrity of the evangelized is respected. In the end, explanation and persuasion should come together, explanation becoming concrete and relevant to the heart's concern and persuasion becoming articulate and perspicuous with regard to the needs of the religious harmony that is God's glory. Probably the best word to describe the means of evangelism is art, not only because this word indicates the sensitivity and skill required of the evangelist, but also because the aim of evangelism is to reveal the beauty or glory of the saving elements of God's creation, including his forgiveness. At this point evangelism as a verbal thing unites with the revelatory function of all art, except that evangelism concentrates on the glory of God in man. Explicitly, evangelism presents the beauty or glory God would work in man, and in this beauty lies evangelism's appeal.

Evangelists have long known that one of the most potent forms of persuasion and the clearest explication of abstract meaning is by example. Even verbal evangelism employs stories as a crucial device. We recall our discussion of Augustine's conversion in the previous chapter and the decisive part the examples of converted Romans played in his life. Christian evangelists inevitably portray the life of Jesus as an example that calls forth imitation.

Imitation is a response to what is at base an aesthetic appeal in the object of imitations. Certain lives have a beauty or glory that calls for imitation. It is usually rather abstract aspects of life that are imitated, such as humility, obedience, acceptance of the love of others or of God, and so forth. Yet the beauty of these imitable features is apparent only in concrete exercises, and the imitation is always concrete.

When a religious community requires that its members be exemplary, this is an expression of evangelistic concern as much as it is a disciplinary measure. The crucial issue concerns what the example should be an example of. In the abstract it is easy to say that the example should portray both private and public religious harmonies that make explicit the adoption of God's forgiveness. In the concrete the exemplary forms of religious harmony are more problematic to determine, for we must determine what can publicly be exhibited by the exemplary person. This is the nature of his dedication.

SECTION D
Dedication

The public form of the inner adoption of the content of faith is dedication. Dedication is the commitment of one's public life and activities to the embodiment of public religious harmony. It is a commitment to citizenship in a religiously fulfilled group. In an institutionalized religion, dedication means, among other things, churchmanship. In all religions, dedication means effort to embody public religious harmony in all groups for which the harmony is deemed appropriate.

Every harmony has a kind of structure. As we noted with regard to the religious harmony of the inner life, there are many kinds of lives that can be religiously harmonious; religious harmony is the harmony of a full human nature no matter what kind of life is led. But religious harmony is not indifferent to the structure of the life led. Regardless of the place, time, or business of the person, his life must incorporate in some way an element of accepting God's forgiveness as well as elements that give expression to all the other factors of the religious life we discussed in the last chapter. Likewise the public harmony embodied in a group may be compatible with many variations in cultural structure; groups differ by time and place, by history, by present conditions, and by function. Groups concerned with religious harmony in a public way may be as limited as families or as large as civilizations.

Like the harmony of the inner life, however, public religious harmonies are not indifferent to the groups that embody them. Whatever the particular function of the group, its religious harmony makes it aim also to be a brotherhood. Furthermore, brotherhood always has particular conditions. These conditions include the structures of appropriating the providential acts that are the basis of the community, the liturgy, and so forth, as well as the group structures of morality that are taken to be essential for public religious harmony. A religious man is one who dedicates himself to the task of embodying the structure of religious harmony that is required to harmonize his particular group or groups.

It is at the point of public dedication that a person might come into sharpest conflict with culture. If culture is taken broadly to mean the nature of the groups for which the religious harmony is a problem, the changes wrought in such groups in order to bring about religious harmony might be cataclysmic. This is especially likely in times like ours when culture is coping with many necessary changes other than religious ones. Innovators of all cultural intents compete with religion for the leadership in reforming society.

We have already spoken of the need of religion to make certain demands of culture, since the culture must be such as to make possible the religious harmony. It is to be emphasized that religion has the public task of reinterpreting its public tenets in terms of the changing conditions of society. Even in groups that have been informed by one religion for generations, changing conditions force the reformation of the group's basic structures, including the ways in which religion is expressed.

On the other hand, it must be emphasized, over against many contemporary thinkers, that culture is essential to religion. Just as religion needs persons to embody the inner religious harmony, it needs cultural groups of persons for its public harmony. It is only in elements that otherwise would be "merely" cultural that the public glory of God in religious harmony can be expressed. When it is claimed that religious people should transcend culture and criticize it, this can safely be taken to mean that religious people should transcend and criticize specific cultural forms. But it need not be taken to mean that culture in general should be transcended. To mean the latter would indicate a belief that there is a significant portion of the world that God could not redeem with the grace of religious harmony. The whole of culture and the natural world is the setting in which man must be religiously harmonious if he is to have that harmony at all. In fact, religious dedication can be seen as a commitment to redeem culture, where the Christian word "redemption" can be interpreted to mean "embody in religious harmony."

In this age when the variation in cultural forms is so apparent, the crucial question for the problem of dedication is, Dedication to what? No practical answer can be given without taking into account not only the differences in the professed ideals of different religions but also the specifics of the groups in question. Something that might promote public religious harmony for one group might destroy it in another. A further complication is the fact that what is relevant, pro or con, to religious harmony in one group might be quite insignificant in another. As groups change or as the focus of religion moves to wider and wider groups, as it does today when religions are having to take account of cultures far different from their historical traditions, the question of the relevance of cultural forms to religion becomes acute. This is not the place to trace out these difficulties. Still, we have seen that religion is not wholly conventional and that it does have a close connection, on the general level, with considerations that stem from our metaphysical discussion. Therefore, we should be able to put the problem of the object of dedication in terms of a general problem of public religious harmony. It is easy to say that religious dedication has as its object the religious service of God; no religion would quarrel with this. But it says too little. To see what is necessary to attain public religious harmony, we must be able to see what the basic public problem of religion is. Our previous chapter oriented its discussion around the task of articulating the nature of the religious problem for the inner life of man. The nature of that problem is that man, inevitably a failure with regard to the norms that should govern his life, takes on the self-defeating task of justifying himself, a task that makes man less than truly human because of the false pride it involves. What is the analogous problem for public religious harmony?

A group is not a personality, but it is made up of individuals who are human beings, or personalities. When the public nature of the group structures the relations between human beings so as to deny, frustrate, or pervert their humanity, the group has a public religious problem. The true nature of a group of persons is the public life of those persons as truly human beings. The public needs of man are many, and for these reasons men exist in groups. But the groups are bad, simply as groups, when they deny the humanity of their members. The denial of humanity is a denial of the essential created nature of groups and hence is a religious problem. The public religious problem, therefore, is the reconciliation of public persons with the true humanity of themselves and their fellows.

SECTION E

Reconciliation

A brotherhood, like a person, is what it is in virtue of a harmony of constituting parts. But the kind of harmony involved in a public group, as well as the kind of constituents, is different from that in a person. It has often been characteristic of philosophers to swing from one to the other of two mistaken extremes in the comparison of groups with persons. On the one hand, there have been those like the idealists who have asserted a near identity in the comparison of personal and group natures. The group, especially the state, is taken to have essentially the same structural features as a person, a spiritual organization according to personal principles of affection and will, and even a consciousness. No one, of course, not even Hegel, meant to assert a literal identity between the structures of persons and states; all agreed that it was the individual citizens and only they who were conscious and that, as a group, the citizens shared some common principles of conscious structure and interpretation. But still, the analogy between person and group is misleading if pressed too far, as it surely has been pressed by popular idealism.

On the other hand, many philosophers have reacted against the identification of personal and group natures to the extent that they have denied any characteristic structure or integrity to groups. Nominalists, for example, who maintain that only individuals exist, once they have given up the view that groups are superindividuals, have little ground to stand on short of saying that groups have "merely conventional" reality. It must be admitted that a group of people is not an individual in any ordinary sense, especially not in the sense that an individual is a physical object; therefore, if only individuals of that sort are what exist, then the reality of groups must be explained away or reduced to elements of the individuals who make them up. But this position, like its opposite, does violence to our funded experience. Although there is a sense in which the significance of groups can be traced to their practical consequences in the minds of persons, this is the same sense in which the significance of physical objects can be traced to their influence on knowers. But this is not to say that either physical objects or groups fail to have characteristic natures of their own with an integrity we must take account of or be wrong about. Some groups, far more than some physical objects, have natures malleable by our volitions; and for other groups, the opposite is true. It is easier to grow roses than to make a group of students wise.

It has not always been the case that social philosophy is based on nominalistic principles, the nominalism of the superindividual or that of the subsocial individual. Prior to the modern period in philosophy the family was taken as the paradigm of a group. But what was paradigmatic in the family structure was the peculiar distribution of authority in the paternal-dependent relation. Under certain conditions this kind of group structure allows for the maximization of human potential; but under other conditions, for example, when the mass of men in the group mature from childhood or dependency, the power structure of the family becomes inappropriate. The rise of democracy as an organizing theme for social groups severely restricted the appropriateness of the family model, and it led to the nominalism of much modern social philosophy. But we have already seen nominalism to be inadequate. What must be done is to elaborate a social philosophy that pays attention to the kinds of differences between the nature of persons or individuals and the nature of groups. This is not the place to attempt that, but we can say some general things about the fundamental structures of groups.

1. *Metaphysical traits of groups.* A group of people is a kind of determination of being. Like any determination, it has many features that it harmonizes into a unity with some integrity. Of the features contained in groups, there are the people themselves, who have both public and private lives; there are physical, political, economic, historic, geographic, and many other conditions of environment; and there are the aims, functions, and traditions of the group, including its own historical institutions and mores. Some groups have other significant features, and some groups may not give great significance to those we have mentioned. The factors work together into dynamic patterns, and if the group has any integrity or stability, even a changing integrity or stability, the patterns are harmonious or coherent.

Now a group can have its worth judged in at least three closely connected ways: in terms of the worth of its aims, in terms of its effectiveness in achieving its aims, and in terms of its quality simply as a group. Here we are concerned most with the last, since all groups, as groups, are harmonies of men, and the ideal harmony of a group is for its members to be united in a way that allows for and perhaps promotes their humanity. Of course, the particular structure of the groups must be determined in large part by the aims they seek and the conditions in which the group exists. Some groups are so impersonal by nature that the public life of their members has relatively little to do with private life. On the other hand, such groups, if good, limit themselves so as not to infringe upon private life. Other groups, such as armies and nations at war, call upon their members to exercise their private lives according to the needs of public life; such groups are good as groups only insofar as they permit the devotion of private life to the public weal to be a truly human way of living. That this is very difficult needs no emphasis today.

This "transcendental" judgment about groups as groups gives a key for understanding the difference between groups and persons. A group is good as a group, regardless of the worth of its aims or its success in their behalf, when it forms the public life of its members so that they can be truly human. Sometimes a group, by virtue of its aim and conditions, is so personal that it fulfills the public humanity of its members and even turns back to foster private humanity, as does a school group. But whereas the aims of a person are to fulfill the various aspects of his humanity, both private and public, the aims of a group are not so much to fulfill the group as to fulfill the public humanity of its members. A group attains its proper harmony for the sake of something besides itself, namely, for the sake of its members. A group does have a nature and integrity of its own, different from the nature and integrity of its members. The standards for the harmony of a group are different from those for the harmony of persons. But the aims of groups are to fulfill the public aims of their members, and the harmony of the group should foster the humanity of its members.

2. *Plato and social morality*. What we have said about the metaphysics of groups is very reminiscent of what Plato says in the *Republic*. A just state, for him, is one that harmonizes its components so that justice is allowed its citizens. Plato conceives of justice in the individual as a harmony of many functions of the soul, both in private life and in public life; this again is quite analogous to the views we have maintained. Plato's theory is indeed attractive in terms of its sensitivity to the very problems we have raised. Although he makes a comparison of persons and the state by discussing justice in each, he never abuses the comparison to attribute personal qualities to the state. On the other hand, Plato does not try to reduce the state to just the individuals involved.

Yet Plato speaks very little about the "religious problem" of a state or group. We would say that the difficulties he cites in establishing a just or properly harmonious state are moral or social and political difficulties, not religious ones. True, he does speak of piety in the *Euthyphro,* and the lesson there seems to be that true piety should take precedence over an abstract and literal reading of justice. Yet it cannot be said that Plato develops his notion of piety to a degree that would be compatible with the demands we have set for a problem of public religious harmony. If, then, we are to maintain that there is a public religious problem, we must give careful consideration to the alternative view that public problems are not religious in the sense we mean.

The problem could perhaps be solved by definition. As we argued above, a religious problem is defined as the problem of being or maintaining one's created nature.[10] As this is a problem for persons, so also would it be a problem for groups, since it seems that groups are significant parts of the created world. A thing's nature is the togetherness of the parts that make it up, and this togetherness, to be a real thing, must be a harmony. Therefore, by definition, the problem of harmonizing the constituents of a group is a religious problem. Moreover, our definition is not an arbitrary one but rather comes out of the whole fabric of our metaphysical and phenomenological discussion.

This solution, however, forces us to penetrate to a fine distinction. It is one thing to face the problem of arriving at a harmonious way of life, where the relevant considerations have to do with how to balance concerns and distribute time and energy. It is another thing to face the problem of coming to terms with and accepting the kind of harmony it is one's own to have. We must be careful to distinguish between kinds of harmony, for example, human, social, and subhuman, and the ways in which these harmonies are embodied. Artists, politicians, bricklayers, and teachers all have different ways of achieving a truly human harmony; and states, clubs, and families are different expressions of public life. The problem a thing has in working out its proper harmony is a moral problem, in the broad sense of that term. When a person chooses a career, a spouse, or a way of life, this is primarily a moral choice, and religious considerations need not be central. To determine the proper structure of a state to provide for fulfillment and justice for the citizens is to consider questions of social norms and morals; it is not to consider religious factors, although religious factors are sometimes important. This is the kind of problem Plato was considering.

On the other hand, when a thing acts so as to deny or pervert its essential created nature, it has a religious problem. When a human being perverts his humanity with pride, or when a group perverts the essential character of the group, those are religious problems. Of course, there are moral difficulties involved, but the essential problem with regard to accepting or perverting a thing's essential nature is religious.

The distinction we are drawing here between the moral and the religious can be put in Platonic terms. Every concrete thing in the natural universe has a nature, Plato claims, in which it participates or which it exhibits with some degree of relative precision and accuracy. The moral problem for each thing is to participate in or to exhibit its nature well instead of poorly. But a thing has a religious problem when its very participation in its nature is jeopardized. Of course, we do not say that artifacts have religious problems, but that is because we give them their natures. Nor do we speak of the religious problems of subhuman natural things, because they lack consciousness to the point where religion is not a matter of responsibility (although some religions do speak of the whole world groaning under the travail of sin, for

[10] See chap. 10.

example). Men and groups of men, however, do have religious problems, and the reason is precisely because through pride men can be less than men and through certain other difficulties groups can be less than groups of men. It is part of the essential nature of a group of men, even a state, that its members be human beings; to the degree that the group or state fails to acknowledge the humanity of its members, it not only fails to participate adequately in its essential nature, which is a moral problem; it also implicitly denies its essential nature, which is a religious problem. If a group solves its religious problem, it still must face the moral problem of working out effective participation; but this does not reduce the religious problem to a moral one.

3. *Estrangement and reconciliation.* Whereas the religious problem of the inner life is that of accepting one's finite nature as imperfect and forgiven, the religious problem of the public life is that of estrangement from one's fellows, since estrangement is a social or group relation that fails to acknowledge the humanity of the persons related. A group is a bad group when its members are estranged from each other.

The concept of estrangement is often used today to articulate the nature of the religious problem. This is a welcome advance, but it has a misleading interpretation. It is often forgotten that estrangement is an affair of the *public* life. Privately man may lose himself through pride, but he may be estranged from himself only by being estranged through his public nature. The possibility of estrangement from others depends upon making some public expression in terms of which we and they can be estranged. To think that only private man can be personal and therefore estranged is a mistake. It is the very disease of estrangement to think that public life must be impersonal. Estrangement is a social affair, depending on a rejection of personal public expressions of persons to each other or to themselves.

It is a commonplace to note that the answer to life's hard problems, especially those of estrangement, is communication, the revelation of heart to heart. Although it is naïve to think of communication as such a panacea, there is an important point in the commonplace; it is, however, the opposite of the point that is usually made. Authentic communication is usually thought to be a problem of true subjectivity, and indeed there must be true subjectivity if there is to be anything to communicate. But the problem of communication itself is a problem of true objectivity; that is, it is a problem of finding a public life in which structures relating persons allow for the humanity of one person to acknowledge, address, and respond to the humanity of the others. Public life, with the possibility of authentic communication it conveys, should be such that people treat each other as truly human beings. A society or group that fails to do this is one whose members are estranged; to be good, simply as a group, it should be a brotherhood (brotherhood is a more comprehensive notion than communication); the move from estrangement to brotherhood is by reconciliation.

How is reconciliation possible? The answer to this question depends upon knowing the answer to a prior question. How is estrangement possible?

Estrangement can stem from two fundamental sources, and they usually co-operate. In the first place, estrangement can stem from the private or inner life of a person. A man can estrange himself from his fellows by withdrawing from or perverting his public life, when that public life perfectly well allows for true brotherhood. But he would do this only from carelessness or from fear. It is a common experience of most of us that true and faithful friendships degenerate into estrangement through carelessness and neglect. Often this estrangement is accompanied by an element of fear at renewing the relationship; this is almost an equally common experience. What we fear is that renewing public life will jeopardize and threaten the humanity we think we have. Again, this is misplaced pride, for our true humanity would profit from the renewal of a truly human association. What is true of friendships is also true of our participation in the public life of much larger groups. We fear to enter public life because it demands that we accept the responsibilities of truly human association, responsibilities that we think threaten our own humanity.

In the second place, estrangement can stem simply from the character of the groups and from the structures of public life into which we are initiated. Although men have considerable power to arrange their groups as they please, and although all groups were once structured by men, none of us was there at the beginning; we are all initiated into a public life with an antecedent structure. To undertake public life at all requires a socialization that conforms persons to an antecedent structure, a process that allows them to take hold on the public. Furthermore, the public life in which men find themselves before they know it is not vague and general, allowing of free and responsible conscious specification. Rather the initial public life is that of the family, and its structures are much more specific and detailed than the wider neighborhood, school, and general culture in which they will live eventually. Families have their specific variations on the national language, their specific traditions and habits regarding the manners of the culture, and selective specifications of personality structures and interpersonal relations from the much wider domain of social possibilities. The particularity of public life in the family, versus the more general possibilities of public life in a culture, is reiterated to just a slightly lesser degree of specificity in the contrast of the public life of a neighborhood or subculture to that of the larger culture. Although it may be true that the structure of the *inner* life of a person moves from the vague to the specific with increasing maturity, the structure of one's *public* life begins with great particularity and moves to more general and tolerant contexts. This means that the development of public life involves a large portion of rebellion against previous restrictive structures. It is often man's misfortune to be born into public contexts that by their very nature estrange him from his fellows. It is safe to say, in this day when the evils of slums and prejudice and social segregation are impossible to ignore, that there are many people who have known no public life but that of estrangement.

Even with the estrangement that results from the *structure* of the public life each man inherits, the *form* the estrangement takes is that of fear of entering into a more human public life. No matter how bad the groups are in which a person has a public life, they will not keep him from meeting people; they may, however, make him fearful of venturing into a truly human association. In the end, no matter whether estrangement stems from the inner life or from a wholly public context, its vicious form boils down to a fear to enter into truly human public relations and groups. One has only to watch the characteristic responses of members of a street gang to see fear of human sensitivity coupled with a need and craving for it.

The religious problem of public life lies at the root of this fear. Why do people fear the loss of their humanity in a public life that calls for truly human association? One would think that this is the very kind of relation to which they would trust their humanity! The fact is, however, that the demands of a truly human public life are too great. No group, no form of public life, regardless of how minimal its impersonal demands, provides a context that allows a person to do all he should to treat his fellows as genuine human beings. No man of social conscience can respond to the human needs of all the people he should help. If he is a northerner and goes to help the Negroes in the South, he will neglect housing discrimination in the North. If he is a southerner who does battle for the oppressed in his own culture, he will neglect the starving millions in India. Even if a person's society had but one other individual, the demands would still be too great. No one can love another so well that he is perfectly sensitive to the other's person. Were love so full that the person would give his whole being to the other, it would still not be enough. A lover who cannot bring himself to give something he has to his beloved suffers terrible and pathetic pain. But for the lover who does indeed give all he has, and finds this not enough, his pain is tragic.

Although only a few people love enough to be in a position to fail as lovers, all of us fail in less intimate situations again and again. The fear of public life is the fear that, upon entering it as we should, we shall be guilty inevitably. Usually we fear that public life will call for more of ourselves than we can give without sacrificing our own humanity. But even if we are willing to give without stint, we shall still fail and be guilty of imperfect public life.

The religious problem of public life is analogous to that of the inner life. In both cases we deny the true nature of the domain because we fear that, seeking it, we are bound to fail. But there is a difference, too. We respond to imperfection in the inner life by misconstruing our nature as higher than finite human reality and as capable of perfecting itself. This is pride. We respond to the imperfection and inevitable guilt of public life by misconstruing its nature as lower than truly human public reality and as not requiring us to recognize the humanity of its members. Yet there is a kind of pride, attenuated as it may be, in our perversion of the public life.

Although it is the *ideal* nature of a group, and of a person in his public life, to articulate social relations such that persons are treated as truly human, it is a fact of actual finite nature that this is impossible. The created nature of a group is that of a social structure wherein people are allowed to treat each other as persons but inevitably fail to do so, not necessarily from ill will but from limitation. We withdraw from authentic public life because of our pride that makes us think that, if only we were to enter public life, we should be able to perfect it. But it is not our nature to be publicly perfect any more than it is our nature to be privately perfect; it seems an empirical fact that we just are not made that way.

To reconcile a man with his fellows in public life, it is necessary first to reconcile him to the kind of thing public life must be—among other things, a domain in which he fails. The proper harmony of public life must be one that includes an actual discrepancy between ideal and fulfillment. At the analogous point in our discussion of the inner religious life, we cited religion's claim that God may forgive man his imperfections. Forgiveness reconciles perfect ideals and imperfect nature into harmony. But it will not do, with regard to the public life, to say just that each man is forgiven, even though that might also be true; for in this case it is not each man who is guilty. Rather it is all men taken together in their public lives. The public life of each man is constituted in large part by his relations with his fellows, and so they must be forgiven collectively. The public life of the group, which is the public lives of all its members, must be forgiven if public religious harmony is to be possible at all. Whether this forgiveness is real is a contingent matter.

Reconciliation is possible only if there is public divine forgiveness. But what is this? Forgiveness is not something that goes on in the mind of God apart from all creation; rather it is something that is the presence of the forgiving creator in his creation. Forgiveness must be an accomplished reconciliation of man's public life. Such an accomplished reconciliation is a brotherhood.

SECTION F

Brotherhood

Brotherhood has been the title of many promissory notes issued in the discussions of this chapter. We must investigate it now under three headings: its nature and demands, its possibility of realization, and the way in which religion proclaims it.

1. *The nature and demands of brotherhood.* The notion of brotherhood has often been misunderstood. The case of Cain is the classic example of this misunderstanding. Cain thought brotherhood meant being his brother's keeper. This was his first mistake. The modern version of Cain's theory is the view that some person or office has charge of the full development and responsibility of other persons. But except in the case of children, such paternalism is misplaced because it denies the responsibility and integrity of the persons dealt with.

It is instructive to determine what misleads Cain and us. Remembering the ideal of public life and groups, we know, as did Cain, that our public lives should be such that the true humanity of all our fellows is acknowledged. On the other hand, it is also apparent that it is public life that evokes or develops true humanity. That is, treating others as human beings is what *makes* them into human beings. It is through social interaction with a person that we develop that person's humanity. Human nature is mainly a social product. Child psychology is good testimony to this; and so are the critical moments in daily life that are decisive in making us truly human beings— these critical moments usually spring from public life. Therefore, it is easy to see how we and Cain come to the view that public life requires us to be not only our brother's keeper but his maker as well.

The difficulty with this view is that, although a person's humanity might take its critical steps in public life, his public life includes more than the influences of other people. A person's public life is constituted in crucial measure by the expressions of his own inner life, and the inner life develops through its adventures into the public domain. Only with small children is public life constituted most responsibly by external influences, and in dealing with small children paternalism is appropriate. But maturation means that a person becomes more and more responsible for his own public life. With maturity, a person takes upon himself large responsibility for the development of his humanity, and to deny him this responsibility is to deny a crucial part of that humanity. It is a mistake to think that it is possible to treat others as truly human beings, if by this we mean *to make* them human beings, without acknowledging that they have an inner responsibility of their own. This is the paradox of public life. We should treat others so as to make them truly human beings; but the responsibility of making them truly human belongs to them as much as to us, and we cannot command their private selves. We sometimes fail to treat others as truly human because they refuse to be treated that way or are incapable of responding humanly. This is the poignancy in the essential limitations and imperfections of the public life.

Our reaction to this is one of pride, for we think that we should be able to perfect our public lives. And we resent our brother's recalcitrance that makes failures of us. Feeling our own failure, we resent the acceptable humanity our brother achieves that is not of our own making. We would take credit for it all. And when we see our brother with some sign of his acceptability and know that we cannot take whole credit, we retreat from the demands of public life to foster his humanity and take up a stone against him. This was Cain's second mistake. It may be that a sharp blow from a heavy stone is more merciful in the long run than the tortures of alienation and dehumanization to which we subject ourselves and brothers today.

We must beware of this false conception of brotherhood, which itself is the source of the very estrangement it tries to combat. A true conception of brotherhood is one that recognizes that true brotherly intimacy involves a respectful distance. A person should devote himself to the humanity of his brothers while he pursues the many functions of the public life. But he should recognize that his public activity can never fully achieve its goal, for that achievement depends on the inner response of his brother; hence, the person must be prepared to let his brother fail. True brotherly love is love that sustains itself through failure and through being failed.

2. *The possibility of brotherhood.* But if men are estranged how are they to be reconciled to true brotherly love? Forgiveness or something like it must be the answer; but what is public forgiveness?

For God to forgive means for him to create in such a way that the created product has a harmony that includes both ideal standards and the failure to fulfill them. That is, for God to forgive is for him to create something actually reconciled to its finitude.

With regard to the forgiveness of public life, for true brotherhood to be possible there must be some created elements that actually reconcile men to the finite limitations of public life and thereby reconcile them to their brothers. These created elements must add up to a public *spirit* that does at least three things: (*a*) it commits the members of the public group to the humanity of each other, (*b*) it commits the members to accept the limitations of public life that might result in their failure and public rejection, and (*c*) it provides public happiness for public creatures. It is always dangerous to use the word "spirit" today, but there seems to be no other term that indicates the kind of pervading element that structures a group in the ways mentioned and that does not at the same time compromise the other structural elements a group has that stem from its aims, its particular membership, the conditions in which it functions, and so forth. The meaning of spirit will become clearer as we discuss its three functions.

a) The first function of the public spirit is to commit the members of the group to the ideal nature of a group qua group—that the group so order the public lives of its members that they treat each other as true human beings. What is of interest here is how the spirit binds a person to a commitment to the ideal, for this is the very ideal that is given up in the state of estrangement. What must be done is to convince the person that his true nature commits him to the ideal. It must become plain that not to take this as the ideal of public life is to pervert one's own nature as a person with a public life to lead. The spirit must articulate in a persuasive way the nature of true public life.

b) The second function of the spirit is to commit the members of the group to acceptance of the limitations and frustrations of public life, limitations that may make them fail the public ideal in many ways. Whereas the first function of the spirit is to commit man to the public ideal, the second function is to commit man to an acceptance of his own inadequacy to the ideal. Whereas the first function of the public spirit is to give man the virtue of duty, the second function is to give him the virtue of humility regarding his own failure. The combination of the two virtues is the willingness to sacrifice.

c) The third function of the public spirit is to give man actual public happiness and to do so in the face of the binding ideals and the inevitable failure. The difficulty in this function of spirit comes with the recognition that to make someone happy is to run the risk of being sacrificed. As lovers know full well, the kind of treatment often needed to call forth crucial human responses is a kind that opens the very being of the lover to the will of the beloved, with the possibility that the lover may be rejected or destroyed. The irony is that one of the things needed to be truly human is to will the happiness of another person. This is what the lover does when he tries to evoke humanity from the beloved. And the means he often uses is to offer his own happiness to the beloved to be willed or destroyed. All dimensions of public life involve this kind of willingness to be sacrificed to some degree or other.

How can public life, when it requires this threat of sacrifice, be made happy as such? The answer must be that man can be made happy in this regard only by being made to see God's glory in public life. If true public life is actual with its obligations and failures, then it is created. Its real harmony is the created artifact of God. The harmonies of creation are the presence of God's glory. Even a public life miserable with the pain of sacrifice may be seen as manifesting the presence of the creative glory of God. This is not to say that man *must* see the presence of the glory of God, for often he does not. If he does see it, it is God who creates him as seeing it, perhaps providentially. If he does not see it, however, a man does not consciously participate in true public life. True public life must involve the reconciliation of man to his finite nature, and this reconciliation is not accomplished without the happiness that is God's glory.

As with inner religious harmony, the reconciliation involved in public religious harmony is reflexive. The harmony reconciling the ideal and man's finite nature is a happiness in that very harmony. Happiness in the harmony constitutes the very harmony man is happy in. It is God's creative (or providential) action that combines harmony and happiness. True public life depends on God's creative action. The forgiveness required in public life is of a piece with the creation of that life.

3. *The proclamation of true public life.* Having discussed what is *required* of the spirit that makes true public life possible, we must still inquire whether true public life is *possible.* It could be that there is no such spirit. As with inner religious harmony, public religious harmony is possible only if it is actual. Whether it is actual is an empirical matter for which we must turn to religion.

Religions seem at first glance to differ considerably in their proclamations about public life. Oriental religions, especially Buddhism, are supposed to regard it as quite unimportant, whereas Western religions are supposed to see it as perhaps more important than anything else. First glances are often deceptive, however, and we should suspect this contrast very quickly, knowing as we do that the most outstanding examples of public sacrifice and blessedness in our day are in Gandhi's community in India. Furthermore, although it might be official belief that finite life, especially in its public dimensions, is unimportant, public life cannot be avoided and therefore all religions articulate some version of its connection with the divine. There is striking unanimity in the belief that there is such a spirit as we have described, and there are striking parallels between the ways that different religions believe the spirit was established.

Most religions agree that the coming to be of the spirit making possible true public life was an act of providence, not just an ordinary element of the creation. They agree that in historical events some divine agency established the spirit or showed men what it was. Buddha established a way of duty, sacrifice, and fulfillment in public life that was institutionalized to the point of monastic orders. Western religions of today all recognize the Old Testament version of the initiation of a public covenant between man and God.

Most religions also agree that the spirit takes its rise from a person, divine or human, but in either case one who is what he is in virtue of divine providence. Buddha, Abraham, Moses, Jesus, Mohammed, all are men whose public lives have a spirit that is incorporated as the binding public spirit of the community. We have already noted the evangelical power of persons as examples of lives to be publicly celebrated and emulated. The aesthetic character of a personal embodiment of the public spirit is very powerful, for it is a concrete way of showing the glory of God. The glory of God, say religions, was evident in these men's lives, and can be present in the lives of those who imitate the founder's spirit. The religions, of course, claim that these men were not "mere" illustrations of a universal spirit but rather were founders of a community that makes the spirit real by carrying it on. We shall return to this in the next chapter.

Listing general agreements does not prove as much as we might like. The best it can do is to lend a broad plausibility to the claim that what we have said about the proclamation of the public spirit is the sort of thing that religions are aiming at. The danger in such lists of general agreements is that they obscure many important differences, differences that the religions might claim are more important than the agreements. Surely it is unfair to say that the Christian's claims about Jesus are on a par with the Muslim's claims about Mohammed, the Jew's claims about Abraham, or the Buddhist's claims about Buddha.

Furthermore, these religions with their mutually exclusive claims cannot all be true. The specific character of the public spirit, if we assume that at least one religion is true, will be much more particular than our general considerations of the functions of that spirit have indicated. But it must be remembered that our concern here is not so much to establish the truth of any one religion but rather to exhibit the plausibility of the metaphysical theory developed in Part One to interpret religion.

13

The Unity of the Religious Life

Since men are individuals, their religious lives must have some kind of unity or coherence. But it is apparent from the experience of religious men that this unity is not a simple thing. Not only do there seem to be many ways of truly religious life, but each individual has many religious concerns that compete with each other for his attention, time, and energy. An experiential approach to the religious life seems to turn up more diversity than unity.

One fundamental diversity in the religious life is the distinction between the inner and the public religious life. It is true that this diversity is not always a competitive one. The distinction is often merely relative and made according to the interests of specific contexts. But a fundamental competition does lie at the root of the distinction. Just as there are public factors that no amount of inner-directed activity can alter, so there are inner and private factors that are impervious to the modifications of public life. Often the demands of both sides are incompatible, at least in their claims on man's being and time. Religious people, especially, tend to be specialists in one side or the other.

The distinction between private and public life is an ambiguous one, as we have duly noted. Sometimes it seems to be a distinction between domains of life or classes of activities. The previous two chapters have had their topics structured with this kind of distinction in mind. In other ways, it is more a direction-oriented distinction, contrasting what lies at the heart of man with what lies outside the heart, that is, the medium through which the heart expresses itself. The discussions of inner faith and certainty and public reconciliation and brotherhood emphasized the latter kind of distinction.

The question of what the total religious harmony for a person is requires that we explore the ambiguity. We have spoken loosely of the inner religious harmony, on the one hand, and the public religious harmony, on the other. There is a sense in which this is proper; but there is also a sense in which it is wrong. The sense in which inner and public religious harmonies are properly *distinguished* is the sense in which the public religious harmony is a harmony of many men collectively and the private religious harmony is the harmony of each individual. The sense in which it is better to speak of *one* religious harmony is the sense in which we note that *each* person must harmonize *his* participation in *both* private and public life. In this latter case, the public harmony that gets harmonized with the inner life is incomplete, since it leaves out the other people; and this is the very problem, that a single individual is only a part of the total public life. For the kind of being that a person is, it seems necessary that the essential harmony of inner and public life must come from the side of the heart, from the faculty of conscious and responsible determination. In this sense, the second kind of distinction is perhaps most important. The religious harmony of the person as a whole, including his inner life and his participation in public life, is a harmony of the humanity a self makes of itself in dealing with the world. To harmonize a life according to the intentions of the heart requires paying attention to a class of highly private and inner problems and to a class of quite public ones. The real problem is that there are two religious harmonies with which a person is concerned: his individual harmony, which includes his inner life and his participation in public life, and the public harmony that includes more people than one but to which his public life makes a contribution.

The upshot of this ambiguity is that a person, trying to harmonize his private with his public life, is often forced to compromise the adequacy of his attention to both sides. This is but another aspect of human finitude, and the failures of neglect to which men are put by this condition are among the failures of which they need forgiveness. As with our considerations of inner and public life, in general the answer to the problem is that to reconcile our own individual human harmony (inclusive of private life and of our participation in public life) with the larger harmony of the public life (which surpasses our own life and whose standards bind us) is something beyond finite power but within God's power. The task of the present chapter is to discuss some aspects of religion that illustrate this thesis.

SECTION A

Discipleship

One of the most commonly recognized forms of religious life is that of the disciple or follower. Religious discipleship means that men pattern themselves after some leader or founder of religion. The last chapter broke off with a discussion of the public spirit as an imitation of the spirit of some religious founder who reconciles public life. The notion of discipleship picks up the thread, adding to public imitation the strand of inner imitation, for discipleship has to do with the imitation not only of a person's public spirit but of his whole religious structure of life as a person. Specifically, discipleship involves the imitation of the master's way of working out the harmony of his private and public religious lives; this harmony is the one closest to the master's truly human nature, and therefore discipleship is the learning through imitation of the way of being truly human.

Discipleship is a peculiar way of life. There are many ways of living that do not involve being a disciple. In fact there are many ways of being religious that do not involve discipleship. But most religions maintain that discipleship is a high level of the religious life and devoutly to be sought. Even Judaism has not lacked for prophetic leaders who attracted and held disciples. In the Rabbinic traditions, the relation of master and disciple has been, if anything, even more marked than in parallel Christian and Islamic traditions.

What is the proper structure of discipleship? As the word indicates, it is a disciplining or ordering of one's life along certain lines. But the word "discipline" has some connotations that do not strictly belong to discipleship. Discipline often means obedience to a set of rules or habits of life that are set over against natural inclinations and ends of people. So, in monastic life, discipline may mean obedience to rules regulating the routine of life and the means that are permissible for attaining things. Discipline is sometimes taken as a set of rules to which one must submit himself to show good will regarding religious authority. This meaning, however, is the very opposite of that involved in discipleship.

To be a disciple is to be a follower of a person. Hence, the discipline involved is an obedience to a way of life. The notion of a way of life is very complex, especially since we mean by it here "a way of religious life." No Christian disciple of Jesus, for instance, would think that he had to be a carpenter because Jesus was one or that he had to dress like or speak the language of a first-century Jew. Most Christians do not even think that Saturday is the Sabbath, although Jesus' way of life regarded it as such. These instances are not what Christians consider to be essentially religious ways of life, although they think that vocation, deportment, language, and liturgy must all be taken into account by the religious life. What is essential is the way in which all these elements of life are harmonized and balanced to make a truly human being. In the case of Jesus, what would count as his religious way of life would be attributes like humility of self-assessment, love of all God's creation, willingness to sacrifice personal advantage to the point of death for the good of God's will, satisfaction that God would turn his bleakest prospects to divine glory, and so forth. To be a disciple in this sense, then would mean to make attributes like these the characteristics of one's own life.

These are personal characteristics, not disciplinary rules. The importance of the distinction is that in the transference from the master to the disciple the characteristics are likely to undergo radical transformations. What might have been a humble gesture on Jesus' part, for instance, for a person of today might be much closer to almsgiving heralded by trumpets. The distinction between times and contexts makes the transference of personal characteristics problematic. It is not at all a case of casuistry—that is, a matter of applying rules of life. It is rather a matter of making concrete the essence of personal characteristics in a context where the conditional features are different from the original. Obedience to such personal characteristics is likely to lead the disciple into situations and commitments far removed from anything that was experienced by the master. In fact, since persons and their characteristics are transformed by moving from context to context, the disciple's behavior on different occasions may seem contradictory when considered from the standpoint of abstract characteristics interpreted as rules for action.

Discipleship has another dimension beyond that of imitation of the master's personal religious characteristics. A disciple is a student of a teacher. A disciple must learn and interpret for himself what the teacher has to say. In Buddhism, for instance, this is the most prominent aspect of discipleship. Since man is such an intellectual creature and since his intellect is so important for his will in guiding his actions through multifarious contexts, imitation of personal characteristics is not enough. Imitation must be coupled with understanding of the nature, relevance, and worth of those characteristics. The whole situation of human life must be interpreted with reference to the problems of attaining religious harmony. The teacher can do this in several ways, but one of the crucial things to be taught must be the belief that is essential for working out a religiously harmonious life—that the creator is present as reconciler. As Hosea put it, the glorious God of Abraham, Isaac, and Jacob behaves like the forgiving husband of an unfaithful wife, continually bringing her home again and restoring her love. The religious tradition, of course, must elaborate and interpret this teaching. But when the religious way of life is essentially that of discipleship, the teaching is contained in paradigmatic form in the personal teachings of the founder.

Obedience to teaching is different from obedience to personal characteristics. Since teaching is a matter of persuasion of truth to be apprehended by the intellect, the intellectual integrity of the disciples must be respected. Whereas a disciple can imitate the master's personal characteristics straightforwardly, he cannot imitate his beliefs and teachings without honest conviction, unless he is to sacrifice the integrity of his human nature, which would be contradictory to the whole purpose of the religious life. It is for this reason that the classic descriptions of the relation between disciple and teacher include far more wrangling and movement from confusion to groping understanding than the "Yes, Socrates; no, Socrates" dialogue we might expect. To be a disciple, or student, involves obedience to the discipline of following out the beliefs of the master with intellectual sincerity. Discipleship in this regard commits one to thoroughness. In the second instance such devotion from the student should lead to agreement and understanding; discipleship cannot nor should not endure if the disciple comes, after long and careful thought, to believe that the teacher is wrong in essentials.

There is yet a third dimension to discipleship beyond those of obedience to personal characteristics of life and sincerity of learning. In simple terms, a disciple is one who carries on the life's work of the master. This may mean either a personal extension of his activities while he is present or a more complete taking over of responsibilities if the master is dead. Being a disciple with regard to the master's mission is a complex thing. It is easy to see how it can be interpreted with regard to the mission in public life. Buddhist monks and the Christian apostles are well known for their public acceptance of their masters' mission. The public mission, we must remember, is that of reconciliation and the establishment of brotherhood in public life. Disciples carry on this work in many ways. Often it is through an organized institution like a church, but not always.

It is harder to see how a disciple carries on the work of the master with regard to the inner life. But if we remember that the aim of the inner life, as well as that of the public life, is to glorify God through the beauties of religious harmonies, then even the inner life can be seen as an arena for the master's mission to be carried on and repeated. Part of the master's public work is to evoke and lay public conditions for the harmony of the inner religious life. The public religious harmony is attained if the structures of the group foster the attainment of individual religious harmony. But each disciple, with regard to his own inner life, seeks to attain religious harmony because that is a fulfillment of the master's work. He extends the master into himself.

One final consideration should be added to this discussion regarding the special significance Christianity sees in discipleship. True discipleship is the way of life that makes men truly human. Therefore, according to Christians, the true master of whom men should be disciples is the actual presence of God creating men to be truly human; to be sure, God is also present in the disciples themselves making them disciples. But the latter is the Holy Spirit; the former, Jesus, is the Son of God, from eternity with all creation, but prior to at least part of creation in the sense that the master is prior to the disciples, creating them as true human beings through being their Lord. For Christians, because Jesus Christ is master, he is creator and redeemer at once.

SECTION B
Public and Private Religion

We are now in a position to restate the problem of the unity of the religious life. There are two unities or religious harmonies that must be distinguished. On the one hand, there is the public religious harmony, which includes all men in the public world who can be harmonized publicly. Many problems of the public religious harmony are not strictly problems of the religious life. Rather, they are political problems. The public problems of the religious life have to do with the individual's participation in the pursuit of the public religious harmony. The second harmony is that of an individual's religious life, a harmony that includes both his private religious problems and his participation in the public religious life. Our concern in the last two chapters has been with the religious life, and the public religious harmony entered our consideration only at the point where it was necessary to indicate the nature of an individual's participation in the public religious domain. In seeking the

unity of the religious life, we are therefore inquiring after the second kind
of unity.

The problem of the harmony of the religious life, however, arises precisely
because the aims of participation in the public religious life transcend the
aims of the individual's harmony. There are times when the demands of the
public domain are such that thoughts of self and even the self's individual
religious harmony should be forgotten. And there are times when the very
possibility of public religious participation requires forgetting the public life
and withdrawing more to the inner self. The unity of the religious life must
harmonize both sets of moments.

In one sense, we must admit that any actual resolution of the problem of
religion in the inner life and in the public life is a harmony. For a life to be
at all, it must be a harmony of sorts, for it is a togetherness of many elements
and is actual. Furthermore, whatever harmony there is, is a glory of God,
since to be is to be harmonious and to glorify God. No matter how much a
person might distort the religious harmony into a merely private thing, or as
is more likely, into a merely public thing, whatever he is, is a harmony and
glorifies God. Lacking religious harmony altogether, a person would still be
something, not truly human, of course, but something. The point is, however,
that just any old harmony will not do. A person should have a harmony that
makes him truly human; any harmony less than this is less than his created
nature. A determination of being has a nature to maintain, and to do this is
its religious problem. Therefore, the harmony of an individual man's religious life has to be a human harmony, and this harmony cannot leave out
attention to either public or private religious life.

How can we determine what a truly human harmony is and conform the
demands of our life's circumstances to it? This is the ultimately practical
question of religion. In one sense, it is really two questions, and there are two
answers to it. One of the questions is, What is the nature of a truly human
harmony? The second question is the more practical one: How does a man
cope with the particular circumstances of his life in such a way as to embody
the harmony?

The answer to the first question, according to religions, is that the nature of
truly human reality is revealed through its beauty as a harmony and that this
harmony is such that persons recognize it as their true essential nature. But
the harmony that is truly human can be revealed fully only in a human being.
A code of laws may help, but ultimately it cannot mark out personal
harmony. The personal revelation of true human reality is the master of
whom religious people should be disciples. Discipleship is the most complete
way people have of determining true human nature.

Given the true master to follow, how can a person cope with the circumstances of his life to unite them into a true religious harmony? This is our
second question. The answer here is more difficult precisely because no rule
or specific direction can be given. Rather the religious life requires something

like a rhythmic alternation between concern for the inner life and concern for the public life. Often these concerns can be blended, of course, and compromised quite nicely. But in critical times exclusive choices must often be made. Furthermore, disequilibrium with regard to public and private concerns is the kind of thing that creeps up on a person without warning. Is not the man tragic who, in his constant devotion to the public affairs of religion, finds that he has lost his soul and become an indispensable bureau? The answer is that he is just as tragic as the man who, in his constant devotion to things of the inner spirit, finds his conviction impotent and his public self useless. The man of religious wisdom is the one who knows when it is time for public religious service and when it is time to retreat to the mountains to study and pray.

The rhythm of public and private life is not a regular one. Public and private circumstances are never regular. Sometimes the demands of one are far more pressing than demands of the other, and often one side makes demands out of turn. Furthermore, a regular rhythm would be an inhuman thing. The elements that must be harmonized in a truly human harmony are constantly growing and developing. Regularity is death to any growing thing when it limits responses to the regular ones; there would be no freedom for creativity. The rhythm of life must be irregular.[1]

It is necessary to note concerning the problem of how to adjust the rhythm of participation in public religious life and concern for the inner religious problems that judgments regulating the rhythm are at root aesthetic ones. They involve the art of normative measure that Plato described in the *Statesman*. Just as an aesthetic judgment is required to recognize harmony, a practical aesthetic judgment is required to organize it. This, of course, is what we would expect. It is because the problem is at root aesthetic that no strict rules of procedure can be given. Nor can a harmony be imitated without aesthetic judgment, for the transference from one life to another requires that a judgment be made that what is harmonious in one is embodied in different form but equally harmoniously in the other.

These two questions, the nature of human harmony and how to cope with

---

[1] The notion of irregular rhythm is one of the most important neglected philosophical topics. It is of a piece with another topic crucial for the answer to the problem of how to harmonize public and private life, namely, how to harmonize a dynamic process, a growing thing that changes. This is especially a problem for understanding responsible human life, for responsibility requires accounting for a harmonious identity that includes past, present, and future and that involves at the same time a completeness of the present moment. The greatest difficulty with Whitehead's Platonism is that he construes patterns and harmonies as applying only to simultaneous realities in actual occasions. But there is more identity in the harmony of a changing process than that of nexus of partial repetitions of patterns. Both of these topics have broader relevance for cosmology and philosophical anthropology than just the concerns of philosophy of religion and must be postponed for more comprehensive metaphysical treatment. It is likely that the next great development in metaphysics will focus on these two topics. As Plato saw, time is the *moving* image of eternity, not a static image, as Whitehead thought.

life in accord with it, are not really so distinct as they may appear. Disciples, for example, come to understand the essential elements in the master's harmony only as they attempt to live a life of discipleship. It is not a matter of first getting an ideal and then finding out how to embody it in oneself. Rather, the ideal is discovered only through attempted emulation. In fact, it is the embodied ideal in the master that creates the truly human harmony of the disciples by making disciples of them. Whitehead expressed this general point with great historical insight. In *Adventures in Ideas,* he lauds Plato for seeing the crucial role that ideals play in the process of history, allowing for the possibility of improvement and rationally controlled progress. But he also lauds the Alexandrian Christians for seeing a crucial metaphysical point that Plato missed, namely, that the divinity of the ideals not only transcends the actual world but is also present in it. Whereas Plato thought that the world was a mere image or imitation of the ideal, the Alexandrian theologians saw that God was actually embodying the ideals in the world and using the embodiments to create the world. Thus God is actually present in the world, not just mirrored by it. The master is divinity creating disciples as truly human beings.

Like all other harmonies, the harmony of a truly human person comes by the creative grace of God. Insofar as man directs its working out, he does so in discipleship to an embodiment of divine human creativity. In adjusting the rhythm of his participation in public and private religious concerns, man's faculty of aesthetic judgment, like all his faculties, is fallible; no one is perfectly human. Yet it is the proclamation of religion that the religious harmony is restored by God's creative forgiveness and that man's bliss and blessedness consist in enjoyment of the fact that God makes man whole.

SECTION C
Religion and the Other Things in Life

Experience forces us to acknowledge at many points that religion is not the whole of life. Or perhaps it is better to say that, although religion is concerned with the wholeness of life, the specific contents have to do with things quite different from religion. We have noted several facets of man, like intellect, emotion, and artistic interests, that are different from religion, and these are only representative of countless more. Wherever there is good to do man should at least try to do it. There are many things besides religion that are of responsible concern to man.

Given the great volume of demands from many sides on a person's limited time, energy, and substance, it is inevitable that the world's many goods, the person's many responsibilities, will conflict and be in competition for his attention. We have spoken in this chapter about the difficulties of harmonizing the demands and responsibilities of the private with the public *religious* life, and these difficulties are great enough. But religious concerns are only one kind of a whole pantheon of claims on a person's attention. There are

Alfred North Whitehead

many aspects of life that have competing private and public sides. And the conflict between private and public is only one of many kinds of conflict to which man's attention is subjected.

Experience also indicates that there are many different kinds of lives to lead. Each kind must face more or less the same responsibilities as the others, but its structure and biases, its aptitudes and faculties, require it to work out a distinctive kind of resolution to the problem. Plato's elaboration of this problem in the *Republic,* with his discussion of the simplified model of three faculties of soul and hence three possible dominant types of personality, is the *locus classicus* for this point. We appreciate fully today the near infinite complexity of the factors that must be weighed and given place in the deliberations about how to live.

Despite the conflicting claims, it is clear that religion claims to be man's ultimate concern and ultimate responsibility. The ultimacy here may well have the connotation of generality, since religion deals with the problem of how man can be truly human, as he was created to be, and this is a more general problem than how to make a living or how to keep a certain friend. General problems, however, are often the most practical, since their ramifications are most pervasive and far reaching. Yet many other aspects of life claim ultimacy, too. Artists, politicians, friends, doctors, and many others argue that their concerns are ultimate and that religion is of only secondary importance. How are we going to adjudicate these claims?

We must first note that, although this is a good philosophical problem, it is not, strictly speaking, a practical problem for religion. Religion's problem is to see to it that the harmony of a person's life is a truly human one, and it must concern itself with harmonizing the private and public approaches to *this* problem. But there are many possible human ways of life, and the deliberations about things like friends and vocations may operate within truly human alternatives. These deliberations are philosophical and not religious, unless, of course, the boundary between a human and subhuman is crossed.

The problem of adjudicating conflicting ends cannot be solved by the view that there is really but one inclusive end of which the specific ends are specializations. If there were but one comprehensive end, then all the specializations of it would have to be commensurable, which seems contrary to experience. The very problem is that the ends are incommensurable.

Nor can it be said that, since the possibilities at any one time do not allow for the compatible realization of distinct goods, there is therefore no responsibility to more than can be realized compatibly. Whatever it is that makes an end good or ideal, it cannot be simply the fact that it is a possibility; therefore it cannot be said that when the compatible realization of several goods is impossible each of them ceases to be good and to make individual claims on man's responsibility. Rather, if they are incompatible, at least some of them will have to be failed and lost. This is part of the finitude and inevitable failure of finite human existence. The view that "ought implies can" is true only insofar as it makes reference to each good individually.

There is no reason to believe that ought implies can with reference to the goods collectively, especially when they may not even be commensurable. Surely the saying cannot be inverted to mean, "if one cannot, then one ought not." These points, of course, require elaboration far beyond the scope of the present work. But they are sufficient to indicate the difficulties with some of the standard attempts to resolve the problem of conflicting responsibilities.

Although it is difficult to maintain the view that there is some comprehensive goal in virtue of which every special end derives its value, it is possible and perhaps even necessary to maintain that there is some transcendental character to all values. Our discussions so far have led us to believe that this character is something like harmony. The point has been developed well by Whitehead in various places.[2] But even if this position can be maintained with an adequate metaphysical defense, it would not resolve our present problem. Though harmony per se might be the abstract character of value, still all harmonies are particular determinate ones, since they must have determinations to harmonize. And there is no a priori way of discovering whether one kind of harmony is more a harmony than another kind; harmonies might still be incommensurable. Besides, until developed much further, the notion of harmony is so abstract as to be of little practical value.

The problem of harmonizing the many conflicting responsibilities of life, like that of harmonizing the religious life, comes down to the development of an aesthetic sensitivity for what is relatively important, as well as the development of a faculty for reconciling oneself to the inevitable failure and loss that finite life entails. We are in a position to give no better answer than that, for a better answer would require that the harmony of life as a whole be based on some determinate principle, which, as we have seen, is contrary to the nature of harmony.

We can, however, point out that although many things might lay claim to ultimacy—art to artistic ultimacy, friendship to the ultimacy of eros, and so on—when religion claims religious ultimacy, this is something special to conjure with. Other domains may be special, too, but their speciality is something different from religion's specialty. Religion's problem is not on a par with the problems of other aspects of life because it involves the crucial relation to the creator. Its problem has to do with the essential identity of man, where "essential identity" means what the thing was created to be. The attainment of essential identity, when the person is as God creates him to be, is the union of the person's happiness and God's glory.

Although religion's problem is man's ultimate concern both in the sense of what is closest to his heart's happiness and in the sense of what has most far-reaching significance for what man is, its practical matters still cannot lay claim to complete dominance over other practical matters. Religion's concerns are demanding enough to take all of one's time and energy; but life has

[2] See, for example, *Adventures in Ideas* (Cambridge: Cambridge University Press, 1933), Chap. XVIII.

more than religion in it. Religion considered by itself is abstract and empty and would provide no inner substance or public enjoyments for man to harmonize. Religion is a rich thing only when life is filled with many other things; then religion has a rich content to harmonize. The shallowness of merely religious people is a well-attested fact. The upshot of this is that although religion might be the most important thing in life, compared with the bulk of matters that claim our attention, religion's share is fairly small. Paying attention to religion is something that must be worked into the harmony of life in a rhythmical way, just as each other abiding concern must be.

To the question, What is the relation between religion and the rest of life? we must say two things. First, we must acknowledge that, given all the human concerns man can have, religion transcends them all in that it is concerned with what makes a man truly human; religion is essential for the proper context of all other concerns. In this sense, religion and nothing else is the ultimate concern of life. But second, we must acknowledge that, since religion has its facets that require explicit care, it is also one of man's many concerns. Furthermore, since religion deals with all the other concerns as the content of life, it cannot displace them from their share of rightful attention without making itself vain and empty. Therefore, religious concerns must be worked into a finite and limited position in the fabric of life, often giving place to the ultimately less important.

SECTION D
Freedom, Love, and Glory

The limitation we found in religion has a positive side. It has often been noted that genuinely religious people seem to enjoy the good things of life as much as, if not more than, people who disregard religion entirely. Furthermore, religious people seem to engage in good works far less from a sense of duty than non-religious people; yet they seem often to enjoy it more. How is this to be accounted for?

Although the phenomenon occurs in most religions, the Christians have a name for it: freedom from the law. This was St. Paul's phrase to describe the state a Christian is in when he accepts salvation as God's free gift in Christ and no longer is bound to work out his salvation in terms of the old legal covenant. As we expressed it above, man is justified by God and not by his own efforts in terms of the moral law.[3] A truly religious man is free from the law in the sense that he is free from having to justify himself by making himself perfect in terms of the ideals relevant to his nature.

We are now in a position to express this in a more general way. The problem of justification is the person's problem of participating well in his essential nature. But his essential nature includes many conditional features

[3] Chap. 12, sec. A.

that relate him contingently to a host of other things. These other things have values that oblige him as norms. Finite existence is so rich and the contingent mass of other things demands so much more of a person than his essential nature can fulfill that he inevitably fails. Human beings, in the face of this failure, are tempted to forget and pervert their essential human natures and pridefully to attribute to themselves essential natures not so finitely bounded. In fact they attribute to themselves a nature that can fulfill the demands of all their infinite variety of obligations; but such a nature would need no less power than the creative power of God that made the harmonious world in the first place. The result of this desperate attempt to participate in a nature that is for all practical purposes omnipotent is the loss of the concrete happiness appropriate to human nature. The misjudgment of man's essential nature is sin, and its correction is justification. The prideful arrogation to oneself of a divine nature competent to meet all obligations is bondage to the law. Only God can free man from this bondage and truly justify him. God can persuade man to accept his true essential nature by persuading him to accept the forgiveness of the failures of that nature. As we have seen, these two persuasions come down to the same thing, for man is persuaded to accept his essential nature when he sees the glory of God embodied there, and it is embodied there when man accepts the forgiveness and the glory.

Accepting and therefore being his essential nature, man is "free from the law." This does not mean that man's obligations in any way cease to be obligatory. It is still man's essential nature to have conditional features that bind him to other beings in an obligatory way. To think that divine justification means that obligation ceases is to make the mistake of antinomianism. Rather, man is simply freed from treating his obligations as the means to his own justification. A truly religious man, that is, a truly human one, does good things not out of a sense of duty to himself but simply out of regard for the good that is to be done. And he enjoys the good that gets done. Furthermore, the religious man is not constrained to concentrate his enjoyment on those things that he does but is free to enjoy all the good things of life around him. This is our account of the phenomenon of the happy religious man.

But there is more to the religious life than just this kind of happiness. It is a commonplace to say that the heart of religion is love. Despite the humanistic sentimentality with which this commonplace has been interpreted, there is a fundamental truth in it. Our metaphysical considerations allow us to give a general definition of love as acting so as to enhance the intrinsic value of the things affected by the action. The intrinsic value of a thing, however, is its peculiar harmony as the determination of being it is created to be. To enhance a thing's intrinsic value, then, is to enhance its being, that is, to make it better what it essentially is. This means that to love a thing is to help create it.

A distinction must be drawn, however, between this sense of creating and the sense in which God creates. God creates from eternity, giving all things their being. But the being of many of the things he creates is determinately related to other determinations of being as the result of those others through the regularities of nature. The sense in which a human lover creates, then, is the sense in which he is one of the determinations necessary for the coming to be of the other created things. God creates through him, as it were. To the extent that love depends on man's free will, he is responsible for setting into motion the regularities of nature that bring about the other created things.

We must ask why a man loves. Love has always been an ambiguous notion because people have recognized two sides of it. On the one hand, love has been recognized as an active thing motivated primarily from within the lover and directed to bring about value in the beloved, even when the beloved is not very lovely. Religion has often remarked on the fact that true love does not require that its object be "worthy" of love, for many of the people who should be loved are quite unlovely indeed. This view is often opposed to Plato's view of love, which says that love is evoked by the beauty or worthiness of the object. Plato's view has a ready answer to the question why we love: we respond directly to the loveliness of the beloved. Plato, however, was careful to point out that what we love in a beloved thing is not what it actually happens to be but rather what its actual being reminds us of—its ideal nature. This qualification should not be forgotten.

To give a metaphysical account of the unity of these two views of love, it is necessary to recognize that the object and motivation of both is a beauty of God's creation. Anything that is, has some harmony or other, and at the root of all harmony is a beauty to be appreciated. Love is a response to the attraction of this beauty. Plato was right in seeing that love needs such a stimulus. He was wrong in thinking that the stimulus had to be something that necessarily transcends the actual being of the thing; anything that is actual has its harmony. Yet, love that is a response merely to the attraction of beauty is just enjoyment; it does not necessarily call forth effort to enhance the value of the beloved. When love does involve effort, it is because the lover sees that the beloved, although possessing the harmony of being, still does not have the harmony of his ideal nature. Plato was right in seeing that people and societies may participate only poorly in their ideal natures. Active love is a response to the beloved's potential participation in his true and ideal harmony. True love of a person is love of him both as he actually is and as he ideally should be. It is a gross reversal to say that we should love every man regardless of what he is just because of the humanity that is in him and that we should love those we especially admire because of what they actually are. This is the mistake of the legendary socialist who loved humanity but hated people. Rather, we should love all men individually because of the harmony in them as they actually are and should love those we especially admire because of their approximation to true humanity as well as because of the harmony in them as they actually are. There is no greater insult, in fact, than to tell the world's unlovelies that we love them because at least they are human. Rather, we love them because at least they have the harmonious beauty of being God's creatures, however perverted they are from true humanity.

Love involves enjoyment, however much work is required to bring about the appropriateness of the enjoyment. The beauty in all the created harmonies manifests the presence of God as creator. This manifested presence of the creator is God's glory, a very rich thing. We apprehend it first in the beauties of the created world, but full appreciation carries us to the mystery of God in his transcendence. Our appreciation begins in delight at the beauty of God's glory and ends in wonder and awe at its depth.

Epilogue

The three parts of our study are strikingly different in style, aim, and subject matter. They might even give the appearance of independent works. But they are not independent. We have argued throughout that the problem of the transcendence and presence of God must be approached from three sides. We have given a speculative theory of God's transcendence and presence, concentrating mainly on transcendence. We have defended the epistemological claims involved in the speculation and have discussed how speculation is related to experience. And we have related our speculation to a large domain of experience, religion; this relation serves both to show the fruitfulness of the speculative theory and to indicate its experiential plausibility. Separately, each part would be abstract. Even with all three parts together, each one is still programmatic and could be expanded indefinitely. Such is the indefinite richness of the worth of reflection.

The parts could have been ordered differently, although not without affecting their internal makeup. We could have taken the experience of religion as the starting point that raises problems for speculative philosophy to answer. In this case, we could have proceeded to show that speculative knowledge is the kind needed to answer religion's questions. The speculative theory would then have been presented as the conclusion. But what this approach would have gained in experiential immediacy it would have lost in philosophical generality and forthrightness.

The separation of the parts, however, and their dependence on each other emphasize an ambiguity that has made itself felt throughout the entire study. On the one hand, we feel that our thought essentially should be of one piece, with no sharp distinction of one domain from another. On the other hand, it is the case that one domain of thought must be used as a test or critic of another and that for this purpose we must maintain the integrity of one side over against the other. This is not a mere academic ambiguity but rather one built into the present intellectual situation. Abstract divisions in thought of all kinds are properly recognized to be signs of artificiality. But we have no way, aside from such divisions, to take up the necessary critical stance. If a way were known to return to the medieval unity of thought that we lauded at the end of Part Two, we should have done so. The situation where philosophy stands opposed to other domains like religion will persist until the fabric of thought is rewoven.

APPENDIX

Real and Conceptual Distinctions

The notions of real and conceptual distinctions can be given greater technical clarification than is appropriate for the running argument of the main text. The distinctions have a peculiar usage in the context of the speculative view defended in Part One.

I call a distinction real when it is between two determinations of being that are determinate with respect to each other and whose harmonies are on the same ontological level. By being on the same ontological level I mean the state of affairs where each determination has essential features over against the other and each has conditional features in virtue of the presence of the other. The harmonies on the same level are those each makes of its essential and conditional features.

It is evident from this formulation that a real distinction is not one that holds between things that are merely separate. In fact, things completely separate from each other cannot be really distinct, for they would not have enough in common to be determinate with respect to each other. Rather, if things are really distinct, then the being of each depends upon the being of the other. The force of this characterization of real distinctions can be indicated in preliminary fashion by two contrasts.

First, a real distinction does not hold between two things that lack conditional features in virtue of each other, since in that case they would not be determinate with regard to each other. It is impossible for us to give instances of such a state of affairs because the very comparison in mind would articulate some mutual involvement and hence mutual determination.

Second, a real distinction does not hold between two things one of which is a proper part of the other, that is, one of the other's essential or conditional features. If it did hold, although each would have essential and conditional features, and although the conditional features of each might be in virtue of the other, the essential features of the constituent determination would not be over against the containing determination. Rather, the essential features of the constituent determination would themselves be constituents of the containing determination, either of its essential or conditional features. The distinction between constituent and whole is not a real one but, as we shall argue below, a conceptual one. The peculiarity of the conceptual distinction is that the harmony of the constituent determination is on a lower level than the harmony of the inclusive determination, not on the same level.

Interpersonal relations illustrate real distinctions quite well. We commonly acknowledge, in light of the work of psychoanalysts and existentialists, that persons develop an integrity and independence of their own over against each other only through long and personally significant involvement with each other. Only people highly determinate in a personal way with respect to each other have integrity over against each other and are really distinct. Without the mutual involvement, or with only impersonal involvement, they are not determinate with respect to each other on the level of their comprehensive harmonies as persons. Furthermore, a personal relationship that subordinates one person to another to an inhuman degree is one in which the subordinated person lacks significant essential features of his own over against the other. The significant personal features that should be essential to him are so much the effect of the other that he is like a long-range extension of the conditional features of the other. Although the subordinated person has essential features of his own as a physical object, on the personal level he is little more than a bunch of conditional features characteristic of the dominant person. Such an interpersonal relationship does not exhibit a real distinction. Of course, with people the complete absorption of one by the other, if not impossible, at least meets considerable dialectical opposition. Hegel has made clear the extent of such a dialectical opposition. Persons are really distinct only insofar as they are sufficiently involved on a personal level, that is, on the level of their comprehensive harmonies, to have essential features over against each other and conditional features in virtue of each other.

Real distinctions are also illustrated by physical objects. Physical objects are separated from each other by space or time or both, not to speak of causal relations, intermediaries, and differences. Consider contemporaneous spatial separation. The essential features of spatially separate things must be over against each other for the things to hold down different positions in space. And the conditional features are mutually determined, at least mediately, because they articulate different positions of the same space. If the space in which each thing exists is so "relative" to the thing that we cannot say that things determine different places of the same space, then by the same token we cannot say they are spatially separate.

Let me conclude this discussion of real distinctions with some remarks about things that must be really distinct for metaphysical reasons. In the first place, every determination of being must have certain constituents that are really distinct from each other despite the fact that they are harmonized together. Every determination must have at least one essential and at least one conditional feature in order to be determinate and *these must be really distinct from each other*. If they were not really distinct, the essential and conditional features would either be indeterminate with respect to each other or one would be reduced to a part of the other. They cannot be indeterminate because the conditional feature must grasp the external determination in a way determinately characteristic of the essential feature and the essential feature would not have a determinate character of its own unless really distinct from the conditional feature. If the essential feature were nothing but a constituent of the conditional feature, then the inclusive determination would have no essential feature over against the determinations with respect to which it is determinate. And if the conditional feature were nothing but a constituent of the essential feature, then the inclusive determination would be in no way different from its essential feature. Therefore, the constituent essential and conditional features of a determination must be really distinct from each other. A determination, of course, might have many essential and many conditional features; but to the extent that these are on the same level and not merely constituents of each other, they are all really distinct from each other, just in virtue of the fact that they are on the same level.

In the second place, if two determinations are really distinct from each other, since they must be mutually determinate with respect to each other they must be included in some more comprehensive harmony. That is, they cannot be together to be mutually determinate unless they are harmoniously together in some sense. There are many kinds of harmony, and some are more tightly bound than others. The real spatial distinction of a person's right hand from his left is included within the rather close harmony of the organic whole. The harmony of two different persons miles apart is much looser in a spatial sense than the unity of right and left hands, but in other senses the community may be harder to dissolve and far more concrete to the people.

The whole realm of determinations of being, insofar as they are determinate with respect to each other, is united in a series of levels of harmony and real distinctions. On each level, the determinations whose harmonies are complete on that level are really distinct. Consideration of the relations between levels of harmonies brings us to conceptual distinctions.

I call a distinction conceptual (of the first order) when it is between two determinations one of which is a constituent of the other and is really distinct from other constituents on the level harmonized by the inclusive determination. I call a distinction conceptual of the second order when it is between two determinations one of which is a constituent of a constituent of the other and is really distinct from other constituents on the level harmonized by the intermediary constituent. A third order conceptual distinction is between two determinations one of which is a constituent of a constituent of a constituent of the other, and so on.

It is evident from this formulation that there is a kind of asymmetry between conceptually distinct things, whereas there are symmetrical relations between really distinct things, for in a conceptual distinction the constituent term is a constituent of the inclusive term and not vice versa. The inclusive term includes the constituent term and not vice versa. Therefore, in speaking of a conceptual distinction we must always be able to specify which term is the constituent and which is the inclusive.

Let X be a determination with constituents M and N. For present purposes it is a matter of indifference which, M or N, is X's conditional feature. M and N are really distinct from each other and conceptually distinct from X. Suppose also that M is really distinct from A and that N is really distinct from B, and suppose that A and B are not constituents in any direct way of X. In this case both M and N would be determinations of being that are determinate on their own without regard to their inclusion in X. But without being included within the harmony of X, M and N would not be determinate with respect to each other or really distinct from each other unless they both were also included as constituents of some further inclusive determination Y. Since M is really distinct from A this must be because both M and A are constituents of some further determination W; and N and B are really distinct because they are constituents of a further determination Z.

Since X is one the same ontological level with W and Z, it is really distinct from them in the following way. Assuming only the connections mentioned so far, X is really distinct from W and Z degenerately. X is really distinct from W insofar as M functions as its conditional feature and N as its essential feature determining it with regard to W; and W has A as its essential feature and M as its conditional feature determining it with regard to X. But it is to be noted that M is conceptually distinct from both X and W, although in different determinate respects, that is, with respect to N and to A respectively. If we assume only the connections mentioned so far, X and W are not necessarily both constituents of some one further inclusive determination. Their real distinction is called degenerate because the harmony of X and W together is only the harmony of M, which unites M's essential and conditional features determining it in real distinctions with A and N. A parallel analysis could be made for the distinction between X and Z.

Since in a degenerate real distinction the same feature is the conditional one of both distinct things and is only conceptually distinct from each, a degenerate real distinction lies between a genuine real distinction and a conceptual distinction. It is not a genuine conceptual distinction because both terms are on the same level, not on the different levels of constituent and including terms. It is not a genuine real distinction because the harmony of the distinct terms is on a constituent rather than an inclusive level and does not allow each to grasp the other with conditional features reflecting the essential characters of each; they share a conditional feature, which is therefore neutral.

A degenerate conceptual distinction is one between two terms one of which is a constituent of a determination really distinct from the other term; but the constituent term is not a constituent of the inclusive term, only of something with respect to which the inclusive term is determinate. Just as there are conceptual distinctions of various degrees, there can be various degrees of degenerateness in conceptual distinctions. And as there are many levels of real distinctions, there can be many degrees of degenerateness in real distinctions. We have only begun to take account of the variations on real and conceptual distinctions.

According to the classical usages of the terms real and conceptual distinctions, a real distinction is one between terms that are distinct without regard to any contribution or function of mind. Conceptual distinctions, on the other hand, are those where the distinction between the terms does depend on some contribution or function of mind. Yet at the same time, there must be a real ground in the things distinguished for the conceptual distinction to be true; otherwise a conceptual distinction would be a fiction, plainly false. To justify the use of the terms "conceptual" and "real" distinctions, I must show how my formulations reflect the classical usage. The case with what I call real distinctions is prima facie clear, I believe. The case with conceptual distinctions is harder, for so far the characterization of conceptually distinct terms has been entirely realistic; that is, the discussion has been in terms of the ground in the things distinguished for the conceptual distinction. What is the contributory role of mind?

Really distinct things can be conceived to be distinct from each other. We can conceive one thing to be genuinely and really distinct from another by conceiving it as the harmony of its essential and conditional features, and we can conceive the other in like fashion. However much the conditional features of a thing depend on and make reference to the other things, they still belong to and are integrated into the harmony of their inclusive determination. The conditional features do not belong to nor are they constituents of the other determination except insofar as they are grasped by the other's own conditional features; and in the latter case it is not the first thing's conditional feature per se that is a constituent of the other thing but rather the other's conditional feature that grasps the first in a way characteristic of the other. True, we cannot conceive of a determination of being without conceiving it to be really distinct from others; so those others are necessary for the being of the first; still they are conceived as distinct.

The case is different regarding conceptually distinct things. We cannot conceive the inclusive term in a conceptual distinction without conceiving the constituent term as one of its proper parts. The inclusive term includes more than any one constituent, or even all the constituents, because it includes the harmony of them all; but it cannot be conceived without conceiving the constituent. We might say that the constituent is an analytic part of the inclusive term. On the other hand, we cannot conceive the constituent term *as distinct* from the inclusive term without conceiving the inclusive term as containing it, for if the conceptually distinct terms are sufficiently connected to be conceived as distinct, we can conceive of the constituent only as a constituent. The constituent term has features precisely in virtue of the fact that it is a part of the inclusive term, namely, those features it has in virtue of being determinate with respect to and really distinct from the other constituent determinations on its own level. It would not be determinate with respect to those others unless it were included with them in the inclusive determination. Therefore, conceptually distinct terms cannot be conceived as distinct in the same sense as really distinct terms can; to conceive one of the terms as distinct from the other is to conceive the other as a part of the first, albeit in different senses of "part" for the different terms.

The contribution of mind to the making of a conceptual distinction cannot be thought of as the addition of some property to what is in fact the real state of affairs. If that were the case, the contribution of mind would be to make a mistake. Rather, the contribution of mind in both conceptual and real distinctions is to articulate what must be conceived in the distinct things to conceive them to be distinct. In the case of real distinctions, it is each thing's own properties that must be conceived, and these are distinct. In the case of conceptual distinctions each thing must be conceived in the other for each to be conceived as conceptually distinct from the other, although the sense in which each is in the other depends upon whether it is the inclusive or constituent term being dealt with. The nature of the inclusive term is conceived as including the constituent term as a proper part. And the nature of the constituent term is conceived as distinct from the inclusive only insofar as it is conceived as having determinations with regard to the other constituents on its own level in virtue of the harmony contributed by the inclusive term. A conceptual distinction is one between terms each of which is conceived in the conception of the other.

Index

Freedom, 29, 81, 90, 103, 153, 205, 216, 244, 254, 301–4; from the law, 301

Freudian, interpretations of religious experience, 125–26, 175

Fulfillment, 222, 230–31, 242, 244, 246, 273

Fundamental dilemma of ontology, 23, 25, 31, 40–42, 64, 91

Future, 115–16, 206

Gandhi, M., 288

Glaucon, 110

Glory, 119, 180, 190, 202, 239–41, 247–53, 275, 277, 288–89, 292, 294–95, 300–304

God, 2, 6, 11, 18, 42, 78, 94–119, 125–26, 138, 142, 146–47, 168–70, 173, 177, 198, 216, 232–33, 237, 277, 292; action of, within the world, 257–58, 260–62, 273–74; conception of, 186, 188–201, 227; connection of, with world refers to creation, 1, 103, 111, 206; creative act of, 1, 94, 97, 103–4, 113–16, 163, 172, 202, 261, 264–65, 268, 288 (see also Creative act); immanence of, 1, 144, 265; intention (or will) of, 103, 202, 228, 264–70; knowledge of, 17–21, 73, 76–77, 84, 90, 96, 136–38, 144–47, 167; and men, 204, 206–10, 213, 219, 221–22, 227, 242, 269; proofs for, 11, 64–74, 90, 126, 177–80; and transcendence, 1, 7–8, 11, 43, 59, 61, 70–90, 94, 116–19, 126, 129, 131, 134–35, 147, 164, 174–75, 177, 183, 194–201, 233, 247, 253, 264–66, 270, 304–6; and world, 1, 11, 42, 77, 97–106, 112, 143–45, 162, 205

Good, 20, 81, 116, 118, 231, 233, 239, 247, 255, 268–69, 297, 299, 301–2; form of, 4, 110, 151, 156–59

Grace, 119, 229, 236, 273–74

Greeks, 4, 192, 223

Group, 259–60, 272–85, 287, 294

Happiness, 247–53, 287–88, 300

Harmony, 49–50, 66, 70, 79, 96, 111–13, 116–18, 150–51, 157–59, 206–12, 216–34, 236, 238–41, 243–50, 254–56, 258–59, 261, 263–64, 270–81, 284, 288–97, 299–303, 307–12

Harris, C. R. S., 62 n.

Hartshorne, Charles, 2, 11, 21 n., 42, 78, 103, 108–9, 117 n., 131, 139 n., 144–47, 172 n., 261, 266, 268 n.; drawing of, 267

Harvey, J. W., 190 n.

Heart, 212, 217, 219, 221–27, 244, 250–53, 290–91

Heaven, 241

Hebrews, 223

Hegel, G. W. F., 6, 8, 26, 28–35, 39, 41–42, 54, 135, 153, 278, 308; drawing of, 27

Heidegger, M., 6, 132

Hell, 240

Hendel, Charles, viii

Heraclitus, 17

Heterogeneity, 135, 149, 157–58, 160–62, 165–67

Hinduism, 230, 253

History, 29, 123, 125, 183, 187, 203, 213, 237, 246, 257, 259, 269, 274, 276, 279, 289

Holiness, 186, 190–95, 200, 227, 239–40, 247, 249, 257

Homogeneity, 149, 157–67

Hope, 210, 218, 219, 228, 230, 235–36, 255, 258, 272

Hosea, 238, 293

Hubris, 223

Humanism, 251

Human nature (human being, true humanity, truly human harmony), 103, 205–10, 216–17, 219, 221–26, 230, 232, 236, 242, 250, 259, 270, 276, 278, 280, 282–88, 291, 293, 295, 299, 301–2; distinction between essential and ideal human nature, 208; see also Man

Hume, David, 106, 268

Ideal, 204, 274, 277, 284–85, 287–88, 297, 299, 303; of explanation, 149–51; of system, 140–43, 149, 156, 164, 166, 185

Idealism, 2, 4, 25, 28, 30, 191, 278–79

Identity, 29, 30, 44, 47–48, 191–95, 200, 251–52, 300

Imitation, 275–76, 289, 291–93

Immanence, 2, 119

Imperfection, 232–36, 245, 250, 255, 258, 282, 284–85

Incarnation, 200

Ontological argument, 70, 129, 191, 193–94
Ontology, 29–30, 32, 34, 48, 61–62, 70, 77, 114, 126–27, 131, 134, 143, 146–48, 151, 154, 157, 160–61, 173, 176, 178, 189, 193–94, 264, 269–70; see also Fundamental dilemma of ontology; Principle of the ontological equality of reciprocal contrasts; Principle of the ontological ground of differences
Order, 156–59; of being, 148–49, 164–66; of explanation, 148–49, 163–66; of world, 268–69
Origen, 6
Otto, Rudolph, 184 n., 190, 197 n.

Page, B. S., 83
Panentheism, 119, 191, 200
Pantheism, 191, 200
Parmenides, 47
Parmenides, 154
Pascal, Blaise, 240–41
Passion, 235–37, 274; see also Concern
Passover, 257
Pattern, 111–13, 213–14, 230–32, 279
Paul, St., 301
Peirce, Charles S., 117, 131, 139, 153, 168, 172, 262; drawing of, 171
Perfection, 222, 231–37, 255, 285–87, 301
Person, personality, 78, 115, 118, 169, 173, 189, 208, 212–13, 219, 226–29, 237, 240, 243, 246, 250, 255, 258, 266–68, 278–80, 285, 289, 291, 295; second, of the Trinity, 100–101, 264, 294
Personal character of God, 42, 98, 114, 119, 188, 191, 199, 253, 258, 264–73
Personalism, 119
Perversity, 221–25, 230, 273, 281, 283, 287, 302
Phenomenology, 132, 201, 281; of religion, 184–87, 190, 192, 195–201, 204, 211, 213
Philebus, 159
Philosophical experience, 168–80
Philosophy and philosophers, 1–8, 76, 88, 94, 106, 117, 123, 125–28, 131–32, 137, 148, 152, 183–87, 190, 193, 195, 202, 204, 216, 231, 241, 244, 278–79, 299; Hegel's view of, 28–29, 31, 153; see also Speculation

Philosophy of religion, 2, 7, 185, 188, 190
Phlogiston, 125
Piety, 169, 175–76, 224, 280
Plato, Platonism, 2–4, 29, 51, 106, 109–11, 135, 151, 154–59, 177, 192, 220, 223, 247, 280–82, 296–99, 303
Plotinus, 81, 83, 86, 158, 192
Pluralism, 43, 47, 49–59, 65, 131, 201
Politics, politicians, 203, 220, 231, 279, 281, 294, 299
Positivism, 123
Possibility, 48, 78, 106, 108–9, 130–32, 144–47, 244
Potentiality, 63, 67, 81, 100, 106, 108–9, 113, 125
Power, 30–33, 42, 78–79, 94, 103–8, 112–16, 119, 161, 172–73, 189, 195–202, 213, 227, 235, 245, 257, 260, 271–72, 291, 302
Pragmatism, 133, 152, 168, 174
Pre-Socratics, 125
Preacher, 203, 244, 274
Predestination, 105, 234
Presence, 2, 8, 11, 55, 170; divine, 2, 59, 61, 72, 76, 83, 94, 98, 116–19, 173, 183, 197, 200, 202, 218, 228–32, 236, 239–49, 259, 266, 272, 285, 288, 294, 297, 304–6
Proslogium, 190 n.
Pride, 223, 225, 235–36, 238, 241, 245–46, 281, 283
Priest, 203
Principle of the ontological equality of reciprocal contrasts, 28, 40–42, 45, 61, 74, 89, 91–93
Principle of the ontological ground of differences, 24, 40, 44–45, 61, 91–93
Privacy, 209, 236, 254, 256, 258–60, 269–70, 272, 274–75, 280, 282–83, 286, 290–91, 294–97, 299
Process philosophy, 78, 108–9
Promise, 235, 238–42, 249, 258–59, 269, 273–75
Proof, 177–80; of the reality of being-itself, transcendent and indeterminate, 63–74
Protestant, 224
Providence, 196, 256–64, 271–72, 288–89
Public life, 176, 180, 209, 236, 244, 258, 272–77, 279–80, 282–91, 294, 296, 299